"Profit and Delight"

Great to meet you!

Best wishes,

Arthur Smyth

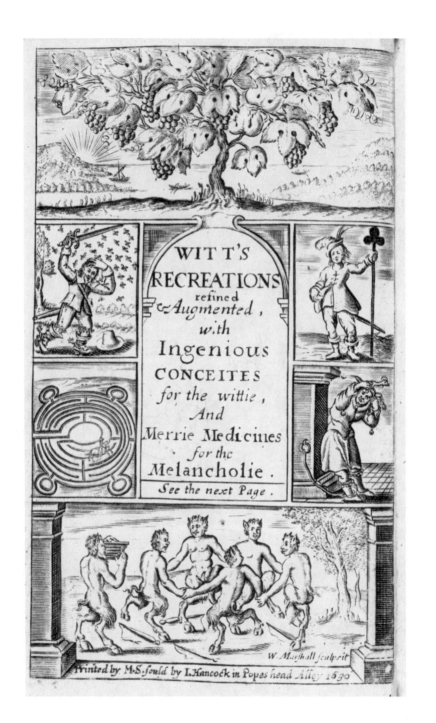

"Profit and Delight"

❡

PRINTED MISCELLANIES
IN ENGLAND, 1640–1682

ADAM SMYTH

Wayne State University Press   Detroit

Copyright © 2004 by Wayne State University Press,
Detroit, Michigan 48201. All rights reserved.
No part of this book may be reproduced without formal permission.
Manufactured in the United States of America.

08 07 06 05 04   5 4 3 2 1

Library of Congress Cataloging-in-Publication Data

Smyth, Adam, 1946–
"Profit and delight" : printed miscellanies in England, 1640–1682 / Adam Smyth.
p.   cm.
Includes bibliographical references (p.) and index.
ISBN 0-8143-3014-2 (cloth)
1. English literature — Early modern, 1500–1700 — History and criticism.   2. Royalists — Books and reading — Great Britain — History — 17th century.   3. Politics and literature — Great Britain — History — 17th century.   4. Anthologies — Publishing — Great Britain — History — 17th century.   5. Literature publishing — Great Britain — History — 17th century.   6. Great Britain — Politics and government — 1603–1714 — Sources.   7. Popular literature — Great Britain — History and critcism.   8. Royalists — Great Britain — History — 17th century.   9. Printing — England — History — 17th century.   I. Title.

PR438.P65S64 2004
820.9'004—dc22
2003023875

∞ The paper used in this publication meets the minimum requirements of the American National Standard for Information Sciences—Permanence of Paper for Printed Library Materials, ANSI Z39.48–1984.

Grateful acknowledgment is made to the British Library for permission to reproduce the frontispieces and title pages from *Wits Interpreter*, 243.k.32, and *Recreations for Ingenious Head-peeces*, 11601.bb.18.

for my dad

Things then did not delay in turning curious.
—THOMAS PYNCHON, *The Crying of Lot 49*

CONTENTS

Acknowledgments — xi

Editorial Note — xiii

Introduction — xv

ONE
Printed Miscellanies: An Opening Survey — 1

TWO
Readers and Readings — 32

THREE
Printed Miscellanies and the Transmission of Texts — 73

FOUR
Politics, Themes, and Preoccupations — 132

Afterword — 173

Appendix
Printed Miscellanies, 1640–1682, Bibliographical Details — 177

Notes — 183

Bibliography — 227

Index — 239

ACKNOWLEDGMENTS

In a book about the circulation and evolution of texts, it seems particularly fitting to begin with an expression of my debts to those people who have helped this project gain shape and momentum.

This book began as a Ph.D. dissertation, and I owe great thanks to Cedric Brown for his guidance and support. Arthur Marotti and Elizabeth Heale were consistently generous with their time and expertise.

Several research institutions helped sustain this project by offering financial support in the form of fellowships: the Huntington Library, San Marino; the William Andrews Clark Memorial Library, Los Angeles; the Folger Shakespeare Library, Washington, DC; the Harry Ransom Center at the University of Texas in Austin; and the Bibliographical Society, London. Thanks to them all. The Wingate Foundation, London, also granted me a generous award which helped the progress of the book. I am also grateful to the staff of the British Library and the Bodleian.

I would also like to thank Tim Amos, Lucy Bending, Karen Britland, Michela Calore, James Daybell, Kathryn Perry, Andrew Stewart, and Stephen Thomson, who in various ways helped me think about researching, writing, and teaching. Thanks, in particular, to Andrew Gordon and Jerome de Groot, who read the whole text and offered great advice. I owe more than thanks to Vittoria Di Palma—my first reader, astutest critic, and best friend. My mum and my brother were consistent with their love and support. But most of all, this book is for my dad, who died a few weeks before the final manuscript was submitted. He informs every page.

EDITORIAL NOTE

All references to Shakespeare's plays are to *The Norton Shakespeare*, ed. Stephen Greenblatt, Walter Cohen, Jean E. Howard, and Katharine Eisaman Maus (New York: Norton, 1997).

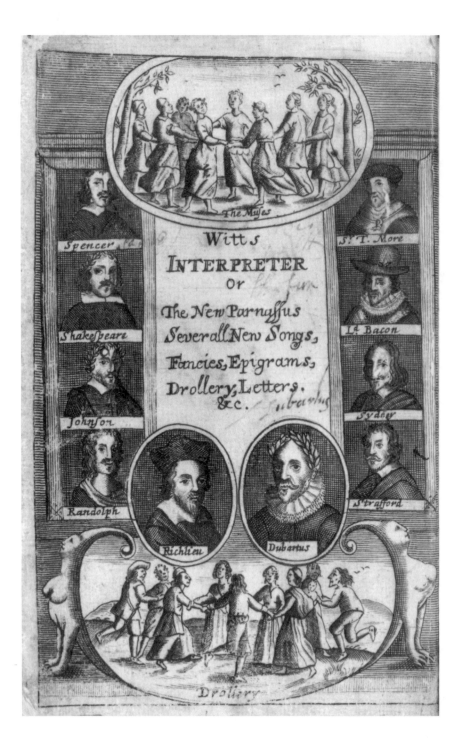

INTRODUCTION:
Thomas Martin's Letters and Poems

I want to begin with an Oxford undergraduate from Chichester.

While studying at New Inn Hall, Oxford, in the mid-1670s, Thomas Martin kept a small notebook. In this notebook Martin transcribed letters and poems: letters between himself and his sister "FS," his cousin "AP," and his friend John Sowter (or Souter); and poems by established and lesser-known authors, along with what Martin rather grandly titles "Verses of my own Composure."[1]

Martin's manuscript survives today in the William Andrews Clark Memorial Library, Los Angeles, and the text suggests a number of topics which run through this present study of printed miscellanies. Of central interest to me is the way in which Martin transfers poems and extracts from printed, public books into his private manuscript. Martin undertakes such acts of textual transmission, it seems, in order to deploy these extracts in his own private letters and in his social interactions. The printed book becomes, in Martin's hands, not a coherent stable whole, but rather a collection of potentially applicable parts. Furthermore, Martin shows not only a readiness to mingle his own poems among these formerly printed works but also an eagerness to adapt and rework printed texts—both habits that implicitly challenge the authority of the original writer.

Written in a swift, fluent, virtually unpunctuated prose—a prose that suggests a proximity between epistolary and oral rhetoric—Martin's correspondence occupies an interesting middle ground between disclosure and opacity. On the one hand the letters trace intimacies: Martin's initial unhappiness at Oxford ("the cares & troubles which I have met with coming to Oxford have so discomposd me"); family tragedies ("[my] aunts death on Friday, & her funerall on Saturday" have "so taken me up ... with greif"); news of his studies ("it being Lent & we accustomed to dispute Ethick questions I thought it not inconveniant or at least unseasonable to read a lecture of Ethicks concerning ye moderation of our desires"); his hopes in love; the excitement of a new friendship unfolding ("his company doth better suit me then any of our countrimens I have yet met with"). "Public" subjects rarely intrude, and when they do, they are bundled at the foot of letters, or hurriedly sketched in postscripts: "Seaven east India ships are arrived with good store of Jewels which is all ye news"; "My Ld Arlingtons house was burnt down to ye grounds last wensday morning 2 a clock & nothing saved there was one cabinet cost £2000 & very rich furniture."

But this attention to personal subjects is accompanied by a coy, allusive tone which undercuts the confessional spirit these topics suggest. Names are dropped; intentions remain unclear; events are placed behind a careful haze. The real subject of the letters is always a reference away. Thus, typically:

> I shall not send y^t letter you saw nor ye verses, but desire you to inform me whither you have received an answer to yours from y^t person you wrote to.

This equivocation was due largely to Martin's anxieties about epistolary privacy—a theme he returns to several times. In a letter to Sowter from the summer of 1674, Martin laments the innumerable mishaps that afflict letters, "not only of being lost but miscarring to those persons whom we desire should not have a view." Indeed, since "it being ye custom in many families y^t he y^t first receives ye letter hath ye perusal we may wish one another together for private conference." Sowter was also troubled by the prospect of unintended readers: he mused on how to avoid prying eyes and reassured Martin that "when you are at Chichester I have a good way to prevent ye interception of letters."[2] The transmission of letters, like the transmission of manuscript verse, was evidently perceived as a potentially unstable process. Like John Donne, Martin was anxious about his texts circulating beyond his control.

The effect of this anxiety is to position Martin's letters uncertainly between the private and the public. The letters gesture at a personal correspondence—the unhappiness, the hopes of love—but remain constrained by an awareness of a potential public readership. (Martin would have been distraught at the present public airing of his prose.)

Yet it is possible to construct a narrative running through the letters. On the cover of the collection Martin writes, "If I am not married within this 8 years Ile never marry," and many of his letters concern both his attempts to woo and the advice on love he dispenses to his friend John Sowter. In particular, Martin's letters show him writing verses for his friend to use—to read? to send? to learn and recite?—when wooing.

Martin was apparently pursuing a woman whose identity, in keeping with the bashful nature of these letters, is cloaked behind a poetic pseudonym. Sowter offered Martin advice:

> As to your resignation of your sweet Theodosia (as you title her) . . . let not your vain imaginations cause such rash resolutions of not sending to her, but goe on in your proceedings & you will find a happy issue of them.

Martin's choice of the name Theodosia suggests an imagination informed by poetic fashion—one thinks of Katherine Philips styling herself Orinda, for instance, or Alexander Brome's addresses to a desirable Theodora. In fact, Martin assumed a poetic moniker himself, as we see when Sowter reassured him that

> They are not private reasons y^t make me think y^t Damons endeavours will find ye desirable affect in courting his sweet Theodosia but from the merits and worth of Damon which are too apparent to be overlooked.

Martin, writing from Oxford, asked Sowter to purchase a book for him in London; the capital's bookshops were, in this instance, better stocked. "Pray send me down ye Female Preheminence written by one Care in 8vo bound in plain Calves leather & I will repay you & thank you for it." There was an initial delay when "time would not permit" Sowter "to goe so far as Fleetstreet for ye book," and Sowter had to wait until "my bookseller got one so yt was a week before I got it, & then I took ye boldness to give it a perusall & therefore was hindred from a speedy dispach." But eventually Martin declared "ye book came safe to my hands for which care of yours I return you deserved thanks & shall send ye money when I know what it cost."

The book Martin ordered was Henry's Care's translation of Heinrich Cornelius Agrippa von Nettesheim's *De nobilitate et praecellentia foeminei sexus*, published in 1670 as *Female Pre-eminence; or, the Dignity and excellency of that sex, above the male an ingenious discourse written originally in Latine by Henry Cornelius Agrippa, Knight, Doctor of Physick, Doctor of both Laws, and Privy-Counsellor to the Emperour Charles the Fifth. Done into English with Additional Advantages, by H.C.* As Sowter's apologetic letter had indicated, the volume was sold in Fleet Street, "*at the Sign of the Bible,*" by Henry Million.

Care's eighty-three-page text is, as the title suggests, an assertion of female virtue. Among many other claims, the book stresses woman's "excellent *Faculties of* Mind, Reason, and Speech"; "the *Dignity* . . . alotted to Woman above Man, by order of Creation"; "the *cleanness* and *purity* of this Sex," particularly when compared to man who "never so well washt, as oft as he washes again, will still leave behind some *filth* and *sordities*"; and woman's superiority in speech ("Did not every one of us first learn to speak from no other *Tutors* than our *Mothers* or *Nurses?*"). Care's prose is peppered with supporting examples drawn from Scripture, history, and nature ("Thus the Eagle, the noblest of Birds, and Queen of all the winged Troops, is never found a *Male*").[3]

Although he ordered the book, Martin intended to pass it on to the object of his amorous advances:

> my own perusal of it being not ye moving cause of my sending for it, but to give it to one to whom these encomiums or rather complemental flatteries may ... seem [appealing].

Martin's resolution "to give it to one" most vividly suggests a literal handing over of the book; an exposition on female virtue was, to Martin's mind, a fitting gift. But "to give it" also suggests a possible recitation of the book's contents—either in conversation or in letters. Martin might well have used Care's text as his own, extracting particularly potent moments to support his own words ("that Character which *Heaven* it self had given of its *Nature*"; "she being the *Loadstone* of Mans Desires")—appropriating parts of this public text to construct his private, epistolary self. Whatever the precise mode of conveyance, Care's text certainly acquired a social function for Martin.

But ultimately Martin was unimpressed with Care's volume.

> I think the author did intend to shew his own ingenuity in giving them preheminence & out of a complement as we do out of a complement give Ladies ye wall or let them set at ye upper end of the table. Yet was he not mistaken with his own perfections then with theirs? else certainly he would have left them to defend themselves, who in his opinion knew as well as ye most convenient time as the best method of doing it.

Martin's hopes to impress his lady with the book fell similarly flat. "ye female preheminence," he wrote to Sowter with bitter understatement, is

> a book I find not much esteemed by ye more discreet & ingenuous sort of females.

As well as requesting help, Martin dispensed advice to Sowter on matters of the heart, and here we see an even more vivid instance of the social function of books. In particular, we see Martin writing poetry for application and use by his friend. Sowter had early on expressed an interest in seeing Martin's verse, and while Martin was initially and dutifully coy—"Your desire of seeing unfinished papers is unreasonable"—he soon assured Sowter he would "bring them down [to Chichester] . . . expect me Friday come seaven . . . you may have a veiw of my imperfections, for I resolve never to trust them to a careless post, or heedless carrier."

Martin soon offered to help Sowter's wooing by composing some encomiums for his intended lady, a Miss Merttins:

let me make one verse or two in her commendation, although having left poetry this year.

Martin sets himself a challenge: not only to return to poetry (a youthful pursuit which maturer men "left"), but also to present his friend with a socially useful acrostic or two. As his letter acknowledges, and as many clanging manuscript examples attest, writing acrostics was no easy thing: "Fancy being kept in bounds & forced to begin every verse with such a letter cannot be so good." Writing from London on 19 July 1676, Sowter indicates that Martin's verse ran into problems.

> Dear Freind
>
> Your kind letter of ye 3^d instant with ye inclosed verses came to hands; I give you many thanks for your pains therein, they were according to their deserves kindly accepted only one of ye chief letters was omitted, which was N, & y^t cannot be well left out, rather ye last which is S, for many times they wrote it without S. But I confess I writ not ye name with all ye letters for it is thus (Merttins) so they are even. If you please to favour me with ye addition or change ye letter S for N. & then it will be Mertin which will do well enough, the last two lines are thus
>
>> Iustly being envied by a Deity
>> Shoots through my soule oh pity or I dye.
>
> I pray make an altera'on & let not any address be made as it is now. (oh pity or I dye).

Sowter, then, asked Martin to change the spelling of the name that formed the basis of the acrostic: requesting that the omitted "N" be added in place of the "S" ("for many times they wrote it without S"). Soon after, Martin writes of "my altera'on of ye last verse instead of a new copy."

This editorial exchange—hammering out a light love verse—highlights the degree to which this poem was the product of a particular social occasion and served a particular purpose. Martin's verse had a precise function: it was written for application, for use—and, as a consequence, reminds us to guard against reading early modern poems as "sincere," or "spontaneous" expressions. As with his reading of Care's book, Martin's verse composition was apparently preparatory for a moment of wooing application, and Martin's manuscript seems to suggest that reading, transcription, and composition were embedded in ideas of social utility. Martin wrote verse to order, to serve a particular function; he read

Henry Care to pepper his prose and his verse with choice phrases, extracting moments with some subsequent redeployment in mind. Such an attitude toward poetry might surprise twenty-first-century readers, and it offers an alternative frame in which to read and understand verse: as applicable and functional. As will be seen, printed miscellanies were in many ways books that invited this kind of employment of literary texts.

While Martin does not transcribe the verses he constructed for Sowter, he does include several "Verses of my own Composure." These are clearly the products of a young university writer interested in and engaged with contemporary, or near-contemporary, poetic fashions. Thus his poems are unsurprising depictions of erotic hopes and doomed wooings ("How oft have I sought my Clarinda in vain"). They engage with popular debates such as "The Lukewarm" lover (does a reticent lover love as intensely as his vociferous counterpart?), recalling Sir Robert Ayton's well-known "No man Love's fiery Passions can approve."[4] They offer Platonic praise of interior over external beauty ("I don't esteem ye glories of a face / Nor well composed looks admire"). They present conventional translations, like "Horace lib, 2 ode 14," beginning "Allas my friend ye hasty years do slide."[5] Like Martin's acrostics for Sowter, these poems often seem to have been written with particular social needs in mind: "To one who desired to see a description of a mans being in Love," for example, might have been born from another friend's request. Martin often included his own poems as gifts in his letters to his sister. He concludes a missive to his "Loving Sister" with the note "Adeu [sic] vain world &c / July 8.74," alerting her to the inclusion of his own "Adieu vain world"—itself a reworking of familiar world-weary goodbyes to life.[6]

Martin's manuscript includes verses by other poets, too—among them, Rochester, Cowley, and Dryden—and a consideration of these poems suggests something of Martin's attitude to authorship and the textual transmission of verse.

Martin must have transcribed this poetry from printed or manuscript collections, or spoken or sung performances. The practice of transcribing fashionable verses into manuscript miscellanies (often commonplace books) peaked in Oxford in the 1620s, but Martin's text, some fifty years later, shows that the trend certainly did not die out. Like its 1620s predecessors, Martin's collection offers a fairly representative slice of the popular verse of the day, including verses from John Dryden's *Almanzor and Almahide*, Dryden's *Conquest of Granada*, and John Crowne's play *The History of Charles the Eighth of France*, as well as verses by John Wilmot, Earl of Rochester. All of these verses also appeared in either popular printed collections of verse—the miscellanies that are the subject of this book—or in manuscript verse miscellanies.[7]

In fact, three unattributed poems which Martin transcribes appear to have been drawn directly from a single specific source—a printed miscellany titled *New Court Songs* (1672).[8] Order, title, layout, and text are all extremely similar, particularly in comparison with other printed appearances of these poems. If this direct movement of materials did indeed occur, it is not surprising that Martin owned, borrowed, or perused a copy of *New Court Songs*. Compiled by Robert Veel (or Vine), this little verse collection was published shortly before Martin arrived in Oxford and was just the sort of vibrant, compact miscellany that proved popular. It also had the added appeal of including verses drawn from contemporary theatrical productions. Martin might well have picked up a copy on one of his trips to London: *New Court Songs* was published at the "Stationers Arms and Ink-Bottle in Lumbard Street, and the Lower Walk of the New Exchange," and Martin wrote of a visit to London during which he went at least as far as "ye 7 Stars in Lubard Street."

All but one of Martin's transcriptions offer no note of author or origin. Reading back from the authorcentric twenty-first century, this apparent indifference to authorship is striking. The lack of ascriptions may have been, in part, the consequence of the manuscript as personal notebook: if Martin knew the authors, an ascription was perhaps deemed unnecessary. Nonetheless, there appears a striking lack of concern for ideas of origin, and, more broadly, for authorship as a means of literary definition. Perhaps the absence of ascriptions suggests Martin understood these poems to be "his"—that the verses had ceased to belong to the original author. Certainly, when Martin includes his own poems alongside work by Rochester and others, there is a relaxed blurring between what might be termed "public" and "private" writings.

Perhaps as a consequence of this relaxed approach to authorship, Martin's renderings of verses by Dryden, Cowley, and Rochester vary considerably from established, "authorial" editions. The poems that appear in Martin's manuscript have titles, layouts, words, and whole lines that vary from printed editions. Such a variance not only strengthens the sense of these texts as poems beyond the control of the original author; it also prompts a consideration of verses as evolving, changing, literary units—as unfixed, malleable texts that might circulate and be read in any number of altered states. Martin's appropriation of Veel's *New Court Songs* similarly suggests poems moving between different kinds of collection, across different kinds of media. This is a point which raises important, complicating questions, not least in terms of this book's methodology. How might we read and understand the appearance of multiple versions of the "same" poem? Do we need to adjust a critical vocabulary predicated on oppositions that include author/reader, original/variant, and writing/reading, when dealing with texts which seem to blur these distinctions?

It is with such issues in mind—with authors challenged; with texts made malleable; with poetry applied—that I turn to printed miscellanies, and a consideration of their significance. Chapter 1 of this book marks out the territory, providing definitions of the printed miscellany, considering the literary traditions from which these books emerged, exploring the kinds of materials included, and thinking about the proposed functions of these books. Chapter 2 is concerned with readers of printed miscellanies: it examines marginal annotations in extant miscellanies in order to suggest ways in which printed miscellanies were read, and, significantly, how these readings differed from the readings prescribed and encouraged in the texts themselves. The subject of chapter 3 is the textual transmission of materials (particularly poetry), and the discussion seeks to explore how texts altered—and with what consequences—as they moved between different kinds of publication. Previous studies of verse transmission have tended to organize their analyses around very broad oppositions such as manuscript versus print—broad oppositions which in fact conceal considerable diversity. This chapter tries to offer a more nuanced account, paying careful attention to particular instances of textual transmission in order to present a precise discussion. The chapter draws, in part, on my online *Index of Poetry in Printed Miscellanies, 1640 to 1682* (www.adamsmyth.clara.net), which catalogs the 4,639 poems in printed miscellanies. Readers will, I hope, find the site useful both as a source of substantiation for this chapter, and, if relevant, as a tool for their own research. Chapter 4 explores the politics of printed miscellanies, examining, in particular, the books' celebrations of royalism, love, misrule, and drink, in relation to the dramatically changing political contexts across the chronological range of this study.

ONE

Printed Miscellanies: An Opening Survey

> There is a great deal of dirt—nasty, worthless trash—
> in the miscellanies of the Restoration, and with this garbage
> I have not chosen to meddle.
> A. H. BULLEN, ED., *Speculum Amantis: Love-Poems from Rare Song-Books
> and Miscellanies of the Seventeenth Century*

DEFINITIONS AND TENDENCIES

NEEDMORE: Can you have occasion to be melancholic, you who are the envy of the Men, and the Darling of the Women?
FREEMAN: What a pox, hast thou lately been reading the *Academy of Complements*?[1]

A lot of people in seventeenth-century England had been reading *The Academy of Complements*. The book went through at least twelve editions between 1640 and 1685, each one larger than the last, and references to it in plays and poems suggest a well-known publication. To twenty-first-century eyes, it is a curious text: a farrago of unattributed poetry, exemplary compliments, "Complementall and amorous Letters," "Questions with their answers resolving the doubts of Lovers," instructions on addressing "the King, or Queenes Majesty," and "A Table for the Vnderstanding of the hard English words." It is a bunched, busy duodecimo, and in it the reader can find stock poetic eloquence, like Needmore's, tailored to suit his or her circumstances. For a *"Protestation of his obedience,"* the text suggests "I shall not all the dayes of my life have a will, which shall not obey yours." To offer wooing praise, the reader might try "Sweet mouth that sendest a musicke rosied breath / Whose every word darts me a living death." And to make *"An offer of Service,"* or voice *"Expressions of Affections,"* or answer questions like "How must a man behave himselfe amongst Ladyes?"[2] *The Academy of Complements* provides fittingly sugared words.

I

Eccentric as this all might seem, *The Academy of Complements* is only the most conspicuous example of a type of publication that proved consistently popular in the mid-seventeenth century: the printed miscellany. Providing clear definitions for the miscellany is a difficult task. Since one of the defining attributes of these texts is their close, often intimate, relationships with other types of books, neat delineation of the boundaries of the printed miscellany is tricky. These books shared interests (and often audiences) with—among many other texts—song books, conduct manuals, commonplace books, manuscript verse collections, ballads, and educational tracts. And so it is perhaps better to offer an accumulation of tendencies rather than hard limits, since hard limits will in many ways prove pointlessly restrictive for a type of publication which embraced variety and merged genres.

Most basically, these texts were small, usually octavo or duodecimo publications of between 100 and 300 pages, bursting with about 120 short poems in English by at least three, and generally many more, authors. While the term "miscellany" in 1615 described "separate treatises or studies on a subject collected into one volume," or "literary compositions of various kinds brought together to form a book," and in 1638 was used to denote "a book, volume, or literary production containing miscellaneous pieces on various subjects" (*OED*), my study takes a variation in *authorship* as its founding definition. While a very few of the multiple author collections I foreground referred to themselves as miscellanies—Abraham Wright called his *Parnassus Biceps* "*a Poetick Miscellany*"—many others did not. My definition of the miscellany, then, is not an attempt to reconstruct a precise mid-seventeenth-century understanding of the word. This difference between early modern and contemporary meanings of the term is a striking reflection of twenty-first-century preoccupations with authorship.

Particularly popular verse forms were the epigram, the comic epitaph, the ballad, the epistle, the lyric, the mock, and the dialogue. The miscellany collections represent a bundling together of writing from diverse sources—commonplace books, printed verse collections, play texts, dramatic or musical performances, song books, ballads, educational tracts, and other printed miscellanies. The material was altered to suit the envisioned purposes of readers; was often set in an educative, generally Royalist, frame; and was offered as an emblem and exemplar of elite, usually courtly, life. Miscellanies generally declare little interest in authorship: poems are titled with loose or noncommittal descriptions, they are almost always anonymous, and they commonly offer variant readings to authorial or "established" texts. On those very rare occasions when ascriptions are offered, they are usually incorrect.

In many (but not all) miscellanies, as in *The Academy of Complements*, verses jostle with a range of other materials: model letters, dictionaries of difficult words, notes of mythology, brief histories, riddles, and jokes.[3] Expositions on "The Gentle Game of Cribbage" come between the origins of marriage and "Accomplished Conceipts . . . To cure corns."[4] And all printed miscellanies—even those which include only verse—exude a sense of gathered diversity.

The most common subject of miscellany musings is love—particularly the torturous sufferings of the snubbed male wooer. Thus verses beginning "Ah Cruel eyes that first enflam'd," "Is she not wondrous fair?" and "Cloris I burn behold and view."[5] But love is not the only subject. Poems praising or criticizing women (particularly extreme beauty or ugliness), lauding friendship, celebrating drink and drunkenness, pleading for sex, and reflecting on death are also common. Overt political or religious commentary is rare—although, as I will discuss in chapter 4, "nonpolitical" topics such as drinking, love, and friendship often acquire a clear political charge. The general tone of printed miscellanies is somewhere between the dutifully educative and the playfully reckless; a studied eloquence mixes with ribald, jesting fun; anxious etiquettes mingle with the scatological. And the effect is dizzying. If these books have any unified voice, it is pitched somewhere between the bawdy, the misogynous, the Royalist, the voyeuristic, the disenfranchised, and the educative. Printed miscellanies are verse collections, models for etiquette, prompt-books for wits, exemplars of elite life, defiant shrieks of misrule.

My chronological parameters are 1640 and 1682. The first, and most popular, miscellanies appeared in 1640, generating a momentum and providing a model for other collections to draw upon; 1682 saw the publication of *Wit and Mirth*, the last printed miscellany, according to my terms, before these volumes dissipated into other kinds of text. The following forty-one titles (first editions listed) represent the printed miscellanies that appeared between 1640 and 1682 and constitute this project's core texts.[6]

Past Studies

A 1928 review of an edition of *Covent Garden Drollery* noted that

> The verse miscellanies of the second half of the seventeenth century may be compared to a vast, and sometimes, it may be confessed, a rank jungle into the tangled labyrinths of which few modern explorers have ventured.[7]

Table 1   Printed miscellanies, 1640–1682

Year	Title
1640	*The Academy of Complements*
	Wits Recreations
1653	*The Card of Courtship*
1654	*The Harmony of the Muses*
1655	*Wits Interpreter*
	The Marrow of Complements
	Musarum Deliciæ
1656	*Wit and Drollery*
	Parnassus Biceps
	Sportive Wit
	Choyce Drollery
1658	*The Mysteries of Love and Eloquence*
	Wit Restor'd
1659	*J. Cleaveland Revived*
1660	*Poems of Pembroke and Ruddier*
	Le Prince d'Amour
1661	*Merry Drollery the First Part*
	Merry Drollery the Second Part
	An Antidote Against Melancholy
1667	*Folly in Print*
1669	*The New Academy of Complements*
1670	*A Jovial Garland*
1671	*Oxford Drollery*
	Westminster Drollery
1672	*Westminster Drollery the Second Part*
	Covent Garden Drollery
	A Collection of Poems
	New Court-Songs
	Windsor Drollery
1673	*Methinks the Poor Town has been troubled too long*
	Holborn Drollery
	London Drollery
1674	*Wit at a Venture*
	A New Collection
1675	*A Perfect Collection of the Several Songs now in Mode*
	Mock Songs and Joking Poems
1676	*A New Collection*
1677	*The Wits Academy*
	The Last and Best Edition of New Songs
1682	*Grammatical Drollery*
	Wit and Mirth

Whether or not we agree that printed miscellanies constitute "a rank jungle," it is indisputably true that "few modern explorers" have waded in with any enthusiasm. A clutch of reprints appeared in the nineteenth century,[8] but editors did not present these texts as objects worthy of serious consideration. "The titles of these books," one commented,

> are replete with delightful promise. *Musarum Deliciae* is potently attractive; *Wit's Recreations* exceedingly fascinating; and *Wit Restor'd* is enough to make one jump for joy.[9]

This interest, however, did not extend beyond an idle curiosity, or a gentle leap. Printed miscellanies were quaint emblems of a curious past, "rarities of 'th'olden time,'"[10] which merited amused attention—collections "as oddly conditioned and tipsily printed . . . as ever poured out of a Press"[11]—but received little or no critical evaluation. Recent scholarship has begun to turn to these texts, but the only sustained evaluation is an unpublished doctoral thesis from 1943. While there have been calls for further studies over the years, recent secondary work, while sometimes excellent, is restricted to discussions within larger projects, or to shorter chapters and articles.[12]

There are many reasons for this critical neglect, including the bawdy contents of miscellanies; the texts' cheap, popular, near ephemeral status; and the fact that miscellany popularity spanned the 1660 line—a date, as Harold Love has noted, that tends to demarcate and separate out research projects.[13] But most crucial of all is the fact that printed miscellanies resist authorcentric scholarship. As will be seen, the collections show little or no interest in dealing with ascriptions or notes of origin, save for the odd nebulous frontispiece reference to Sidney or Raleigh. They reprint texts already in circulation in print or manuscript form, and they often introduce textual changes to these materials. Since original authorship and context have been the persistent organizing principle for literary-historical scholarship, where the version closest to the writer's hand is deemed the reading most worthy of study and all other versions corruptions of this "right" original, printed miscellanies were doomed to neglect.[14] When early commentators come to sum up these collections, it is with an implicit suspicion of their illegality—of these collections as storehouses for broken, third-hand goods; or, at least, a sense that these anthologies were not playing by the rules. "*Stolen* from Chaucer," one disapproving annotator scratches in the margin of his book.[15]

Authors, Publishers, Popularity

Since one of the defining characteristics of the miscellany is the effacement of authorship, discovering the original writers of inclusions is often difficult, and sometimes impossible. It is also paradoxical, since supplying ascriptions runs counter to the central tenet which underpinned, and to my mind renders significant, miscellany composition: a resistance to authorcentric reading. Nevertheless, the following tables reflect those authors that I have been able to link, with confidence, to miscellany poetry.[16] The first table indicates the numbers of miscellany appearances by each poet. The figures include variant or duplicate copies of poems and so do not necessarily correspond to the number of different poems in printed miscellanies by the cited author. (These tables consider first editions of miscellanies.)

Table 2 Number of appearances of poems by writers

Poet	Appearances of Poems	Poet	Appearances of Poems
William Strode	71	Thomas Flatman	14
Ben Jonson	66	Thomas Jordan	14
Thomas Carew	61	Samuel Rowlands	14
Henry Parrot	56	John Mennes	12
William Hickes	53	John Pyne	12
John Fletcher	47	James Shirley	12
George Wither	44	Aphra Behn	11
Alexander Brome	40	John Hall	11
John Dryden	37	William Davenant	10
James Smith	34	John Heath	10
Charles Sedley	28	William Shakespeare	10
George Etherege	24	Robert Herrick	9
Richard Corbett	23	Henry Wotton	9
Sir John Davies	19	John Ashmore	8
William Cartwright	18	Robert Hayman	8
Thomas Bastard	17	Dr Henry Hughes	8
John Donne	17	Jasper Mayne	8
John Suckling	17	Samuel Pick	8
William Munsey	16	Walter Raleigh	8
Francis Beaumont	15	John Wilmot, Earl of Rochester	8
Henry Fitzgeffrey	15	Richard Brome	7
John Harrington	15	William Browne	7
Henry King	15	Edward May	7
Robert Ayton	14	George Morley	7

Table 2 *(continued)*

Poet	Appearances of Poems	Poet	Appearances of Poems
Robert Wild	7	Richard Lovelace	6
William Wycherley	7	Thomas Shadwell	6
Thomas D'Urfey	6	Abraham Wright	6
John Grange	6		

Now, in some ways these figures are misleading as indicators of popularity since several of the writers cited occur many times in one text and hardly at all in others: their figures reflect more the predilections—or sources—of a single compiler, and less the status of the author's work in general miscellany circulation. Thus it is worth considering the number of *different* miscellanies in which a poet's work appears. This gives a much better indication of how widely circulated his or her work was. Thus, the following table.

Table 3 Number of appearances of writers in different texts

Poet	Different Miscellanies	Poet	Different Miscellanies
Ben Jonson	18	Henry King	8
Thomas Carew	17	Charles Sedley	8
William Strode	15	James Shirley	7
Alexander Brome	13	James Smith	7
John Dryden	13	Aurelian Townshend	7
John Fletcher	13	George Etherege	6
Robert Ayton	10	William Hickes	6
Richard Corbett	10	John Donne	5
John Suckling	10	John Mennes	5
William Cartwright	9		

Notably absent in this latest table are George Wither and Henry Parrot: their apparent popularity in table 2 is misleading since all of Wither's poems appear in a single text (*The Marrow of Complements*), and all but one of Parrot's appear in another (*Wits Recreations*). Thomas Bastard, William Munsey, John Pyne, Henry Fitzgeffrey, and to a degree William Hickes are also less widely distributed than their initial figures in table 2 might imply. Robert Ayton is the most conspicuous mover in the other direction: his fourteen identified occurrences in printed miscellanies occur across ten different texts. This is largely due to the fact that two poems by Ayton—verses beginning "Wrong not sweet Mistris of my heart" and "No man Love's fiery Passions can approve"—were very popular, each appearing in print four times. Ben Jonson, Thomas Carew, William Strode, Alexander Brome, and Richard Corbett are high on both lists.

These tables of poets imply an alternative literary canon of writers, and it is worth contrasting those early modern poets most widely read in mid-seventeenth-century miscellanies with those most widely read, studied, and discussed today. Certainly there are notable differences. William Strode, most popular of all writers in the printed miscellany—and almost certainly the most circulated writer in early-seventeenth-century manuscript—has received scant critical attention. His poems were not edited until 1907, and there has been no published edition since.[17] Similarly, the work of Alexander Brome and Richard Corbett must have exerted an influence on seventeenth-century readers more significant than existing scholarship might imply. For scholars interested less in (largely arbitrary) notions of aesthetic value, and more in the cultural influence of writers, there is a compelling case to be made for new studies of Strode, Brome, Corbett, and their quietened contemporaries. Ben Jonson occupies a unique position as the recipient of similarly high levels of attention in the seventeenth-century printed miscellany and the twentieth-century scholarly text. The early modern popularity of contemporary university favorites such as William Shakespeare, Philip Sidney, and Edmund Spenser came via other types of publication, rather than the printed miscellany.

It should be stressed, however, that since almost all miscellany poems were printed unascribed, compilers and readers were probably not aware with which poets they were dealing. Of course this does not mean Strode's influence was any the less; rather, it means that his work was read as a scattered series and not as a work unified about his name. It seems the poems most likely to move into miscellany print were those popular in manuscript circulation, or in other printed miscellanies; those appearing in play texts; those dealing with love, sex, women, drink, or revelry; those of a short, compact, witty structure. The author of the poem was not *in itself* a crucial variable; thus, Strode's poems were popular in miscellanies because they had flourished in earlier manuscript collections to which printed miscellany editors sometimes turned. His name—in many cases unknown—did not determine their fate. Poems which were long, dense, and difficult, which had not appeared before in some medium, or which related to a constrictingly specific scenario were types of verse much less likely to appear in miscellany print.

Printed miscellanies rarely do more than hazily allude to the origins of the materials they print. Many, particularly earlier, miscellanies boast a reliance on manuscript collections: *Wits Interpreter,* for instance, was "ransack'd from private papers"; *J. Cleaveland Revived* was "at last publisht from his Original Copies"; and *The Academy of Complements* came replete with talk of "Jewels" once "lockt up," now "presented to thy view or fancy."[18] Such prefatorial puffing should be treated with caution: it is part of an attempt to connect these popular texts with elite contexts—a process sustained in title-page evocations of "the *Spring Garden, Hide Park,* the *New Exchange,* and other eminent places" as the source of inclusions (*The Mysteries of Love and Eloquence*). But it does appear that some compilers drew on manuscripts, and particularly manuscript verse miscellanies, often the products of university circles. Of the 4,639 poems contained in the forty-one printed miscellanies, 1,010 also occur in Bodleian manuscripts—and mostly in manuscript verse miscellanies. Now this is not to say that in all cases those manuscripts were the very sources compilers turned to for their printed texts; but such a high figure demonstrates the overlapping worlds of printed and verse miscellany, and it is probable that *some* of these manuscripts supplied the printed collection. Later miscellanies tend to stress their close relation with current London songs: they present themselves as samples of contemporary urban culture and their declared but nonspecific sources are the streets and theaters of their time. Such miscellanies often turned to plays, extracting songs or prologues and presenting them as discrete verses. Sometimes their provenance is noted; usually not. Printed miscellanies also made use of *other* printed miscellanies—removing poems from rival collections and thus strengthening the sense of connection between miscellanies that we will see later as an emerging theme.

Printed miscellanies were usually sold in the area of London around St. Paul's Churchyard. At least forty-three individuals were involved in the production of these texts, as publishers, printers, or sellers.[19] But I think we would struggle to talk meaningfully of these names as forming anything like a unified "printed miscellany group." Those names that recur across a number of publications tell different stories. There are some "publishers" (the term was often an imprecise blurring of printer, editor, and publisher at the time) who appeared to specialize in printed miscellanies, taking advantage of the popularity of these collections and producing several texts. Nathaniel Brooke (or Brooks or Brookes) published *Wits Interpreter* (1655), *Sportive Wit* (1656), *Wit and Drollery* (1656), *Mysteries of Love and Eloquence* (1658), and *J. Cleaveland Revived* (1660).[20] With Robert Pollard he also published *Wit Restor'd* (1658). And Pollard himself published *Choyce Drollery* in 1656. Other miscellany publishers are names not normally associated with such cheap popular books. Humphrey Moseley, better known for the first collected editions of Milton's poems and the works of Cartwright, Crashaw, Davenant, Denham, Donne, Fanshaw, Howell, Vaughan, and Waller,[21] also published *The Card of Courtship* (1653), *The Marrow of Complements* (1655), and the hugely popular *The Academy of Complements* (1640). Then there are the little-known names who seem to have specialized in these kinds of texts—and, consequently, to have remained obscure. Most enticing is William Hickes (or Hicks), known as Captain Hickes, who compiled *Oxford Drollery* (1671), *London Drollery* (1673), *Grammatical Drollery* (1682), and two books of jests. He was evidently a maverick entrepreneur: born in Oxford into a poor family, Hickes worked as a tapster in the Star Inn, Oxford; as a retainer for the Lucas family in Colchester at the start of the English Civil War; as a clerk to a Deptford woodmonger; as a (would-be) dancer and dancing instructor; and as a military tutor to youngsters. Hence the title "Captain." He was, descriptions note, "a sharking and indignant fellow,"[22] and he turned to publishing, and in particular to miscellanies, later in his career.

Sources suggest printed miscellanies were very popular books. Many of the texts were reprinted in later, augmented editions. Most popular of all was *The Academy of Complements*. Originally published in 1640, it also appeared—in an expanding form—in 1640, 1641, 1645, 1646, 1650, 1654, 1658, 1663, 1664, 1670, 1684, 1685, 1705, 1727, 1750, 1760, 1790, and 1795.[23] *Wits Recreations* was printed in 1640, 1641, 1645, 1650, 1654, 1663, 1667, and 1683. Sixteen miscellanies, in all, reappeared in new, usually expanded, editions.[24] Publisher Nathaniel Brooke has left details of a print run for one of his miscellanies. His *Sportive Wit* landed him in trouble with the committee for the regulation of printing for its alleged "scandalous, lascivious, scurrilous and profane matter."[25] When questioned on *"the 19th day of April 1656, before Sir John Barkstead knight, lieutenant of his highness's Tower of London,"* Brooke noted

> there were 1000 of them [*Sportive Wit*] printed, but he did not receive so many, but received 950, or thereabouts, and hath disposed of 700 of them.[26]

This suggests swift and significant sales. And print runs may have been as high as 2,000 copies—the maximum allowable print run at the time—for other texts.

If print runs imply popularity, printed miscellany prefaces reinforce a sense of commercial success.[27] They commonly invoke a busy, competitive market for their publications: *Folly in Print*, in its section "To the Reader," notes

> The whole world (imaginably) is but one great market; and all mankind in it, are distinguished into buyers and sellers, who either truck for, or buy Commodities; particularly in Books.[28]

Specifically, collections of poems appear everywhere:

> the once exalted Scene is at this present level'd, other Poems have come forth in such throngs, that our English world is satiated with them . . . such as ingenious persons, cannot have the patience continually to be afflicted with.[29]

This sense of a world drowning in print is a prefatorial refrain which, we will see, some miscellanies actually adopt as a condition that renders their efficient summarizing necessary.

Note also *Holborn Drollery*'s lamentations that

> Books of this Nature [i.e., printed miscellanies] should come out as frequent as the *Philosophical Transactions*, since two or three *Prologues*, and as many *Epilogues*, with some few *Stanza's* Venerable for their Antiquity, are their Ingredients.[30]

Other writings reflect the apparent popularity of miscellanies. A verse beginning "I'll go no more to the Old Exchange" discusses the New Exchange and its splendid array of *a la mode* items. Referring, most likely, to printed miscellanies, the poem notes, "There's curious Book of Complements, / And other Fashions strange."[31]

Self-Presentation of Printed Miscellanies

Variety, marrow, sum, choice, harmony, complete, garland, collection, storehouse, magazine, academy, finest, public: these are the words printed miscellanies most frequently use in descriptions of themselves to prospective readers. While miscellanies juggle with a wealth of other terms, these are certainly the most common. And what emerges through these moments of self-definition is a tension: a tension between, on the one hand, the complete, and on the other, the fragmentary; between printed miscellanies as both the summation and the select.

Typical is the declaration that the miscellany is "choice." *Parnassus Biceps* offers "Choice Pieces of Poetry"; *Wits Interpreter* originates from the "private Papers of the *Choicest Wits*."[32] The term is resonant with notions of selection, abridgement, gathering. Florio likens choice to "a culling" or "a sifting out";[33] Randle Cotgrave to the "exquisite," the "exact," the "daintier," the "picked."[34] The word generates legitimacy precisely because it resists ideas of the total. Two other very common terms in miscellanies suggest corresponding connotations of selection and refinement: "marrow" (*Marrow of Complements*), from the "pith or harte . . . in bones, in hearbs and shrubs," indicating, more generally, "the inward partes of the heart or minde"; and "garland," from a gathering of flowers. Both words litter miscellany prefaces, and both imply acts of editorial discrimination: a plucking out of the choice, the ripe, the key. "Marrow" might also suggest a growing out from this central point: in dictionaries the word is glossed as "Graine or corne wherof to make bread," and, by extension, "The seed of generation."[35]

Yet, simultaneously, there is a celebration of these texts as collections whose virtue lies in their clear *lack* of discrimination. Printed miscellanies are described as public storehouses—a term often used to suggest a kind of thesaurus, but also evoking rooms stocked with meat, corn, butter, and apples, not fine rarities or jewels, and associated with safety and security, not exclusivity.[36] Texts are defined as repositories, or "Magazin[es] richly furnisht."[37] The frequent stress on "variety"—perhaps the most common claim of all—is similarly resonant with notions of range, not rarity. To the early modern reader, "variety" suggested "diversitie," "mutabilitie," "change," "difference."[38] Collections which laud variety celebrate the virtue of an expansive reading that resists confinement to a limited (if choice) number of fixed models. Similarly, miscellanies which offer themselves as "complete"—a common but unexplained claim—evoke a notion of a total, and therefore nonselective, reading. Thus: "others have been bold to affirm that to compleat this Volume, they could not imagine what more could be added or invented."[39]

This tension between the select and the total is best articulated by *The Marrow of Complements*, as it collapses into contradictory claims: the book is "*the Summe and Marrow of all former contrivances of this nature, and yet not with the least dependencie upon any of them*"—at once an accumulation ("Summe"), an essence ("Marrow"), and an entirely distinct collection ("*not with the least dependencie*").

This paradoxical emphasis is part of a larger uncertainty about the kind of text miscellanies constitute. We see a correspondingly anxious equivocation as miscellanies try to establish some kind of known literary language with which to describe themselves. Miscellanies nervously shuffle through a range of metaphors in their moments of self-presentation: metaphors of food ("This little Booke is like a furnish't feast, / And hath a dish, I hope, to please each guest"[40]), or childbirth ("It took its birth from them"; "I am confident this *Volume* will live"[41]), or jewels, or gardens, or poesies of flowers, or inns, or previously locked cabinets,[42] or women (*Bristol Drollery* is "a fresh Country Muse come up to Town / Which you on easie tearms may make your own").[43] There is a sense of compilers clutching at every available way of presenting a text in the pursuit of some kind of known, established vocabulary.

A similar anxiety is implied by printed miscellanies' lumbering attempts to establish a sense of literary precedence. Since generally precedence, not novelty, generated early modern literary legitimacy, prefaces consistently begin by recalling traditions—by positioning themselves in relation to some standard practice—with statements like "It hath been such an hereditary practice,"[44] or "Those who appear in Print, do commonly praesuppose,"[45] or "the common strain of the Epistles Dedicatory,"[46] or "I have often observ'd how ineffectually (almost) all Books are Dedicated,"[47] or "The Mode of clapping an Epistle before a Book is to acquaint the Reader what is therein provided . . . [and I am] unwilling to deviate from the Principles of my Profession."[48] In the course of a few pages, *Wits Interpreter*'s breathless preface connects its text with, among other traditions, love, nationalism, Royalism, the socially eminent, social utility, inclusivity, exclusivity, food, birth, sexual purity, gardens, publishing accuracy, and manuscript culture.[49] But rather than providing any clear literary precedent, these hurried graspings construct a sense of profound uncertainty about where, exactly, printed miscellanies might find a known genealogy.

With history apparently unable to supply a clear sense of precedent or tradition, printed miscellanies had to work hard to build a contemporary group identity—to present themselves as a distinct, identifiable publishing phenomenon. Thus compilers make clear the relationship between their book and similar collections, and so attempt to explain themselves as part of a publishing genre. Sometimes connections are drawn directly. *Mock Songs and Joking Poems* proclaims itself a product of "*the Author of* Westminster *Drollery*"[50]—defining itself, then, in terms of another printed miscellany. *The Marrow of Complements*, as we have seen, comprises "the Summe and Substance of all Books of this nature hitherto divulged."[51] And *London Drollery* opens its epistle to the reader with

> *The other Drolleries going so swift away,*
> Why should I think that this should make a stay[52]

which makes apparent a sense of group.

But the near neutral tone of these claims was exceptional. Texts normally denounce rival texts in an angry tone. A publication from 1673 asks the reader whether there be not *more* and *better Songs* in this *little* paper, than he ever found in *any* of the *Drolleries,* whether *Westminster, Windsor, Coventgarden, Holborn, Epsom-Wells, &c.*[53]

Wit and Mirth attempts to distance itself from other texts when it notes that there is not

> in any one Volume so small the like variety of excellent *Poems,* suitable to every humour, except such as delight only in seditious and scandalous Lampoons, or in debauch'd and obscene Ribaldry.[54]

And *The Mysteries of Love and Eloquence* sustains this tone of despair when it deplores the quantity of bad rival texts debasing the miscellany market:

> the several simple Pamphlets that have treated so surreptitiously of this subject, exacted this employment from me, as I could not but be highly incensed, to see them [i.e., readers] so cheated and baffled by such specious pretenders, but most wretched performers of what they undertook. I will not vex my Reader with the Names or Titles they are distinguisht or dignified with, I hope by this time all Ingenious Persons have learnt sufficiently to detest them.[55]

But these definitions through denunciation of course rely on a sense of correspondence with other texts. *The Mysteries of Love and Eloquence* expects readers to recognize the (detestable) other collections; and by resolving to outdo these other works, this miscellany signals its coincidence of intention, form, audience. An alleged supremacy depends on comparison and thus a degree of equivalence. And so in the act of distancing, these printed miscellanies invoke the similarity—and sense of group—they purport to avoid.

This simultaneous recollection of and distancing from a sense of collective identity is sustained in *The Wits Academy* (1677). It explicitly names connecting texts:

> *The Title of this Book I must confess is little different from that piece of weather-beaten Antiquity, vulgarly known by the once famous Name of,* The Academy of Complements[,][56]

then deplores the construction of similar books:

> *exemplary works are for the most part very laudable, especially when we make an imitation on those which have been Famous, Learned, and Nobly extracted, &c. Yet in undertakings of this Nature, imitation is only deem'd to be the barren products of a thred-bare Fancy, and that which a Man can't properly call his own.*[57]

Such efforts to hammer out a sense of the printed miscellany as a recognizable publishing phenomenon—to position the collections as members of the same bickering family—enforce this sense of an anxiety about literary legitimacy.

Precedents for Printed Miscellanies

While to early modern compilers printed miscellanies were apparently difficult to define, and to twenty-first-century eyes these texts confound generic categories, printed miscellanies clearly grew out of certain literary traditions.

Manuscript commonplace books provide perhaps the most obvious precedent. Commonplace books were normally private manuscript collections of observations and excerpts assembled from a range of sources, arranged—in their most organized form—across an alphabetical list of headings. Thus one Joseph Baildon organized his materials—his "Flowers divine and human serving to adorn discourse, mainetaine argument, beautifie both speech & writeinge and to make a man liue happily, and dye blessedly"—under headings that included Creation, Man, Soul, Woeman, Tyme, Eternitie, Synne, Death, and Sabbath.[58] At the heart of commonplace book rationale were notions of selection, appropriation, and use: readers were to gather, organize, and redeploy *sententiae*. Commonplace books were tools for organizing knowledge, educational aids which gathered and grouped a diversity of information into manageable, malleable, applicable pieces. They encouraged readers to plunder life and texts for their profitable moments—to read and observe, and so "Like chesse-nuts sweet, take . . . the kernell out";[59] to "Marshall thy notions," in the words of Thomas Fuller, "into a handsome method";[60] or, as *The Mysteries of Love and Eloquence* mockingly put it, to "turn down the page, transcribe, and for the present subsist on such slender notions."[61]

Whitelock Bulstrode (1650–1724), controversialist and mystical writer—not to be confused with Bulstrode Whitelock (1605–75), keeper of the great seal—reminded himself of the importance of bringing such method to his studies of life; in a note in his own commonplace book, dating from September 1689, Bulstrode wrote

> In ye World, what I meet with extraordinary or Usefull, I committ to writing, y^t on Reflection I may be able to give some accompt of Men & things. In Reading I should observe (but my broken Minutes, will not permitt it) this Method.

> First be Comon-Place; in a generall booke, under proper Heads, what I finde remarkable 2dly sett down what I finde new, & fitt to be remembered, wch one should review at ye End of ye Weeke, & then more exactly Digest it; 3dly be sett downe in another little booke s^{ies} [subjects], y^t I know not; in Order to be Informed, when I meet wth men capable.[62]

Bulstrode's method was unusually ambitious—too ambitious, presumably, given his "broken Minutes." But the principles of his study—the seeking out of the "Usefull"; the cataloging of extracts "under proper Heads"; the relentless ordering of experience; the anticipation of new topics to come—would have been familiar to most seventeenth-century readers. Commonplace book practice was prevalent: in *Love's Labour's Lost*, Sir Nathaniel "Draws out his table book" after hearing, from Holofernes, "A most singular and choice epithet";[63] and in his *Diary*, Pepys notes that "my lord told me [of] . . . his father's many old sayings that he had writ in a book of his."[64] In his *Anatomy of Melancholy*, Robert Burton lamented the lack of any such system in his own reading.

> This rouing humour . . . I haue euer had, and like a ranging Spaniel that barkes at euery bird hee sees, leauing his game, I haue followed all sauing that which I should, and iustly complaine, and truly . . . that I haue read many books but to little purpose, for want of good method, I haue confusedly tumbled ouer many Authors in our Libraries, with small profit, for want of art, order, memory, iudgement.[65]

Also popular were printed commonplace books—either books with a series of printed headings, under which the reader could enter his or her own *sententiae*, such as John Foxe's *Pandectae locorum communium* (Basle, 1557);[66] or fully prepared collections that offered readers the benefits of a dissected, cataloged anthology, while demanding none of the industry of compilation. Significantly, though, this latter variety was often augmented by readers who inserted their own observations in the margins of the book: the commonplace book was as much process as product. Thus a copy of John Marbeck's *A Booke of Notes and Common places . . . collected and gathered out of the workes of diuers singular Writers* (1581) has a reader's brief comments on "The nature of A Tragedie."[67]

Printed miscellanies follow commonplace book conventions in several important respects. Both kinds of text generally show little interest in author or origin: these collections are more concerned with possible future applications of materials than with speculations on sources or origins. The structure of miscellanies often mirrors commonplace books' distribution of inclusions across sections—*The Academy of Complements* sprinkles its offerings across "Pearles of Eloquence," "Choice and faire Flowers," "Complementall and Amorous Poems," and "The Garden Knot of faire and rare Letters of Complement."[68] And in terms of function, commonplace book rationale—the practical application of poetry; the plundering of texts for useful *sententiae*—was sustained in printed miscellanies which advertised themselves as storehouses of poetry and prose which might be pressed into action: "if rightly directed," printed miscellanies "are most absolutely useful."[69] Manuscript verse miscellanies—often, in effect, commonplace books without the system—were similarly close to printed miscellanies. These collections, like their printed counterparts, assembled poems with little consistent regard for author or original contexts and with a free editorial hand. Generally associated with members of Oxford (particularly Christ Church) or, to a lesser extent, Cambridge Universities, or with students at the Inns of Court, these manuscripts shared a taste for the bawdy, the witty, the scurrilous. And they often included a striking range of nonpoetic items: it is quite normal to find Carew poems squeezed in between doodles, riddles, accounts, and potted prose.[70] Printed miscellanies are similarly busy texts. Letters to lovers jostle with puzzles, dialogues, and verses; "Complementall Expressions towards Men" blend with "Letters for all Occasions"; "A short Table of delightful Fictions of the Heathen Poets" mixes with "Fancies, Devices, and flourishing Expressions on Love-Tokens, &c."[71]

In fact, printed miscellanies sometimes explicitly advertise themselves as ready-made commonplace books. The 1650 edition of *The Academy of Complements* mocks the gallant who feels aggrieved that this printed collection

> should rob him of his Commonplace Book; he hangs down his head, and bites his Lip for indignation; and to write seriously, tis a plain case, this Gallant is utterly undone, and sequestred of all; he pursued his Mistriss with such Language, writ thus, sung the same songs, used the same Fancies, and was soe happy as to win admiration from such set forms. Alas poor Gentleman! so Bates *first learnt his Majesties* Hocus Pocus *tricks, and after printed them, and the man of Feats never appearing in his Calling again, there the Common-wealth lost a good subject.*[72]

Presented thus, *The Academy of Complements* is both destructive and constructive: destructive in that this gallant's formerly secret rhetorical techniques are popularized and his efficacy in love is thus destroyed; but constructive in that such previously cloistered modes are conveyed to the general reader. The mocking tone of this preface and the record of the loss of "a good subject" leave the reader uncertain as to whether the destruction of this gallant, like the destruction of

Bates, is a cause for celebration or regret. Either way, this miscellany occupies—displaces might be a better term—the place of the manuscript commonplace book.

John Cotgrave's *The English Treasury of Wit and Language* (1655) stakes similar claims for the former cultural position of the commonplace book. This text, while not a printed miscellany, is an anthology of excerpts, "*Collected Out of the most, and best of our English Drammatick Poems;* [and] *Methodically digested into Common Places For Generall Use.*" By presenting itself as a printed commonplace book, *The English Treasury* suggests it is the only practical way for readers to deal with the great expansion of printed books:

> *if* Salomon *could say, That the reading of many Bookes is wearinesse to the flesh, when there none but Manuscripts in the world: How much is that weareinesse increased since the art of Printing has so infinitely multiplyed large and vast volums in every place, that the longest life of a man is not sufficient to explore so much as the substance of them, which (in many) is but slender? Extractions therefore are the best conservors of knowledge, if not the readiest way to it.*[73]

Cotgrave's text has as a founding principle the conviction that seventeenth-century readers, faced with an explosion of printed material—faced with, in Robert Burton's words, "a vast *Chaos* and confusion of bookes"[74]—required pragmatic organizing tools. Collections of prearranged extractions—ready-prepared commonplace books—were offered as the best means of gathering "substance" from this "chaos and confusion." William Winstanley's *The New Help to Discourse* (1672) is similarly convinced of the need for summaries in a culture newly satiated with printed books. Describing himself as "the Bee to extract Honey out of the flowery Writings of several Authors," Winstanley declares

> Thou hast here ... the pith and marrow of many Voluminous Authors of that bulk and bigness, that many people have not time to read them, more have not money to buy them, and therefore by that means, seeing the tediousness and chargeableness of attaining knowledge, break off their Journey at the beginning of the Race, and despairing of attaining to the end, begin not to run at all; by which means when at any time, (as few so low but sometimes do) they come into company of knowing persons, they are feign to fit like dumb Images or Statues, for fear by speaking they betray their ignorance.[75]

Winstanley's collection boasts "Great store of matter in few sheets compris'd," and, like the desire of Marlowe's Barabas to "inclose / Infinite riches in a little roome," it is indicative of early modern culture's desire for the total to be, somehow, briefly expressed, for complete knowledge in the face of an apparently unmasterable sprawl of texts.[76] Like Cotgrave's *English Treasury*, and like Winstanley's book, printed miscellanies were in part a consequence of commonplace book rationale meeting the daunting reality of the mass market of print.

Printed miscellanies also developed out of the practical educative spirit of the conduct manual tradition which had helped to establish the notion of advancement—primarily but not always social—through personal study.[77] Henry Peacham's *The Complete Gentleman*, first published in 1622, is perhaps the best-known example of this kind of text. But Peacham's text in many ways occupied a very different cultural position to printed miscellanies. The book was originally written for "the priuate use of a Noble young Gentleman my friend," and it aimed to ensure that "euery Noble or Gentle-man" was "attaining . . . the most commendable qualities that are requisite" according to their rank. Such education had, in recent times, grown "deplorable," due to "the remisnesse of Parents, and negligence of Masters in their youth."[78] The book was defiantly not about the redistribution of such knowledge to a broader reading public—what Peacham terms "that pestilent ayre of the common breath."[79] The book's chapter on poetry illustrates this different approach, offering not a series of applicable excerpts, but rather a broad history of verse with a heavy concentration on classical Latin poets. The only mention of writers from 1558 onward comes in a cursory final paragraph:

> In the time of our late Queene *Elizabeth* . . . were *Edward* Earle of *Oxford*, the Lord *Buckhurst*, *Henry* Lord *Paget*; our *Phoenix*, the noble Sir *Philip Sidney*, M. *Edward Dyer*, M. *Edmund Spencer*, M. *Samuel Daniel*, with sundry others; whom (together with those admirable wits, yet liuing, and so well knowne) not out of Enuie, but to auoide tediousnesse I ouerpasse. Thus much of Poetrie.[80]

Texts which combined Peacham's emphasis on education through reading, with the pursuit of a public dissemination of knowledge through print, were closer in spirit to printed miscellanies. Stephano Guazzo's *The Civile Conversation*, published in George Pettie's English translation in 1581, is an example of this kind of text. Guazzo's book was a middle-class counterpart to Baldassare Castiglione's *Il libro del cortegiano* (1528; translated in English as *The Courtyer* in 1561), and offers model dialogues of the kind seen in later printed miscellanies. One copy now in Austin, Texas, contains extensive early modern manuscript notes which suggest a reader consuming the book with a sense of subsequent application in mind.[81] Gervase Markham's sprawl of practical guides such as *The whole art and trade of husbandry* (1614) and *The English House-Wife* (1649) offer other instances of this blend of reading and practical utility. Printed miscellanies, with their frequently invoked emphasis on "Profit and Delight," their stress on advantages to be gained through reading, and the social functions of their verse, develop this tradition.[82]

Printed miscellanies also have an ancestral link with the sixteenth-century miscellanies such as the now fragmentary *The Court of Venus* (1538), Richard Tottel's *Songes and Sonnettes* (1557), *The Paradyse of Daynty Deuises* (1576), Francis Davison's *A Poetical Rhapsody* (1602–21), and "dictionaries" of verse like Robert Allott's *Englands Parnassus: or the choysest flowers of our moderne poets* (1600). This latter collection organizes its (attributed) poetic inclusions under a range of headings: Albion, Angels, Ambition, Affliction, Art, Audacitie, Avarice, etc. At a similar time, and in a similar vein, there appeared a quartet of collections of prose maxims and precepts: Nicholas Ling's *Politeuphuia, Wits Common-Wealth* (1598); Frances Meres's *Palladis Tamia. Wits Treasury* (1598); Robert Allott's *Wits theater of the little World* (1599); and *Palladis palatium: wisedoms pallace. Or the fourth part of Wits commonwealth* (1604). All these collections offer "worke gathered out of diuers learned Authours," presented as "epitomized histories [for the reader] to æmulate . . . and to make right vse of their examples."[83] Meres's *Palladis Tamia* provides little summaries of the works of classical authors—a few lines that extract a clear, unequivocal moral: "As Swans seeing what good is in death, do end their liues with singing: so ought all good, and honest men to do. *Cicero.*"[84]

These books by Ling, Meres, and Allott certainly share some similarities with later printed miscellanies. In terms of the range of materials, the presentation of extracts, and the gathering of work by various authors, often altered, unascribed, or wrongly attributed, there are clear continuities. However, later printed miscellanies are generally less rigidly organized—gone, usually, are the precise commonplace book headings, and if sections are granted titles, they are rather looser (the "Pearles of Eloquence" or "Choice and faire Flowers" of *The Academy of Complements*) than dissecting litanies of "Angels" and "Afflictions." There was a striking difference of tone, too. The Elizabethan collections often had an overt seriousness of purpose largely absent in their mid-seventeenth-century relatives. Their attitudes to their poems were more deferential, distant, learned: while there was still the notion of gaining from books, the envisaged advancement was generally not social but moral. Extracts were presented as exemplars, not quotidian conversational or amatory devices, and the collections remained removed from the chaotic editorial improvisations of *Wits Interpreter* and its squabbling family of texts.[85]

The tendency of printed miscellanies to employ a language of woods, trees, and horticulture suggests a relationship with the classical "silva" tradition.[86]

The silva (Latin for wood or forest) was a "collection" genre, originally—in models such as the Roman poet Statius's *Silvae*—a miscellaneous gathering of poems with a defining absence of order, coherence, or system. Its influence can be seen in early modern collections such as George Gascoigne's *A Hundreth Sundrie Flowres* (1573), divided into sections of "Herbes" and "Weedes" in the edition of 1575, and Ben Jonson's "Forest" and "Under-woods." As Frans De Bruyn has demonstrated, the silva genre provided an important model for Baconian collections of scientific writing—writing which emphasized particulars, rather than wholes; miscellaneity, rather than system; a ranging, expansive, receptivity to supplement, rather than a limiting pursuit of definition. For Bacon, and, later, for the Royal Society, writing which resisted order and which, in effect, drew attention to its systemless miscellaneity, had an intellectual honesty which coherence and categorization would always betray. The silva, and Bacon's celebration of its unsystematized miscellaneity in works such as *Sylva Sylvarum: or a Natural History* (1627), provided an intellectual defense of the orderless collection as a form. And while printed miscellanies make no explicit connection with this silva tradition, their use of a vocabulary of forests, trees, and gardens, suggests a link. In *Parasceve,* Bacon likens the silva to a "Store-house"[87]—a term printed miscellanies repeatedly use in their own self-definitions.

"Admirably Useful": The Declared Purpose of Printed Miscellanies

Some texts loudly proclaimed a lack of any apparent serious aim: readers are told to do no more than "Read, Laugh, and enjoy";[88] that "the publishers have no designes beyond thy pleasure,"[89] and that collections are only "Variety of Songs, full of Mirth and Pleasure, / For Young-Men and Maids to read at their leisure."[90]

A lack of seriousness was not an apolitical stance. In particular, the kind of pleasure these texts suggest—a pleasure full of drink, mirth, ribald humor, disengagement—was in some ways a powerful attack on Commonwealth and particularly Puritan ideology. This is apparent in *Wit and Drollery*—"invented purposely to keep off the violent assaults of Melancholly, assisted by the additionall Engines, and Weapons of Sack and good company"[91]—which equates its happy purpose with the woes of contemporary England.[92]

Of those texts which do propose a clear purpose, some declare textual duties. They stress an interest in preparing a high-quality edition to counter other baser rivals whose poor texts do "as much dishonour of our English Wit, as if Don's Poems were turned into Dutch."[93] We are told over and over that *this* miscellany, unlike those corrupt others, is "*Collected with the greatest care, and printed after the most Correct Copies.*"[94] There is an emphasis on a duty to poetry and, more broadly, an obligation to the English language. One compiler styles himself an editor

> who is zealous for the honour of our Language ... who bewailes those weake essayes that have been made by others to this purpose.[95]

In this respect, printed miscellanies recall Tottel's *Songes and Sonnettes* (1557), which proudly asserted its duty to proving the poetic worth of the English language, particularly in comparison with "the workes of diuerse Latines, Italians, and other[s]."

> That our tong is able in that kynde to do as praiseworthy as ye rest, the honourable stile of the noble earle of Surrey, and the weightinesse of the depewitted sir Thomas Wyat the elders verse, with seuerall graces in sondry good Englishe writers, doe show abundantly. It resteth nowe (gentle reder) that thou thinke it not euill doon, to publish, to the honor of the English tong, and for profit of the studious of Englishe eloquence, those workes which the ungentle horders up of such treasure haue heretofore enuied thee.[96]

A later edition of *A Collection of Poems. Written upon several Occasions,* from 1693, notes in its address from "The Publisher to the Reader" that

> The *French* have lately Publish'd Five or Six Volumes of their choicest Poems, by Several Hands; but I must beg, that this Collection may not be thought to be done in imitation of them. We are pretty well recovered from the Servile way of following their Modes; and this Publication is an effect of Emulation, to shew, That as the *English* Genius and Language for the *Drama* and for *Epick Poetry,* has been granted, infinitely to excel theirs; so we have no less the Advantage in the less, tho' nice Productions of the Nature of these Collections. Their Gallantry and Courtship is what we justly condemn as Foppery; and their Panegyricks are made up of nothing but Intolerable Dawbing: whereas in this Collection you will find Performances of the Sublimest Fancy, Govern'd by Solidity of Judgment, and Polish'd by the utmost Delicacy of Art.[97]

Almost 150 years after Tottel's celebration of "Englishe eloquence," collections of poetry in English still anxiously asserted their legitimacy against a European context. Some printed miscellanies offered themselves, in part, as contributors to this process of justification.

But more common than either the defiant pledge of purposelessness, or this nervous celebration of Englishness, was the printed miscellany's promise that it was socially educative. Text after text claims to be a practical handbook fit for application: to present the manners and customs of a social elite to the general reader. Such miscellanies are, we are told, manuals of etiquette and style—"as every way beneficiall to thee,"[98] and full of

> such nimble applications, [which] if rightly directed, are most absolutely useful; and that those which have been adorned with such qualifications, have had such tall advantages over others, as seldom or never fall short of their ends.[99]

This collection offers

> Addresses, and set Forms of Expressions for imitation; Poems, pleasant Songs, Letters, Proverbs, Riddles, Jeasts, Posies, Devices, A la mode Pastimes, A Dictionary for the making of Rimes, Four hundred and fifty delightful Questions, with their several Answers. As also Epithets, and flourishing Similitudes, Alphabetically collected, and so properly applied to their several Subjects, that they may be rendred admirably useful on the sudden occasions of Discourse or Writing. Together, with a new invented Art of Logick, so plain and easie by way of Questions and Answers, that the meanest capacity may in a short time attain to a perfection in the wayes of Arguing and Disputing.[100]

As this collection's tireless title page indicates, the precise nature of these "nimble applications" varies. Sometimes the texts envision readers enjoying significant political advancement through the re-presentation of miscellany rhetoric. Among the many and varied inclusions in *The Academy of Complements*, for instance, is a brief but audacious exposition titled "*Stiles and Tearmes used to* the KING, or QUEENES Majesty, either in our Speech, or in Superscriptions of Petitions directed to them." This section describes how the reader might manage various kinds of generally written interactions with the monarchy. It is conduct advice taken to the highest point of application. We find that "*If you present anything,*" the act must be prefaced with "May it please your Majesty"; "*If you write in forme of a petition to the King,*" the prose must begin "May it please your Majesty to understand, or to grant."[101] In later editions of this same book the theme is explored further, as the reader is initiated into the intricacies of offering "*A tender of service to ones Soveraigne,*" or "*An humble addresse to a great Lord,*" where the reader is encouraged to employ epistolary prose such as "I must entreate you to pardon my boldnesse, in that I, who am a stranger, have presumed to come to visit you, being invited thereunto by the fame and report of your noble vertues. . . ."[102] *Wits Interpreter,* similarly, dictates how to address a duke, an earl, a marquess, and a viscount.[103] (In both books it is generally written, not oral, eloquence that is suggested, indicating a sustained distance between reader and royalty.)

If the plea for service is the most striking miscellany inclusion, the plea for love is the most common. Miscellanies are full of chunks of (generally oral) stock eloquence which a wooing male might place before a female. *The New Academy of Complements* declares that if the reader is intent "*To bear* Loves *Arms, and follow* Cupids *Tent,*" the miscellany will teach him

> *how to speak her fair, to write, and wooe.*
> *Last having won thy Mistriss to thy lure, I'le teach thee how to make her love endure.*[104]

In fact there is considerable slippage between the language of political service and the language of love: a vocabulary of love often shapes political pleadings, and a politicized lexicon of rank, deference, service, and etiquette frequently informs amorous pleadings: "To *the most gracious Queen of my Soul*"; "To *the most illustrious Princess of my Heart*"; "To the Countess Dowager of my Affections"; "To *the Baroness of my Words and Actions.*"[105]

To enable wooing there are general, set sentences—"Pearles of Eloquence," in the words of *The Academy of Complements*—which offer broad prose flatteries such as "*Lady,* Your forme doth so ravish beholders that you seeme a heavenly creature in a mortall carcasse." There are also more particular models of praise which present descriptions "On her face . . . hair, brow, fore-head, eyes, smiles." Such an extended blazon is very common. One collection dissects its subject into more than twenty parts and offers praise on each: "*On her Face*" ("You are the Beauty without parallel; in your Face all the Graces, and in your Minde all the Vertues are met: he that looks upon your milde Aspect, were it the most savage creature, would derive a new Nature from your Beauty"); "*On her Eyes and Lips*"; "*On her Beauty*"; on her hair, locks, forehead, face ("So full of majesty, that *Aurora* blushes to see a countenance brighter then her own. Her Face is full of Sun-shine"), looks, smiles, cheeks, breath, chin, tongue, brow, neck, words, voice, arms, hands, and breasts.[106]

The nature of the interaction, more than the appearance of the woman, often organizes miscellany praise. Thus there are nuggets of courting prose distributed under various headings pertaining to particular social moments: "*Upon his Absence*"; "*Protestations of Love*"; "*Vpon her Beauty*"; "*In admiration of her goodnesse*"; "*On her leaving him*"; "*To accuse in a letter*";[107] or, more particularly still, "*The lover having adopted himselfe Servant to a beautie that would make him believe she hath vowed Chastitie, may thus informe her by Letter.*"[108] There are verse witticisms to accompany acts of gift-giving: "*Upon a Scarf presented*" ("Take this scarf, bind *Cupid* hand and foot, / So love must ask you leave before he shoot"); "*Upon a Fan presented*"; "*On a pair of Gloves presented*" ("Fairest, to thee I send these Gloves, / If you love me, leave out the G, / And make it a pair of Loves").[109]

And there are models of wit and eloquence framed for certain specific environments; thus, a series of short conversational pieces guides the reader about what to say at "*the Horse-Races,*" with headings like "*The Gentlemen to the Jocky,*" and "*After Starting.*"[110] Another provides resources for entertaining at home: "*Before Dinner*" ("*Sir,* be pleas'd to seat your self there, that is the place which is appointed for you"); "*After Dinner* ("*Sir,* You will excuse your bad entertainments").[111] *The Mysteries of Love and Eloquence* purports to depict, among other things, "*The Mode of* Hide Park," and includes a narration of a couple's courting dialogue as they move through the park: he invites her into his carriage; she accepts; he recounts the latest news (the text leaves blanks which might allow the insertion of names: "Madam, they say, Sir *Charls* ———— hath put off his mourning-weeds, and appears this day in the Park with a new Coach and Livery"); they proceed to the ring, where "Fruiterers, who are bold Wenches, offer oranges and cherries; he buys the latter." There is a sense of the distant in all this: "Hide Park," the courtship, and the news of "mourning-weeds" constitute, to a degree, vignettes of other lives, with the reader positioned as voyeur, peering though the carriage windows. But there is also the impression that readers might genuinely employ these models. As the courting man and woman travel in the coach round the ring, we are told with endearing literalism how

> Much discourse cannot be expected from that restless motion of Wheels and Horses, it being onely a preparative for treatement talk; neither indeed in that place of Observation, is more required, then onely as occasion serves, to tell your Lady, *That is my Lord such a ones Coach; That's my Lady such a one; That's Squire such a one.* And then when opportunity offers itself, to say, *Your humble Servant; my Lord; Your most humble Servant, Madam.*[112]

The reader, it seems, is positioned somewhere between voyeur and participant.

Not all miscellany compliments relate to love. There are materials that concern male friendship (a male-female or female-female friendship is never considered): "Complementall Expressions towards Men" such as "Sir, Without a

Complement, I am your Friend, and that one word speaks me wholly yours," and headings which offer words pertaining to particular scenarios: "*Comfortable Advice to a Friend on the death of a Son, or other near Relation.*"[113] There are also applicable inclusions designed to generally impress an audience and raise one's social stock. Thus there are "flourishing Similitudes and Comparisons, for the better imitation, admirably applied to their several Subjects" such as "*Success is a rare paint, it hides all ugliness.*"[114] There are tricks: "Pretty Conceits," including "*To heave up a Bottle with a Straw*"; "*How a Peare, or an Apple may be parted into many parts without breaking the Rind*"; "*How to tell a man his Christian name though you never saw him before*"; "*How a man may put his finger in, or wash his hands in melting Lead without danger of burning.*"[115] There are jokes ("*Q. Why are Tobacco-shops and Bawdy-houses conincidents? A.* Because smoak is not without fire").[116] There is a (baffling) exposition of "Cardinal Richeleiu's Key to his manner of writing of Letters by Cyphers." There are explanations of games, including drinking games; rhyming games like "that pleasing Pastime called *CRAMBO*" which depends upon "The more expeditious finding out of any Rime"; and "the Joviall al-a-mode sports and games, that are most celebrated by Persons of Honor," such as "*Crosse-purposes,*" "*the Lovers Alphabet,*" and "*Gliphing.*" The latter "chiefly consists in the quick pronouncing of a sentence, hard to be uttered without a wanton or some other unlucky kind of merry mistake . . . the mistakes may the sooner produce laughter."[117] There is a guide to "The Art of Reasoning, A new Logick," which provides a chapter-by-chapter explanation of logic. (This rather dry contribution was cut from later editions.)[118] There are brief summaries of the origins of "geometrie," hunting, and husbandry, as well as potted dictionaries of classical mythology.[119]

Miscellanies are just the kind of text Henry Peacham would have condemned: writing some twenty years before the printed miscellany boom, Peacham's *The Complete Gentleman* deplored "the common Education; which is, to weare the best cloathes, eate, sleepe, drinke much, and to know nothing."[120] The elite gloss that printed miscellanies promised to convey—the ability to offer up "flourishing Similitudes and Comparisons"; to play at crambo; to expound, briefly, from a potted dictionary of mythology—is precisely the kind of fashionable, superficial social education Peacham attacked.

Even those books in which the purveyance of social grace is not the explicit intention, poems were presented as products of prestigious locations and coteries, and as exemplars of the excellent: "Composed by the best Wits that were in both the Universities"; "By Sir *J.M. Ja:S.* Sir *W.D. J.D.* And other admirable Wits"; stored with complements "that are, and have been lately in request at Court, and both the Theatres." Miscellanies are presented as alluring conveyers of social status; desire is a key term in their prefaces and title pages.

Instances of female agency within these political and amatory contexts are very rare. Printed miscellanies do sometimes include women among their imagined readers: *A Jovial Garland* offers itself "For Young-Men and Maids"; *The New Academy of Complements* is intended for "both Sexes"; and *The Marrow of Complements* confidently predicts the

> *Citizens Wife . . . (in her closet) will peruse me with more veneration than she would* Perkins *or* Playford.[121]

And there are a few moments when this inclusion is sustained within the dialogues and poetry of the collections: among "Letters for all Occasions," there are models such as "The Lady to her Lover, in defence of her own Innocency."[122] But such instances are rare, and even these cases generally present females reacting to—defending against—earlier male initiatives. Thus, a verse titled "*A Maide or Widdow having long beene in league with one that (seemingly) was her faithfull friend, and now finding him inconstant, and affianced to another, may thus take notice of his perfidiousneße.*"[123]

Miscellanies overwhelmingly imply male readers and agents, and construct females as the passive recipients of praise. Indeed, the socially mobile woman is often invoked as a figure of transgression, both comically and as a serious warning about the misapplication of miscellany materials. *The Mysteries of Love and Eloquence* laments the fact that

> a wench of fourteen, with a few Dramatical *Drayton* and *Sidney* Quillets, put to the *non plus* a Gallant of thirty; I may safely depose on it, that I have heard such a Lass defeat a Gentleman of some years standing at the Inns of Court.[124]

We see this alarm articulated most vividly in John Cotgrave's *Wits Interpreter*. Cotgrave disdainfully distances his book from collections by those "late Scriblers" which invite a broad readership. In particular, he denounces the idea that his book might help the humblest chambermaid to rise up the social ladder. In eager, busy prose, he comments:

> Not to trouble the *Reader* with many instances, I will present him with an *Impossibility*, which some of our late *Scriblers* most strongly hold forth; and what it is, think you, but an *Art of Complementing*, which they obtrude on the *under-Wits*, and amongst the rest they have more especially seduced a Favorite of

theirs y'cleped the *Chambermaid* to make her believe, she may be easily completed with *offensive* and *defensive terms* of *Language*, so to manage her *Wit* as if she were at a *prize* . . . Our little *English World* hath of this kind to many *presidents*.

Cotgrave was probably aiming his wrath directly at *The Academy of Complements*—a text which regrets that "Chambermaids and waiting-Gentlewomen . . . are often constrained to blush, in ignorance, for want of Complements."[125]

Of course actual readers did not necessarily match this constructed demographic. As chapter 2 will discuss, there is clear evidence of females reading printed miscellanies, and, in general, of readers and reading practices falling well outside the models miscellanies prescribe. But the present discussion is concerned with miscellany constructions, not the evidence of actual reading practice, and in this sphere females are rarely included as active participants.

Cotgrave's desire to discourage the reading chambermaid and, in general, to limit female agency, is part of a larger concern about the legitimacy of miscellany readings. When *The Academy of Complements* includes "A miscellaneous present of Similitudes, Comparisons, and Examples," the text stresses that such material is "selected for the Readers *discreeter* application."[126] And that "discreeter" is important, since it suggests the citing of recycled lines had a dubious status—that miscellany readers might display the wit, but not the means by which the wit was acquired. And we can see this attitude elsewhere—this sense that miscellany learning was a process which had to be concealed. In "*Occasioned by a Lovers presenting a Copy of Verse to his Mistresse*," a woman reacts angrily when she realizes she is being offered second-hand wit:

> And now faith tell me, what Poet has hired you to put off his Verses, you bring nothing of your own besides the tune . . . Come I know some penny Rimer or other hath sold you a stock to set up with, to save delayes of printing, take you out of this way, and you have no more time in you then a dying Swan, though less melody.[127]

Printed miscellanies appear to be walking a precarious tightrope: they offer model dialogues which prepare the reader to nimbly deny a reliance on model dialogues. In *The Marrow of Complements* (1655), the editor notes how readers will not admit to a perusal of miscellanies—but will, in private, quickly turn to such collections.

> *I know* Socrates (*though perhaps in private he sport with his* Cattamite) *will cast a frowning countenance upon these Amorous pieces:* Diogenes *will be dogged,* Cato *censorious and* Curio *currish; but this is onely a varnish to their (clandestine) venery, for in private the*

crabbedst Crittick of them all will with more willingnesse peruse these facetious fancies . . . they will not blush to make me their Tutor.[128]

Much humor in printed miscellanies is generated through what one collection calls "Mock . . . And Drolling Letters" that derive their comedy from depictions of attempted interactions across the social hierarchy. Particular scorn is directed toward the lower-class male attempting to woo the higher-class woman: thus, "*A Broom-man in Kent, to a young Lady of quality, whom he fell in Love withall, beholding her in a Belcony,*" where the young "Broom-man" is assigned appropriately debasing pleadings like "I would give all the old Shoes in my Sack to enjoy the happiness of your sweet company." The same collection includes "*A Country Parson to a rich Farmers Daughter in the same Village,*" and "*A Countrey Bumpkin to his Mistress.*"[129] This is a collection that laughs at the absurdity of cross-class dialogues, but at the same time has the prospect of social advancement as its raison d'être. There is a kind of self-loathing at the heart of printed miscellanies.

"Well Said, *Academy of Complements*": Depictions of Miscellany Readers

Dramatic representations of miscellany readers suggest the notion of applying materials from these collections, particularly in amatory social contexts, was well established and ripe for bathetic comedy. Such scenarios consistently present miscellany readers as gauche young men of low but aspiring social rank, ineffectually turning to (most frequently) *The Academy of Complements*, or some such text, for clumsy wooing compliments, and laborious reworkings of once-delicate lines.[130]

William Cavendish's *The triumphant widow* (1677) provides a representative construction. In act 3, Codshead ("a Coxcomb") recites

> As I was saying, Madam, you are a pretty Thief, and steal every bodies heart, no man can keep a heart in quiet for you.

To this, Lady Haughty replies

> Did not you steal that out of the Academy of Complements, Mr. *Codshead*?

Codshead denies the charge ("No, as I hope to be saved") and tries to continue his wooing words. But wit does not come easy, and he starts to stumble through his half-remembered lines:

Madam, your Eyes hum—your bright Eyes hum—have so enslaved me, that, hum, hum—I can no longer call my heart my own ... And then that stately and majestical Forehead adorned by, or rather adorning those curles—hum—those snares for hearts ... Peace, I have a thousand commendations more for you, as that your breath is a heavenly dew, sweeter than Eastern Winds—hum—that o're the flowry Gardens blow—hum, ha—or than the choicest Arabian Gums.

Codshead's lexicon—hums aside—is in fact extremely close to the vocabulary offered in *The Academy of Complements:* his "Your teeth like—hum—Oriental Pearls" recalls "Within the compass of this holow sweet, / Those orient rankes of silver Pearles doe meet"; his "your snowy Breasts" bring to mind "snowie flesh." And Codshead's whole repertoire evokes, in general, *Academy* lines such as "Her brests those Ivory Globes"; "Her bright Browes drive the sunne to clouds beneath"; "Her eyes the contradictors of the night."[131]

The printed miscellany, here, and in other dramatic depictions, supplies viscous, sickly praise, and the clumsy male wooer is rendered foolish. (As Codshead splutters his lines, Lady Haughty declares, "These commendations come not from your heart, you hum and pause, and seem to be in pain.") Furthermore, not only does a dependence on miscellany eloquence suggest a lack of wit; such a reliance also amounts to the breaking of etiquettes of eloquence and courtship. While the Lady's suggestion that Codshead did "steal" the words deflects back the accusation that she is "a pretty Thief," it also suggests that the plundering of miscellany wit is a dubious, illicit activity. We see this in Codshead's failed attempts to convince that these lines are his ("I am a Son of a Whore, Madam, if they be not from my heart"). Such an anxiety recalls those model dialogues in *Wits Interpreter* which depict speakers being chastised for employing model dialogues—and, in general, printed miscellanies' laughter at those cross-hierarchy interactions which they, apparently, seek to enable.

This same construction—printed miscellanies supplying tired lines for tired wits, who fail to impress their would-be lovers—is seen repeatedly in later seventeenth-century plays. The debunking of the wooer's lapidary praise, in particular, emerges as a refrain. Alert recipients of miscellany lines respond with a weary dismissal, and the wooers emerge as not only rejected but also uninformed, unsophisticated, and unconvincing. The gap between the ornament of the wooer's eloquence and the curt irritation of the recipient creates a moment of acute bathos. Thomas Forde's *Love's Labyrinth* has Doron extracting recycled wit from "the Nichodemus Of Complements, that's a sweet book, 'tis a very magazine of Poetrie, a store-house of wit," to which Carmilla offers a cool, tired, dismissive "What small Poet have you hired to make a miracle of my name?"[132] In Richard Brome's *A Joviall Crew, or, The Merry Beggars*, Rachel characterizes foolish suitors as those that

> tell us, Ladies, your lips are sweeter [than sweetmeats], and then fall into Courtship, one in a set speech taken out of [Nicolas Breton's] old *Britains Works*, another with Verses out of the *Academy of Complements*, or some or other of the new Poetical Pamphletters, ambitious onely to spoile Paper, and publish their names in print.[133]

Far from enabling grand social advances, printed miscellanies mark out their readers as unrefined, ignorant, absurd, and so enforce a sense of social hierarchy as something fixed and certain. Thus these dramatic representations position printed miscellanies not as transformative texts—a potential miscellanies often proclaim—but as collections that emphasize social difference and limit mobility. *The Academy of Complements*, far from adorning readers "with such qualifications," seems to function—in these dramatic depictions—as a badge of exclusion.

As a consequence, to be accused of depending on miscellanies is a damaging charge. In Isaac Bickerstaffe's *Love in a village* (1763), act 2, scene vii, an ornate speech ("The sun seems to have hid himself a little, to give you an opportunity of supplying his place") is met with the deflating "Where could he get that now? he never read it in the academy of compliments." The speaker is indignant:

> Come don't affect to treat me with contempt; I can suffer any thing better than that.[134]

Of course, such caricaturing, dramatic constructions only tell us so much. The purpose of Codshead, Doron, and this last indignant speaker is to generate comedy, not necessarily to represent actual reading practices. To begin to detect the traces left by real seventeenth-century readers is a more speculative project—but a compelling one. It is the task of chapter 2.

TWO

Readers and Readings

... is not the leaf turn'd down
Where I was reading? Here it is, I think.[1]
Julius Caesar

Please do not
... write in or mark any item.
... *The British Library reserves the right to remove a reader's pass
if regulations are contravened.*
A REMINDER TO READERS, British Library

Who Read Printed Miscellanies?

The few studies that have examined printed miscellanies usually suggest an audience of young town gallants of good family, perhaps engaged with university or Inns of Court educations, and fidgeting dissolutely at the fringes of court or establishment life.[2] Certainly some contemporary references evoke this kind of reader. One 1675 character collection describes the town gallant as that "Bundle of *Vanity*" resembling

> a kind of *Walking Mercers shop* ... made up of Complements, *Cringes, Knots, Fancies, Perfumes,* and a thousand *French* Apish tricks.

"His whole Library," we are told,

> consists of *The Academy of Complements, Venus undress'd, Westminster Drollery,* half a dozen *Plays,* and a bundle of *Bawdy* Songs in *Manuscript*.[3]

Printed miscellanies, in this collection's world, were snapped up by foppish males—"the smooth effeminate silken tribe"[4]—who liked nothing better than the affectation of Continental fashions, and who used miscellanies as one more jewel to ornament their costume. In Thomas Otway's *Friendship in Fashion*, the absurd Sir Noble Clumsy "had all *Westminster Drollery* and *Oxford Jests* at his Finger ends."[5] *Westminster Drollery* is a printed miscellany; *Oxford Jests* is a related text, a collection of prose anecdotes compiled by William Hickes, dancer/captain/tapster/poet.

Miscellanies themselves, in their prefaces and poems, often exude this sense of the young urban male reader preoccupied with wit, women, and wine: "the Youthful Gentry," those "ingenious Lovers of Poetry" who frequent "the Play-House," who "with *Bacchus* . . . [are] jolly," who fall for "The Beautiful Chloret Suprized in the Sheets."[6]

But printed miscellanies were and are eminently mockable texts. Their grand but flawed sense of exclusive self-importance invites ridicule and stereotyping. Proposing a homogenous (and absurd) class of readers is thus tempting, but surely misleading. Such a proposition rests on the assumption that the readers constructed in preface and title page matched actual readers, implying the world described in verse—the world of young male wooers and court gallants—was the world lived by readers. In fact, the very popularity of printed miscellanies demands a more nuanced consideration of readership since it suggests texts were subject to many different readings.

One also needs to understand that compilers were in many ways obliged to construct a sense of exclusivity for their printed texts. Much has been written about the "stigma of print": about the widespread early modern perception of print as an ungentlemanly medium.[7] This perception, it has been argued, was constructed at court where poets like Wyatt and Surrey composed for a "coterie audience," stressing the secondary, almost frivolous, nature of their verse and avoiding the discrediting descent into print with its commercial connotations. Thus George Puttenham, in *The Arte of English Poesie* (1589), named Raleigh among "a crew of Courtly makers, Noble men and Gentlemen of her Majesties owne servaunts, who have written excellently well, as it would appear if their doings could be found out and made publike with the rest."[8] Manuscript, in contrast to popularizing print, was resonant with exclusivity and privilege, and as Castiglione had suggested, manuscript verse was a complement to the dancing, singing, gaming, and civilized conversation that supposedly made up life around the Crown.[9] Even writers who sought to make a living directly from the pen and so kept an eye on the commercial advantages of the press were acutely conscious of its connotations and frequently affected some of the self-effacement typical of their courtly counterparts. They might stress their delay in moving to print, or their youthful rashness, or the urging of friends, or some other means to display contrition. In dedicating his printed collection "To the truly noble Edward Pepes, Esq," the editor of *Wit and Drollery* was aware he was treading a dangerous path. "I am not ignorant," he wrote, "how you shun these vulgar ways of being made public."[10] If manuscript was often accompanied with associations of secrecy and the elite, print was frequently figured as the baser, popularizing medium.[11]

In fact such an analysis lacks a necessary specificity: not all printed texts suggested the same negative connotations, and if we are to locate an early modern stigma of print, we should at least acknowledge the degree to which it varied according to types of publication, author, and historical moment.[12] A folio devotional work and a duodecimo sonnet collection must have generated different connotations, and we see in Shakespeare's plays *particular types* of printed text—most frequently ballads—inducing negative, populist connotations. Cleopatra, fearing for her reputation, imagines that "scald rhymers / Ballad us out o' tune"; Benedick declares that if it is "prove that ever I lose more blood with love than I will get with drinking, pick out mine eyes with a ballad-maker's pen." Chapbooks foster similar associations: "Beauty is bought by judgment of the eye, / Now uttered by base sale of chapmen's tongues."[13] It is perhaps more useful to replace the "stigma of print" with the "stigma of the populist," since it was not the medium itself that most commonly induced nervous prefatorial justifications, but the process of being rendered widely read by unknown readers. (Thus a privately circulating printed book would not generate perceptions of the debased.)

So when compilers of miscellanies came to produce their books, connotations surrounding popular print put them in a difficult situation. Their medium was the small, cheap, printed book—the epitome of the commercial, which might well "Ballad us out o' tune." Hence the compiler's anxiety that readers of the later 1650 edition of *The Academy of Complements* should

> *Receive it with washed hands, and without a prejudicate opinion; for whatsoever thy censure was of it before, it was then well approved of, as this tenth Edition declares, which now carries so much state with it, as not to stoop to thy Censure.*[14]

The writer goes on to describe those readers who desire this collection, but feel shame at the prospect of buying a cheap, popular printed book:

> *I have met with other downe-right Delinquents; the first of them is bashful, he is ashamed forsooth to step into the quaint edifice of our Academy; he will not buy it himself, but sends another to procure it for him, and playes least in sight; Like a Wench that spreads her fingers wide before*

her face, that she may see, if it were possible, the obiect more modestly, which otherwise she must flie from: So this new eclips'd Gentleman that sees and will not seem to see, reads this Volume in his study more privately than his Prayer Book, and perhaps with more devotion, though he will not let the world know so much, for feare his phrases should grow common: it is his Diary, he looks oftner in it than on his Watch: in a word, he accounts of it as the Jewel of his practice, and the sum of his most refined conversation: This, Reader, is my publike enemy, but my secret friend.[15]

Yet despite these perceptions, compilers fashioned their miscellanies to convey a sense of the desirable, the profitable, the exclusive.

Thus prefaces frequently cite that select and generally young, urban, male readership we have discussed as part of a larger attempt to evoke an exclusive milieu. (It is worth noting that the construction of a young town gallant readership lent social legitimacy in the seventeenth century but for twentieth-century scholars served only to condemn these texts as playgrounds for idle wits.) Compilers connected their books with prestigious places: thus *The Mysteries of Love and Eloquence ... As they are manag'd in the Spring Garden, Hide Park, the New Exchange, and other eminent places*; thus *Wit at a Venture* as "Clio's Privy-Garden"; thus *Holborn Drollery*'s declared context as "Grayes-Inne-Walkes."[16] (By contrast, Matthew Stevenson's collection of poems called *Bristol Drollery* admits to a relative provinciality: "Why does any there [i.e., in Bristol] pretend to Wit?," the prefatorial verse asks, and "Do's not the Author tell us flat and plain, / Such a dull foggy Air do's clog the brain?"[17]) Miscellanies stressed links with the eminent: *Wits Interpreter* prints sketches of Philip Sidney and Francis Bacon (although the pictures bear little relation to the contents of the book); *The Harmony of the Muses* boasts that "The Fancyee of so many letter'd and unequalled men are here united into Piece," and that it contains work by "many incomparable Witts."[18] In fact, *Sportive Wit* specifically warned readers that certain rival miscellanies used the eye-catching names of Sir John Mennes and James Smith to sell books, while offering little of their work: "these worthy persons are likely to suffer by Copies, to which their names are shortly to be affixed: Papers only to be protested against."[19] The charge was perhaps directed at *Musarum Deliciæ: or, the Muses Recreation ... By Sr J.M. and Ja:S.* (1655), but the indignation did not stop *Sportive Wit*'s title page from itself enigmatically promising inclusions by "*a Club of sparkling Wits, viz. C.J. B.J. L.M. W.T. Cum multis aliis—*."

But at the same time, it was clear that a few pennies in the bookseller's purse would enable anyone to clamber up these various manifestations of the "*English Parnassus.*" Introductions and title pages thus lurch between that sense of the exclusive that might counter debasing connotations and addresses to the commercially desirable mass reader. *The Mysteries of Love and Eloquence*, we remember, offered the modes of *"Wooing and Complementing; As they are manag'd in the Spring Garden, Hide Park, the New Exchange, and other eminent places."* It proudly asserts that

> the contributions of several persons of Honor, as well by their particular prescriptions, as also of their choisest Manuscripts, built up this Volume. It took its birth from them.[20]

Yet it simultaneously claims to contain

> Addresses, and set Forms of Expressions for imitation; [and] Poems, pleasant Songs, Letters . . . Together with a new invented Art of Logick, so plain and easie . . . *that the meanest capacity* may in a short time attain to a perfection.[21]

The Marrow of Complements was a book

> Fitted for the use of *all sorts* of persons, from the Noblemans Palace to the Artizans Shop,[22]

and *The Academy of Complements* promises aid to all levels of social intercourse: "from the king to persons of the most inferior ranke or qualitie."[23] *The Card of Courtship* boasts many a court-like phrase, yet was *"fitted to the Humours of all Degrees, Sexes, and Conditions."* It dedicates itself "To the longing Virgins, amorous Batchelors, blithe Widows, kind Wives, and flexible Husbands, *of what Honour, Title, Calling, or Conversation soever, within the* REALM of GREAT BRITAIN."[24] *The New Academy of Complements* offers itself "For Ladies, Gentlewomen, Courtiers, Gentlemen, Scholars, Souldiers, Citizens, Country-men, and all persons, of what degree soever, of both Sexes."

As this large quotation indicates, the implied readership might include women readers. They are suggested in other texts, too: in *A Jovial Garland* ("For Young-Men and Maids"), *The New Academy of Complements* (for "both Sexes"), and in William Wycherley's play *The Country Wife*—where Mrs. Pinchwife, finding the bookseller without the desired "six-penny worth" of ballads, requests "*Covent-garden-Drollery*, and a Play or two."[25] This is an exchange not only interesting for its allusion to female readers: it also implies a degree of cultural equivalence between printed miscellanies and ballads, and suggests the potential rural readership of such texts.

It should be said, though, that when women are mentioned as potential readers they usually form a constituent of a more generally democratic readership: that is, they are rarely cited as a *discrete class* of readers, rarely explicitly addressed, but included—when they are included—as a component of wide readership. There are few moments when active female readers are vividly invoked, and, as chapter 1 suggested, those depictions of female readers tend to present females reacting to—defending against—prior male initiatives. When a distinct class of female reader is addressed, it is in the context of a comic, mock preface. Thus *"To those Cruel Fair Ones, that triumph over the distresses of their loyal lovers,"*[26] which depicts the world through poetic commonplaces and portrays females as harsh oppressors of love-struck males.

But caveats aside, miscellany prefaces do at least gesture toward a wide readership that might be termed "middle class" in its broadest sense. Thus while John Cotgrave invokes an elite readership—they "oughtest to be Ingenious"—he simultaneously embraces them as strangers, as unknowns, as "whosoever thou art."[27]

The vitality of the publishing industry similarly suggests a great range of readers. According to David Cressy, early modern London literacy rates may have reached 80 percent[28]; the area around St. Paul's Cathedral was alive with booksellers and literary entrepreneurs;[29] and miscellanies were relatively inexpensive, selling for 1s 6d or less.[30] Neither was a strong market for these texts the preserve only of London: Oxford, Cambridge, Lincoln, Salisbury, Exeter, Worcester, Winchester, and Canterbury all had booksellers who might well have carried miscellanies.[31] Studies suggest that regional bookshops kept running accounts with London suppliers and were well stocked with recent publications.[32] Printed miscellanies were almost certainly readily available to many.[33]

Manuscript marginalia in miscellanies enforce this sense of readers drawn from a wide cross section. Markings suggest some texts passed from reader to reader—or owner to owner—and were thus subject to a diversity of readings. One copy of *Wits Recreations* bears the signatures of "John Williams," "John Prichom," "William Willett," and the magnificently named "Josephus Scerm."[34] Another includes the manuscript note "William Wynne Ellin Wynne 1680,"[35] denoting, probably, a book circulating within one family and perhaps readers of different ages. Across the opening pages of a copy of John Playford's *An Introduction to the Skill of Musick* (1674)—a book in many ways occupying a similar cultural position to a miscellany—are various scribblings, including apparent notes of ownership: "Thomas brak" [?], "Anne Pole," "Alice Trollop . . . / Thomas Pole . . . his / Booke."[36] These last two texts suggest female readers, as does "Hannah Lea / is my name / Ha." in a Bodleian copy of *Wits Interpreter*.[37] Clumsy attempts at calligraphy, scribblings, and doodles[38] imply child readers, or readers with little education, and evoke a context away from those educated town coteries printed miscellanies often imply. Of course such scribblers might not have been readers. Paper was expensive, and cheap books might function as useful scribbling pads; annotators could well have had little interest in the printed materials in the center of the page. But this was surely not true for all annotators.

If manuscript markings imply readers were not all young town gallants ensconced in taverns or on the fringes of court, being lascivious, witty, and drunk, so does the tantalizing case of Leonard Wheatcroft. As chapter 3 will discuss, Wheatcroft was a Derbyshire yeoman whose late-seventeenth-century manuscript miscellany includes verses copied directly from various printed miscellanies.[39] His notes record fascinating instances of stanzas lifted from printed collections—with no notes of provenance—jostling with his own poetry. There is no knowing how representative he was, no knowing how many other Wheatcrofts there were who are lost to us now, but this single instance is surely important. It shows a close reading, as well as appropriation, application, and use, of printed miscellanies by an individual whose social and geographical position would exclude him from audiences normally constructed by both seventeenth-century compilers and twentieth-century scholars.

"To Father the Brat of Another's Brain": Why Were Printed Miscellanies Read?

As chapter 1 suggested, printed miscellanies advertise themselves, in part, as practical handbooks,

> Wherein *Ladyes, Gentlewomen, Schollers,* and Strangers may accommodate their Courtly Practice with most Curious Ceremonies, Complements, Amorous, High expressions, and forms of speaking, or writing.[40]

Miscellanies are portable tutors, "alwayes ready to furnish you with the best expressions of choice complementall language," and, in particular, able to provide that crucial virtue, eloquence:

> a principall part in a well qualified man . . . [since] it adornes our discourse, gives a grace and life to our actions, opens us the gates and dores to the best company, and puts us in such esteeme as well 'borne spirits ought to arrive too.

Through the careful study and application of these "richest Iewels," the reader might attaine to the quality of such worth that thou mayst learne from it to cure thy dumbenes, to discourse confidently with thy friends, *and assuredly to tender thy wit and service to those thou shalt have occasion to acknowledge, especially in the Court,* where neatenesse and curiosities of all sorts, and principally of speech is to a sillable exactly studied.[41]

But what, exactly, did this mean? Did it mean that through reading printed miscellanies readers gained a genuine chance of social, even court, advancement? While historians suggest that there was at this time a sense of opening social opportunity,[42] the notion that readers of *The Academy of Complements*—a book which was hugely popular and widely read—might all trip off to court is patently absurd. But the book's grand claim does introduce a theme that runs through reader constructions in many miscellanies: the sense that while compilers might talk with a straight face about the court or coterie opportunities a perusal of their text would yield, readers envisaged rather different purposes.

Readers' manuscript marginalia provide a possible way of assessing how readers actually approached printed miscellanies. If we are to judge from references in plays and poems, writing in the margins of some kinds of book was common practice. Richard Brome, acerbically pondering the fate of Sir John Suckling's grand folio edition of *Aglaura*, paid particular attention to the physical appearance of Suckling's work, and the wide margins bordering the print: "This great voluminous Pamphlet may be said / To be like one who hath more hair than head." Brome speculated on the likely responses of readers to such a text and, specifically, to those seductive bands of space running round the print. "By this large margent," Brome writes,

> did the Poet mean
> To have a comment wrote upon the Scene?
> Or else that Ladies, who doe never look
> But in a Poem or in a Play-book
> May in each page have space to scrible down
> When such a Lord or fashion came to Town;
> As Swains in Almanacks their counts doe keep
> When their cow calv'd and when they brought their sheep.

Brome's verse posits three models of marginal annotation: the dramatic commentary, the note of news or fashion, and the record of accounts. These models have a varying degree of correspondence with the text itself. The marginal space might be, respectively, a site for reflection on the text; a space to be used as blank paper, for entirely unrelated notes; or a place for notes that relate to but do not engage with the printed text. While the type of marginal annotation varies, and while Brome was invoking particular reading models to ridicule Suckling's book—thus Ladies, whose readings are limited and light, and whose concern is only fashion, and thus rural, uneducated Swains—the verse does at least suggest that marginal annotation was common practice. "Ink is the life of Paper," Brome notes, "'tis meet then / That this which scap'd the Presse should feel the pen."[43]

The metaphorically marginal—the repressed, the silenced, the excluded—have, of course, been foregrounded in many recent scholarly studies, but work on literal textual margins has only recently emerged as "a field [but] . . . not yet a discipline, or interdiscipline."[44] Even more problematic is the unwarranted conflation of these two uses of the term which has led to assumptions that notes in textual margins were by their nature discordant, dissenting, outside, occupying not only the textual edges but also the boundaries of thought and orthodoxy. In the seventeenth century this need not have been the case.

Several recent studies have very usefully opened up the sustained study of readers' marginalia. H. J. Jackson's *Marginalia: Readers Writing in Books* is (I believe) the only broad, sustained account, and conveys a marvelous delight in its subject. For my purposes, however, the book's utility is constrained by its starting date of 1700 (although brief mention is made of earlier practices). William Sherman's *John Dee. The Politics of Reading and Writing in the English Renaissance* provides both a careful survey of Dee's reading traces and an account of recent scholarship on the history of reading. H. R. Woudhuysen's *Sir Philip Sidney and the Circulation of Manuscripts, 1558–1640* offers some valuable notes.[45] And the book-length study of Jonson's annotations of Spenser by James A. Riddell and Stanley Stewart is valuable for a focused consideration of a canonical reader/writer.[46] Yet despite this interest, and despite the quality of these accounts, it is still true that studies of marginalia have generally focused only on canonical names (save for some moments in Jackson's book). Thus Coleridge's handwritten marginalia, or Jonson's, or Dee's, have been dissected, explained, and printed;[47] but that study of anonymous readers, silent save for the whispers of manuscript traces in a few printed books, has yet to be written.

About one in three printed miscellanies I have examined contain some form of manuscript addition, and many of those contain sustained marginal notes—like the Bodleian *Wits Interpreter*, with an "X" or "XX" against almost all its poems.[48] The nature of these interventions varies: from simple crosses or lines which indicate moments of interest, to signatures and dates and impenetrable doodles, to more elaborate additions, alterations, and variations.[49] Perhaps the first point to note is that manuscript additions in printed miscellanies imply, I think, a sense of individual ownership, and of private readings. The markings that occur most commonly—crosses, ticks, slight alterations, highlighted passages, scribbled additions—all suggest a close and private relationship between reader and book. Marginal notes give little thought to later comprehensions and do not attempt to construct systems of reference for subsequent readers. They suggest a familiar, intimate, solitary reader; they reflect personal predilections; they infer rereadings rather than new readers; and they are generally opaque, implying much more than they state. Adding dates and names to books—common practice in printed miscellanies, and, of course, in many other texts—conveys this sense of the book as an individual's private property. A collection of texts now in the Bodleian has neat manuscript notes on its title pages: "Bought at Oxo. 12 March. 1688–6d"; "bought at Oxon 26 Feb 1688–6[d]."[50] These accompany the roll call of names penned in printed miscellanies: Charles Wersley ("his Booke 1672"), Reginall McNabes, William Biggs, Edward Jones, John Wallworth, Henry Bradshawe, Joseph Boweson ("Booke").[51] When later owners come to add their name to the book (and this is fairly common practice; miscellanies, like other books, did pass from owner to owner), earlier names are often cancelled out.[52] Thus when one owner of a 1667 edition of *Wits Recreations* wrote "William Willett is my name / and with my pen I wrot the same / 1682," he was careful to cross through two previous signatures.[53] One copy of Robert Allott's *England Parnassus: or the choysest Flowers of our Moderne Poets, with their Poeticall comparisons* (1600) includes not only nervous assertions of ownership ("James Brownhill ye right owner of this booke"), but also, perhaps, the dismissal of a former reader: "James Brownehill is ye right Owner of this Booke: and Hee Had it . . . from Mr Bhild [?] Oaks Aprill: in 78."[54] Marmaduke Hodgeson's *A Treatise of Practical Gauging* (1689) has the title page note "Richard Streete domeney 1721," but a later reader has undercut this proud assertion with the addition "hee is a rouge you know well Enough."[55]

A copy of *Wit at a Venture* from 1674 did stay in a family but even then "Ellin Wynne," who wrote her name and "1680" on the title page, was careful to delete "William Wyenne," written before.[56] Of course there is also evidence of books as communal objects, particularly within a family, as was perhaps the case with a 1684 edition of *Wit and Mirth*, whose title page declared "John Emmerson / Wescome / His Books / Given him by / Wil^m Wescome / Novem—the 12 / 1747."[57] But these collective moments are variations from the theme.

If, in general, a sense of private readings emerges through marginalia, this sense is also implicit in many poems in these books. A popular inclusion in miscellanies is the text which takes advantage of the typographical sophistication of the printing press to play with the relationship between the meaning and the physical shape of words and poems. The apparent meaning of the poem is wittily enforced or undercut by the image the words form on the page. The poem beginning "Round about all in a Ring" arranges itself in a circling fashion; "Ever in a wand'ring Maze" zigzags across the page.[58] There are poems whose meanings change according to whether they are read horizontally or vertically, like William Strode's "I hold as faith," whose assessment of Catholics depends on the path taken by the reader's eye—either positive (read vertically) or negative (read across).[59] *Wits Interpreter*'s "*Of women in a double sense*" alternates between misogyny and praise according to the reader's interpretation of layout.[60] And in *The Card of Courtship*'s "Emblematical Fantasticks; More emphatical and numerous then all ever yet printed," images replace words at key moments in poems: thus the last two words of "A Shepherd sat beneath a Tree" are replaced with a picture of a tree.[61] The same verse includes images of, among other things, a bow and arrow, a heart, two birds, a snake, and a sun.

The significance for reading habits is that the full meaning of all these poems cannot be conveyed through spoken expression. Only silent, solitary reading which appreciates words as both signifiers of meaning and visual objects can properly express the poems' wit.

This sense of an intimate readership is particularly striking since it sits in such contrast to the communal world portrayed in printed miscellanies. The miscellany milieu is the coterie of friends—"Sir *J.M. Ja:S.* Sir *W.D. J.D.* And other admirable Wits";[62] its stage the shared tavern ringing with "*Jovial* Poems, *Merry* Songs, *Witty* Drolleries."[63] In miscellanies verses are often accompanied with notes of known tunes, functioning like musical scores: "Catches, To the Tune of A Boat, A Boat, Haste to the Ferry," or "A Ballad on King James; to the tune of When Arthur first in Court began."[64] While it would be dangerous to assume an exact equivalence between the world constructed in printed miscellanies and the world lived by readers, printed miscellanies suggest a culture that was partly literacy-based—with an emphasis on solitary, silent reading, and with books as private objects—and partly oral, with a stress on the communal performance of texts.

Aside from an intimate sense of ownership, the overwhelming impression one gets from manuscript additions is that the margins of printed miscellanies were seen as general spaces ready to be filled with anything useful—as sites where readers might "interscribe any other compendious Apothegme, at pleasure and leisure."[65] Sometimes aphorisms are noted: in a Folger *Wits Recreations*, one reader has scribbled "Man wisdoum ouer cometh Althings,"[66] in keeping with the spirit of this educative miscellany, perhaps, but not drawn from the particular printed poems it accompanies. Material was often added which had little apparent connection with the printed poetry. Records of accounts occur in several texts: rows of figures jotted down margins or at the end of sections. Occasionally these records spill over the print; in one book they are scrawled upside down across the back of the title page.[67] Readers sometimes seem to use books as diaries. Robert Allott's *Englands Parnassus: or the choysest Flowers of our Moderne Poets, with their Poeticall comparisons* (1600) includes the manuscript addition "Randle Houlbrooke at Mr Crevillions house the next doore to the silver house ouer against Sta[ple?] Inn In Houlburne." This is perhaps a record of a social appointment, perhaps a note of the place of purchase.[68]

Particular texts induced this kind of use. Almanacs, for instance, were often used as a framework into which personal records might be inserted. A reader of Thomas Trigge's *Calendarium Astrologicum: or an Almanack for the Year of our Lord, 1666* used the printed book's calender as a kind of diary, adding manuscript notes opposite the printed text, such as "5th June to meet Mr Robt ffolley," along with some sketched details of the visit. The future tense indicates the book was used as a prompt, like a modern pocket diary, rather than as a site for reflection or retrospective self-accounting.[69] William Sherman has shown how John Dee added his own notes to a printed almanac, Joannes Stadius's *Ephemerides novae*. Dee's additions are more spectacular: where the former annotator had "to meet Mr Robt ffollet," Dee includes "I rid to Windsor, to the Q. Maiestie."[70] But the practice, and the conception, of the printed book as an organizing frame for personal notes is essentially the same.

Readers used space in their books to practice calligraphy, too, rehearsing signatures on the title page and occasionally throughout the book, or copying the printed titles of poems underneath. There are doodles which take a printed word from title or verse and fill margins with variations. The style of these additions can vary, from a neat, diligent hand to the loose, unreserved ink of a child's pen. A copy of *Westminster Drollery* is decorated with scribbles, repeated words, zigzags, and signatures.[71] One reader took the title page of *The Academy of Pleasure* and used it as a model, sketching "Acad" underneath; a *Wits Recreations* reader carefully duplicated the title "A Ballade"; in another copy, a reader copied "on a poore poet" in a faltering hand; in a third, next to "369. Possessions," a reader has doodled "pposseessiioonnss." In a *Musarum Deliciæ* "women" is written next to a printed "Women." In another book a reader repeatedly wrote the number eight next to page 83; a few pages later the same hand sketches the letter "M" in big, looping script.[72] Another text includes a reader's attempt to draw what looks like a calendar in a spare half page. Under the printed text, rows and columns are ruled and numbers added in each box. But something went wrong, evidently, or patience grew thin, as the whole thing is furiously scrawled out under wild arcs of ink.[73]

It is a pleasant paradox that these texts, now diligently kept from unscholarly eyes in the hush of university libraries, were once the subject of scribblings, doodles, litanies of the mundane. And that they were does much to suggest their early modern cultural position. Not only does the condition of these books indicate frequent reading, consultation, *use*, but readers so literally conflating poetry and the everyday also implies that these collections were in fact quotidian texts. Printed miscellanies were not held in careful reverence—witness the torn pages, the splashes of ink, the thumbed corners. The edge of the page did not mark a boundary between verse and life, but a place where connections between them were vividly portrayed.

Readers were also quick to add material directly related to the text. Gervase Markham's practical guide books—in some ways cousins to printed miscellanies—often include manuscript additions by readers. *Markham's Methode . . . Wherein is Shewed his approued Remedies for all Diseases whatsoeuer . . .* [afflicting] *Creatures seruicable for the use of man* has lengthy prose notes added by a reader,[74] sometimes a related comment scribbled in the margin (on page 8, next to "Methods for curing of all diseases in Horses, &c.," the news that "an handfull of hempseed in his oates is very good for a cold"); sometimes more than a page of dense text offering alternatives to the printed word.[75] A British Library copy of Markham's *The Complete Farriar* is littered with similar notes that suggest a reader regarding their printed text as a site for depositing useful, themed knowledge. "For a strayne," a manuscript addition notes at the very end of the volume, "A penniworth of linseed oyle 4d worth of *Turpen Oyle* beate them together & rub itt in well. Then take Acquavita & putt upon itt & hold a hott barre of Iron to itt."[76] To a copy of John Playford's *Choice Ayres, Songs, and Dialogues to sing to the Theorbo-lute, or Bass-Viol* (1676) a reader has added a verse to the bottom of the title page (with no note of its author, Edmund Waller): "Goe lovely rose tell her y^t wast her time and mee / When I resemble her to thee how fare and ~~seet~~ sweet / She shemes, to bee: tell her, to sufer her self to be des . . . "[77] The page has been trimmed, and the verse is cut short.

The same type of accumulative reading is evident in manuscript additions to printed miscellanies. Sometimes additions are clear attempts to fill in lost details: a reader of *Wit Restor'd* (1658), next to a reference to a Wadham butler, has noted, "The first Butler of Wadham Coll. of kin to ye founder."[78] On one

Musarum Deliciæ title page, where the text is ascribed to "Sʳ J.M. and Ja: S.," a manuscript addition expands, "Mr John Mennes and Dʳ James Smith."⁷⁹ *A Collection of the Newest and Most Ingenious Poems*, published in 1689, often prints blank spaces for character names in its poems, and a reader of a Bodleian copy has carefully added in the missing letters.⁸⁰ So too with a copy of *Wits Recreations*. After

> But waking felt he was with Fleas sore bitten,
> And further smelt he had his shirt be——

a reader, anxious to remind himself of the wit of the piece, has added "shitten." And after the lines,

> So turning from him angry at her heart,
> She unawares let out a thundring——

"fart" was noted. Around a sketch of six clothed animals in the poem "*The Drunken Humours*," the reader has carefully labeled each figure: "Lion," "Asse," "Dogg," "Swine," "Ape," "Fox."⁸¹

But most additions are more substantial than this, and imply a conception of books as incomplete collections to which more should be added. In "A SONG," in *Westminster Drollery the Second Part*, the reader seems to have intervened to "complete" the verse: at the end of stanza one—eight lines, to the other stanzas' ten—a manuscript couplet is added, consistent with the verse's rhyme scheme, reading

> I did I doe I still must loue
> which showes a constant mind.⁸²

A Bodleian copy of *Wits Interpreter* has "An Epitaph. On a Taylour that dyed of the stitch" written in the margin next to a printed series of anonymous Ben Jonson poems ("*On a hungry Captain*"; "*On Groyn*"; "*For a pair of Gloves*").

> A Taylour in this grave doth lye,
> That by the stitch did live and dye,
> Longest his lives thread might have been,
> But death with his shears came in between,
> Wound up his bottom, bound up ₍ʰⁱˢ₎ feet,
> And sewed him upon his winding sheet.⁸³

This appears to be an expanded version of a punning couplet that appears in *Wits Recreations* (1640):

Here lyes a Taylour in this ditch,
Who liv'd and dyed by the stitch.[84]

The six-line manuscript addition certainly maintains the playful, witty tone of the anonymous Jonson pieces with which it shares the page. Perhaps the reader sought to catalog his new find (or his own composition, based on the *Wits Recreations* couplet), with a view to plucking it out at a fitting moment—and that page of *Wits Interpreter*, with its complementary verses, offered a natural home. This instance of marginalia shows a reader happily adding to a printed book— viewing the printed collection as a start, not a closed completion, and as a useful depository for profitable poems. A copy of *Wits Recreations* now in the British Library also displays a reader's verse additions. After the printed "*On Button the Grave-maker*"—"Ye powers above and heavenly poles, / Are graves become but Button-holes?"—a manuscript addition continues "Man's but a Button by my Soul / The grave a very Button-hole." Similarly, the sensational "*On Joan Truman who had an issue in her legge*" is followed by a handwritten "She needs not fear hir children they may begg: / Sinc all hir issue was in hir swolne legg." The same text includes several examples of Latin couplets penned after printed verses which deal with similar themes.[85] A Folger copy of *Wit Restor'd* from 1658 prints the satirical verse "To the Duke of Buckingham," to which a reader has added "Bee Joifull Felton, for thou hath laid in dust pride ambition . . . and lust."[86] Miscellanies were not perceived as definitive, closed, or set, but as expandable collections.

John Cotgrave's *The English Treasury of Wit and Language* (1655) is a collection of excerpts from verse dramas. One copy in the British Library has numerous additions written on pages interleaved between the printed pages. (While the printed extracts are in verse, the manuscript additions are in prose.) Thus, the printed heading "*Of Death*" (70) has notes on the facing inserted page, including "To hold up ones hands in marble or kneele in brasse; to tast eternity & an unknowne fate." "*Of Folly, Fools*" (106) has manuscript additions that include "To whom good & solid discourse would be as ye sun amongst the blind." "*Of Prudence, Wisdome*" (242) has the insertion "One y^t weighs her behavior & her words in ye golden scale of discretion." After the final printed page, inserted pages with manuscript additions continue the text, with new headings, consistent with the style of the printed text ("Of mathematicians Instruments mathematics Conjurer"; "Wellcome"; "Kisses"; "Deseases Pox wounds") and a continuation of page numbers. The titles of these manuscript additions at the end of the book have been inserted into the opening printed "Alphabeticall Table of all the

Common Places contained in this Book." Not all the inserted pages have been filled: this copy of Cotgrave's book was apparently conceived as an ever-expanding collection. Spaces anticipate a continuing process of augmentation.[87]

But just as readers appeared eager to add poems to the foundations the compiler had laid—viewing books, then, not as objects to revere, but to expand and enhance—they also seemed interested in breaking down verses into their constituent parts to extract particular sections. In fact, the most common manuscript addition is the small note expressing interest in a section of the book: a cross, a tick, a "good" in the margin, or, in the case of a Folger copy of *Wits Recreations*, the repeated and endearing "I like" beside various poems and parts of poems.[88] (Folger MS Va 85, an octavo manuscript miscellany compiled between about 1600 and 1670, indicates a contrasting assessment: next to "Musicks Duell, English'd by Mr Crashaw," on page 13, is the marginal note "This Poem is very ord$_\wedge^i$nery.") A 1663 edition of the same text in Oxford includes pointing hands drawn in the margins at various points[89]—not perfect hands, it should be said: some have four fingers, others are blurred, while some point, bizarrely, away from the text, to the space outside the book.[90]

Sometimes these marks allude to whole poems. When they do, subjects covered are diverse, but most frequent are female beauty, deformity, hypocrisy, or cruelty; marriage; satirical pieces on various professions (most commonly lawyers); epitaphs (mock or otherwise); and just about anything bawdy. Those pointing hands indicate an interest in the claustrophobia of love, in the nature of epigrams, in sex, in avoiding paying debts, in female hypocrisy, and in wishing for a silent wife. Different readers, naturally, display different interests. Manuscript additions to a Bodleian copy of *Wit and Mirth* indicate an attention to family inheritance;[91] a copy of *Wits Interpreter* has manuscript marks next to "To take Partridge," "Another way to take Partridge," "Another way to fox any Birds," and "To take Fish the same way";[92] while marginalia in *Wits Recreations* in the Folger suggest a reader with an unusual penchant for poems about long beards.[93] A copy of *The New Academy of Complements* includes symbols next to various verses, in the body of the text and the index, that attempt to group by topic.[94] Such practice suggests a reader eager to rearrange the text—to pluck out those poems of interest to him—and so construct his own anthology. A reader of *Westminster Drollery the Second Part*, similarly, has added a sequence of numbers above certain poems, indicating the compilation of a new, personal collection, drawn from the printed text.[95] A copy of RECREATION FOR *Ingenious Head-peeces* includes faint traces of a reader's list of poems, numbered in ascending order.[96] And an earlier edition of this same text has manuscript additions which cross-reference epitaphs by subject, grouping poems that dealt with Prince Henry, women, wives and marriage, cobblers, butlers, lawyers, chandlers, usurers, and (inevitably, given common jokes at the time) Welshmen.[97]

However, marks of interest more often suggest that readers of printed miscellanies were drawn not so much to complete poems but to passages within verses. A Folger copy of *Parnassus Biceps* demonstrates a reader who has drawn vertical lines or brackets in the margins next to twenty-four parts of poems. Only one whole poem is marked in this book: William Strode's extremely popular "How To Choose A Mistresse" (beginning "Her for a Mistresse would I faine enjoy"). In general it is phrases, single lines, or couplets that receive marks, some of them double scored to emphasize particular interest.[98] A reader of *Westminster Drollery the Second Part* carefully and neatly underlined all the sexual references that could be found in the book (and there are many).[99] A Bodleian *Wits Recreations* has marks and sketches of small flowers next to parts of verses.[100] The passages marked are diverse in nature but there appears to be something like a sustained interest in quick wit: the telling pun, the phrase that rings with a sense of aphorism, the tidy paradox—these are the lines that receive the attention of the pen. Style, or turn of phrase, seem rather less significant; interrogations of the meaning of a whole verse are very rare. There is no sense of *disputing* with author or subsequent readers. We do not see—as we often do in contemporary annotations—debates in the margins between readers squabbling over interpretations of the text. Rather, we see readers marking (and removing?) particular *sections* of poems—like that reader of *Wits Recreations* who showed an interest in removable, requotable bawdy wit ("her back-part spake low-dutch")—and small paradoxes, such as "most true in change," and "a little gulfe," and "made it deeper by a teare."[101] *Westminster Drollery the Second Part* has lines next to phrases which ring proverbial and are fit for detachment and reapplication in new contexts—"who tryes no Circle, may mistake the Center," "Fruition is the Comfort of the Bride," and, in a variation of the popular expression "to dine with Duke Humphrey," meaning, to go without food, "with *Humphry* I sup."[102] The marked "she that is faire doth seldome prove unkind" recalls Iago's improvised wit "She never yet was foolish that was fair, / For even her folly helped her to an heir" met by Desdemona's "These are old fond paradoxes, to make fools laugh i'th' alehouse."[103] Readers sometimes attempt to distill a poem down to a single useful aphorism: like that reader of *A Perfect Collection of the Several Songs Now in Mode* who reduced "The secret lover" to "fortune prodigious."[104]

Of course there are some marked passages which do not conform to any comfortable generalization. For example, a reader of *Westminster Drollery* who often isolated the predictable also marked the incongruous "entertaine you in a shed."[105] Passages like this remind us of the speculative nature of this discussion—of contexts forever unknown, of motives unrecoverable.

However, it is possible to suggest with more certainty that readers were interested in sections of poems more often than wholes; that they displayed a readiness to isolate and remove lines; and that they regarded poetry as an accumulation of potentially useful parts. And this interest in removing key lines or ideas, perhaps for some later retelling, is actually advocated in a four-line verse by Robert Hayman, printed in *Wits Recreations* as "To a verse reader":

> Thou say'st my verses are rude, ragged, rough,
> Not like some others rimes, smooth dainty stuffe;
> Epigrams are like Satyrs, rough without,
> Like chesse-nuts sweet, take thou the kernell out.[106]

Hayman's lines themselves recall Francis Bacon's note that apothegms "serve to be recited upon occasion of themselves . . . if you take the kernel of them, and make them your own."[107] The *New Academy of Complements* (1669) reflects a similar, dissecting attitude to texts in *"Mock Song 8"* on page 90—a poem composed entirely of proverbial lines which, en masse, mean little or nothing and seem to joke at a culture of aphorisms.[108]

Henry Edmundson's *Comes Facundus in Via. The Fellow Traveller Through City and Countrey. Among Students and Scholars. At Home and Abroad* (1658) emphasizes the potency of this rhetoric of brevity. Edmundson notes that

> *more life there is in these* [aphorisms], *and more efficacy, to move men then in a long Speech made for state and Ostentation, which often dyes in its birth. These make a stronger* Impression *in mens mindes; and are more quickly received because of their acutenes; as a sharp-pointed Instrument enters easier and goes farther then a flat dull and broad one; and these obtain a firmer* Retention; *as Nails not only enter easier but stick faster . . . These are* Democritus *his Atomes; and a world of benefit is built upon such little things.*[109]

In keeping with this tendency of readers to fracture poems, marginal notes suggest that print was not regarded as a medium which fixed or excluded. Readers altered texts to create new readings. Occasionally annotations switch what seem to be simple slips of meaning. A reader of *Parnassus Biceps* changes "without devout care" to "withall devout care"[110]; notes in *Wits Interpreter* adjust *"Astroph. Did you not once Lucinda view"* to *"Astroph. Did you not once Lucinda view* vow"—a change justified by the verse's rhyme scheme.[111] A British Library *Wits Recreations* has manuscript notes changing "He payes too door" to "He payes too

Dear";[112] a reader of a copy of *The Academy of Complements* (1650) has changed "*On his Mistris walking in the Sun*" to "*On his Mistris walking in the ~~Sun~~ snow*"—the most common title of this verse, by William Strode;[113] and a *Wit Restor'd* reader changes "Strong which mirth nothing shall controul" to the more common "Strong mirth which nothing shall controul."[114] Other alterations imply less the correcting revision and more the imposition of reader interests. A *Wits Recreations* text alters "On a Clowne" to "On a Minister."[115] *A Collection of Poems*, printed in 1672, has manuscript marks altering "Let every married Man, that's grave and wise" to "Let every married Man, that's *Rich* and wise"; a few lines later "To teach and to instruct his Family" becomes "To teach and to *Increase* his Family."[116] A Folger copy of *Wit and Mirth* has at one point the name "Jemmy" crossed out and "Billy" written underneath,[117] perhaps an attempt to personalize the poem to suit particular circumstances. In a *Wit and Drollery* text from 1682, the "Midnight" of "Mother Midnight given this" is underlined, and "Mosely" penned above.[118] A 1641 edition of *Wits Recreations* prints "On Annas a newsmonger":

> *Annas* hath long eares for all news to passe:
> His eares must needs be long for hee's an asse.

Underneath the verse is the manuscript note "Fannatics / in Genere[l]," a note indicating a desire to read this—to apply it—in a more general, inclusive fashion.[119]

In several texts stanza numbers within poems have been added, normally to longer poems (a twelve-page verse in *Sportive Wit*;[120] a three-page poem in *Wit and Mirth*[121]). Numbering stanzas alludes, perhaps, to the memorizing of verse, with labels functioning to render learning more manageable. It may suggest a reader intending to refer back to a specific stanza—to select one section of the poem rather than dealing with the whole. Numbering here could function like an index which dissects the contents of a book and allows for the extraction of parts. Alternatively, readers might have been interested in the subsequent *reordering* of the poem. One particular manuscript verse collection in the Folger Library contains an example of precisely this process. It includes a transcription of Roger L'Estrange's "The Liberty of an imprisoned Royalist" which it entitles "Contentment"—the verse beginning "Beat on proud billows."[122] In the center of the page the stanzas are written with numbers above. But to the left and right are alternative sequences of stanza numbers—different readings, then, based on the same poem. An accompanying note at the top of the page explains that these "Double fig[ures]" are required since "The written order is confused." Here, then, the numbering of stanzas enables easy textual manipulation: readers of printed miscellanies might well have marked their texts with the same restructuring motive in mind. One copy of Nicholas Ling's *Englands Helicon* (1614) contains pins which have been skewered through the top of three pages.[123] The pins—like multiple bookmarks—suggest not a linear consumption but a reading which interrupts the text with precise dissections.

When readers do alter poems, then, they tend not to be concerned with the aesthetic considerations of improving the verse as a poem, as, perhaps, some modern annotators may be.[124] Neither was there a sense of disputing what the printed page had to offer; there is no sense of antagonism, of competition between print and ink—no notion of better readings. Rather, what emerges is a perception of poems as frames into which readers might fit predilections and interests of their own, of poems as malleable units ripe for rewriting. Thus, for some readers, if a verse could be made more bawdy, then it was changed in that direction; for others, if an attack on churchmen, or women, or courtiers, or lawyers could be developed, then the verse was altered accordingly. Reading verse was a process of appropriation.[125]

An apparent lack of interest in disputing meaning is important for any explanation of why women read these explicitly misogynist texts, as marginalia and title pages suggest they did. Elizabeth Heale notes that the Devonshire Manuscript contains moments when female readers seem to have penned modifications or even answers to instances of male misogyny.[126] Perhaps women readers of printed miscellanies responded with similarly contesting readings, taking their *Wits Interpreter* or their *Academy of Complements* and intervening to counter the sustained assaults on women. More likely, I think, was the notion that gender was only one variable of definition: particulars of class, wealth, location, family, physical appearance, and so on provided others. And so it may have been that women reading misogynist poems—particularly misogynist poems which place the subject in an exaggerated rural setting ("Meg of the Milk paile ... Doll of the Darie"), or focus on her humbling social status ("On Luce Morgan a Common-Whore"), or size ("On Fat Peg"), or ugliness ("On an ugly Woman")[127]—would have felt a strong sense of *distance* from the ridiculed subject, not proximity. In this way, women readers would become implicated in a culture of misogyny.

Alongside an interest in adding to texts, in removing parts of poems, in altering verse to suit the reader's context, are manuscript additions that allude to possible moments of use. A *Wits Recreations* has "may 6th" written next to poems about braggarts, women, and long hair.[128] Adding a date like this suggests an interest in the appropriation of verses for some event—some future occasion when these poems could be employed—now unknown. A reader of a copy of *Wits Recreations* has labeled stanzas in the verse "Of Melancholly" alternately "Coh" and "Dy."[129] Presumably these titles refer to voices, "Coh" representing, perhaps, "Chorus." Such a marking seems to imply the extraction of the verse by a reader with an interest in the performance of the text, or at least the idea that here is a poem which ought to be considered as a duet or dialogue. In one copy of Tottel's *Songes and Sonnettes* (1557) a reader has added tune titles to several of the printed poems.[130]

Not surprisingly, given a seventeenth-century approach to books which looked forward to future reworkings of sections of verse, notes of authorial origin are not common. When nineteenth- and twentieth-century readers intrude on texts they are pedantic in foregrounding authorial ascriptions. They mark texts with fretful notes of authorship and censorious cries of plagiarism. One can almost see the blood rising in one later annotator of *Doctor Merry-man: Or, Nothing but Mirth* who wrote beside one section "*Stolen* from Chaucer," in angry, angular ink.[131] Another reader, next to *Wit Restor'd*'s "A Song in commendation of Musicke," asks "Who is the *Author* of this beautiful Song?"[132] Seventeenth-century readers would be unlikely to note such a question. Readers did sometimes add a name to a verse,[133] but there is only one text I have come across which shows persistent evidence of this.[134] In general, readers seem comfortable with the notion of poems as units which circulated freely, generally devoid of constricting definitions like author and origin. Given readers' apparent interest in appropriating poems or parts of poems for their own purposes, it seems likely that potential future contexts rather than the original circumstances of composition interested them.

Indeed, readers were apparently familiar with the realities of verse transmission, when poems passed from text to text, often liberally adapted as they moved, and unfettered by ideas of single ownership. Above *Choice Drollery*'s "On a Sheepherd that died for Love" (beginning "*Cloris,* now thou art fled away"), a reader has added "Joviall Drollery p:15."[135] And this verse does appear on pages 15 and 16 of *Sportive Wit*—a text whose running title, at the top of the page in the first half of the book, is "*Jovial Drollery.*" The reader's uncensorious note might be read as an indication of an awareness and tolerance of verses moving among collections. Furthermore, evidence from contemporaneous manuscripts suggests that readers accepted the notion of texts existing in multiple states—of the "same" poem being altered, rewritten, restructured. Bodleian MS Ashmole 36–37 includes a version of the lengthy ballad which celebrates "The

Blacksmith." To the original numbering of stanzas penned by the copyist at the time of transcription, a later hand has added an alternative ordering. In this new sequence, verse 11 is labeled 23; 12 is labeled 11; 13 is 12; 16 is 13; 18 is 16; 21 is 18; 22 is 21, and so on. This second set of numbers corresponds to the stanza order found in several printed texts, including *Wit and Drollery, Merry Drollery the Second Part, An Antidote,* and *Wit and Mirth.* What appears to have happened was that an owner of the manuscript came across this other version—in one of these texts or in a now lost related manuscript—compared the two and noted the variant forms. Significantly, the original stanza order is not deleted; there is no imposition of "right" over "wrong," no hierarchy of readings, and both versions seem to coexist peacefully.

Folger MS Va 96, a circa 1640 miscellany compiled by an Oxford man, suggests a similarly relaxed receptivity to texts simultaneously existing in multiple versions. There are several moments when the original transcription is supplemented with lines which do not replace the earlier text but instead offer alternative versions. In "An Elegie on the death of his Sister," attributed to "Robt: Thomson" and beginning "The glimmering tapers dropping 'bout thy hearse" (f.12r-v), "Poynted with briny periods" is augmented with the alternative "fflow in disioynted Numbers"; "I will not shedd a teare" is offered as a different possibility to "I will not waste a teare"; and "who mourning for the dy'd" is offered as a variation on "that weeping for the dy'd."

So, then, we can perhaps begin to generalize about the type of readings these manuscript markings suggest. They hint that these books were private spaces; that they were employed as useful sites for storing information of any variety; that they were regarded as incomplete collections to which readers might add poems from other sources, textual or otherwise. Manuscript marginalia imply an interest in breaking poems down into constituent parts, in the removal of parts, in new contexts; readers' notes suggest a willingness to alter and adapt. Collectively, these traits imply active, interventionist readers, showing little reverence for these printed books, and giving less thought than we might imagine to issues of original context, authorship, or significance.

Chapter 1 outlined some of the connections between printed miscellanies and commonplace books, and the reading characteristics discussed above strengthen this connection. The type of manuscript marginalia observed suggests a reading practice shaped by commonplace book culture, as readers mark sections of printed texts, perhaps extracting them for entry into some other, personal collection—appropriating sections of verses for future contexts. Perhaps readers were carrying out just this sort of transfer: one Folger manuscript

(Va 308) contains emblem poems clearly copied directly from later editions of *Wits Recreations*; the aforementioned Leonard Wheatcroft—Derbyshire yeoman and manuscript compiler—drew his wit, in part, straight from printed miscellanies; and Pepys, on 24 November 1660, "fell to entering those two good songs of Mr. Lawes, *Helpe, helpe, O helpe* &c. and *O God of heaven and Hell* in my song book—to which I have got Mr. Childe to set the base to the Theorbo. And that done, to bed."[136] But more significant, I think, than speculating on the precise destination of parts of poems and suggesting every annotator was a manuscript compiler, is the observation that readers *thought* in terms of selection, dissection, alteration, and use: manuscript marginalia in printed miscellanies suggest structures of reading informed by commonplace book thought.[137] While readers might not have been marking texts as a prelude to actual transference to some personal notebook, their markings do imply a way of reading that grew out of an interest in this transference.[138]

If manuscript markings suggest a seventeenth-century perception of printed miscellanies as objects to augment, to dissect, to make one's own; if the margin did not constitute a sign of exclusion but a welcoming of variation, supplement, addition; if marginal space was, in other words, not vacuum but potential plenum, this was an attitude which printed miscellanies themselves seem to have endorsed. Poetry and its accompanying materials were presented as quotidian tools, as things enmeshed, absolutely, in the social. These books' structures affirmed readings which might add, alter, even remove, and they display, I think, at least an implicit conception of poetry as an accumulation of potentially profitable parts.

Printed miscellany inclusions were offered as applicable and useful. In *Wits Interpreter* poetry is just one—albeit the largest—of eight classes of education which "compleat our English *Gentry.*" Poetry is presented alongside, among other things, "The Art of Reasoning, A New Logick," "Accurate Complements," "New Experiements and Inventions," "Letters A la mode," and "Cardinal Richeleiu's Key to his manner of writing of Letters by Cyphers."[139] Poetry is positioned within a wider genre of instructional or exemplary writing, and assumed similar functions to explanations of logic, tricks, model letters, or revelations of codes.

A sense of use and the related idea of selection were strengthened through the practice of retitling poems to emphasize an applicable context: "A Complementall Rhapsody, Meriting presentation to any Noble Mistresse, the Lover desirous to illustrate the Beautitude of the (feigned) Elizium"; "A mayd or widow being forsaken, may thus certifie her false friend by Letter"; "The Lover angry at his Mistreß unsufferable contempt, may (if he will) thus vent himself, in an invective manner."[140] *The English Treasury of Wit and Language* (1655) organizes its contents around an alphabetical list of ever-pertinent headings: "absence," "affection," "anger," and so on. Readers might quickly find the topic that interested them without considering the text as a coherent whole. Indexes were increasingly common in this type of text—"Half of your book is to an index grown," one verse notes, "You give your books *contents,* your reader none"[141]— and functioned with a similar effect, encouraging readers to deal in parts, not wholes, and serving, as lines by Richard Niccols imply, to carve up the text like a commonplace book. He

> Who is not, yet to some may seeme, profound,
> And little reading serue, if in this case,
> The bookes kinde index bee his common place.[142]

Printed miscellanies also entertain the notion of verse as something negotiable and unfixed—an idea that, we have seen, some manuscript marginalia imply. We might note verses that demonstrate an awareness of poetry as something that is not closed, or final, or fixed, but open to addition and alteration: verses like "*A Rural Song, the third and fourth verses being lately added*";[143] "*KISSES, with an Addition,*"[144] which follows the six lines offered in *Wits Recreations*[145] with an additional eighteen; and "*Bagnall's Ballet, supplied of what was left out in Musarum Deliciae,*"[146] which supplements "*Tom Bagnalls* Ballet," from *Musarum Deliciæ.*[147]

Texts actively encourage readers to manipulate and alter printed words. *The Academy of Complements* promises readers

> thou hast choise and select complements set thee downe in a forme which upon an occasion offered thou may imitate *or with a little alteration make use of.*[148]

Wits Recreations' "On Paulus" demonstrates a similar attitude to textual ownership as it describes how poetry, once in print, "must the peoples not the authors bee"[149]—like Hamlet's observation that his words ("I eat the air, promise-crammed. You cannot feed capons so") once spoken, are not "mine now."[150]

Also interesting is the 1667 miscellany *Folly in Print*, a text which, as its title page suggests, comically subverts editorial norms.

> Whoever buyes this Book will say,
> There's so much Money thrown away:
> The Author thinks you are to blame,
> To buy a Book without a Name;

> *And to say truth, it is so bad,*
> *A worse is nowhere to be had.*

Its section of errata contains corrections for the usual minor slips ("Plunders" for "Plunder"; "where" for "when"), but also notes more substantial variations which comically sustain the theme of subversion.[151] Where the main text has "with a little thing for a certain" we are offered "With a certain thing they call." Instead of "Where Hopkins rimes the people sing," notes suggest (the rather bizarre) "Hopkins jiggs the soltheads." And in place of "then I affirm'd under my hand" we are presented with the intriguing "his pike shrinks in his hand." There are other, similar cases too. And the comedy rests on the notion of alternative readings which are not simple slips of typesetting—not straightforward cases of correcting an error which somehow obscures or distorts the right text, but rather an acknowledgment that these poems could and did exist in various states and that the existence of these various states did not constitute a contradiction. Now of course it might be said that since these notes appear in a section of errata, they represent precisely the imposition of correct reading over error. But I think the concept of notes of errata was rather looser than that. In Edward Phillips's *The Mysteries of Love and Eloquence*, there is a short address on the subject:

> Courteous Reader, there are some more Errata's besides these committed, but since it is a custom to print Errata's and few or none takes notice of them, I intreat thee favourably to pass them by, and as thou readest, correct them by thy own judgement.[152]

Not only does this passage suggest that notes of errata were usually ignored, but by articulating the notion of textual malleability—"correct them by thy own judgement"—and thus invoking variant versions, Phillips's address upsets any right-wrong binary the mere existence of notes of errata might seem to imply.

Texts as alterable units imply reader intervention, and this was encouraged, I think, through the common rhetoric of text as female and reader as male, an aspect of what Harold Love describes as the "deep-rooted metaphor which sexualised the material of writing, paper, as female and the acts of reading and writing as displaced versions of sexual domination of the female by the male."[153] The act of reading becomes an act of voyeurism when *Bristol Drollery* presents itself as a young country female new to town and speculates of the female/book, "Her two leaves wou'd be open'd, and perus'd."[154] *The Marrow of*

Complements, a guide to would-be suitors printed in 1655, includes a section entitled "Venus Naked," which lavishly displays the female body, part by part, in written form *"for an Amourist, whoo desires to praise his Mistresse perfections from head to foot, or to particularize."*[155] Never considering the subject as a whole, it individually details nineteen physical characteristics including hair, visage, lips, shoulders, breasts, belly, and finally "A Secret."

But such fashioning goes beyond voyeurism. *Bristol Drollery* casts itself as "a fresh Country Muse come up to Town"; "the young gallants" are asked to "Receive her kindly," and may "on easie tearms . . . make [the book their] own."[156]

This passage conjures text as passive female, reader as dominant male, and reading as a sexual act ("on easie tearms may make your own"). *Holborn Drollery*, subtitled "The Beautiful Chloret surprized in the Sheets," employs just these kinds of rhetorical maneuvers. The preface presents the book as Chloret addressing her "Worthy Gentlemen":

> That I may engage your Civilities, send for me to your Chambers, carry me into your Walks or to the Play-House, I am at your service . . . I know you will use me kindly: for I am young, and a stranger to the Town: as for my Beauty and All that, I must submit to your judgements, since Beauty in us, is but the Idol of your own fancies, which you first make and then worship.[157]

Inclusions such as these conflate the text with an eroticized female. By inviting readers to, in Chloret's words, "use me kindly" and by noting that readers may, in *Bristol Drollery*'s words, "on easie tearms . . . make [me] your own," the reader—conjured in these prefaces as, generally, male, young, and lustful—is granted a position of dominance over a passive text, and intervention in that text is thus implied.

The authority of the reader over the text also increased as printed miscellanies began to address the reader in terms previously reserved for the patron. Early miscellanies tend to separate reader and patron as distinct categories. *Wits Recreations* of 1640 offers a powerful assertion of social hierarchy by creating a sharp disparity between noble patron and lowly reader. It dedicates itself "To the Nobly accomplished FRANCIS NEWPORT Esquire, Sonne and Heire to the Right Worshipfull Sir *Richard Newport* Knight and Baronet,"[158] and the publisher stoops low as he bows and signs "who am Sir your obsequious servant Humphry Blunden." The reader, by contrast, is treated with an almost contemptuous candor. "The Frontespeice discovered" is a somewhat labored explanation of stock images, such as "The Devious Horseman, wandring in this

Maze" which "Shewes Error, and her execrable ways." It creates a sense of an unlearned audience. So too does talk of duping ignorant readers, a clear concern with book sales ahead of quality, and the styling of reader as "guest,"[159] dependent on the hospitality and kindness of the publisher and not the subject of courteous discourse.

But in other texts, this clear-cut opposition between lofty, revered, and specific patron and lowly, foolish, anonymous reader, is blurred. In *The Mysteries of Love and Eloquence*, compiler Edward Phillips does dedicate his book to a kind of patron figure: he is "emboldned to prostrate these my Devoires at . . . [the] feet" of those "Bright Stars of Beauty,"[160] his female audience. And, like *Wits Recreations*, he persists in addressing the reader separately, with a

> short Advertisement to the Reader, by way of Introduction, for his better understanding of the Mysteries of Eloquence and Complementing.[161]

But while the distinct "patron"-reader divide persists, the nature of that patron has changed from named individual to (effectively anonymous) group. *The Academy of Complements*, similarly, does not dedicate itself to an individual patron, but does address "the Ladyes and Gentlewomen of England" in the rhetoric and vocabulary of traditional writer-to-patron discourse. The book, for instance, "can arrive at no greater perfection of happineße than your favour,"[162] and the writer seeks

> only that you would grace it with the influence of your propitious smiles, which cary in them a secret power, not only to cherish and advance the object whereon they reflect, but also to endeare it into others opinions.[163]

But these echoes of patron-seeking dedications were accompanied by an attempt to distance the book from just such addresses:

> Let other workes covet their Patrons and Mæcenaßes, to derive from them a golden sprinkling of their bounty; whilst this shall express an ingenuity beyond such vulgar intents, and in a brave and free manner sacrifice it selfe to your acceptance and service.[164]

Here, then, we see a petition to a general, somewhat undefined group, not figured as readers (their address follows after), but not specific, identified patrons, either. It comes in the rhetoric of the traditional patron address, but simultaneously distances itself from "such vulgar intents." It feels something like a change before completion: like compilers moving away from one mode of presenting their books toward an uncertain other.

This equivocation, this sense of uncertainty about the book's guardian, is gone in later books. Now readers are squarely addressed as the protectors of a text's fate, with the same techniques as were (earlier) practiced on individuals like Francis Newport.

In "To the (unbiassed) Reader" in *The Marrow of Complements*, "Philomusus" thanks the public's "candid acceptance" of "My former Indeavours in matter of this nature." For this

> I acknowledge my selfe obliged in all the bonds of grateful service.[165]

This is the language of writer-patron, redirected to readers. "Philomusus" continues:

> if your noble dispositions shall like well of (or if you will but reasonably respect what your selves have drawne me to) I shall be nothing displeased at others cavills, but resting my selfe contented with your good opinions scorne all the Rabble of uncharitable Detractors.[166]

More explicit still is *Folly in Print*. This text concludes its address "To the Reader" with an assertion of the publisher's dependency on him, figured in (literal) writer-patron terms. The book

> 'tis now expos'd to thy censure; If it meet with generous Patrons, I am oblig'd to serve you agen, and better, from your incouragement.[167]

It is no coincidence that later texts more frequently give voice to this reader-as-patron condition. Publishers were hesitantly coming to terms with the nature of their medium and the new conventions it demanded. Earlier texts, more anxious to counter the stigma of print, and more closely connected with university manuscript miscellanies, attempted to position themselves in an elite milieu. The individual patron figure was a useful badge to evoke this. But later texts, less contrite about their medium and clutching precedence as their justification, were candid in realizing that their fate depended on the unknown reader. Other collections, somewhere between the two positions, dedicated themselves to socially prestigious but anonymous groups who were not quite figured as readers. Printed miscellanies between 1640 and 1680, then, moved uncertainly between seeking the protection of the traditional patron figure and the anonymous mass reader. And in applying the perceived functions of the patron to the reader, the authority of the reader increased. Rather than suggesting passive, dutiful readers, this shift encouraged readers to consider their relationship with the text as one of control and dominance.

Implied versus Prescribed Readings

"Usefulness" is frequently presented as a virtue of miscellany contents. John Cotgrave boasts his book "will be incomparably usefull."[168] *The Mysteries of Love and Eloquence* frames its verse contents in terms of instruction and application. It promises the careful reader "Profit and Delight" through "Epithets, properly fitted for immediate use."[169] When Edward Phillips addresses his preface "To the Youthful Gentry," he assures the reader he "hath, as I may rightly call it, a Magazin richly furnist, for his dispatch of any of those high Concernments, *Cupid* or *Mercury* shall at any time instate him in";[170] his book, he writes, is of "such nimble applications [which], if rightly directed, are most absolutely usefull."[171] In much the same way, Joshua Poole's *The English Parnassus* defines the lyric as that "which is of such extent, that it may be made use of on any occasion."[172] And Geffrey Whitney's *A Choice of Emblemes and other Devises* includes a similar emphasis:

> The volumes great, who so doth still peruse,
> And dailie turnes, and gazeth on the same,
> If that the fruicte thereof, he do no vse,
> He reapes but toile, and neuer gaineth fame:
> > Firste reade, then marke, then practise that is good,
> > For without vse, we drinke but LETHE flood.[173]

But this term, "use," was subject to different interpretations, and we can sketch a contrast between understandings implied in frontispiece and preface, and the expectations readers themselves brought to their texts. Title pages imply that the employment of a few lines from these collections, presented as products of court elites, will smooth the path to court; they suggest that these poems are fit for reapplication by readers in the same court settings evoked in the books. But this is clearly not possible: printed miscellanies are texts available for anyone; they advertised their accessibility—were "revealed to the weakest Iudgement"[174]—and thus commercially they stood as emblems of an almost total *lack* of exclusivity.

Reader understandings of these texts still rested on the idea of usefulness, but not of the reading-your-way-to-court type suggested in *The Academy of Complements*. Rather, readers, I think, perceived miscellanies as collections of verses which might be appropriated, applied, and used in the readers' own contexts. That is, not as a means to grand social climbing; not even as an education in the sense of opening opportunities. Rather, poems were useful units which might be taken, altered, and reemployed amid a reader's particulars. Readers took courtly wit and suited it to their circumstances; they did not change their circumstances to suit courtly wit. A reader of "Cardinal *Richlieus* Key, his manner of writing of Letters," "Another manner of Character difficult to be understood," in a 1662 edition of *Wits Interpreter,* has added manuscript writings showing he was practicing the secret writing these pages display.[175] He was not, then, approaching these "elite codes" as remote badges of exclusivity that had no relevance for him; but he was surely neither intending to employ them in Richlieu's lofty contexts. Rather, the reader trod the middle path, regarding these codes as potentially useful, applicable tools, but within his own contexts.[176]

In fact, beneath their dazzling prefatorial promises of advancement, printed miscellanies themselves suggest a corresponding sensitivity to the maintenance of hierarchy and degree. Take *The Mysteries of Love and Eloquence.* While its prefaces talk of

> *the Court, and such eminent places as* Hide Park, *the* Spring Garden, *and the* New Exchange, *and set Meetings at Balls*

—places which *"are esteemed the fittest Schools of Ceremony and Complement"* for the socially prestigious—they also seem to suggest that other social ranks should know their status and limits. That is, while the reader can observe courtly practice, he should understand that this text does not provide an opening to those circles. Context is crucial, and the reader's context will not change. The courtier

> *if discretion be not wanting . . . will not fail to conform himself to the mode and condition of the place that he is to exercise his Genius in.*

Other, lower, social ranks should understand this same loyalty to hierarchy.

> *Complements do not suit with all places, nor with all sorts of men; it ill beseems a Mechannick to play the Orator; that urbanity which becomes a Citizen, would relish of too much curiosity in a Countrey-man; and that Complement which gives proper grace to a Courtier, would cause derision if presented by a Merchant or a Factor. The Statesman requires a graceful and grave posture, whereas in ordinary affairs of Traffique, it were indiscretion to represent any such state. Thus I might instance from the Madam to the Chamber-maid.*[177]

What this text offers, then, is a display of the customs of the elite—indeed, those customs dissected and made "plaine and easie" for even "the meanest capacity"[178]—along with an assertion of rank. Compiler Edward Phillips's simultaneous advocacy of studied eloquence and social stability means that the manners of the social elite can still offer nondidactic, adaptable lessons even while readers' contexts do not change.[179]

This means that while prefaces might imply an opening up of the previously exclusive—a widening of the doors to court—these texts simultaneously barred those very doors and enforced notions of social difference. By raising the issue of court access, the impossibility of that access was surely made apparent, explicitly apparent in the case of *The Mysteries of Love and Eloquence*, and these collections became vignettes of far-off lives. Thus *Wits Interpreter* has connections, clearly, with the conduct book tradition, but it also serves as a powerful reminder of essential social differences: it is "A sure Guide . . . In which briefly the whole Mystery of those pleasing *Witchcrafts* of *Eloquence* and *Love* are made easie"; and yet it deals with "compleat[ing] our English *Gentry.*"[180] It is both an apparent opening up of the previously exclusive and an assertion that these are specifically "Gentry" matters to which, we remember,

> none but the *Intelligent,* such as are the *Muses friends,* ought to ascend.[181]

And I think one can also see in this final emphasis on rank, hierarchy, and stability something like last-minute nerves at the implications of readers acquiring new modes. Perhaps it is right to interpret this ambiguity as to the precise function of *The Mysteries of Love and Eloquence, Wits Interpreter,* and other similar books, as just that: an unresolved and anxious uncertainty about the social implications of these texts. Like the alarmed cries of socially conservative nobles when the democratizing potential of the printing press became apparent, the literary entrepreneurs responsible for many of the printed miscellanies were perhaps disturbed at the latent force for change their texts contained.[182] Thus, with typical schizophrenia, *The Mysteries of Love and Eloquence* offers a whistle-stop education in eloquence as transformative as "the Chymists Elixar." And yet the book insists that "Complements consist not of Conges, Cringes, Salutes, superficial Discourses, foolish Repititions, or frivolous Extravagances; these are but the shadows, which they that use forget the substance."[183]

We should note, too, that miscellany boasts of "use"—what we might call their conduct manual strain—and thus their apparent sense of the possibility of social mobility, decline over time. Later texts are often not offered as storehouses of "such nimble applications, [which] if rightly directed, are most absolutely useful";[184] no longer are readers promised they "cannot wish for that favour, which you may not gather" from these books.[185] Later miscellanies often offer their poems as songs—plain and simple—or once-dismissed catches, unaccompanied by talk of social advancement.[186] Attempts to connect with the court also peak in 1650s texts and decline thereafter: contrast their contorted conjurings of "the *Spring Garden, Hide Park*, the *New Exchange*, and other eminent places,"[187] and "those Admirable Accomplishments that compleat our English *Gentry*,"[188] with later miscellanies which casually offer themselves as "Mocks to several late Songs about the Town"[189] or products of both "City and Country"[190] or as collections with no allegiance to place at all: *A New Collection of Poems and Songs* (1674) claims only to be "Written by several Persons,"[191] and there is the almost comically vague *A Collection of Poems, Written upon several Occasions, By several Persons* (1672). Even those texts which do maintain an emphasis on application concentrate much more on an applicability within, not across, layers of social hierarchy. Thus, rather than "*Stiles and Tearmes used to the* KING, *or* QUEENES *Majesty*," *Wits Academy* (1704) offers "*A Father's Letter to his Son at School in the Country*"; instead of "*A tender of service to ones Soveraigne*," the collection presents "*A Letter from a Citizen to his Friend in the Country so send him up an Apprentice*," "*A merry Letter to invite a Friend to the Tavern*," and "*A Country Farmer's Son to one of his Neighbour's Daughters*." The volumes's discussion of "*Superscriptions for Letters, suitable for all Degrees and Qualities of Men and Women*" does begin with notes of decorum for addressing the monarch, the nobility, and "other Dukes," but these are quickly dismissed and the bulk of the material focuses on the gentry, lawyers, "kindred and relations," lovers, and "ordinary Friends and Acquaintances."[192]

The gradual shift away from ideas of court applications had much to do with compilers' increasing confidence about the legitimacy of publishing printed miscellanies. Positioning texts near conduct manuals, and creating connections with court, were, to a degree, midcentury strategies to efface the stigma of popular print by placing the books within a frame of respectable tradition. Early printed miscellanies feel deeply insecure: their frantic attempts to connect with as many established publishing traditions as possible suggest compilers anxious about their lack of precedent. As fiercely competitive prefaces make clear, later miscellanies were increasingly aware of specific rival texts,[193] and while this may have fueled vituperative introductions, it also fostered a more fundamental sense of calm as to the validity of the verse miscellany as a publishing venture. Consequently, desperate clutchings at precedents declined.

But these were the beginnings of later developments. For earlier texts, and for most subsequent books, notions of use remained fundamental. In Thomas Forde's *Love's Labyrinth*, act 5, scene 6, we see such a miscellany put to use. Doron, intent on wooing Carmila despite his flagging wit, turns to his "magazine of Poetrie, [his] . . . store-house of wit":

> DORON I think I am provided now, if Poetrie will do't, my Carmila is mine; these witty knaves, what fine devices they have got to fetter maidens hearts? . . . there are some secret charms in these same verses sure. Let me see here what I have got. Ha Carmila, look here, I think you'l love me now.
>
> *Reads.*
>
> CARMILA—A Miracle.
>
> CARMILA A miracle, for what, Doron?
>
> DORON Why, a miracle of beautie, and I think you'l be a miracle of folly, if you don't love me now.
>
> CARMILA What small Poet have you hired to make a miracle of my name.
>
> DORON Nay, I have more yet, and better, that I found in the Nichodemus Of Complements, that's a sweet book, 'tis a very magazine of Poetrie, a store-house of wit; do but hear them Carmila. . . . Now Carmila, you must imagine that 'tis I, and only I, say this to you, and none but you: for the unhappy wag ha's so fitted my fancie, as if 'twere made for no bodie but me.

Doron then offers a series of wheezing compliments that had actually appeared in *Wits Recreations* (1640) as verse number 222:

> Excellent Mistris, brighter than the Moon,
> Than scowred pewter, or the silver spoon:
> Thine eyes like Diamonds shine most clearly,
> As I'm an honest man, I love thee dearly.

But his efforts are rebuffed:

> Had it been your own mother-wit, Doron, I could have like't it well: But for you to father the brat of another's brain, is too ridiculous. I like your love much better than your hackney lines.

The comedy rests on an understanding of the printed miscellany as a provider of wit for the specifics of the reader's (Doron's) problems. The lines have a practical function for Doron—to get the girl—but are not a means to change his position in society in the way some miscellanies suggest. Doron's blundered wooings suggest that appropriation (inclusion within existing circumstances), more than transformation (the changing of circumstances), defined readers' attitudes to these texts.

Printed Marginal Notes

How, then, do *printed* marginal notes relate to these ideas? Assessments often suggest they functioned as a means to limit interpretative possibilities—to impose *a* reading, and thus to prevent readers from being active, autonomous participants.[194] To a degree these conclusions come as a consequence of the foregrounding of Ben Jonson, whose printed notes formed part of his sustained attempt to use the press to order and contain readings of his work—to ensure his readers "reade it well: that is, to understand."[195] He first printed notes in his 1604 *Part of King James His Royall and Magnificent Entertainment*.[196] Jonson's notes do nothing, really, to clarify the text for the reader, to open up possibilities for varying judgments; rather, they function to frame the text in a learned, almost impenetrable, classical past. With such a frame the reader is denied any latitude, and Jonson's printed words, now heavy with heritage, become immovable. Similarly, notes surrounding *Sejanus* were attempts to protect Jonson from misinterpretation, from *wrong readings*: the Latin notes and allusions to sources again provide a dense, classical frame.[197] A history of biblical annotation in the early modern period would, I think, suggest similar attempts to render the reader weak and passive.[198] Cervantes' *Don Quixote* writes of the printed marginal note, "if it serves no other purpose, at least that long catalogue of authors will be useful to lend authority to your book at the outset."[199]

There seems to be a tension, then, between such established practices of printed annotation and the type of reading printed miscellanies suggest. Printed notes, as exemplified by Jonson, resist the notion of the reader determining the function of a piece; printed notes attempt to create for the text a stability which renders fracture and appropriation textual abuse. But printed miscellanies, through their structure and their manuscript additions, indicate a very different approach to reading.

I want to conclude this chapter by looking at two poems printed in various miscellanies in the second half of the seventeenth century which, in contrasting ways, engage with these competing ideas of marginal notes. They are significant poems because they are accompanied by printed marginal notes which in different ways—and contrary to Jonson's notes—undermine attempts to control readings and introduce a new chaotic frame in which to position poetry.[200]

The poem beginning "Here lies William de Valence," titled "*Old Soldiers*" or "*On the Tombs of Westminster Abby*," was printed in various forms in miscellanies including *The Mysteries of Love and Eloquence, Sportive Wit, Wit and Drollery* (second edition), and numerous editions of *Wit and Mirth*.[201] Its lengthy prose preface tells us the verse is the story of a visit to Westminster Abbey on some

> *Easter* Holy days: for now *Sisty,* and *Dol, Kate* and *Peggie, Moll* and *Nan* are marching to *Westminster,* with a lease of Prentices before them; who go rowing themselves along with their right arms to make more haste, and now and then with a greasie Muckender wipe away the dripping that bastes their foreheads. At the dore they meet a croud of *Wapping Sea-men, Southwark Broom-men,* the Inhabitants of the *Bank-side,* and a Butcher or two prickt in among them; there awhile they stand gaping for the Master of the Shew, staring upon the Suburbs of their delight, just as they view the painted Cloath before they go in to the Puppet-play: by and by they hear the Keys, which rejoyces their hearts like the sound of the Pancake; for now the Man of comfort peeps over the spikes, and beholding such a learned auditory, opens the Gates of Paradise, and by that time they are half got into the first Chapel (for time is then very precious) he lifts up his voice among the Tombs, and begins his lurrey in manner and form following.[202]

There ensues, in some 240 lines of verse (276 in *Sportive Wit*), the guide's commentary around the abbey as he points out the tombs of the illustrious and infamous. But what is particularly interesting is the use of the margins, for here we find not instructions on how to read—not notes obdurately framing the central text—but small, printed descriptions of the asides of the tour party as they travel around the abbey. Thus after the voice of the guide offers

> This is the Dutchess of *Somerset,*
> By name the Lady *Ann,*
> Her Lord *Edward* the sixt protected,
> Oh! He was a Gallant Man

the marginal notes print

> *Tom. I have heard Ballad of him sang at Ratclif Cross. Mol. I believe we have it at home over our Kitchen mantle-Tree.*[203]

The verse continues

> This was Queen *Mary,* Queen of *Scots,*
> Whom *Buchanan* doth bespatter,
> She lost her Head at *Tottinham,*
> Whatever was the matter.

The asides comment

> *Dol. How came she there then? Will. Why ye silly Cate could not she be brought here, after she was dead?*

A little later the central verse reads

> Two Children of King *James* these are,
> Whom Death keeps very chery.
> *Sophia* in the Cradle lies,
> And this is the Lady *Mary*.

In the margins is

> *Bess. Good Woman pray still your Child, it keeps such a bawling, we can't hear what the man say.*

And beside a reference in the poem to "Queen *Elizabeth* of great Fame" is the note

> *Sisty. That's she for whom our Bells ring so often, is it not Mary? Mol. Ay, ay, the very same.*

There are others, too, all vividly contrasting with the balanced verse in the center of the page, not only through their jaunty, spontaneous, irregular tone which diverges so effectively from the guide's steady rhymes, but also in terms of form (the notes are in prose) and appearance (they are printed in italic script). The reader, confronted with this text, is, initially at least, left in an uncertain state. Are there two pieces here, or one? What is the relationship between margin and text? Is this a poem about Westminster Abbey, or a poem about responses to it, or a poem about the relation between the two? Should commentary and verse be read apart, or conflated as one? Where, precisely, does authority lie?[204]

The effect is to offer a frame for the central verse which does not limit or contain but invokes a world outside. The alternative voices which speak from the margins imply the external: they point from the text, outward to new contexts that are glimpsed and uncertain and free. As notes they differ in effect from much printed marginalia: where Jonson's notes fix his text in a tight interpretative structure—controlling, defining—these marginal words loosen the ropes that tie poems down. They use the textual margins as a bridge between verse and world, and position the poem somewhere between the controlled center and a chaotic outside.

The second poem worth considering for its creative dealings with textual margins is by James Smith, a chaplain, described variously as a rouge, a wit, and a man, in the words of a legal brief from 1633, "much given to excessive drinking." His verse *The Innovation of Penelope and Ulysses* circulated in manuscript in the

1630s but later found its way into printed miscellanies, appearing in *Wit and Drollery* (1656) and *Wit Restor'd* (1658).[205] It is a mock poem based loosely on Ovid which satirizes those pedantic, haughty, talentless versifiers Smith seemed to see everywhere.

The poem mocks, in part, through bad lines: Smith's comically lumbering verse epitomizes the writing of those he seeks to attack with stumbling couplets like

> List to my dolefull glee, o list I say,
> Unto the Complaint of Penelopay.[206]

Smith's friend John Mennes, in a prefatory verse, makes the target clear:

> Blush, Blush, for shame, yee wood-be poets all,
> Here see your faces, let this glass recall
> Your faults to your remembrance.

But the poem also assails its targets through the use of printed notes. Straight-faced printed notes which look, at first, like they are doing just what many did: creating a learned, stable, didactic frame in which to position a text. But these are notes which, in purporting to affirm, to fix, to limit, to confer status, embody what Smith regarded as all the faults of the pot poet with pretensions to grandeur.

The notes mock attempts to invoke a learned heritage. "There the Author translates out of Ovid," one note records, "as Ben Johnson do's in Sejanus out of Homer." There are notes attacking false learning: in line one the word "Cliptick" is accompanied by "The harder the word is, the easier it is to be understood." Similarly, the kind of aphoristic but hollow wit prevalent in this poetry is imitated: "As a pudding ha's two ends," Smith's notes record, "so a smock ha's two sides." There are notes which mockingly demystify the poet's strategies. The line "That have or sense to hear or use of eares" is followed by "In varying the use of the senses the Author shewes himselfe to be in his wits." And when the word "list" is written twice we read, "Being twice repeated, it argues an elegant fancy in the Poet." Lazy attempts at erudition are sarcastically exposed: after mention of "twelve Cælestiall Signes," we are told, "There the Author shewes himselfe to be well versed in the Almanack"; "And pinch'd her cheeks to make the redde bloud stream" is footnoted "For distinction sake, because many mens noses bleed white blood." When lines make no sense at all, the notes offer "To make false English, argues as much knowledge as to make true Latin." And a particularly clanging couplet is followed by "Better falsifye the Rime, then the Story, &c."

The obvious effect of all this is to comically but brutally expose what one preface calls that "crue of Scriblers that with brazen face / Prostitute art and worke unto disgrace."[207] But the process of ridicule goes further than this. Smith's work not only derides a certain type of writer; it goes some way to demystifying poetry and, in particular, subverts the role of the marginal note as a didactic vehicle for controlling effect, meaning, and, ultimately, reading. While notes were employed by some to determine a deferential model of reading—to establish a dominant text and a submissive reader—Smith's anarchic commentary lowers the status of both poet and verse. His notes are at once comic and unsettling; his verse is, in Massinger's words, "A temple built up to facetious mirth,"[208] but his notes are whispers in the ear of the reader which tell of the artifice of that being read.

Some Conclusions

Roger Chartier and Guglielmo Cavallo, introducing their *A History of Reading in the West*, draw a distinction between attitudes to print and attitudes to electronic texts. Print culture, they suggest, enforced

> a strict limitation on the reader's ability to intervene in the book. Since the sixteenth century ... The print object imposed its form, structure and spaces on the reader, and no material physical participation on the reader's part was supposed. If the reader none the less wanted to inscribe his presence in the object, he could do so only surreptitiously, by occupying the spaces not occupied by type in the end sheets, blank pages and page margins.
>
> All this changes with the electronic text. Not only can readers subject texts to a number of operations (they can be indexed, annotated, copied, shifted from one place to another, recomposed); they can become co-authors. The distinction between writing and reading and between the author of the text and the reader of the book, which had been immediately discernible in the printed book, now gives way to a new reality.[209]

These are provocative paragraphs for my account of printed miscellanies. While it is true that a macro assessment of the impact of print is likely to describe a force for textual stability and reader exclusion, a more focused study of one particular type of text—in my case, the printed miscellany—highlights the fact that these generalizations are just that: broad generalizations that, inevitably, efface moments of irregularity and difference. Traditional conceptions of print as a force for fixity and closure, with readers correspondingly deferential—"surreptitious"—in their moments of interaction, need some modification when printed miscellanies are considered. Readers read—and miscellanies encouraged them to read—in a manner we might call active, or interventionist: a type of reading that regarded poems as potentially useful objects to dissect, extract, adjust, and apply in the reader's own contexts. Printed miscellanies did not create readers with a preoccupation with authorship or original contexts; they did not impose "a strict limitation on the reader's ability to intervene in the book," nor did they claim to definitively fix their texts: "material physical participation on the reader's part *was* supposed." Even printed marginal notes—often seen as blatant attempts to set and limit readings—sometimes constructed alternative dialogues between margin and text and dealt creatively with issues of textual authority.

What is striking is that these active and interventionist approaches to texts match, fairly closely, the kind of readings Chartier and Cavallo consider characteristic of interactions with digital technology. In the interactions between early modern reader and miscellany, and between twenty-first-century reader and e-text, "books" are not closed, nor excluding, nor fixed. Texts are never complete: further reader alterations are always latent; new texts lurk in the margins, and in the menus. Printed miscellanies and e-texts were and are malleable units of potential—not ossified literary forms that prohibit alteration.

The reasons why both media elicit(ed) similar reading methods has much to do with the fact that both forms were and are not fully established as legitimate and illustrious means of conveying texts. Printed miscellanies were regarded as texts of dubious authority and status—as cheap, popular printed books which paradoxically sought to confer and exude exclusivity. The position of electronic texts is similarly uncertain: the Web's principal virtue—accessibility—robs it of status (Internet publications are still regarded with suspicion on a résumé), and just as manuscript had a social status that some early printed books did not, contemporary printed books have a perceived legitimacy which electronic publications generally lack. And in both cases, the text's lack of status induced, and induces, empowered readers. "The stigma of printed miscellanies"—more useful, here, as a term, than the too general "stigma of print"—and "the stigma of the electronic" are parallel forces for debasing texts and so constructing dynamic readers who feel little deference before an eminent text, and who consequently quickly intervene.

Clearly, in printed miscellanies we have texts which particularly lent themselves to active, interventionist readings, since they played down authorship as an organizing principle for writing and played up the notion of readers appropriating and applying texts within their contexts. But other texts surely invited similar modes of consumption. Certainly, if we narrow down the features of printed miscellany readings to a salient three—that print did not fix the text absolutely and did not prevent reader interventions; that readers saw books as an accumulation of potentially useful parts, not a single stable whole; that authorship and original context were not the principal means of literary definition they were to become—then these were characteristics which, I am sure, were prevalent in popular readings of ballads, prose romances, conduct manuals, plays, drolls, chapbooks, and collections of jests, proverbs, and riddles. And an emphasis on appropriation, extraction, adaptation—this conception of cultural items as malleable units, and readers' contexts as (largely) stable and formative—was also a defining characteristic of popular culture more generally.

So if these readings of printed miscellanies are not to be considered exceptional, but rather representative, early modern ways of conceiving and reading texts, it seems historians of the book have often greatly overestimated what they might call the immediately revolutionary capacity of print to fix, set, and stabilize—reading back twentieth-century notions of print onto early modern understandings.[210] The real immediate significance of print lay in its rapid dissemination of texts to readers previously excluded from the widespread circulation of literature. This was frequently observed at the time, as both a force for good—"For such as in the lowest form they may by the help of *Book-ushers*, climb to the highest pitch of Knowledg"—or, more typically, as a potentially dangerous means toward democratization—"Learning is a thing that hath been much cried up and coveted ... especially in the last century ... people of all sorts though never so mean and mechanical ... aspire to book-learning."[211] But the influence of print on ways in which readers engaged with texts—ways in which books were regarded, and authorship was understood; ways in which poems were used, and readership was performed—was less immediate.

Printed miscellanies clearly played an explicit role in this dissemination of texts to new readers, and it is thus particularly interesting that while socially conservative noblemen feared this apparently radical democratization, one of the primary significances of printed miscellanies was in fact their paradoxical enforcement of social hierarchy. Although printed miscellanies apparently usher readers toward exclusive worlds, their real emphasis lies in the need for readers to appropriate elite wit within their own contexts: since *"it ill beseems a Mechannick to play the Orator,"* since *"that Complement which gives proper grace to a Courtier, would cause derision if presented by a Merchant or a Factor."*[212] Printed miscellanies thus illustrate the capacity of what we might term "aspirational texts"—texts which imply a reader hoping for social advancement—to discourage and therefore presumably limit mobility: a strain which is, I think, an underestimated quality in early modern conduct literature.

Since printed miscellanies claim to represent texts that originated in court circles, they enacted, at least theoretically, a transfer of elite culture to a popular readership. What is interesting is that we have seen "popular" readers reading these texts in different ways from members of those more eminent contexts of origin. Rather than pondering original, court contexts, readers appropriated texts within their own environment, making the formerly elite texts relevant to them. In other words, the same texts were subject to different readings, according to some sense of social status. *Wits Academy*'s title page constructs a correlation between reading modes and social hierarchy: it is a book "helpful for the inexpert to imitate, and pleasant to those of better Judgement, at their own leisure to peruse." Thus the transfer of texts between court and public, which potentially weakens notions of the exclusivity of these divisions, was accompanied by some awareness of rank or context that found expression in modes of textual consumption, which strengthens the significance of hierarchy. The ways in which readers adapted and extracted poems, the ways in which they read, were influenced by a sense of their relative social position.

And this is important, since it seems to support Roger Chartier's compelling hypothesis that it is not necessarily a difference in book ownership that reflects (and induces) social hierarchy, but rather the different ways the same books might be read. "A retrospective sociology," Chartier writes, "that has long made the unequal distribution of objects the primary criterion of the cultural hierarchy must be replaced by a different approach that focuses attention on differentiated and contrasting uses of the same goods, the same texts, the same ideas."[213] What makes popular reading, in other words, is not the book, but the ways in which the book is read.[214] Printed miscellanies, by offering the anonymous reader the elite discourses of court and, simultaneously, by stressing the need to adapt materials to the readers' nonelite contexts, encouraged just these sorts of differentiated uses of the same texts.

THREE

Printed Miscellanies and the Transmission of Texts

He was, let us not forget, almost incapable of ideas of a general, Platonic sort. Not only was it difficult for him to comprehend that the generic symbol dog *embraces so many unlike individuals of diverse size and form; it bothered him that the dog at three fourteen (seen from the side) should have the same name as the dog at three fifteen (seen from the front).*
JORGE LUIS BORGES, "Funes the Memorious"

Authors and Textual Fixity

Methinks the Poor Town Has Been Troubled Too Long (1673) opens with a meditation on the efficacy of print technology and, startlingly, the declaration that *"Errour* is an *accident* so *inseparable* from the *Press."* The preface proceeds to explain.

> And a very little consideration will shew us the *impossibility* of its being *otherwise;* for ... even the *Author* of a Song himself *forgets* how he *first* wrote it; or if he *remembers,* he will rather *comply* with a *common received mistake,* than seem *singular* in endeavouring to *Correct it.* Nor is this all; for, if a Song be brought to the Test, ever so *uncorrupt,* yet if it has but the least inclination to *smuttiness,* it lies at the mercy of the *Prover* to be *altered* as he thinks convenient: which alterations are imputed to the Publisher, who thereupon is cursed by all that are concerned in the abuse: and laugh'd at by all that are not.[1]

The passage is doubly striking. First is its emphasis on the inability of print technology to fix and stabilize texts: its contention that *"Errour"*—that is, the alteration of the poem—"is an *accident,* so *inseparable* from the *Press."* Second is its stress on the author's disempowerment: the writer has ceased to exercise control over his or her verse, and is forced to cede authority to readers. He or she "will rather *comply* with a *common received mistake*, than seem *singular* in endeavouring to *Correct it.*"

This equation of the printing press with both textual instability and a lack of authorial control may seem surprising to readers familiar with scholarly narratives that position the press as a force for a new textual fixity and the rise of the author, but *Methinks the Poor Town* is in fact representative of attitudes generated in printed miscellanies and in many other seventeenth-century texts. In Walton's *Compleat Angler*, Piscator demonstrates a similar indifference to the authority of the writer when he prefaces a rendition of "Farewell ye gilded follies" with a brushing aside of authorship: "But let them be writ by whom they will." As if to enact this indifference, the 1653 edition of Walton's text notes "some say [the verse is] written by D[r]. D.," while the 1661 edition has "some saw written by Sir *Harry Wotton*, who I told you was an excellent Angler."[2]

When printed miscellanies were deemed to have transgressed limits of decorum and legality, the law elided poets from printed miscellanies and, instead, deemed stationers, compilers, and printers accountable for these collections.[3] When *Sportive Wit* offended the sensibilities of the Interregnum government, official records note that

> Nath. Brookes, stationer, at the Angel, Cornhill, had the book printed; that John Grismond of Ivy Lane, and Jas. Cotterill of Lambeth Hill printed it, and John Phillips wrote the epistle dedicatory.[4]

Printers, publishers, and editors were punished; texts were seized and publicly burnt; but authors were not deemed accountable. When the issue of authorship was raised, Brooke is reported to have replied that the text is

> only the collection of sundry papers, which he procured of several persons, and added together for that purpose. Being asked the name of the particular persons, who are authors of any of the said poetry? saith, that of one Walter Wasse he received the maid's portion, the hunting of the gods, and several others therein contained. The rest he had from several other musicians and other persons, and put them together as aforesaid.[5]

Brooke's vagueness is striking, and even those he does cite ("Walter Wasse"; "musicians"; "other persons") appear to have been suppliers of texts of poems, but not authors in our contemporary sense.

If the law ignored poets in anthologies, the texts themselves were similarly unconcerned with precise ascriptions: poems were rarely accompanied by a poet's name; those very few ascriptions were often wrong; and title pages boasting specific contributors often misrepresented the book's actual contents. There was some interest in invoking particular writers. The frontispiece of *Wits Interpreter*, for instance, promises work by, among others, "Spencer," "Shakespeare," "Randolph," and "Sydney." But such names were an attempt to lend prestige to cheap, popular miscellanies. Compilers' efforts to prove a specific literary connection were half-hearted or even nonexistent. Indeed, it was social eminence, not literary credibility, that seemed crucial. Nathaniel Brooke sold *Wits Interpreter* on the basis of it containing the work of "so many eminent witnesses both Native and Forrayn, all Souldiers, Statesmen and Poets."[6] Its frontispiece includes "T. More," "Ld. Bacon," "Strafford," and "Richlieu": names to evoke an imprecise and largely nonliterary sense of respectability.

The low status granted to authorship was further encouraged by the sometimes uncertain position of the compiler as originator, owner, or point of definition for the miscellany. Some texts draw a clear distinction between "we poor Collectors" and "our Authours, the Poets themselves." While the compiler might "know 'em all pretty familiarly, and call 'em *Jack*, *Tom*, &c. where-ever I meet 'em," he does not suggest a blurring of roles or authority.[7] Another editor is quick to draw a distinction between compilation and authorship:

> I made bold to elect you for to Patronize these my rude and undigested Lines; though I do confess they are none of mine own; for I gathered them out of the hands of the youthful and sprightful Youngsters of these times.[8]

But there is a tension here, which is powerfully exploited in other miscellanies. While the compiler calls the poems "none of mine own," he simultaneously declares them "my . . . lines." And while he styles the collection a work of others, he delivers it to his dedicatee "as a part of my cordial affections."[9] Is this text his, or the (unknown but vividly invoked) poets'? How, exactly, are compilers and poets positioned?

With a similarly nebulous conflation of textual authorities, *Wits Interpreter*'s frontispiece promises the work of "Johnson," "Randolph," and others, yet compiler John Cotgrave calls the collection of poems "these my *Endeavours.*"[10] *London Drollery* and *Grammatical Drollery* are both "By W[illiam] H[ickes]," despite their inclusion of work by many poets.[11] E[dward] P[hillips] styles himself "Author" of *The Mysteries of Love and Eloquence*, but he presents the words of other writers.[12] And the compiler of *The Academy of Complements*, cloaked behind the anonymity of "Philomusus," concludes "The Authors Preface to the Reader"[13] with the "wish . . . that thou mayest inioy as much pleasure in the perusing of it, *as I had to pen it.*"[14]

This uncertainty of authority was heightened in some works by compilers including their own work amid the poems of others. Abraham Wright includes six of his own poems in his *Parnassus Biceps*.[15] Wright's poems are unascribed and it is left to the modern-day scholar (with lots of time) to observe his unspoken blurring of compiler and poet. Not so with William Hickes, who in *Oxford Drollery* couples verses "by the most Eminent and Ingenious Wits of the said University" with "The First part, composed by W.H."[16]

Without authorship as a means to define and therefore stabilize poems—without authorship as a pin to fix verse to a single "right" text—poems printed in miscellanies display a high degree of textual malleability. As this chapter hopes to make clear, miscellany printings of what might traditionally be seen as the "same" poem often appear in various forms: titles vary wildly; layouts are modified; tunes appear, disappear, or change; lines are cut or added or reworked; stanza and line orders switch; words and lines appear radically altered; distinct poems are conflated or blurred; ascriptions are dropped or, in some cases, altered. The reasons for the introduction of such changes clearly varied: alterations might be made to suit texts to the reader's envisaged contexts, or to advertise some potential use for the poem, or to align the text with a changed political climate. But the key point here, I think, is that such textual instabilities were not simply the products of slips or errors (although of course slips and errors did play a part). Rather, transcribers, compilers, and, subsequently, readers willingly disrupted the texts they read, quite deliberately reworking the materials they encountered.

Printed miscellanies make little attempt to conceal this culture of sanctioned textual variance. Most printed miscellanies openly celebrate the evolving and by implication unfinished state of the verse they convey: thus those poems such as "*A Rural Song, the third and fourth verses being lately added*," and "*KISSES, with an Addition*," and those many miscellany encouragements to readers to "with a little alteration make use of" the inclusions.[17] The marginal annotations of readers suggest that they willingly embraced this notion of printed poems as alterable, developing, latent.

While scholars have noted the variant texts miscellanies convey, analysis has been rather more limited. A preoccupation with authorial versions has generally relegated printed miscellanies to little more than occasional providers of spectacularly "bad texts." For many recent editors, printed miscellanies are valueless corruptions of authorial originals. Indeed, there is something like a duty to purge the world of these versions that are, in the words of one editor, "grossly corrupt," "degenerate," and "corrupt to the point of nonsense."[18] (The persistent and by no means exceptional use of a highly charged vocabulary of hygiene, morality, and even mental illness in this sort of textual survey is well worth a study in itself.) Other critics are more inclusive, and several articles narrate the sort of textual histories in which printed miscellanies play a part. In 1945, J. B. Leishman attempted the Herculean task of constructing a relationship between the many versions of Henry Wotton's "You Meaner Beauties of the Night."[19] However, these various readings are only interesting to Leishman as a means to identify the original, authorially sanctioned text. Miscellanies, for Leishman, are valuable when they allude to the initial text from which they depart, and thus are worthy of study only when they efface their own difference. The same paradoxical obscuring of variant texts is apparent in a more recent discussion by Ted-Larry Pebworth, whose meticulous bibliographical work does not fundamentally shift his interest from the missing "authoritative edition."[20] Even Mary Hobbs's compelling plea for scholars to take variant readings in manuscripts more seriously is undercut by her justification that these texts shine light on "authorship . . . and [the] reliability of their particular line of textual transmission."[21] Variant readings in manuscripts, in other words, have value when they reclaim that first, "original," "right" text. Such a methodology ultimately shrouds the variants it seems to reveal. While Hobbs hedges the term "corrupt" with quotation marks, she still uses the word and thus invokes a hierarchy of textual validity.[22] As long as textual histories are pursued only as a means to construct authorial versions—as long as variant texts are conceived as the dust that needs sweeping away to reach the authorial text—printed miscellanies, and their culture of variance, will continue to be obscured.

This chapter argues that since early modern readers did encounter wildly varying versions of poems, the erasure of such variations by later scholarship misrepresents the reading experience of the seventeenth century. It is anachronistic to replace the textual heterogeneity miscellanies conveyed with a unity and stability. Thus, we might instead complement an authorcentric approach to literature with a methodology that considers these various manifestations of a poem. (And I would stress *complement*: I am not proposing an end to authorcentric scholarship, but rather an alternative—and to my mind a more appropriate—set of principles and methods.) We might adopt a methodology which places emphasis on texts as *read*, not just *written*, cultural items. Contemporary bibliographic theory might define such an approach as "socio-centric."[23] This methodology rejects ideas of "corrupt" or "wrong" copies—avoiding a ceaseless prioritizing of the authorial word—and instead embraces textual variations as a means to understand how poems were published, circulated, consumed. Textual difference ceases to be an obstruction to understanding and emerges instead as potentially instructive, providing clues about the status and function of verse. Within such a methodology, printed miscellanies acquire a new significance.

Re-Presented Poems

At the heart of this chapter is an online *Index of Poetry in Printed Miscellanies, 1640 to 1682* (www.adamsmyth.clara.net). The *Index* catalogs all of the 4,639 poems in first editions of the forty-one printed miscellanies across seven fields: first line, last line, text, date, title and pages, number of lines, and (where known) author. The *Index* may be consulted in two ways: as browsable tables, organized alphabetically by first line, last line, or author; or as a keyword searchable index, where searches are possible across any or all fields.

Such a resource obviously opens up a range of research projects, but in this discussion of verse transmission the *Index* is useful to indicate which verses appear in more than one miscellany in order to begin a tracing of poems across texts.[24] The figures for duplicate verse in printed miscellanies are as follows:

number of times a poem appears in a miscellany	*number of instances*
once	3301
twice	392
three times	111
four times	41
five times	6
six times	4

Thus 1,335 (that is, [392x2] + [111x3] + [41x4] + [6x5] + [4x6]), or 28.8 percent, of printed miscellany poems appear more than once. This high incidence of reappearing verse shows that reprinting was fundamental to miscellany editorial techniques, and that the transmission of verse between texts was thus an essential, identifying characteristic of printed miscellanies.

The four verses that appear six times—those most popular poems in mid-century printed miscellanies—are those beginning "Let Souldiers fight for pay and praise," or "Bacchus, Iacchus, fill our braines" (by Aurelian Townshend—despite a Ben Jonson ascription in *Wit and Mirth*—and originally composed for a 1636 court masque);[25] "Keep on your Mask [or Vail], and hide your eye" (by

William Strode, conflated with a verse by Thomas Carew in *Wits Interpreter*); "Why should we laugh and be jolly" (by Alexander Brome); and "Why should we boast of Arthur and his Knights." The six verses appearing five times are those beginning "Beauty and Love once fell at odds"; "Give o're foolish heart and make hast to despair"; "He that marries a merry Lasse"; "I Can love for an hour when I am at leasure"; "Of all the Trades that ever I see" (usually titled "The Blacksmith" and probably composed by members of the so-called Order of the Fancy); and "Oh love, whose power and might." Significantly, to only four of these ten poems—the most popular and so widely read poems in this genre—can I lend an author.

The forty-one poems appearing four times are those verses beginning

"A wife I do hate"	William Wycherley
"Adieu to the pleasures and follies of Love"	
"Am I mad O noble Festus"	Richard Corbett
"Aske me no more whither do stray"	Thomas Carew
"Blind Fortune, if thou wantst a guide"	Martin Harvey
"Cook Laurel would needs have the Devil his guest"	Ben Jonson
"Disdain me still"	William Herbert
"Forgive me Jove"	
"From the fair Lavinian shore"	Robert Davenant
"Go(e) you tame gallants"	Robert Wild (also attributed to Thomas Randolph)
"Hang sorrow and cast away care"	
"Her for a Mistress fain I would enjoy"	William Strode
"How charming are those pleasant pains"	
"How happy is that prisoner" ("How happy the . . . ")	
"I always resolved to be free"	William Hickes
"I doat, I doat"	William Cavendish
"I keep my Horse, I keep my Whore"	Fletcher/Jonson/Middleton (in *The Widow*)
"I saw fair Chloris walk alone"	William Strode
"I went from England into France"	Thomas Goodwyn
"If any so wise"	
"If shadows be a pictures excellence"	Walton Poole

"Let Fortune and Phillis frown if they please"	
"Make a Noise"	
"No man Love's fiery Passions"	Robert Ayton
"Now that the Spring"	
"Peace Cupid, take they Bow in hand"	
"She that will eat her breakfast"	Matthew Mainwaring
"Sir Eglamore"	Samuel Rowlands
"Stay shut the gate"	
"The thirsty Earth"	Abraham Cowley
"The wit hath long"	William Strode
"There was three cooks"	
"Tis late and cold"	John Fletcher
"To friend and to foe"	
"When a woman that's buxom"	
"When first my free heart"	
"When I shall leave this clod of clay"	
"Whil[st]e Alixis lay prest"	John Dryden
"With an old Song"	
"Wrong not dear Empress"	Robert Ayton
"You meaner beauties" ("Ye glorious trifles")	Henry Wotton

Many of these poems are well known to scholars; others perhaps less so. Their popularity in print may have been due to a range of factors: their presentation of popular topics like the Petrarchan sufferings of love, drink, defiant jollity, and bawdiness; their inclusion in play texts; their previous popularity as broadside ballads; their appearance in other printed miscellanies which supplied related texts; their popularity in manuscript transmission in university and Inns of Court contexts. The purpose of the following discussion is to consider the significance of these kinds of factors on the circulation of texts in the seventeenth century, and by considering such variables, to try to bring to a discussion of verse transmission a useful specificity. Thus, rather than simply noting that texts altered as they moved from manuscript to print, or that manuscript versions appear particularly susceptible to change, discussion will focus on a number of kinds of textual transmissions in an attempt to offer a more precise account of what happened to printed miscellany texts as they circulated. Specifically, discussion will focus on eight kinds of textual evolution: editors' attempts to regularize and rewrite verses for a new, broad audience; the textual fortunes of poems that had experienced a particularly high manuscript circulation; the transmission of answer and mock verses; the relationship between ballads and printed miscellanies; the influence of music and memory on textual transmission; the fates of songs and poems drawn from dramatic performances and printed play texts; the relationships between printed miscellanies and their manuscript counterparts; and the evolution of texts between apparently distinct genres of writing.[26]

Editors Broaden the Audience

Aurelian Townshend's verse beginning "Victorious beauty, though your eyes" is an unusual verse of praise.[27] Written, perhaps, as an address to Catherine, wife of the second Earl, William Cecil, the poem initially celebrates the power of the addressee's beauty, but then proceeds subtly to undercut this testimony by suggesting the narrator in fact loves another who in turn might steal some hearts from the addressee. Thus, the final two stanzas declare:

> Thy conquest in regard of me
> Alas was small, but in respect
> Of her that did my love protect,
> Were it divulg'd, deserv'd to be
> Recorded for a Victory.
>
> And such a one, as some that view
> Her lovely face perhaps may say,
> Though you have stolne my heart away,
> If all your servants prove not true,
> May steal a heart or two from you.[28]

This is, then, a poem that depicts a rare, triangular relationship between narrator, addressee, and true love: a narrator praises a "victorious" powerful woman, but complicates that praise by drawing attention to his other love. The poem is engaging precisely because it reworks the familiar dynamics of praise from narrator to single subject.

When this complex poem appears in printed miscellanies, there are significant alterations. *The New Academy of Complements* prints just the first stanza of Townshend's verse. As a result it offers a straightforward description of the narrator's captured heart with none of the subsequent triangular complications. The effect is like offering the first eight lines of a sonnet without the entangling final six. *Wits Interpreter* does produce the whole text but with considerable changes. There are spluttering moments of bathetic emendation: "Victorious beauty, though your eyes / Are able to subdue an hoste," becomes "Victorious beauty, though your eyes / Doe conquer when you sit or rise." But more significant are apparent editorial interventions that attempt to replace the triangular relationship of Townshend's original with a more familiar binary between narrator and addressee.

If we return to the penultimate stanza, we can note an instance of this kind of reworking. This is that point where, in earlier manuscript versions, Townshend's verse introduces the second subject, his true love:

> Thy conquest in regard of me
> Alas was small, but in respect
> Of her that did my love protect,
> Were it divulg'd, deserv'd to be
> Recorded for a Victory.

The verse (and the whole poem) hinges around "but in respect / Of her"—that textual moment when the initial praise of the "Victorious Beauty" is rendered frail by being positioned in relation to the narrator's prior, constant other love. *Wits Interpreter* (1655), by contrast, offers:

> The conquest in regard of me
> Is small, but in respect of thee
> (Which if divulg'd) deservest to be
> Recorded for a victory.

The complicating and crucial "but in respect / Of her" is flattened to "in respect of thee," which makes little sense. And the line "Of her that did my love protect" is cut. Editor John Cotgrave seems to have worked to produce a simpler text—a text offering a more predictable celebration of a female subject, with no reference to a third party. But the attempt to simplify to produce this general text resulted in a stumbling, sometimes contradictory piece. Rather like John Benson's heterosexualizing editorial interventions in Shakespeare's Sonnets, Cotgrave clumsily worked to regularize the love scenario on display.[29]

This kind of textual alteration—the flattening out of the idiosyncratic in pursuit of the generic—was characteristic of many printed miscellany editorial interventions. And predictably so, since these collections were compiled with a broad readership in mind, and with an emphasis on the potential application of materials by readers. As a consequence, the jaggedly particular—in Townshend's case, the complications between narrator, female subject, and true love—was of less use than the known, the general, the predictable.

This strain of editing that rendered the specific generic was most common with the retitling of verse. Complex details of origin were dropped in favor of simpler, functional, more general framings. In *Wits Interpreter*, Ben Jonson's "Epitaph on Elizabeth, L.H." becomes "On a Gentlewoman"; "On Captain Hazard the Cheater" is "On a Cheater."[30] Sir John Harrington's epigram "A good answer of a Gentlewoman to a Lawyer" is offered as "Upon a Lawyer."[31] Sometimes miscellany titles are more carefully explanatory: Amorphus's song from *Cynthias Revells*, untitled as a distinct verse in Jonson's *Workes*, is offered as "*For a pair of Gloves.*"[32] Other titles give readers a clear sense of how and when the poem might be employed. Thus, for instance, "A mayd or widow being forsaken, may thus certifie her false friend by Letter," or "The Lover angry at his Mistreß unsufferable contempt, may (if he will) thus vent himself, in an invective manner."[33] (But this movement toward clear or generalized titles was not always maintained. A verse by William Hickes, for example, in his *Oxford Drollery*, is accompanied with the magnificently specific heading "An Elegy on the death of John Seamore formerly a Tailor, but lately Water-caryer, Feweller and Porter to Mr. Brome Whorwood at Halton near Oxford, Drown'd in his Moat on a Christmass eve in a great frost, he was seventy years old.")[34]

Editors of printed miscellanies did not only attempt to flatten or generalize verses in an attempt to produce more commercially compelling texts; they also altered the subject of poems in an effort to anticipate reader preferences. James Howell's "An EJACULATION To my CREATOR" seems to have received just this sort of revision. The poem, as it appeared in *Poems On several Choice and Various Subjects*, tells of the narrator's longing for God.[35] This 1663 text begins:

> As the parch'd Field doth thirst for Rain
> When the Dog-star makes Sheep and Swain
> Of an unusual Drowth complain,
> So *thirsts* my Heart for Thee.

When the poem appeared in *Wit at a Venture*, eleven years later, a few textual emendations had produced a distinctly secular version.[36] Now titled "Grief for Absence," the verse has shifted from a devotional song to God to a lament for an absent lover. Thus:

> As the parch'd field doth thirst for rain,
> When the Dog-star makes sheep and swain
> Of an unusual drowth complain,
> So thirst I to see thee again.

And where Howell's text concludes

> Or as the Teeming Earth doth mourn
> In Black (like Lover at an Urn)
> Till *Titan*'s quickning Beams return,
> So do I *mourn, mone, pant* and *thirst*
> For *Thee* who art my *Last* and *First*

Wit at a Venture offers

> Or as the troubl'd earth doth mourn
> In black (like Lover at an Urn)
> Till *Phoebus* quickning beams return,
> Whilst I in dire impatience burn.

The substitution of "Whilst I in dire impatience burn" for "For *Thee* who art my *Last* and *First*" sustains the movement of the poem away from the devotional and toward an established, known, Petrarchan poetry of love. So does "Phoebus" for "Titan": the former a more familiar reference in stock verses of love. These changes were quite possibly introduced in order to construct a verse more likely to appeal to the reader of popular printed miscellanies—those more interested in familiar poems of love than poems of faith.

We can detect a similarly free, strategic editorial hand in *Parnassus Biceps*. Editor Abraham Wright includes a version of Henry King's highly popular lamentation "On Prince Henry's Death" ("Keep station nature, and rest Heaven sure"). But the text is missing lines fifteen to twenty-four. The reason for this can only be guessed at—but it seems likely that ten lines beginning "Cease then unable Poetry, thy phrase / Is weak and dull to strike us with amaze,"[37] and which go on to lament the inability of verse to convey true profundities of sadness, were judged unsuitable for a collection intended to display poetry's power, and "that Ocean of Wit, which flowed from those two brests of this Nation, the two Universities."[38]

As well as altering texts with their readers' predilections in mind, editors of printed miscellanies might create new verses through the conflation of previously distinct texts. "*To his Mistresse*" in *Parnassus Biceps* is, in effect, a cobbling together of (an unusual reading of) Thomas Carew's "In her faire cheekes two pits doe lye"[39] and a shortened version of William Strode's "Keep on your mask." A new, forty-line verse is constructed—unascribed to anyone. The opening ten lines of "A Perswasive Letter to his Mistress," in *The Mysteries of Love and Eloquence* (1658), are similarly the product of conflations:

> Sweetest, but read what silent Love hath writ
> With thy fair eyes, tast but of Loves fine wit,
> Be not self will'd; for thou art much too fair,
> For death to triumph o're without an heir;
> Thy unus'd beauty, must be tomb'd with thee,
> Which us'd lives they Executour to be;
> The Flowers distill'd, though they with Winter meet
> Lose but their show, their substance still is sweet.
> Nature made thee her seal, she meant thereby:
> Thou shouldst Print more, not let the Copie die[.]

These lines are in fact the final couplets from five sonnets in Benson's 1640 edition of Shakespeare's poems.[40] They were combined with other lines, perhaps written by compiler Edward Phillips, or perhaps borrowed from some other text.

If editors were quick to construct new poems out of formerly separate verses, they often also plucked smaller sections from larger poems, printing fragments as complete, discrete texts. *The Academy of Complements*, for instance, apparently removes six lines from Michael Drayton's "*Alice* Countesse of Salisbury to the blacke Prince," published in *Englands Heroicall Epistles* (1598).[41] Drayton's original poem reworked the legend of Edward III's wooing of the wife of the First Earl of Salisbury, and her honorable resistance. *The Academy* retitles the lines with the generic "On a modest faire one," and creates a discrete six-line celebration of "Beauty [as] ... an attyer t'adorne sweet modesty." The new poem is shorn of any referents to its original textual or historical context. The same miscellany, just a few pages earlier, offers the final couplet from a song from Sidney's *The Countesse of Pembroke's Arcadia*: "As without breath no pipe doth move, / No musicke's kindly without Love." In Sidney's text the verse is presented as the shepherds' song in the First Eclogue, beginning "We love, and have our loves rewarded"; *The Academy*, however, presents the final two lines as a distinct verse, unascribed, and headed "Of Musicke and Love."[42] (Of course, *The Academy* might well have transcribed this couplet from a manuscript which offered an already dissected Sidney text: as Woudhuysen's *Sir Philip Sidney and the Circulation of Manuscripts* demonstrates, many of Sidney's poems appear in manuscript in this fragmented form. But even if the miscellany was not the initial agent of textual fracture, *The Academy* certainly perpetuated and disseminated this culture of fragmentation.) A few pages later, *The Academy* offers a couplet "On Virginity": "Like untun'd golden strings faire women are, / Which lying long untoucht will harshly Jar." The lines originate (with some alterations) in Marlowe's *Hero and Leander*.[43]

Perhaps the most striking example of the persistent fragmentation of a single text comes in *The Marrow of Complements*. While *The Marrow* assures readers that its inclusions were "never before published,"[44] this was a familiarly hollow boast. *The Marrow* in fact draws heavily on numerous printed (and almost certainly manuscript) publications: the list of writers whose works are silently plundered is lengthy, and includes, among many others, Ben Jonson ("Underwoods"; *Time vindicated to himselfe* [1640]), William Shakespeare (*Merry Wives of Windsor, Much Ado about Nothing, Love's Labour's Lost, As You Like It, Twelfth Night*), Francis Quarles (*The virgin widow* [1649]), William Davenant (*Love and Honour* [1649]), Jasper Mayne (*The amorovs warre* [1648]), and Robert Herrick (*Hesperides* [1648]).[45] But of all these sources, George Wither's *Faire-Virtue, the Mistress of Philarete* is the most regular supplier of texts.

Wither's *Faire-Virtue* was first published three decades before *The Marrow*, in 1622, and a later edition appeared in 1633.[46] The publisher of the 1622 edition noted that these early Wither poems, "composed many yeares agone," circulated widely in manuscript and arrived in Marriot's hands "without a Name." Wither himself was anxious to suppress publication since the

> lightnesse of such a *Subiect*, might somewhat disparage, the more serious *Studies*, which he hath since vundertaken. Yet, doubting (this being got out of his Custodie) some imperfecter *Coppies* might hereafter be scattered abroad in writing, or, be vnknowne to him, imprinted: He was pleased (vpon my importunities) to condescend that it might be published, without his *Name*.[47]

Of *The Marrow*'s 152 poems, all of which appear with no note of ascription or origin, forty-six come from Wither's *Faire-Virtue*. The most sustained borrowing appears in *The Marrow*'s "*VENVS NAKED. Instructions for an Amourist, whoo desires to praise his Mistresse perfections from head to foot.*"[48] This offers a sequence of nineteen short poems that blazon the would-be lover from "Her haire," "Her Eyes," "Her Chin," to "Her Mouth," "Her Breasts," "Her Navell," and, finally, "A Secret." Each of these poems is composed of lines taken from the same section of *Faire-Virtue*, separated out, and with the addition of a clarifying title. Now, it is possible that *The Marrow* turned to an intermediary text for these materials and not directly to *Faire-Virtue*—indeed, this is possible for almost all the transfers I discuss. But the number of lines that appear in both collections, the lack of the kind of textual variants that come from lengthy circulation (slight changes in word order, punctuation, and so on), and the fact that a single section from *Faire-Virtue* provides all the poems in "*VENVS NAKED*"—all these factors suggest a direct borrowing.

Often *The Marrow* poems are straight, sequential liftings from *Faire-Virtue*. "2. Her Brow," for example, reprints a *Faire-Virtue* couplet virtually unaltered: "Beauty there may be descride, / In the height of all her pride." Sometimes there is a slight rewriting of materials. Thus a *Faire-Virtue* couplet—"And her lips, that knew no dullness, / Full are, in the meanest fullness"—is removed and adjusted to produce "7. Her Lips. / Her soft Lips doe shew no dulnesse, / Full they are, in meanest fulnesse."[49] There are also moments when *The Marrow* constructs its blazons by conflating lines and couplets from different moments from this *Faire-Virtue* sequence. "1. Her haire," for example, beginning "There's her haire with which Love angles," draws six lines from distinct moments in a longer section of *Faire-Virtue*.[50] "8. Her Teeth," beginning with the wonderful "These are in such order placed," is similarly the product of a fusing of nonsequential lines.[51]

It is important to stress just how common these acts of textual carpentry really were. To focus on the few examples above is to imply an exceptional status for these instances, but this is not the case. Textual alteration and fragmentation were not eccentric moments of difference, but defining characteristics of miscellany compilation. Indeed, a miscellany culture of variance was the norm against which moments of the precise, steady reproduction of whole texts stood as exceptions.

There is one other instructive case of miscellany editorial practice, concerning the treatment of Ben Jonson's printed poetry in *Wits Interpreter*. While *Wits Interpreter* turned to numerous, diverse sources for the majority of its material—assembling a true "store-house" of gathered diversity—it also drew *directly* on the 1616 or the 1640 printed *Workes* of Ben Jonson. This is never openly declared; indeed, Cotgrave asserts "whilst I was in Town to attend the *Press,* I crossed out whatsoever had bin formerly published."[52] But, as with *The Marrow of Complements*' claim of uniqueness, the truth was very different: *Wits Interpreter* printed poems that had already appeared in many books, including Thomas Carew's *Poems* (1640),[53] Robert Herrick's *Hesperides* (1648),[54] Richard Lovelace's *Lucasta* (1649),[55] and Thomas Deloney's *Jack of Newbury* (c1597).[56]

But beyond this general editorial tendency to draw on the previously published, there are two compelling strands of evidence to suggest Cotgrave turned directly to *The Workes*.⁵⁷ First, *Wits Interpreter*, pages 314 to 317, offers thirteen consecutive Jonson poems which appeared sequentially in *The Workes* (in "Epigrammes"), numbered XII, XX, XXI, XXV, XXXI, XXXVII, XXXIX, XLI, XLII, XLVI, XLVII, LVII, and LIX. Pages 304 to 305 print epigram numbers LXII, LXIX, LXXXVII, and XC. Thus, while *Wits Interpreter* does not print the *complete* sequence of epigrams in *The Workes*, its ordering is still consistent with *The Workes'* layout. Second is an insightful case of Cotgrave's carelessness. In the 1616 edition ("Epigrammes," p. 777, no. XXXI), "ON BANCK THE VSVRER" is a simple satirical four-line poem:

> Banck feeles no lamenesse of his knottie gout,
> His monyes trauaile for him, in and out:
> And though the soundest legs goe euery day,
> He toyls to be at hell, as soone as they.

But *Wits Interpreter*, page 315, offers the apparently inexplicable "*On a Usurer*":

> *Bankes* feels no lamenesse of his knotty gout,
> His monies travel for him in and out.
> Twere madness in thee to betray thy fame
> And person to the world, ere *I* thy name.

This last couplet is not the product of a rush of literary self-belief in Cotgrave. It is, in fact, the last two lines of "TO PERSON GVILTIE"—the poem printed *directly above* "ON BANCK THE VSVRER" in *The Workes*. Copying the latter, Cotgrave must have accidentally scanned back four lines and conflated the two to create a new poem.⁵⁸

If, then, it can be said with some confidence that *Wits Interpreter* used *The Workes* (either the 1616 or the 1640 edition) as its source for some of its inclusions, what evidence do we have of Cotgrave's editorial techniques when dealing with a printed source? Do we detect a new reverence for these supposedly stable, excluding versions? Does *Wits Interpreter* support Walter J. Ong's argument that printed texts were regarded as final, unalterable truths, in contrast to manuscripts, which invited alteration and were, implicitly, equivocal, uncertain documents?⁵⁹ Do the particulars of Jonson's verse in *Wits Interpreter* support or contest ideas of the emergence of a distinct culture of print that demanded a new exactitude? In particular, what does Cotgrave's miscellany suggest about the cultural status of Jonson's *Workes*—a collection often heralded as iconic in the establishment of the printed book, and of the author?⁶⁰

Perhaps unsurprisingly, Cotgrave's miscellany has a much more relaxed relationship with its printed source than these theories imply. As well as alterations to punctuation, spelling, layout, and titles, there are frequent changes to the verse, too, many of which result in new readings. "*On something that walkes somewhere*" (*Wits Interpreter*, 309) is a version of Jonson's epigram II. It tells of a meeting at court between the narrator and a grave figure who calls himself "A lord . . . buried in flesh and blood." For most of the poem the two versions are close, with only punctuation and orthographic differences. But where line six of *The Workes* reads "*And such from whom let no man hope least good,*" Cotgrave's version is "*And such from whom let women hope much good.*" This appears to be a bawdy rewriting designed to produce a verse more engaging to a wider readership.

There are other instances of significant variations. While the final line of "*On an English Mounsieur*" has "Dayly to turn in *Pauls,* and halfe the trade," *The Workes* (epigram LXXXVIII) offers " . . . and helpe the trade." In the context of the rest of the poem, Cotgrave's line makes little sense. Similarly, in the opening of "*To Wooall a Knight,*" a version of Jonson's "TO SIR LVCKLESSE WOO-ALL" (XLVI), the Knight's "wast wife" has become "vast." "*To Sickness*" has seven significant alterations from *The Workes*; "*On a Gentlewoman*" has six in only twelve lines; "*On Giles and Jone*" has seven; and "*On a waiting Gentlewoman*" five (including "soule" for "foole," "love" for "tast," and "fate" for "face").[61]

Even those instances of textual alterations which seem less the product of deliberate editorial intervention and more an accident of Cotgrave's carelessness in compilation are instructive. They suggest that compilers did not treat print with a new reverence; that editors turned to print as they turned to manuscript—selecting passages, not wholes—and treating texts with no great caution, with errors creeping in. Of course we should remember that Cotgrave, as a compiler of miscellanies—he also produced *The English Treasury of Wit and Language*, a collection of excerpts from verse dramas, in 1655—had a vested interest in the fracture of texts. But in printing these unstable "Jonson" poems, *Wits Interpreter* and its forty sister publications conveyed to their reading public a notion of literature that placed little emphasis on stability or closure.

Such textual instabilities must affect *The Workes*-embodied Ben—fixed, monolithic, excluding—often proclaimed "decisive" in the history of the book and of authorship. Certainly this image of Jonson as the Controlling Author is challenged by the reality of the treatment of verse—of *his* verse—in anthologies at this time.[62] Here, we see those poems carefully set in Jonson's printed *Workes* being treated with relative nonchalance: separated, slackly copied, deliberately changed. And while it must be stressed that printed miscellanies—the center of attention in this project—are only small voices in a larger, louder cultural debate, they are voices worth hearing for their consistently antagonistic position to narratives that propose the emergence of print as a medium of, *necessarily*, a new exactitude. While Jonson, who exhorted his readers to "take care, that tak'st my booke in hand, / To reade it well: that is, to understand,"[63] would surely have been dismayed at the various versions of his poems in manuscript and print,[64] students of early modern writing can embrace this textual diversity as a real opportunity for a more detailed understanding of how writing was read in seventeenth-century England.

High Manuscript Circulation

Printed miscellanies frequently boast a reliance on the manuscripts of the socially elite. *Wits Interpreter* declares that it draws, in part, on the work of eminent men—"*all Souldiers, Statesmen and Poets*"—and that "*these sheets of paper . . . are printed from their own Manuscripts.*" *The Mysteries of Love and Eloquence* maintains not only that the volume comprises "the contributions of several persons of Honor," but that, in particular, "their choisest Manuscripts, built up this Volume. It took its birth from them, to whom with a most sincere gratitude it doth again humbly dedicate it self."[65]

Such assurances should be read with extreme scepticism: they were part of an attempt to lend legitimacy and status to cheap printed miscellanies. As we have seen, when the law demanded that the compiler of *Sportive Wit* list his sources, Brookes could only cite "one Walter Wasse . . . several other musicians and other persons."[66] There was no sign of a direct borrowing from eminent authors or collectors.

But while printed miscellanies probably did not turn to those "choisest Manuscripts" "of several persons of Honor," they certainly did include poems which had proved popular in manuscript circulation. This is not surprising: editors of printed miscellanies were engaged in a commercial activity and so naturally sought to offer fashionable poems, making the interesting assumption that poems popular in manuscript would be poems popular in print. The duplication of materials across manuscripts and printed miscellanies reflects, at times, a direct reliance on those manuscripts. In particular, compilers seem to have drawn on miscellanies and commonplace books of the sort compiled by Oxford undergraduates in the 1620s and 1630s, and as a result printed miscellanies offered public versions, thirty years later, of these kinds of manuscripts.

What traits can we discern about miscellany printings of verses which had enjoyed a high manuscript circulation? The unattributed verse beginning "O Love whose power and might" was highly popular in manuscript transmission: it made a dozen appearances in Bodleian manuscripts alone, and also emerges in Huntington and Folger texts. The poem wittily undercuts a conventional poetry of love—and, in the process, conforms to another conventional model. The verse works by repeatedly invoking a familiar wooing plea, and then subverting those romantic intentions through jolting, bathetic intrusions. Thus:

> Grant pity, or I die,
> Love so my heart bewitches,
> With grief I howl and cry;
> Oh how my Elbow itches.

and

> What ist I would not do
> To purchase one sweet smile?
> Bid me to *China* go,
> 'Faith I'le sit still the while.[67]

With such a wide manuscript distribution, versions of the text are predictably varied. A brief comparison of two manuscripts serves to highlight this persistent level of textual variation. Folger MS Va 124 is a circa 1630 poetical miscellany that belonged to Richard Archard. Folger MS Va 162 is a similar collection, probably belonging to an Oxford student around 1650. Both manuscripts include the verse but in noticeably different forms. The former titles the verse "Dr Dun to his m^{rs} y^t scorn'd him," and offers a fifty-two-line text.[68] The latter presents the poem as "Mr Poulden's delight of N. Coll. in Oxon" and offers a shorter twenty-eight-line text.[69] Individual lines vary. Where Archard's text offers "None euer yet withstood," the 1650 manuscript has "Noe power euer withstood"; for "Your dresses finely wrought," there is "Your tresses that were wrought"; for "With waues of daily weeping," "With floods of dayly weepinge" for "I know that I shall dye," "Grant pitty else I dye." And there are numerous other moments of textual change. Not radical departures, perhaps, but cumulatively significant, and representative of the variety of versions of this poem preserved in manuscript. Other versions offer attributions: to "Mr Polden of New College," "Mr Lawson of St John's Colledge," "John Hoskins."[70]

Printed miscellanies reflect this wide and variable distribution: textual differences among the six printed miscellany manifestations are persistent and, collectively, significant.[71] Line numbers vary (fifty-two, forty-four, and twenty-eight lines); the stanza order switches wildly as sections are dropped and reordered. *Folly in Print* (1667) includes two stanzas absent in all other printed miscellanies. And there are important differences between individual lines—as the following comparison of particular lines from the poem in two printed miscellanies indicates (notable differences in bold):

Wit and Drollery (1656)	*Folly in Print* (1667)
Oh Love, whose power and might	
No Creature ere withstood,	None **every** yet withstood,
Sole Mistress of my heart,	Sole mistress of my **rest**
Grant pitty or I die,	**I think that** I shall die
Tears overflow my eyes	Tears overflow my **sight**
With flouds of daily weeping,	With **waves** of daily weeping;
Her Tresses that were wrought,	**Your** tresses **finely** wrought
My loving heart hath caught,	My **silly** heart hath caught
But think men still will flatter,	But think **that I do** flatter,
He struck my heart to day,	He **hit me 'o ther day**
A Turd in *Cupid's* Teeth.	A T— in *Cupids* teeth.
I vow I love you ever,	I vow I lov'd **her** ever,
But yet it is no matter.	And **fain I would be at her.**

What is striking here is the persistent degree of variation between the two texts, and the cumulative effect of such variations is, I think, significant. What these miscellany versions suggest is the degree to which the textual instability of the manuscript miscellanies and commonplace books is sustained into print ("finely wrought"/"wrought"; "waues"/"floods"; "I know that"/"Grant pitty else"). Rather than fixing the poem in a single, stable text, printed miscellanies served to duplicate, disseminate, and render public the textual volatility that characterized the more restricted manuscript circulation of this verse. In this instance, printed miscellanies were important not for unifying texts around a single reading, but in perpetuating a culture of textual variation—in (paradoxically) fixing a culture of instability. Indeed, there are several instances of a single printed miscellany offering multiple, contrasting versions of the same verse. Sir Robert Ayton's "Wrong not dear Empress of my heart" appears twice in *Wits Interpreter,* with considerable differences: once as "To his Mistresse by Sir Walter Raleigh," accompanied with Raleigh's "Passions are lik'ned best to floods and streams"; once, more simply, as "To his Mistress."[72] William Strode's "Keep on your vail and hide your eye" also appears twice in this single book, as "*To a Lady unvailing her self*" and "*On a Mask.*"[73] Print technology not only disseminated cloistered texts to a larger reading audience, it also disseminated an accompanying culture of textual variation and instability.

Answers and Mocks

> 1669 these Mr Boss of Hode made concerning my
> Cozin Leonard Sprakeling: see my answere to them, 4 leaues
> foreward ... These are in answer to a parcel of verses made
> by John Boss of Hode Ely of my Coz Leonard Sprakeling.
> see the copy 4 leaues backward. Aug 1669.
> Marginal notes by Henry Oxenden, next to two poems
> in his manuscript miscellany.[74]

Sir Robert Ayton's verse beginning "No man Love's fiery Passions can approve" declares that a "milde and luke-warme zeale in Love" is preferable to those "fiery passions" which fail to yield "pleasure & promotion."[75] The verse scoffs at lovers affecting a rhetoric of death and destiny: we love as we wish, Ayton's verse declares, and no more. The poem was highly popular, appearing in four printed miscellanies,[76] and it is easy to understand why. The poem is, in effect, an answer to the thousands of lines (including some by Ayton) that had previously proclaimed, with ruthless monotony, their "fiery passions," their powerlessness to "destiny," their various deaths from love. It is an answer to the figure of the doomed, love-struck poet: histrionic, silks asunder, Petrarchan conceits flowing like sweat off his brow.

In *Oxford Drollery* we find a reply to Ayton's answer. "The Answer to Loves fiery passions" is a point-by-point refutation of the issues raised in the original verse which turns Ayton's vocabulary back to discredit the charge that a *via media* love is best. Thus, to Ayton's opening "I like of milde and luke-warme zeale in Love," *Oxford Drollery* declares a hate for "Luke-warmness in an Amorist." When Ayton's verse mocks ideas of dying of love—

> And how can any dye of that disease,
> Whereof himselfe may be his own Physitian?

—*Oxford Drollery* replies

> *Nor may we love or nor love as we please,*
> *Since Cupid's Laws commands mens disposition,*
> *For I have known men die of that Disease*
> *Of which himself to others was Physieian.*

And so on, through each of Ayton's cynicisms.

But the anonymous *Oxford Drollery* text presents us with a paradox. The wit of the poem depends upon its specific engagement with Ayton's verse: the answer poem names the original in its title ("The Answer to Loves fiery passions"), employs much of the original's language, and an appreciation of the wit of the piece requires a reader who perceives and understands this correspondence. But *Oxford Drollery* does not actually include "No man Love's fiery Passions." We are left with an answer verse whose meaning depends upon a recalled but absent poem. Such an omission alludes, I think, to one of two things: either to the looseness of miscellany compilation (would not a careful editor gather the two poems together?; does not the omission merely indicate a slack text?), or, more compellingly, to an assumed contemporary knowledge by readers of the original verse (in other words, printing of the first was deemed unnecessary because readers were already familiar with it).[77] Miscellany compilation is certainly often imprecise, and surely some separate answer poems allude to the quick, careless editor; but it is so often the case that miscellanies offer answer poems which declare their correspondence to an absent original that an assumed popular knowledge of the catalyst poem is vividly implied. We see a similar dependence on significant reader knowledge in miscellanies that print only abbreviated first lines ("Here's a Health to his Majesty with a Fa la la, &c"),[78] tunes ("Farewel unkind one, since you so design, &c"; "To the Tune of I'le tell thee Dick, &c"),[79] and titles ("The Fire on London Bridge, &c"; "Against Fruition, &c").[80]

It is not always the case that miscellanies offer distinct and solitary answers. Sometimes poem and answer are coupled, as was the case when *New Court Songs* followed "A SONG in Love in a Wood"—sixteen lines from William Wycherley's play, beginning "A Wife I do hate"—with "The ANSWER" (beginning, "A Wife I do adore").[81] *Wits Interpreter* provides three consecutive pairs of poems, each offering an assertion and a refutation of the need to act swiftly and decisively to gain a woman's heart. Thus, in the first pair, the stanza

> *Unlesse thou cast thy lure,*
> *Or throw her out a crain,*

> Thou seldome shalt a falcon or
> A taffel gentle gain

is answered in the opening stanza of the subsequent verse ("*Answer ex tempore*"):

> Although you cast the lure,
> Or flingest forth thy train,
> No falcon but some haggard kite,
> Or bussard thou shalt gain.[82]

Answer poems might be even more specific than this. One untitled verse which depicts a nervous narrator coyly fumbling through words of love is immediately followed by the dissecting "*Answer to the third stave*," which lambasts such reticence and declares

> A young Wench loves a Lad that's bold,
> And not a simpring noddy.[83]

But more typically, as the *Oxford Drollery* instance suggests, answer verses are printed without the original. Thomas Gansforde's "A description of Women" ("All you that women love . . . ") appears in *Wits Interpreter*, but its answer—"Women are cloth, and you are moth"—does not.[84] William Bond's "*An Answer to the Letter of the Cloake*" appears in *Parnassus Biceps* unascribed and alone.[85] "O Love whose power and might" appeared in six miscellany printings; the answer, "Your Letter I receiv'd," appeared in only four. The poem beginning "She lay all naked in her bed" is printed as a single verse in *Wit and Drollery* in 1656, but in the second, 1661, edition, this verse is separated into "A Song" and "An answer, being a dreamed."[86]

A separation of verse and answer is perhaps an unsurprising characteristic of manuscript transmission: manuscripts generally circulated within relatively restricted environments, and an informed readership, sharing the same knowledge, expectations, and assumptions, is to be expected. Thus we see that "Hence all ye vain delights" and William Strode's answer "Return my joys and hither bring"—two of the most popular poems to circulate in seventeenth-century England—appeared in twenty-three manuscripts in the Bodleian and British Library but appear together in the same manuscript only five times.[87] In eighteen manuscripts the two sections did not travel together. But what printed miscellanies show is that the same suggested reader knowledge—the same sense of readers being able to construct correspondences between this new answer and a known, remembered earlier verse—existed well outside the close circles of manuscript circulation, like universities and Inns of Court.

The same separation of verses applies to mocks or parodies (sometimes termed "imitations"), a genre which grew out of—and in some ways replaced—this tradition of answer poems.[88] Mocks used the same tune and rhythm as their named source, but offered alternative words. Here the wit of the piece relies heavily on the often comic discordance between original and mock; poems thus demand a cognizant readership, able to draw connections. A 1683 ballad attacking Sir Roger L'Estrange titled "Towzer Discover'd; or a New Ballade on an Old Dog That Writes Strange-Lee," is set to the tune "Oh how unhappy a Lover am I." By citing this lament of unrequited love from Dryden's *The Conquest of Granada*, the ballad announces the song it parodies—and the radical disjunction between Dryden's delicate love elegy and the lumbering attack on L'Estrange which begins "How unhappy a Mastiffe am I" would have sharpened the ballad's satiric edge.[89] Richard Corbett's attack on Puritans beginning "Am I mad O noble Festus" similarly gained witty intensity by being set, in one miscellany, "To the Tune of Tom a Bedlam"—thus invoking the hugely popular verse tale of mad Tom, come "Forth from my sad and darksome Cell, / . . . To see if he can ease his distemper'd brain," a tune popularly associated with the ridicule of a libel victim.[90]

Mock Songs and Joking Poems is a collection "of Mocks to several late Songs about the Town" which specializes in just this kind of substitution of the bawdy for the decorous. Thus, "A Drunkard I am, and a Drunkerd I'le dye" is, as the title notes, "A Mock to a Lover I am, and a Lover I'le be. *And to that Tune*"[91]—a poem which appears in *Westminster Drollery*[92] and *Windsor Drollery*.[93] Thus the poem beginning "I pass all my hours in a shady old grove"[94]—sometimes ascribed to Charles II—is transformed into "I Pass all my hours with a dingy old Punk."[95] Thus "Tobacco I love, and Tobacco I'le take"[96] is offered in place of the decorous "A Lover I am, and a Lover I'le be."[97] Such mocks are not confined to this collection. Other printed miscellanies offer many similar reworkings: a mock to "Oh Love whose power and might" appears in no less than five printed miscellanies; Marlowe's "Come live with me and be my love" is rendered "Come live with me, and be my Whore."[98] "Come my Daphne, come away," a song from James Shirley's *The Cardinal* that was popularized in three printed miscellanies, provided the model for a number of different mocks, including "In imitation of Come my Daphne, a Dialogue betwixt Pluto and Oliver" ("Come Imp Royal, come away"); "A Drunken Mock, to come away my Daphne"

("Come my bully-rock away"); and "A Mock-song to Come my Daphny" ("Come my durty pug away").[99]

In order to generate their wit, such mocks had to vividly invoke and then subvert the decorous poems they reworked. Their relationship to the original poem was thus equivocal: the mocks engineered an undermining, but an undermining that relied on a vivid rendering of the uncorrupted original. And since these mocks, like the answer poems, generally cite but do not print the original that is reworked, the reader's knowledge of these verses is once more presumed. As a result, these texts suggest that many popular poems were etched on the memories of the broad, anonymous readership to which texts like *Oxford Drollery* were directed, and that a reference to a title or a first line would conjure at least the outline of the poem. Printed miscellanies were in dialogue with, and relied upon, this vivid oral culture, and their usually abbreviated (or coded) appeals to this oral culture makes apparent the amount of material, and the degree of cultural context, which is lost to the twenty-first-century reader. Furthermore, by disseminating poems that had often previously only circulated in manuscript—by opening the gates to waves of possible models for answers and mocks—printed miscellanies themselves fostered this level of public knowledge of verses and enabled a culture of printed answers, mocks, and parodies to flourish.

"The Blacksmith"

This reliance on a now largely effaced oral culture is vividly apparent in the history of one of the most popular poems in printed miscellanies: that verse, simply titled "*SONG*" in its debut miscellany appearance, which tells—over and over and over, across twenty-seven stanzas—the many virtues of the blacksmith. Through references to classical mythology, proverbial wisdom, rival professions, and the geography of London, we are presented with wave after wave of reasons to admire these men. "Of all the Trades that ever I see," the poem begins,

> There's none to the Black-smith compared may be,
> With so many severall tools works he.
> *Which no body can deny.*
>
> The first that ever Thunderbolts made,
> VVas a Cyclops of the Black-smiths trade,
> As in a learned Author is said.

> *Which no body, &c.*
>
> . . .
>
> The fairest Goddesse in the Skies,
> To marry with Vulcan did advise,
> And he was a Black-smith grave and wise.
> *Which no body, &c.*
>
> Vulcan he to doe her right,
> Did build her a Town by day and by night,
> And gave it a name which was *Hammersmith* hight.
> *Which no body, &c.*
>
> . . .
>
> The common Proverb as it is read,
> That a man must hit the naile on the head,
> Without the Black-smith cannot be said.
> *Which no body, &c.*
>
> Another Proverb must not be forgot,
> And falls unto the Black-smiths lot,
> That a man strike while the Iron is hot.
> *Which no body, &c.*

And with clanking puns at the expense of various professions, we read

> Though your Lawyers travell both neer and far,
> And by long pleading, a good cause may mar,
> Yet your Black-smith takes more pains at th' Bar.
> *Which no body, &c.*
>
> . . .
>
> If a Scholler be in doubt,
> And cannot well bring his matter about,
> The Black-smith he can hammar it out.
> *Which no body, &c.*

The verse concludes with a rousing chorus:

> Now heres a good health to Black-smiths all,
> And let it go round, as round, as a ball,
> VVee'l drink it all off, though it cost us a fall.
> *Which no body, &c.*

"The Blacksmith" appears in four printed miscellanies.[100] Unusually, some of these texts offer a precise literary and social context in which to place this verse. *Wit Restor'd* ascribes "The Blacksmith" to *"some of the Modern Familie of the Fancies"*— a reference to that group of drinkers and wits who followed the model of Ben Jonson's tavern societies and met in the late 1620s and early 1630s. Tim Raylor's *Cavaliers, Clubs, and Literary Culture*—to which this discussion of "The Blacksmith" is indebted—offers the only sustained (but still speculative) account of this "Order of the Fancy."[101] Raylor suggests a club membership of, most notably, James Smith, Sir John Mennes, James Atkins, Philip Massinger, William Bagnall, Robert Herrick, and Sir John Suckling. Behavior was evidently boisterous but the ideology was far from radical: the unifying theme was a sense of exclusion from positions of influence. In Raylor's words, members were "disgruntled younger sons of gentlemen and alienated intellectuals, all of whom had reason to feel dissatisfied with their families and with their position in society."[102] Members of the group sought not radical political or social change but simply inclusion, and there was consequently an implicit assertion of the significance of those elusive establishment positions. The group's most extreme behavior seems to have been Sir John Mennes's habit of riding home on the back of an unfortunate citizen after a night of hard drinking.[103]

In fact, *Wit Restor'd* does more than ascribe the poem to this boisterous, communal author. The book also places the verse within a larger literary sequence. The verse before "The Blacksmith" is "THE INNOVATION OF *Vlysses* and *Penelope*," a very free reworking of the first epistle of Ovid's *Heroides*, with the addition of comic footnotes.[104] This poem concludes with the lines

> The Iron-Age, quoth he that used to sing?
> This to my mind the Black-Smith's Song doth bring
> The Black-Smiths, quoth *Ulisses*? and there holloweth
> Whoope! is there such a Song? Let's ha't.
> It followeth,

And there then follows, immediately, "The Black-Smith. As it was sung before Ulysses and Penelope at their Feast, when he returned from their Trojan Wars, collected out of Homer, Virgill, and Ovid, by some of the Modern Familie of the Fancies."[105] Here, then, "The Blacksmith" is presented as a sung, communal verse amid a broader literary project. These literary contexts also evoke something of the original circumstances of composition, too—the world of Ulysses calling for a group song close to the world of "The Order of the Fancy" and its disenchanted young revellers.

This club context—this emphasis on "The Blacksmith" as a product of the disenfranchised, a marker of a restless dissatisfaction with the contemporary—was crucial for the later politicization of this verse. Since there was no note of this club context in broadside ballad or manuscript versions of the text, printed miscellanies were the medium sustaining a sense of the verse as a communal, aggrieved, drink-assisted song, and so enabled subsequent political appropriations.

At the foot of a manuscript rendering of "The blacke-smiths' Song" are the words "To the tune of Greene sleeues," the name of a melody to which the words were to be sung.[106] A popular ballad with a known melody was often invoked to supply the tune for a new verse, as a precursor or shorthand to a full musical score. In fact, 163 poems in printed miscellanies invoke a specific accompanying tune in this way, and *The Rump* (1660) mockingly alludes to this fashion when it sets "THE FOUR-LEGG'D ELDER ... To the Tune of *The Lady's Fall*, or, *Gather your Rose-Buds*, and 50 other Tunes."[107] The manuscript citation of "Greene sleeues" is no surprise since this was an extremely well-known melody; the earliest reference to it comes in the *Stationer's Register* on 3 September 1580 when Richard Jones was licensed to print *A Newe northern Dittye of ye Ladye Greene Sleves*, and it was common ever since.[108] But, typically, "The Blacksmith," once popular, began to replace "Greensleves" as the referent for its tune. ("Which no body can deny" was also used as a title.) *An Antidote against Melancholy* (1661), for example, includes the poem "The BREWER. A Ballad made in the year, 1657. To the Tune of the Blacksmith."[109] And in the evening of 23 April 1660, Samuel Pepys listened as his Lord "fell to singing of a song made upon the Rump, which he pleased himself with—to the tune of *The Blacksmith*."[110]

While "The Blacksmith" became an established name for this particular tune, "Which no body can deny" proved popular as a refrain for poems, appearing thirteen other times in printed miscellanies. These verses also employed the structure of "The Blacksmith," with a three-line verse plus refrain. Significantly, they generally shared an overtly political tone—including "The Rump" in *Merry Drollery the Second Part* (1661); "The Protecting Brewer" *Merry Drollery the Second Part*; and verses beginning "In few words I'le describe a Fanatick knave," "The Papist cannot take one oath," and "I mean to sing of Englands fate."[111] Two 1660 anthologies of political ballads, *Ratts Rhimed to Death* and *The Rump*, include many verses drawing on the legacy of "The Blacksmith," using both its title to indicate the tune, and its refrain and verse structure. And these verses are similarly explicitly political. The former includes, among many other post-Blacksmith verses, "A Display of the Headpiece and Codpiece of Valour, of the most Renowned, Colonel *Robert Jermy*, late of *Bafield* in the County of *Norfolk*, Esq; with his son Captain *Toll* by his side; now on their way for *New-England*. Or, the lively description of a dead-hearted fellow. *To the Tune of a* Turd, *or the* Black-smith."[112]

The political agenda articulated by these Blacksmith-influenced poems is reasonably consistent: overwhelmingly, these poems present Royalist lamentations for better times gone by, or rueful satires on 1650s Republicanism. Thus, for example, "The Protecting Brewer" or "The Brewer's Praise," which appeared across a number of publications, gives voice to the popular and disparaging 1650s description of Oliver Cromwell as the beer-drinking son of a tapster:

> Of all the Professions in the Town,
> This Brewers trade did gain renown,
> His liquor once reacht up to the Crown,
> Which no body, &c.[113]

The original perception of "The Blacksmith" as a product of a disenfranchised group was crucial in politicizing its tune, structure, and chorus in this particular way. The original ballad had no overt ideology of opposition, only really taking swipes at oft-abused "snuffling Puritans" and a contemporary "when so many Hæresis fly about, / And every sect growes still more in doubt." While there is no hard political philosophy, the verse does construct a vague but discernible sense of protest, through its vivid evocation of a lifestyle of the "Roreing-Boy who . . . swaggers, & drinks, & sweares and rayles"; through criticisms of those who try to curtail such excesses; and through the refrain, with its rousing, communal opposition to deniers. This sense of common resistance must have been crucially strengthened through association with the original circumstances of the composition of "The Blacksmith" and here printed miscellany texts played an important role, since they—unlike broadside ballads and extant manuscripts—offered the verse as a product and marker of an aggrieved, disenfranchised club. Those various post-Blacksmith poems were thus in part drawing on these miscellany reconstructions of the original circumstances of composition of "The Blacksmith"—circumstances which emphasized a politics of community, resistance, and an assertion of the forbidden. This resentment at disenfranchisement was a powerfully amorphous sense of grievance that could be reapplied in new contexts. Originally, it expressed distress at the authors' personal exclusion from positions of influence; but later, in the 1650s, in poems like "The Rump" and "The Protecting Brewer," it acquired a greater resonance and was used to convey a specifically pro-Crown, anti-parliament agenda.

More generally, what this swift survey of Blacksmith manifestations suggests is the capacity for a particular melody and verse structure to become established and recognized signifiers of meaning. Invocations of either melody or verse form conjured the sense of injustice, disenfranchisement, and opposition that accompanied the original Blacksmith verse. Such markers are particularly intriguing since their connotations are entirely implicit: the meanings surrounding the Blacksmith melody were known, shared, and embedded in the oral culture of mid-seventeenth-century England, and so a spelling out of their significances was not necessary. Consequently, such significances escape the twenty-first-century reader unless a history of the Blacksmith verse is constructed. Other ballad tunes must have also suggested frames of allegiance in which to position their accompanying verses. Thus when printed miscellany verse includes titles like "A CATCH, To the Tune of, Old Poets Hipocrene Admire"[114] or "A Ballad on Queen Elizabeth; to the tune of Sallengers round,"[115] particular meanings—political, social, literary—were surely being conveyed.[116] Future research might attempt to interrogate the meanings conveyed by particular melodies and verse forms.

There is in fact one vivid instance of an individual appropriating the form of "The Blacksmith" to convey his personal grievances. William Houlbrook was a blacksmith who was arrested and prosecuted for Royalist sympathies in July 1659.[117] After paying a fine he was eventually released from Newgate prison, but his sense of injustice was such that he wrote *The Loyal Black-smith and no Jesuite*, published in 1660 and 1677 as

> A True Relation how I *William Houlbrook* Blacksmith of *Marleborough* was betray'd by Coronet *George Joyce*, who carried the King prisoner from *Holmby;* and of the unjust imprisoning of me: And my several examination before *Bradshaw*, and his bloody Crew; With my Answers unto all of them, as you may read in the following Discourse.

At the end of the second edition of the book in 1677, Houlbrook includes "The Black-smiths Song of *Marleborough*," an eleven-stanza poem praising his profession which follows the Blacksmith model—including one stanza drawn directly from "The Blacksmith" and eight verses that appeared in a subsequent Black-smith verse.[118] And Houlbrook followed this verse with another, titled "A Song on the Author," which once again adopts the Blacksmith verse model. The first stanza reads

> *William Houlbrook* is my name
> And for his Loyalty suffer'd shame,
> For which the *Rump* was much to blame,
> *Which no body can deny*, &c.

The verse is truly dire—a later stanza continues

> And now I dwell in *Marle-borough* Town,
> Who for my suffering had never a Crown,
> And yet I am of some renown,
> *Which no body can deny*, &c.[119]

But Houlbrook's significance is not aesthetic. He offers a neat illustration of that conception of poetry as something to be appropriated by readers—appropriated and reshaped according to the particulars of their environments. Houlbrook's verse also suggests that "The Blacksmith," while having obvious professional significance for him, was a verse form known to convey a sense of grievance, exclusion, and resentment. And in drawing on these connotations, Houlbrook was relying on a chain of significance which dated back—via printed miscellanies—to the Order of the Fancy's communal, drink-assisted, grievance-laden composition of the 1620s.

Music and Memory

> Well remembered, honest Scholer
> ISAAC WALTON, *The Compleat Angler*

In Isaac Walton's *The Compleat Angler*, a group of friends decide to

> draw cuts what Song should be next sung, and who should sing it. They all agreed to the motion, and the lot fell to her that was the youngest and veryest Virgin of the company; and she sung *Franks Davisons* Song, which he made forty years ago, and all the other of the company joined to sing the burthen with her; the Ditty was this,

Bright shines the Sun, play beggars play,
here's scraps enough to serve to day . . . [120]

As Walton's text proceeds through these dialogues among the angler Piscator, the "falkner" Venator, the hunter Auceps, and others, the reader is repeatedly reminded of the intimate relationship between memory, musical performance, and poetry: the book is full of resolutions to "sing another Song in praise of Angling to morrow night," to recall a "Song . . . with mettle . . . choicely fitted to the occasion."[121] Many of these songs appear as verses—often with no note of a musical setting—in printed miscellanies. "*Franks Davisons* Song" is a verse from Francis Davison's *A Poetical Rhapsody* (1602), and it also appears in two printed miscellanies.[122]

An overlap between poems in printed miscellanies and lyrics in songbooks is common, and texts seem to have moved in both directions. John Playford's *The Musical Companion, in two books* (1673), for instance, prints dozens of poems popular in printed miscellanies, including William Strode's hit "I saw fair Cloris walk alone," reduced from ten lines to an economical four, with music by "Mr. Christopher Simpson."[123] The editor of *Poems of Pembroke and Ruddier*, John Donne Junior, noted in his prefaces to the volume that in order to gather his materials, "which were chiefly preserved by the greatest Masters of Musick," he

> was fain first to send to Mr. Henry Laws, who furnishing me with some, directed me for the rest, to send into Germany to Mr. Laneere, who by his great skill gave a life and harmony to all that he set.

Similarly, the editor of *Sportive Wit* noted the volume's materials came, in the most part, from "several other musicians."[124]

We see many other reminders of the mixed cultures of music and verse. Throughout miscellanies, the terms "poem," "sonnet," and "song" are used interchangeably, and verses frequently cite opening lines of ballads as referents to known melodies, inviting readers to supply a remembered tune. Printed miscellanies celebrate a lifestyle suffused with the semipublic musical performance of poetry, and readers are encouraged to "*drink* and be *merry*, dance, *Joke*, and *Rejoice*, / With *Claret* and *Sherry*, *Theorbo* and *Voice.*"[125]

This intimate connection between music and poetry had significant consequences for the transmission of materials.[126] Verses set and performed to music were prone to particular kinds of textual changes, and I would like to focus on three characteristic evolutions. First, since musical settings often separated lyrics into distinct parts, there was a tendency for printed miscellanies drawing on musical settings to offer only part of a former song. Second, verses set to music were often reworked to match the needs of particular performances. As a result, characteristics of the poem—the identity of voices, for example—were often changed, as the resources and occasion dictated. Printed miscellanies maintain some of these changes in the versions they convey. And third, poems performed to music might induce memorially constructed transcripts some time after the moment of performance. Since printed miscellanies often drew on manuscripts which recorded these performances, they offered to a larger public texts with these kinds of alterations. A look at some miscellany manifestations of Ben Jonson's "The Musical strife; In a Pastorall Dialogue"—that poem beginning

"Come with our Voyces, let us warre"—provides an opportunity to examine these three models.

Jonson referred to this poem when, in his wine-loosened *Conversations with William Drummond*, he remarked that "The most common place of his repetition was a dialogue pastoral between a shepherd and a shepherdess about singing."[127] The verse appears in the second edition of *The Workes of Benjamin Jonson* (1640), in "Under-woods."[128]

The 1640 text of the poem is a dialogue between an assertive female and a cautious male. The female calls for them to join and sing together—a singing that will prove so powerful as to

> stay the running floods?
> To make the Mountaine Quarries move?
> And call the walking woods?[129]

The male hesitates, suggesting first that her voice alone is sufficient, and then that her singing might prompt angels to mistake heaven for earth, and *"fall againe."* The verse concludes with the female's reassurances that angels will not fall but *"May wish us of their Quire."*

In addition to this *Workes* text, "Come with our Voyces" appears in three other printed books, all of them miscellanies: *The Harmony of the Muses* (1654), *Wits Interpreter* (1655), and *The Marrow of Complements* (1655).[130] As Figure 1 illustrates, "Come with our Voyces" appears in these printed miscellanies with considerable textual variations. While *The Workes* presents the verse within the context of the collected oeuvre of Ben Jonson, none of the three miscellanies includes an ascription to Jonson—or anyone else. None makes any mention of the poem's original literary context. The title shifts radically. Instead of "The Musicall strife; In a Pastorall Dialogue," we have, variously, "Two Gentlemen inviting each other to sing," "*On a Lady Singing*," and "*A Song in parts, by* Endimion *and* Julietta." What was once, in Jonson's words, "a dialogue pastoral between a shepherd and a shepherdess" becomes something rather different in each printed manifestation.

The verse as dialogue also changes. *The Workes'* stanzas are carefully allocated to "SHEE" and "HEE," and each speaker's position is clear and consistent— "SHEE" asserts the need to sing, and reassures; "HEE" voices doubts and fears. *The Harmony of the Muses* and *Wits Interpreter* drop these stanza headings, lessening the clarity of dialogue. And in *The Marrow of Complements*, gender roles are reversed: here, an assertive male, Endimion, calls on a nervous female. It is Endimion who declares "Come with our voyces" (line one) and "Lets mix our

Figure 1. Four printed versions of "Come with our Voyces, let us warre."

The Musicall strife; In a Pastorall Dialogue.   *On a Lady Singing.*

SHEE.

Come, with our *Voyces*, let us *warre*,
    And challenge all the *Spheares*,
Till each of us be made a *Starre*,
    And all the world turne *Eares*.

Come with our voices let us war,
And challenge all the Spheares,
Till each of us be made a Star,
And all the world turn eares.

HEE.

At such a Call, what beast or fowle,
    Of reason emptie is!
What Tree or Stone doth want a soule?
    What man but must lose his?

SHEE.

Mixe then your Notes, that we may prove
    To stay the running floods?

Mix then our notes that we may prove
To stay the running floods,

To make the Mountaine Quarries move?
    And call the walking woods?

To make the mountain quarries move,
And call the walking woods.

HEE.

What need of mee? doe you but sing
    Sleepe, and the Grave will wake,

What need of me? do you but sing,
Sleep and the graves will wake;

No tunes are sweet, nor words have sting,

No voice so sweet, no words have sting,

    But what those lips doe make.

But what your lips do make.

SHEE.

They say the Angells marke each Deed,
    And exercise below,
And out of inward pleasure feed

Some say the Angels mark each deed
We exercise below;
And out of inward passion feed,

    On what they viewing know.

On what they see or know.

HEE.

O sing not you then, lest the best
    Of Angels should be driven

Sing you no more then, lest the best
Of Angels should be driven,

A Song in parts, by Endimion *and* Julietta.   *Two Gentlemen inviting each other to sing.*

Endimion.

Come with our voyces let us warre,　　　　Come with our Voyces let us warre,
Till each of us be made a starre,　　　　　　　and challenge all the Spheares,
And challenge all the Spheares,　　　　　　Till each of us be made a Starre,
Till Tygres shed salt teares.　　　　　　　　　and all the world turn Deares.

Julietta.

At such a call, what beast or fowle,
What tree, or stone doth want a soule?
What man but must lose his
lesse he of reason emptie is.

Endimion.

Lets mix our notes that we may prove,　　　Mix then our Notes that we may prove,
To make the mountaine Quarries move;　　　to stay the walking floods,

To stay the running floods,　　　　　　　　To make the Mountain Quaries move,
And call the walking woods.　　　　　　　　and call walking the Woods.

Julietta.

What need of me, doe you but sing　　　　What need of me, do you but sing,
And touch with art the quavering string,　　Sleep and the Graves shall wake;

Sleepe, and the Grave will wake,　　　　　No voyce hath sound, no voyce hath string,

And stones will sence partake.　　　　　　but what your lips do make.

Endimion.

They say the Angels marke each deede,　　They say the Angels view each deed,
And doe on inward pleasure feede,　　　　　who exercise below,
Till ravisht they doe grow　　　　　　　　And out of inward passion feed,

With what they view below.　　　　　　　　in what they see or know.

Julietta.

Oh sing not you then, lest the best　　　　Sing we no more then, lest the best
Of Angells, wishing such a feast;　　　　　of Angels should be driven,

Figure 1. *(continued)*

To fall againe; at such a feast, *Mistaking earth for heaven.*	To fall again at such a feast, Mistaking earth for heaven.
SHEE.	

Nay, rather both our soules bee straynd,
  To meet their high desire;
So they in state of Grace retained,
  May wish us of their Quire.
	Nay, rather let our notes be straind,
	To meet their high desire,
	So they in state of grace retaind
	May wish us of their quire,

—Jonson *Workes* (1640) "Under-woods," 173.	—*Wits Interpreter* (1655), 94–95.

notes" (line nine). Julietta defers: "What need of me" (line thirteen), "Oh sing not you then" (line twenty-one). The three miscellanies also alter pronouns, to considerable effect: "Mixe then your Notes" (*Workes*, line nine) becomes "Mix then *our* Notes" (*The Harmony of the Muses*, *Wits Interpreter*) or "Lets mix *our* notes" (*Marrow of Complements*); "O sing not you then" (*Workes*, line twenty-one) becomes "Sing *we* no more then" (*The Harmony of the Muses*).[131]

The three printed miscellanies omit whole stanzas. *The Harmony of the Muses* and *Wits Interpreter* do not print the second verse, and, as a consequence, derail the alternating dialogue structure carefully maintained in *The Workes*, where male answers female. In *The Marrow of Complements*, the final stanza is not printed. Thus, what had been the penultimate stanza in the other editions—that verse beginning "Oh sing not you then"—now has the final word, and the whole tone of the piece alters as a result. The verse concludes with a call *not* to sing.

At other stages of the verse, words are altered to produce new meanings. In *The Workes*, the male expresses anxiety that their song might cause the angels "*To fall againe; at such a feast, / Mistaking earth for heaven.*" But *The Marrow of Complements* presents a reverse movement. Here, Julietta worries that their song might result in the angels being "driven / To fall from earth to heaven."

Entirely new lines are introduced—most vividly, once more, in *The Marrow of Complements*. *The Workes*' "*And all the world turne Eares*" (line four) becomes "Till Tygres shed salt teares." "*No tunes are sweet, nor words have sting*" (line fifteen) is rendered "And touch with art the quavering string" (line fourteen). "*And exercise below*" (line eighteen) becomes "Till ravisht they doe grow" (line nineteen).

Figure I. (*continued*)

Should once againe be driven
To fall from earth to heaven.
	To fall again at such a feast,
	Mistakes Earth for Heaven.
	
	Nay, rather let our Notes be straind,
	   to meet their high desire;
	So they in state of Grace retaind,
	   shall wish us of their Quire.

—*The Marrow of Complements* (1655), 27.	—*The Harmony of the Muses* (1654), 62–63.

Jonson's poem was often set to music—Trinity College Cambridge MS B.14.22 includes a score under the verse—and the striking textual variations that printed miscellanies convey suggest, in different ways, the influence of music and of memory on the transmission of the verse.

The omission of stanza two ("At such a call . . . "), and the consequent derailing of consistent, alternating voices, is a feature of both *The Harmony of the Muses* and *The Marrow of Complements*. Herford and Simpson suggest that "Come with our Voyces" began as a six-stanza musical duet between two women, and that Jonson later revised the verse, "making it a singing-match between a shepherdess and a shepherd, inserting a second stanza and giving it to the shepherd."[132] It is certainly true that of the manuscripts and printed texts that omit the second stanza—that are, according to Herford and Simpson, versions of Jonson's *earlier* text—none offers a cross-gender dialogue: they are all either for two women,[133] for two men,[134] or are presented with no note of a dialogue.[135] Among this group of texts are the only Jonson ascriptions we find, suggesting this earlier version circulated relatively close to the author. According to this thesis, *The Harmony of the Muses* and *The Marrow of Complements* offer versions which connect back to this earlier text, while *The Workes* and *Wits Interpreter* offer versions of the later, restructured version of the poem—including the second stanza, and presented as a dialogue between male and female. Thus the inclusion of "At such call" in *The Marrow of Complements,* and its exclusion in *The Harmony of the Muses* and *Wits Interpreter,* reflects the two-staged "publication"—to use Harold Love's definition of the term as the making public of texts[136]—of "Come with our Voyces."

But there is another possible explanation for the omission of stanza two, if a musical setting of the poem is considered. Songs set for multiple voices, where lyrics were sung across a number of performers, were highly popular. In *The Musical Companion* (1673), John Playford offers an explanation of this kind of setting.

> I thought it necessary for Information of some Songsters who are not well acquainted with the Nature and Manner of Singing Catches, to give them these Directions: First, a Catch is a Song for three Voyces, wherein the several Parts are included in one; or, as it is usually tearmed, Three Parts in One. Secondly, The manner of Singing them is thus, The First begins and Sings the Catch forward, and when he is at that Note over which this [:S:] Mark or Signature is placed, the Second begins and Sings forward in like manner, and when he is Singing that Note over which the said Signature is, the Third begins and Sings, following the other, each Singing it round two or three times over, and so conclude. This kind of *Musick* hath for many Years past been had in much estemation by the most Judicious and Skilful Professors of *Musick*, for the Excellency of the Composition and Pleasant Harmony.[137]

Playford's model describes the dispersal of a song across three voices, with three singers apparently drawing from a single score. Sometimes, in arranging their compositions as part songs—a variation on the catch, with each voice only singing *part* of the lyrics—compilers of music texts wrote separate parts for each singer, each part, on a separate sheet, containing only the lines for that particular voice, along with brief (two- or three-word) cues. Rather than offering a single, complete score, this transcription process produced as many scores as there were voices, each one a fragment of the single song. Dialogues, in particular, were often distributed this way. After copying one stanza of his setting of Alexander Brome's "Stay shutt ye gate" in his songbook, Edward Lowe, organist of Christ Church, noted "the rest of ye words are in my pocket Manuscript."[138] Lowe's transcription fragmented the poem into two texts. This (quite common) kind of textual dispersal meant later copyists might draw on one of those single parts, rather than the complete score, and, as a result, encourage fragments to circulate as complete texts—just as a later transcriber might have found Lowe's "rest of ye words" in his "pocket Manuscript" and copied them as a complete verse. The final song in *Love's Labour's Lost*, performed by Ver and Hiems (Spring and Winter)—"When daisies pied and violets blue"—is printed as two separate verses, nonconsecutively, in both *The New Academy of Com-*

plements and *Windsor Drollery*.[139] This separation might well reflect a previous separation of the song into two distinct parts.

We see just this kind of dispersal of Jonson's verse across a number of manuscripts that provide a musical setting. One manuscript, collected around 1660 for a public performance in Oxford, separates the verse into three voices, each written as a separate text, with cues.[140] Instructions for the "Violin to play with the voices in yᵉ Dialogue at yᵉ Schooles Saturday" follow. A reader who finds only the first part of three would be faced with a verse which lacks stanzas two, four, and six. Another manuscript divides the lyrics between two voices and sets it to music by John Wilson, first Heather Professor of Music at Oxford, 1656–61.[141] If one separate part was read in isolation, the reader would experience only that strand of the dialogue, and stanzas would be lost. The omission of stanza two in *The Harmony of the Muses* and *The Marrow of Complements* might have come as a consequence of this sort of textual fragmentation, with the second stanza being, at some stage, separated off to another part. Alternatively, a scribe faced with a complex of cues might prefer the direct transcription of a single part to the expansion of cross-references. Again, lines would be lost. Or perhaps a listener was drawn to a particular part and copied down only that fragment of the verse.[142] Of course, we cannot be sure of the textual history of Jonson's verse, but such speculations about the dialogue's fragmentation into parts stand as useful reminders of this aspect of verse transmission.

Perhaps the most striking instance of the retitling of this verse comes in *The Harmony of the Muses*. Where *The Workes* prints "The Musicall strife; In a Pastorall Dialogue" between "Shee" and "Hee," *The Harmony of the Muses* offers "*Two Gentlemen inviting each other to sing.*" It seems possible that this change in title reflects a particular performance of the verse: the alternative title, introduced by the compiler of *The Harmony of the Muses* or, more probably, a compiler of a source on which this text drew, may reflect a particular musical performance when two male singers appropriated what had been a dialogue between shepherd and shepherdess. Perhaps the inversion of gender roles in *The Marrow of Complements*, where an assertive male calls on a nervous female, reflects a similar altering of the text to fit the resources of an occasion. (Or perhaps the editor, trying to compile a book that would prove a commercial hit, feared his frail male readers could not endure the scenario as depicted in other texts, and reversed the politics.)

Alterations to stanza layout and possibly the omission of stanza two may also have been an attempt to "regularize" the verse in line with fashion. Conventional dialogue-song form begins with voice A, proceeds to voice B, and concludes with the two joining together.¹⁴³ Jonson's dialogue is unusual in that it does not follow this form, eschewing the final resolving duet and preferring, instead, the alternating voices throughout. So versions which impose a new form may be pulling the poem in the direction of more standard dialogues. Thus Bodleian Mus b1, John Wilson's folio songbook, orchestrates a more traditional joining together of the voices at the end of the verse.

Apart from the omission of stanza two, and the various retitlings, there are also numerous moments when words and lines vary across the miscellany texts. Some look like straightforward slips in transcription or the products of mishearings at a performance—by compilers of miscellanies, or by the compilers of the manuscript sources on which miscellanies drew. Thus "And all the world turn *Deares*" (*The Harmony of the Muses*) for "*And all the world turne Eares*" (*Workes*). New lines were also produced through (presumably accidental) conflations of distinct half-lines. Compare two printings of stanza six:

Workes	*Marrow of Complements*
HEE.	*Julietta.*
O sing not you then, lest the best	Oh sing not you then, lest the best
Of Angels should be driven	Of Angells, wishing such a feast;
To fall againe; at such a feast,	Should once againe be driven
Mistaking earth for heaven.	To fall from earth to heaven.

The latter's "Of Angells, wishing such a feast" looks like a compound of "Of Angels should be driven" and "To fall againe; at such a feast." But even such "slips" are instructive, since they tell us something of the status of this poetry (that it was not writing that required meticulous copying), and they tell us something of the way printed books were produced (with haste and a loose hand).

But beyond these small switches, there are several new and largely unprecedented lines. *The Marrow of Complements* suggests a significant and deliberate rewriting of the verse. Perhaps the editor preferred his or her own lines to Jonson's original; perhaps lines were changed to make the verse more pertinent to a specific occasion. These are possible explanations, although there is little obvious logic in the inversions, and the new lines' gains are unclear. More compelling, I think, is the hypothesis that this unique text alludes to a flawed memorial reconstruction of the verse.

The role of memory in the circulation of poetry is highly significant.¹⁴⁴ When, in Walton's *Compleat Angler*, Piscator requests a song of "cheerful Spirit," Viator recollects some

> Verses that were made by Doctor *Donne* . . . to shew the world that he could make soft and smooth verses when he thought them fit and worth his labor.

These lines—actually, a parody of Marlowe's "Come live with me, and be my Love"—particularly please Viator "because they allude to Rivers, and fish and fishing." After their recitation, Piscator congratulates him on this act of recollection:

> Well remembered, honest Scholer, I thank you for these choice Verses, which I have heard formerly, but had quite forgot, till they were recovered by your happy memorie.

As an expression of thanks, Piscator promises to regale Viator with "some observations of the *Eele*."[145]

The editor of *The Marrow of Complements* was, I would suggest, similarly dependent on a memorially constructed text. Certainly the number of lines inverted in relation to other readings suggests a text half-remembered, rather than a consistent and conscious rewriting. So too do new lines which echo—aurally and conceptually—but do not duplicate phrases found in other versions: "Should once againe be driven" (*Marrow*, line 23) recalling "Of Angels should be driven" and "To fall againe" (*Workes*, lines 22–23); "And stones will sence partake" (*Marrow*, line 16) reminding readers of "Of reason emptie is! / What Tree or Stone doth want a soule?" (*Workes*, lines 6–7)—all indicating an attempted but imperfect remembering. The new and largely unprecedented lines—

Workes	Marrow of Complements
And all the world turne Eares.	Till Tygres shed salt teares.
No tunes are sweet, nor words have sting	And touch with art the quavering string
But what those lips doe make.	And stones will sence partake.
And exercise below,	Till ravisht they doe grow

—perhaps constitute moments when the editor, tired of scratching his head for recollection, substituted his own words for the blanks his memory returned. The evident popularity of the poem meant the editor would have known the general *shape* of the verse, and would recognize its commercial viability for his printed collection. Through a combination of remembered lines, blurrings, confusions, and novelties, the editor of *The Marrow of Complements* might thus have attempted to construct that verse he had read in other miscellanies, had seen in manuscript, had perhaps heard in performance, was *sure* he could remember, if he could just merge those two half-lines, fill out those couple of blanks with a few words of his own, try to remember what it said *there* . . .

Dramatic Performances and Play Texts

On 7 November 1667 Samuel Pepys saw his first performance of what would become one of his favorite plays: Davenant and Dryden's reworking of *The Tempest*. It was, Pepys noted, a play "full of so good variety that I cannot be more pleased almost in a comedy."[146] Pepys was particularly captivated with Ferdinand and Ariel's echo-song ("Go thy way") in act 3, scene 4:

> a curious piece of music in an echo of half sentences, the echo repeating the former half, while the man goes on to the latter; which is mighty pretty.

Some six months later, at another performance of the same play, Pepys decided to transcribe the song. "Between two acts," he writes,

> I went out to [the actor] Mr [Joseph] Harris, and got him to repeat to me the words of the Echo, while I writ them down, having tried in the play to have wrote them; but, having done it without looking upon the paper, I find I could not read the blackhead. But now I have got the words clear.[147]

Two things seem particularly significant about Pepys's note. First is the impression that the detachment of particular moments from a play was by no means an exceptional activity. There is a sense of the routine about Pepys's record of "having tried in the play to have wrote them," and in fact during other performances of this same play Pepys worked at extracting other small sections. On 3 February 1668, at the Duke of York's house, Pepys "took pleasure to learn the tune of the seaman's dance." While I am not suggesting that all audience members were furiously scribbling transcriptions of songs and speeches, the notion of extracting parts of the performance was by no means extraordinary.

The second significant feature is the evident *difficulty* of accurate transcription from a performance: Pepys's first attempt left him with nothing but a scrawl "I find I could not read." Since most playgoers would not have had the opportunity to ask for a repeat recitation from the actor, other manuscript records of songs from *The Tempest*—and, in general, other manuscript transcripts of oral transmission—were presumably often loose and approximate, full of changes, slips, estimates.

If Pepys's description offers a model for performance transcription—as both common and difficult—we might test this model against the circulation of moments from plays in printed miscellanies which appear to have been products of just such instances of copyings from performances.

Printed miscellanies certainly appear to confirm the impression that such acts of textual fracture were common. Play songs and verses regularly appear as discreet poems in printed miscellanies. And while we certainly cannot assert that all come from sources originating with a playgoer, like Pepys, struggling to "writ them down," the very many examples of excerpts from plays offered as coherent, complete poems suggests a culture of extracts, some of which surely originated with performance transcriptions. Among the many instances are verses beginning "A wife I do hate" from William Wycherley's *Love in a Wood*; "After so many sad complaints to us" from the prologue to Thomas Killigrew's *The Parsons Wedding*; and "How happy's that Prisoner" from *Cromwell's Conspiracy*.

A fourth example of a play song appearing in miscellanies comes from John Dryden's *The Conquest of Granada by the Spaniards: In Two Parts*, and it is worth pausing to check the miscellany manifestations of this verse against Pepys's other characteristic of song circulation: the difficulty (and hence looseness) of transcription. The song beginning "How unhappy a lover am I" is a dialogue from act four of Dryden's play. The verse offers a male who laments that his love for Phillis will remain unrequited since "All my hopes of Delight / Are another man's Right"; and an advice-giving female who counters with the comfort that, first, Phillis "Is as wretch'd and more / And accounts all your suff'rings her own," and second, while Phillis's "Honour deny'd" their love "in life, / In her death . . . [Phillis] will give to your love."

Through the evidence of extant letters we are able to fix the date of the first performance of the play to early January 1671.[148] Printed publication of the play came later: Henry Herringman entered *The Conquest of Granada* in the *Stationer's Register* on 25 February 1671, and it appeared in 1672.[149] But between these moments of performance and printing, the song appeared in both *Westminster Drollery* and *The New Academy of Complements*.[150] Like Pepys's "echo of half sentences," "How unhappy a lover am I" was thus quite possibly transcribed from a performance and reached the compilers of these two miscellanies via, perhaps, a meandering route. This is by no means certain: it was reasonably common for manuscript play texts to be made public before printed play texts appeared (actors might circulate copies among friends; companies might sell manuscript play texts to raise money, or might present such texts to patrons), and such texts could have provided a preprint circulation of the song. However, this scribal publication was much more a feature of pre-1641 theaters; by 1660, as Harold Love notes in his very useful discussion of the scribal publication of drama, "Restoration theatre companies, with their repertoires secured by royal edict, had no reason to oppose the print publication of plays."[151]

If we assume (with an air of the tentative) that the 1672 quarto provides an accurate representation of the song as it was performed in 1671—acknowledging, however, that this was not necessarily the case—then we can check miscellany readings against this play text to establish the degree of variation between performance and those first miscellany printings which perhaps relied on oral transcriptions.[152] The song in *The New Academy of Complements* recalls the theatrical performance by labeling its speakers "*Almanz.*" and "*Queen.*," but it includes two textual variants (in the second stanza, "affords" for "allow," and in the fifth, "Powers" for "Gods"). The song in *Westminster Drollery* expands on these variations to produce a significantly altered text. Here the verse is titled "A Dialogue between two friends," and a melody is noted—"Tune, How severe and forgetful is old age." The speakers are assigned single initials—enigmatically, "R" and "W"—and there are persistent textual differences: in addition to the changes noted above, there is, in the first stanza, "whilst" for "while"; in the second, "As" for "But," and "helpless state" for "hopeless Estate"; in the third, "Yet" for "For"; in the fourth, "comfort" for "pleasure"; and in the final stanza, "For the souls do meet freely above" for "For the Souls to meet closer above."

While the meaning of the verse is substantially maintained, these alterations certainly do have an effect on our reading. Where Dryden's play offers "Since her Honour allows no Relief, / But to pity the pains which you bear," *Westminster Drollery* prints "Since her honour *affords* no relief, / *As* to pity the pains which you bear" (my italics). The difference is conceptually significant: the latter's "As" shifts the meaning from the comforting thought of her pitying his grief to an emphasis on her refusal to feel any pathos. Similarly, the apparently minor substitution of "Yet" for "For" in the third stanza constructs a new significance: where the play offered "I have try'd the false Med'cine in vain, / For I wish what I hope not to win," *Westminster Drollery* prints "I have tried the false *Medicine* in vain, / *Yet* I wisht what I hope not to win." Not only does the expanded "Medicine" add an extra clumsy syllable to the line, but the new "Yet" repositions the second line *in opposition* to the first.

Indeed, several other songs from this Dryden play appeared in miscellanies before the play was published, and they exhibit similar levels of significant textual variation. Before appearing in quarto publication (part 1, act 3), the song beginning "Beneath a Myrtle shade" also appeared twice in a single printed miscellany: *Westminster Drollery*. The three texts—quarto play and the two miscellany versions—offer highly significant differences which in places radically alter the meaning of the verse. The quarto describes Phillis as a "bright Vision"; *Westminster Drollery*'s first text styles her a "bright Virgin." The quarto has "Her every Grace my heart did fire";[153] *Westminster Drollery*'s first version offers "Her ev'ry part my heart did fire"—a more corporeal reworking of her virtues. Upon waking, the speaker claims the vividness of his dream has rendered his imagined love real, and thus that—according to the quarto—"Fancy, the kinder Mistress of the two, / Fancy had done what Phillis wou'd not do!" But in *Westminster Drollery*'s second text, we are offered the intriguing "Fancy the kinder Mistris of the two, / I fancy I had done what *Phillis* would not do." And where the play text concludes "Asleep or waking you must ease my pain," this miscellany version reads "Asleep or waking I must ease my pain."

If transcriptions stemming, originally, perhaps from a performance are characterized by a textual malleability that often resulted in these significantly different miscellany texts, transcriptions which derive from printed play texts display far fewer moments of textual variation. Middleton's *The Widdow* was written about 1616.[154] Printed publication, however, did not come until 1652, when a quarto edition appeared: *The Widdow A Comedie. As it was Acted at the private House in Black-Fryers, with great Applause, by His late Majesties Servants*. In act 3, scene 1, Latrocinio, "the chief Thief," muses on a song to sing. He suggests "Come my daintie Doxes"—a witty reference to a song in Middleton's *More Dissemblers beside Women*—but Ansoldo complains, and in doing so hints at the success of the play, with "Oh, that's all the Country over sir, / Ther's scarce a Gentlewoman, but has that prickt."[155] Latrocinio selects another song—"Well, here comes one I'm sure you never heard then"—and sings the verse beginning "I keep my Horse, I keep my Whore."

This song is a celebration of the highwayman's trade which lauds the itinerant but rich lifestyle ("I traverse all the Land about . . . / With Partridge plump, with Woodcock fine / I doe at midnight often dine"), the disengagement from quotidian commercial transactions ("I take no Rents, yet am not poor"), and the sexual conquests ("And if my Whore be not in case, / My Hostesse daughter h'as her place").

The song appears in four printed miscellanies, the first of which, *Wits Interpreter*, appeared shortly after the 1652 printed publication of the play text, and it seems that this miscellany turned directly to the 1652 play text for this song.[156] What is striking across these four miscellany texts is the lack of significant textual variations. There are only a few very minor moments of variation: "travel" for "traverse," for instance, or "Hostler" for "Ostler." A study of these minor moments of variation suggests *Wits Interpreter* and perhaps *Choyce Drollery* turned directly to the 1652 quarto for their material, and transcribed with a high degree of precision, and that *The New Academy of Complements* and *Windsor Drollery* perhaps drew, in turn, on *Choyce Drollery*. Such movements indicate that the printing of a song in a play text did not set that individual song within the firm frame of that publication: the printed publication of a song did not permanently embed that song in its accompanying dramatic or textual frame, and so end that song's circulation history as a separate text. Rather, the printed quarto induced other printed versions of the song as compilers continued to pluck songs from their dramatic (printed) contexts. Yet, at the same time, since the level of variant readings is very low, the 1652 quarto seems to have been a force for the relative stability of these texts.

As a result, we are prompted to consider something like a paradox about this particular kind of print and verse transmission: the 1652 printed quarto did not curtail but in fact *induced* textual fracture and the transmission of a constituent part of the play; yet transmission, due to the availability of the 1652 printed text, was marked by textual stability. In the scenario discussed here, the appearance of a printed text of a poem or song did not necessarily slow down the circulation of copies of that poem or song, but it did tend to produce more stable texts. What emerges is a position that resists the simple notion of print as fixing and stabilizing, but alerts us to a more subtle model: of print, in this instance, as a force encouraging both textual fracture of plays and a relative stability of those fractured parts. The popularity of folio single-sheet prologues, excerpted from plays, illustrates this capacity of print culture to work as a force in opposition to the textual and aesthetic unity of plays. Examples of these kinds of publication include a 1683 text containing the "PROLOGUE to *Dame Dobson* the *Cunning Woman.* Spoken by Mrs. CURRER," and "EPILOGUE to the Same! Spoken by Mr. JEVORN"; or, in 1684, "THE EPILOGUE TO *Mr.* LACY's *New Play,* Sir HERCULES BUFFOON, *or the* Poetical Esquire. Wrote and Spoke by J.H. Com." Often the play from which the excerpt originated is not named. One 1683 text containing the "PROLOGUE. Spoken by Mrs *Cook*" has a reader's manuscript note which supplies this effaced detail: "To ye Tragedy of Valentinian 20 Feb 1684/3."[157]

Printed and Manuscript Miscellanies

Printed miscellanies frequently turned to manuscript miscellanies and commonplace books for their texts, and even when there is no clear direct correspondence between printed collection and manuscript, the cultures of print and manuscript clearly overlap.[158] Huntington Manuscript 116 is a neat, small, bunched, verse miscellany—the property, we might infer from the many Oxford references, of an Oxford (perhaps Christ Church) undergraduate compiler, assembling materials some time in the 1620s. It is a thoroughly typical early-seventeenth-century verse miscellany, full of largely unascribed favorites by William Strode, Robert Ayton, Thomas Carew, Henry King, Thomas Randolph, and Richard Corbett. Of the manuscript's 270 poems, 115 also appear in printed miscellanies, including the popular "A maiden fair I dare not wed"; Robert Ayton's "Wrong not dear Empress of my heart"; and William Strode's "I saw fair Chloris walk alone."[159] Another manuscript, a large folio poetic miscellany usually assigned to the playwright and theatrical manager Thomas Killigrew but actually the work of a number of hands, includes 406 poems. Of these, 147 appear in printed miscellanies.[160] While there is no evidence to suggest *direct* textual borrowings between the Killigrew text and printed miscellanies—although this might have sometimes occurred—the high number of common poems does demonstrate the degree to which the cultures of manuscript and print were linked.

This cultural overlap is well illustrated by the many manuscripts which adopt characteristics of printed books, just as early printed books had sought to mirror manuscript appearances. The manuscript of Henry Calverley, of Ergholme, Durham, is typical in this respect. The text includes notes drawn from Fuller's *Church History*, and they begin "THE / CHURCH-HISTORY / OF / BRITAIN; / From ye Birth of / IESVS CHRIST, / Untill ye YEAR / MDCXLVIII. / Epitomised from Fuller. / HENRICUS: CALVERLEY. / 1658." Subsequent pages have a running title of "The Church-history of Britain."[161] Huntington Manuscript 93, a verse miscellany, opens with a title page similarly penned in the style of a printed book: "Dayly Obseruations / both / Diuine & Morall / The First part. / by / Thomas Grocer, / . . . 1657."

Within this general culture of overlappings between manuscript and print, direct borrowings among texts also emerge as printed miscellanies sometimes turned to particular manuscripts to supply their texts. Huntington Manuscript 198 part 1 provides an example of this process. The manuscript is a 205-page folio verse miscellany, dating from the 1630s, and is written in a single hand, with sheets of different shapes and sizes bound together. It is notable for its fifty-two John Donne inclusions. It appears that John Donne Junior's *Poems of Pembroke and Ruddier* (1660) drew directly on this manuscript for some of its contents. Sequences of poems in this manuscript very closely match sequences of verses in the printed miscellany[162]; the degree of textual variation between manuscript and printed collection is extremely low; the printed volume follows the manuscript in its ascriptions; and many of the common poems are sufficiently rare to enforce a sense of direct borrowing.

The prefaces to *Poems of Pembroke and Ruddier* cite two sources for the volume's texts: first, "the greatest Masters of Musick," including "Mr. Henry Laws" and "Mr. Laneere"; and second, the dedicatee of the volume, "The Right Honorable Cristiana, Countess of Devonshire, Dowager"—a well-known Royalist literary patron and wife of William Cavendish, Second Earl of Devonshire—who had "been so careful to preserve, & now command to be published, these elegant Poems."[163] Perhaps Huntington Manuscript 198 part 1 was in some way connected to one of these two sources.[164] The unusually high number of accurate authorial ascriptions in the manuscript—among the names are Beaumont, Carew, Corbett, Donne, Herbert, Herrick, Jonson, and Randolph—suggests a proximity between compiler and the kind of literary context which the Countess of Devonshire encouraged. The subject matter of many of the manuscript's poems enforces this sense of a socially elite, poetic coterie, too—poems such as "To thy Lady Mary Wroth for writeing the Countes of Montgomeryes Urania"; "The Coppy of A Rodomantathe sent by the Duke to the house of comons 28. Ju: 1628"; and "Obsequis to the Lady Ann Haye," ascribed to Carew.[165]

The manuscript miscellany of Leonard Wheatcroft, a yeoman from Ashover (1627–1706), is, like Henry Calverley's epitomized Fuller or Thomas Grocer's "Dayly Obseruations," a manuscript whose structure—a long section of love verses, followed by funerary elegies and epitaphs, and including a running title—mirrors the design of a printed book, and, in particular, of a printed miscellany.[166] Indeed, it seems very likely that Wheatcroft included, alongside his own verses, materials he extracted directly from *Wits Recreations*: eight poems in the first nineteen pages of Wheatcroft's manuscript derive from *Wits Recreations*, and while it is not certain that Wheatcroft drew directly on this popular text, similarities of order and text powerfully suggest such a correspondence. Here, then, printed miscellanies, rather than fixing texts and halting manuscript circulation, actually extended it to a social and geographic space (a yeoman's rural Derbyshire) far from the expected environments of verse circulation.

Wheatcroft's probable borrowing from *Wits Recreations* is one of several extant instances of this printed miscellany apparently furnishing a later manuscript collection. Folger Manuscript Va 308 is a late-seventeenth-century, early-eighteenth-century verse miscellany bearing the signatures of both "Thomas

Boydell" and "John Boydell."[167] It offers a typically eclectic range of materials: poems; recipes for making counterfeit gems; a giant quintuple Latin and triple English acrostic "On the glorious Passion, & Resurrection of our Lord, & Saviour, Jesus Christ"; several (rather poor) drawings (a horse, two deer, various profiles of faces, a tree, several compasses); an epitaph on Buckingham "Inserted in Derby: . . . Mar. 23. 1720." The collection suggests a preoccupation with language: there are notes on shorthand, and a dialect sketch called "A Yorkshire Dialogue between Will a Wally" is followed by "A Clavis to the foregoing Dialogue," which offers a short dictionary of Yorkshire dialect terms, beginning "Ackwards, i.e. Backwards. / Agye. Aside. / . . . Asta. As thou / . . . Barn. Child."

This interest in language is sustained, most spectacularly, in a series of extremely elegant shape poems. These verses use the spatial layout of the poem to wittily enforce the subject. Thus, a poem that exhorts its reader to follow love, and "leave denying, Endless knotts let Fates be trying," is written in the shape of a twisting rope. Another poem substitutes letters, numbers, and symbols for words, beginning "If V 2 I, as I 2 V am true." And a third verse once more uses its appearance—the words sketched on an entwining ribbon—to physically enact the message it suggests:

> THIS is Love, & worth commending, Still beginning, never ending . . . ensnareing . . . In a Round . . . In and out, whose every Angle More, and more doth still entangle . . . loveing Twineing Arm, exchangeing kisses, Each partakeing others blisses . . . Never breaking, ever bending. This is love and worth Commending.

On the facing page, a series of faltering beginnings to sketches—a sun, a rose, a saw, what looks like a snake—suggest some other project, quickly abandoned.

These intricate materials were products of textual transmission. A close examination of the edges of the two shape poems reveals heavy scoring—indeed, a part of the page has fallen away as a consequence. Such score marks indicate a tracing from some other text: the compiler marking the shape of the rope and ribbon on the manuscript before following the lines with ink and subsequently adding the words. *Wits Recreations* supplied the model to trace and follow. All these images appear within a few pages of each other, in this miscellany's "Fancies and Fantasticks" section, and the dimensions correspond precisely to the manuscript version.[168] John Boydell—"John" is sketched twice on these pages—must have turned to a copy of *Wits Recreations*, traced through the printed page onto the manuscript, and filled in the details afterward. While the shapes are traced and therefore duplicate the printed image very closely, the words were added in a freehand and are looser in their spatial correspondence to their printed source. We can even assign an origin to the half sketches on the facing page—the sun, rose, saw, snake. These are drawn from another poem in *Wits Recreations*, three pages after the ribbon verse, which wittily substitutes symbols for words: an image of the sun and a rose for the line "The sun arose"; a saw to render "I saw two lovers"; a coiled serpent for "snake." Boydell must have begun to sketch these images after his three laborious, dutiful transcriptions, but soon gave up. Compared to the twisted rope and ribbon, the penmanship is lazy and imprecise, and the snake is scored through with a diagonal line.[169] It is interesting, however, that this interrupted transcription is in many ways the most compelling of the group—its sense of a copying cut short vividly suggesting a moment of generation.

In fact, Boydell's miscellany yields several more instances of the direct transmission of materials from *Wits Recreations*. The manuscript's section headed "Epigrams" plucks its eighty-eight poems straight from the first 204 epigrams in *Wits Recreations*.[170] The order is generally retained, and the level of textual variance from the printed source is very low: occasionally a title is modified, but there are few other alterations. Boydell's major change to the poems is that he renders many of them wholly or partly in shorthand. But there is no doubt that he is turning, once more, to *Wits Recreations* for his materials.

A few pages on, the compiler draws on this same printed miscellany, laboriously copying both the image of a jaunty soldier and the two long poems from *Wits Recreations*' "*The Welsh mans praise of Wales.*"[171] Once again, score marks round the edge of the manuscript drawing, and the proportions of the manuscript and printed image, suggest a tracing. Next, Boydell turned to *Wits Recreations*' "Epitaphs," transcribing, in order, many poems taken directly from the printed source. As with the epigrams, many of these poems are wholly or partly translated into shorthand; once more the level of textual variance in full English versions is extremely low.[172]

And there are other places of connection between Boydell's manuscript and earlier printed miscellanies. Of the first sixty-five poems in the manuscript, fifty-nine also appear in *Windsor Drollery* (1672). (After the sixty-fifth, Boydell's manuscript introduces a new layout—the page divided into two columns, broadside ballad-style—and turns to other, uncited sources for the subsequent epigrams.) And while the relationship is not as clear-cut as Boydell's use of *Wits Recreations*, the degree of overlap between these two collections is remarkable. In particular, Boydell's manuscript constructs sequences from poems that appear within a few pages of each other in *Windsor Drollery*. Thus the opening eight poems in the manuscript appear in *Windsor Drollery* as poem numbers nine, one, twelve, thirteen, twenty-five, twenty-six, twenty-eight, and thirty-one. Furthermore, textual variants between print and manuscript are extremely low. Boydell, like most transcribers, prefers short forms (thus "y^e" for "the," "y^{ts}" for "that's"); but these are the only consistent differences between his collection and *Windsor Drollery*. Occasionally, a stanza is omitted—as is the case with Boydell's version of Alexander Brome's "Let the bowl passe free."[173] Perhaps Boydell was displeased with the stanza (it begins "The King we'll not name"); perhaps he cut a verse to ensure this poem ended neatly at the foot of the page (and Boydell does seem to prefer such spatial regularity). But more striking is the manuscript's retention of unusual features: where *Windsor Drollery* offers a title, Boydell's manuscript follows it—*Windsor Drollery*'s "Song 31. JAMES and SUSAN" is rendered "8. James, & Susan"; "Song 149. Prisoners of Ludgate's Song" is transcribed "26. Prisoners of Ludgate's song." And even patterns of layout are often maintained.

Boydell's manuscript provides one other striking instance of the transmission of materials from printed miscellanies. In addition to the poems discussed, Boydell's collection also includes a few pages of brief prose notes on a range of tricks and illusions: details of how "To wash one's hands in melted Lead," "To hinder a man from swallowing Meat," and, remarkably, "To make people seem headlesse." And it seems extremely likely that Boydell was turning to *Wits Interpreter* to furnish these novelties. This printed miscellany includes all the tricks Boydell mentions, in the same order, and in strikingly similar prose. Thus, for instance, Boydell's manuscript explains how "To cause a cup to stick to his Lips":

> Mingle y^e milk of a ffig-tree with Gum Tr$_\wedge^a$gacanth, & anoint y^e brims of y^e cup, & when 'tis dry it will not be see: giue the cup full of Liquor, where you design: & obserue y^e effect.

Wits Interpreter reveals how "*To cause the Cup to stick to a mans lips, that it can hardly be pulled away*":

> Take the Milk of a Fig-tree, and mingle it with Gum Tragacanth, and anoint the brims of the Cup with it, which when it is dry will not be seen. Then give it to any one full of Wine to drink, and it will before he has done drinking, stick to fast to his Lips, that it will be impossible to pluck it away.[174]

To ensure "That a Woman shall not eat," Boydell's manuscript recommends that the reader "Take a little green Basil, & conveigh it privately under ye Dish." *Wits Interpreter* offers a fuller rendering of essentially the same advice.

To make a Woman that she shall not eat the Meat set upon the Table.

To do this, take a little of the green *Basil*, and when one bringeth any Dishes of Meat unto the Table, put the same Herb secretly under one of the said Dishes of Plates, that she see it not, and as long as the Herb lieth so upon the Table, the Woman shall eat nothing of the Meat in that Dish which covers the Herb.[175]

And Boydell's plot "To make people seem headlesse"—"Break Arsenick very fine, & boyl it with Sulphur in a couered Pot, & kindle it with a new Candle"—is close to *Wits Interpreter*'s scheme:

Break Arsenick very fine, and boyl it with Sulphur in a cover'd Pot, and kindle it with a new Candle; and the standers by will seem to be headless.[176]

All the other tricks Boydell notes are present, in similarly close but expanded forms, in *Wits Interpreter*—all from the same section, and often offered as successive pieces. The case for direct transmission from printed to manuscript miscellany is not as watertight as with the *Wits Recreations* materials. There may have been a common text supplying both collections independently—a text such as *Hocus Pocus Junior. The Anatomy of Legerdemain* (1654, fourth edition), which offered accounts of these kinds of sleights of hand. There may also have been intermediary texts between printed and manuscript miscellany. But the correspondence is, nevertheless, striking. Boydell seems to have been drawing his tricks from *Wits Interpreter*, moving through the section titled "Pretty Conceits," extracting eye-catching offers, and noting them down in a summarized form.

Boydell's persistent dependency on printed miscellanies as suppliers of materials raises a number of important points for a consideration of relationships between printed and manuscript miscellanies.

Textual transmission is typically presented as the flow of materials from the cloistered manuscript to the popular printed text. Like water, transmission—it is supposed—follows the path of least resistance. But Boydell's text suggests quite the opposite to this democratizing model. While *Wits Recreations* dates from the 1640s, Boydell's manuscript originates between about 1690 and 1730 ("Some Lines taken out of the Satyr against Wit. 1700."; "Inserted ... Mar. 23. 1720"),[177] and so the movement of materials must have been from print to manuscript. In fact, Boydell is not unusual in this respect. Wheatcroft's reliance on *Wits Recreations* suggests a similar model, as does the poetic miscellany associated with Thomas Killigrew, many of whose 406 poems were already in print.[178]

Now, this movement of materials is important not only because it reverses the normal path of verse transmission; it also complicates that notion—common in histories of the book—of manuscript as (relatively) private and prior to public print. *Wits Recreations*, like most printed miscellanies, positions itself as a force for the public dissemination of formerly restricted texts; but Boydell's collection functions to "reprivatize" these public texts. What we see is the movement of materials from a cheap, portable, popular, readily available printed miscellany to a large personal manuscript.

The fidelity of Boydell's manuscript to its printed source—even in the case of complicated visual set pieces—also adds another caveat to that sweeping notion of manuscript as an inevitably loose, careless medium, in contrast to fixing print. Boydell's collection often displays a stability many printed texts do not match. And, more generally, Boydell's manuscript also reminds us how items other than verse (images; prose) circulated among collections.

But lurking behind all this is a puzzling question of motivation: why did Boydell draw at such length from these printed miscellanies? Constructing a manuscript compilation of extracts from various separate texts makes sense: the manuscript becomes a "storehouse" of useful pieces otherwise distributed across a number of manuscripts, printed books, and memories. Transcribing from a rare text, on loan, is also logical. But to draw so persistently, and so carefully, from *Wits Recreations*, and *Windsor Drollery*—texts which were cheap, portable, popular, and which themselves offer anthologized verse plucked from various sources—is puzzling. Boydell in all probability owned a copy of *Wits Recreations*, *Windsor Drollery*, and perhaps *Wits Interpreter*: so why bother spending such effort transferring poems to manuscript?

Boydell's occasional translations into shorthand could offer a partial explanation: Boydell might conceivably be using poems from *Wits Recreations* as raw material to practice on. But Boydell only translates a minority of the poems he transcribes—most are retained in full English. And there are easier ways to practice than to transcribe, so dutifully, poem after poem. Similarly, the manuscript could possibly have functioned as a copy book, with Boydell practicing his penmanship. But this is not entirely convincing: why omit, for instance, some poems from transcription?

What Boydell's collection does suggest is that the same materials in a manuscript collection were regarded very differently than when in a printed book. Different media, in other words, constructed different notions of ownership. While Boydell almost certainly owned *Wits Recreations*, he still laboriously transferred materials. This suggests that the act of transfer rendered the poems the property of the compiler in a way the mere ownership of a printed book could never do. While Boydell rarely personalizes the poems by introducing formal textual alterations, the process of transcribing these poems to his manuscript miscellany created a new type of relationship with the materials. Thus, perhaps, the surprising transfer of materials from cheap, popular printed book to manuscript.

One further, spectacular instance of transmission is worthy of note. The manuscript miscellany of Sir John Gibson (1606–65) of Welburn, York, was compiled during Gibson's years as a Royalist prisoner in Durham Castle—"The House of my Pilgrimage. / The House of Bondage"—between 1653 and 1660. Into his manuscript Gibson has pasted several images, literally cut from printed books. Among these is the well-known picture of cadaverous Death, holding an hourglass and an arrow, accompanied by a Latin couplet translated as "The Muses works stone-Monuments outlast; / "Tis wit keeps life, all else Death will down cast." Gibson could have obtained this image from several publications, including later editions of *Wits Recreations,* where it appears in precisely this form.[179] Around the image Gibson has added his own lines of verse: down the left side of the page the words "I dye to live, and liue to dye"; down the right, "That I may liue, eternallye"; and above the image, "Death when to death a death by death hath giuen, / Then shall be op't the long shut gates of Heauen."[180]

Here, then, is a literal instance of both the conflation of the cultures of print and manuscript, and of the perhaps surprising movement of materials from print to manuscript. Gibson's physical fragmentation of his printed books is striking, but it stands as a fitting symbol for the kind of textual fractures and transmissions in which printed miscellanies played such an important part.

"This Is in Verse Somewhere": Slippages in Genre

As we have seen, within this culture of re-presentation it was not only poetry that moved between texts. Images and prose riddles of the sort that interested Boydell might experience a similar transfer. So too might dialogues. Several exemplary speeches in *The Mysteries of Love and Eloquence* (1658), for example, reappear in a slightly altered state almost a century later in *The New Academy of Compliments: Or, The Lover's Secretary* (1750) —not a printed miscellany, but a book that grew closely out of this tradition of popular print conveying elite eloquence. We could note:

1658 *Mysteries of Love and Eloquence*, 41	1750 *New Academy of Complements*, 13
"After Dinner. / Sir, You will excuse your bad entertainments, otherwise we must oblige our selves to make you a better. / Sir, Your Entertainment hath been very good, there hath been no fault, there is no need of excuses. At least you may assure your self to have been lookt upon with a respect, and to have been cordialy receiv'd. I wish I could testifie my affection to you in a thing that were more worthy of you. Sir, I have had so many testimonies of your favour that I am ashamed that I have not bin able to give you better acknowledgements, which I shall be ready to do, when you are pleas'd to honour me with your commands. At present I humbly thank you for my entertainment and kiss your hands."	"At the End of Dinner. / A. Sir, pray excuse your bad Entertainment at this present, and another Time we shall endeavour to make you amends. B. Truly, Sir, it hath been very good, without any defect, and therefore needs no excuse. A. However, your Welcome was hearty; and I shall desire to testify my cordial affection some other Way more worthy yourself. B. Sir, I have so many Testimonies of your good Will, that I am ashamed it lies not in my Power to requite the least of them. I will expect when your commands shall give me Opportunity to do it, and so I thank you for my good cheer, and humbly take my leave of you."

It is unclear whether the latter text simply drew directly from the former—which the sense of close paraphrase, of slight rewriting, suggests—or whether some other text(s) stood between these volumes. Either way, these reappearing conversational set pieces are another reminder that textual transmission was not restricted to verse.[181]

The degree of reworking between these two appearances is not substantial, and the two texts are essentially close: while there are persistent minor variants, both texts offer careful complimentary eloquence, suited to a particular occasion, and both belong to the same genre of writing. But in other instances of the transmission of printed miscellany materials, alterations were considerably more striking, and textual malleability might sometimes shift the very genre of the writing.

There is a twelve-line verse that appears in *Wits Interpreter* (1655) as "Of Books and Cheese." It is a bizarre poem—in part, I think, the witty product of humanist educational drills that asked students to align wildly different things (why black is like white, why short is like tall). The verse—admittedly no classic—concludes "No Cheese there was that ever pleas'd all feeders, / No Book there is that ever pleas'd all readers."[182] About twenty years later, in a collection titled *Coffee-House Jests* (1677)—a work cobbled together by that former dance instructor and miscellany compiler William Hickes—the same material appeared, not as a poem this time, but as prose anecdote number 186. It begins "There's no two things in the world so like, as eating of Cheese and reading of Books." The text proceeds to explain how this is: how no men can agree on the type of cheese they prefer just as "in the reading of Books, one says 'tis too long, another too short... a third of meet length," and so on. Next to a British Library copy of the anecdote a reader has added: "This is in verse somewhere."[183]

It seems, then, that Hickes's prose anecdote derives from a poem already in popular circulation. The path might well not have been direct—although the resourceful Hickes, compiler of three printed miscellanies, must have known of the highly popular *Wits Interpreter*, and might well have turned to it for sources. (We know, from Hickes's frequent inclusion of his own verses in his published collections, that he was not shy of working up materials with his own pen.) But whether this instance alludes to a direct transfer or to larger paths of transmission, the reworking of the verse attests to the fundamental malleability of circulating texts to the degree that genres might be rendered loose and temporary. What we see is not simply the odd textual variant—a switched title, a dropped stanza, a reworked final line. Rather, we see the complete reworking of materials into new forms of writing.

This kind of transfer of materials across genres—in this case, from epigram to prose anecdote—is by no means unusual. The same sort of evolution occurs as poems become songs, and, frequently, as texts evolve in their movements between printed miscellanies and collections of dances.

John Playford's *The Dancing Master* offered "*plain and easie Rules for the Dancing of Country Dances, with the Tune to each Dance, to be playd on the Treble Violin.*" It was a highly popular collection, running through eight editions between 1651 (where it was published as *The English Dancing Master*) and 1728. In the process, the collection grew from 100 to more than 900 dances.

For each entry, *The Dancing Master* prints a title, a starting position for dancers, a musical score, and then dance instructions. Thus, "Cuckolds all a row"—a dance for four—is accompanied with the notes

Meet all forwards and back—Stand for a strain played once—That again—
Stand for a strain played twice—Turn back to back to the Contrary Women
faces again, go about the Contrary Women not turning your faces—Stand for
a strain played once—Turn back to back to your own, faces again, go about
your own not turning faces—Stand for a strain played twice.

Playford presented his book as a record of current country practice—the collection's function was to document and disseminate, not to innovate—and *The Dancing Master*'s titles and tunes often came from well-known poems, and in particular from popular ballads. Since printed miscellanies often also draw on and circulate ballads, many of the titles of dances in Playford's book appear in printed miscellanies as full verses—with no note of melody or dance. Thus "Cuckolds all a row," for instance, is printed in *A Jovial Garland* as "SONG LXVII. Cuckolds all a row."[184] (And evidently the dance was a hit: Pepys noted that at a New Year's Eve ball, in 1662, Charles II called for "Cuckolds all away" as the first of the country dances and led the company in "the old dance of England.") Similarly, dances headed "Blew Cap," "Broome—The bonny bonny Broome," "Drive the cold Winter away," "The Gun," "Jack Pudding," along with many others, are cited as dance titles in *The Dancing Master*, and as tunes or poems in printed miscellanies. Playford's collection also includes a dance titled "Jog On"—which appears as "A Catch" in two printed miscellanies, and, originally, as a song in Shakespeare's *The Winter's Tale*.[185] In a similar fashion, another Playford collection, *The Musical Companion, in two books* (1673), prints tunes to many of the poems that appear in printed miscellanies—including William Strode's highly popular "I saw fair Cloris walk alone," Robert Davenant's "From the fair *Lavenian* shore," and Aurelian Townshend's "Victorious Beauty" (with music by "Mr. *William Webb*").

Such genre slippage not only occurred between texts. Within the course of a single printed miscellany we see the same sort of blurring between epigrams, ballads, epitaphs, jokes, verse epistles, riddles, dialogues, prose letters, potted histories, games, anagrams, tricks, codes. Very often printed miscellanies conflate what to us might seem distinct kinds of writing, and in so doing, challenge conventional ideas of genre. In *The Mysteries of Love and Eloquence* genres evolve into one another. Like the lumps of clay in Ovid's *Metamorphoses*, verse letters become prose letters become poems; lyrics merge into aphoristic couplets which merge into proverbs; "Jesting and Jovial Questions" become "Set Forms of Expression inserted for imitation" and then "A Dictionary For The finding out of any Rime." These shifts in genre are gradual, and throughout this evolving text clear division seems unimportant: the book moves through broad stages but the edges of these stages are uncertain. To call them ill-defined would be to imply that conspicuous distinction is a lacking necessity. But it is not. Rather, readers are offered various genres which merge and slip and evolve under what the title page calls "the Arts of Wooing and Complementing."

The evolution of the cheese-book poem into a prose jest, and the shift of "Jog On" from Shakespearean play song to miscellany verse to dance title, might stand as emblems for this chapter's consideration of the movement and instability of texts. Certainly, these histories exemplify the three most important features of all the textual developments I have tried to narrate: the textual malleability, the resistance to authorcentric readings, and the blurrings of genres.

Each of these features raises compelling questions about the way early modernists (and others) have tended to organize academic research. In particular, these characteristics call into question our modes of describing literary texts. Miscellanies challenge, or at least complicate, the claim of authorship as the organizing principle of literary studies; they render dubious the privileging of particular genres of writing over others; they contest the notion of the passive, acquiescing reader; and they nuance, critique, or in some cases overturn many of the existing binaries that serve to organize literary research. These binaries include public versus private; author versus reader; writing versus reading; even, in the cases of books with marginalia, manuscript versus print.

These neat, stable classifications have in the past worked to obscure many kinds of writing, and many kinds of readers, by constructing a canon that is overwhelmingly authorcentric; that privileges certain stable, identifiable genres; that gives little thought to the reader and the reception of texts. Miscellanies, in their resistance to these tenets, emerge as potent sites for locating voices that have been previously hushed. More fundamentally still, miscellanies invite us to reconsider the principles that have structured our study of texts.

The very fact that just about every early modern manuscript miscellany is library cataloged "Commonplace book, ca. 1620"—often wrong on both counts—is emblematic of this gap between ways of describing, and the rich texts themselves. If the significance of miscellanies, whether manuscript or print, is to challenge ideas of genre, of authorship, of reading, it is important to find ways of discussing these texts, rather than simply positioning them as momentary aberrations from an established norm; rather than simply plugging miscellanies into those fixed modes of criticism which will only serve to flatten out these texts' potentials. By offering this chapter's very detailed discussion of miscellany versions of texts, I have tried to avoid this flattening out, and to resist a collapsing back into obscuring binary oppositions.

As I noted earlier, past discussions of miscellany texts have been largely (although not wholly) limited to outraged rejections cast in a lexicon of the "corrupt" and "degenerate," or to more considered textual histories which nevertheless use miscellanies to plot a path back to the author and, in so doing, cover their miscellany tracks. I have attempted to use printed miscellanies' resistance to traditional ways of describing texts not, as has been the case in the past, as a reason to ignore them, but rather as an opportunity to discuss precisely the kinds of neglected texts, readings, and readers that they suggest.

In trying to offer a more sustained consideration of verse transmission and miscellanies, I have tried to offer a methodology grounded in the precise discussion of particular texts. Of course such a pursuit of the particular has its problematic corollary. I began this chapter by quoting from Borges's fiction about "Funes the Memorious," whose ability to comprehend, absolutely, each single moment meant he was constrained to a kind of immobility beneath the weight of his rememberings.

> A circle drawn on a blackboard, a right triangle, lozenge—all these are forms we can fully and intuitively grasp; Ireno could do the same with the stormy mane of a pony, with a herd of cattle on a hill, with the changing fire and its innumerable ashes, with the many faces of a dead man throughout a long wake.

Consequently, Funes "was not very capable of thought. To think is to forget differences, generalize, make abstractions. In the teeming world of Funes, there were only details, almost immediate in their presence."[186]

Funes died of congestion of the lungs, but I am not proposing death through detail, nor that we should clog our conclusions with only single precisions, and never move toward something larger. But I am suggesting we might tread a more careful path: that we might, through a greater attention to a text's particulars, nuance those established terms of literary definition that have, in the past, served to obscure many kinds of literary activity.

FOUR

Politics, Themes, and Preoccupations

FIRST WORDS: "STUFFED WITH PROFANE AND OBSCENE MATTER"

On 25 April 1656, a committee meeting to discuss the respectability, or otherwise, of *Sportive Wit* concluded

> that the book contains much scandalous, lascivious, scurrilous and profane matter—that the Lord Mayor of London and the other Commissioners for regulation of printing cause all copies thereof to be seized wherever they are found, and deliver them to the sheriffs of London and Middlesex, who are to cause them to be publicly burnt, with those copies already seized.[1]

Those involved in the book's publication—"Nath. Brookes, stationer, at the Angel, Cornhill, had the book printed; John Grismond of Ivy Lane, and Jas. Cotterill of Lambeth Hill printed it, and John Phillips wrote the epistle dedicatory"—were fined and called to "attend Council next Tuesday." A second printed miscellany from 1656, *Choyce Drollery*, met an equally censorious fate. Two weeks after the incident above, on 9 May, it was declared that

> The Lord Mayor of London, and the other Commissioners for regulation of printing, [have decided] to cause all the copies of "Choice Drollery, Songs, and Sonnets"—a book stuffed with profane and obscene matter, tending, to the corruption of manners,—to be seized wherever they are found, and delivered to the sheriffs of London, who are to order them to be burnt.[2]

Scholars have not generally treated printed miscellanies with the seriousness "The Lord Mayor of London, and the other Commissioners for regulation of printing" evidently did. Partly this stems, I think, from the assumption that mirth, mockery, and bawdiness—topics endlessly rehearsed in the pages of these anthologies—were empty retreats from the world offering little to interest the historian. What Interregnum authorities labeled "scandalous, lascivious, scurrilous and profane matter" is dismissed as a playground for idle wits—as, in the words of one survey, "a chapter—or footnote—in the history of literature, not in the history of politics."[3]

"It may be said," another account decides,

> that this verse does not tell us much about the conflicts of those years ... We must look elsewhere for the expression of religious fervour, and there is little political bitterness here, and none of the anguish of fratricidal war.[4]

Miscellanies, to these commentators, are amusing, perhaps—and certainly good for a quote or two—but ultimately little more than peripheral texts: divorced, fundamentally, from ideas of politics or power.

In fact, the distance miscellanies attempted to introduce between themselves and their contemporary context lies at the heart of their significance; their wit, comedy, and decadence were not an abdication of a seriousness of intent, but rather the conscious adoption of an alternative vocabulary which attached mirthful labels to serious concerns. And thus I think a correspondingly careful consideration of such strategies will begin to answer that call by recent scholars, including Timothy Raylor, for a study of the politics of printed miscellanies.[5]

Royalty, Re-Presentation, and Association

The second edition of *Wit and Drollery* (1661) opens with a note that recalls those earlier burnings. "This sort of Wit," it observes,

> hath formerly suffered Martyrdom; for *Cromwell*, who was more for polity than Wit, not only laid the first Reviver of these Recreations in the Tower, but also committed the innocent Sheets to the mercy of the Executioners fire; as being some of them too kind, as he thought, to the Royal Partie.[6]

Miscellany "Wit" and "Recreations" are here aligned with an overt kindness "to the Royal Partie"—and certainly a Royalist sympathy is one of the more striking preoccupations of printed miscellanies. Numerous poems openly celebrate kings, queens, and their families, and a vocabulary of Royalism expresses excellence in beauty, literature, and art.[7] Indeed, there is evidence of Royalists in exile reading printed miscellanies. The Anglican Divine Michael Honywood, in exile in Utrecht in the late 1640s and 1650s, lent books to other English Royalist exiles and kept a manuscript catalog of these transactions. Among the recorded books are "Witts Recreations 1645" (the third edition), lent twice to

English readers, and "Sr. J. Mennes, &c. poems 120" (probably *Wit and Drollery, Musarum Deliciæ*, or *Wit Restor'd*).[8]

Within this miscellany Royalism, two themes, in particular, emerge as prominent. The first is royal births. We read, for example, five celebrations in *J. Cleaveland Revived*: "*Upon the birth of the Duke of York*"; "*To the King*"; "*To the Queen upon the Birth of one of her Children*"; "*To the Queen*"; and "*To the Queen, upon the Birth of her first Daughter.*"[9] The second is what might be termed royal returns. Again, in *J. Cleaveland Revived*, we find "UPON THE KING's Return from Scotland" ("Return'd? I'll ne'r believ't, first prove him hence . . .") immediately after the prefatory verses.[10] *Parnassus Biceps* includes "*Upon the Kings Returne to the City of London.*"[11] *A Jovial Garland* includes a celebration of Charles II's return to the throne,[12] and *Oxford Drollery's* final poem, "*On King James's Death*," laments his passing, recounts his virtues, and concludes with a familiar consolation borrowed from nature's endless restoration: "then turn you from the west / And see the new Sun rising in the east.[13]

Many of these poems were originally written for official university verse collections which celebrated Royalism in the 1630s and early 1640s, such as *Solis Britannici Perigaeum* (1633), which welcomed the King's return from his Scottish coronation, and *Horti Carolini Rosa Altera* (1640), published to mark the birth of Henry, Duke of Gloucester.[14] When re-presented a little later, in midcentury printed miscellanies, these kinds of poems become much more provocative. *Parnassus Biceps'* "*Upon the Kings Returne to the City of London*" begins "Sing and be merry King *Charles* is come back," and was first written "*when he* [Charles I] *came last thether from Scotland and was entertained there by the Lord Mayor.*" But its 1656 printed miscellany form presented the verse in a new political context: post-regicide, with the future Charles II abroad in the Low Countries. New interpretative possibilities open up. The verse might have been read as nostalgia for this original return from Scotland; as mourning for Charles I; as lamentation for the future Charles II's current *lack* of return; as a plea for that return; as implicit criticism of Interregnum government; or, perhaps most likely, as some combination of all these views. Similarly, those poems celebrating royal births acquire a particular currency in the 1650s. *Parnassus Biceps'* printing of James Shirley's "*On the Princes birth*," for example, attains a new defiance in 1656, conjuring potential royal rebirths alongside celebrations for past royalty.[15] In fact, the effect of countless celebrations of royal births, particularly when the child is unnamed, is to construct a notably *vague* sense of royal virtue which acquires potency for reapplication because of that very lack of particularity. That Charles I and II shared a

Christian name meant post-regicide praise for the former might invoke hopes for the latter, and, in general, lead to new possibilities for readings.

Central to the mechanics of these anthologies is the re-presentation of existing poems. A consideration of miscellany themes and politics must remember that verses offered in new contexts yield fresh readings: poems that had appeared, years earlier, in manuscript collections as more moderate expressions of orthodoxy might later, re-presented in midcentury texts, carry new currency. The allegiances of printed miscellanies can only be properly interrogated in this light of meaning as the product of not just text, and of not merely text and *single* context, but of interactions between poem and changing environments. When we read of *"The Gallants of the Times,"*[16] in other words, we must ask, *which times?* and appreciate that this verse's resonance will shift as the answer changes.[17] When we read Aurelian Townshend's verse beginning "Bacchus, Iacchus, fill our braines"—originally written for a court masque—across *Wits Interpreter* (1655), *An Antidote against Melancholy* (1661), *Merry Drollery the Second Part*, *A Jovial Garland* (1670), *Windsor Drollery* (1672), and *Wit and Mirth* (1682), we should understand that each printing opens up new possibilities for interpretation. So too with the oft-discussed Parliamentary fart poem. Originally written in 1607 after a nonverbal contribution in the House of Commons by Henry Ludlow during a reading of a Lords message on the union, the verse (and fart) were presented as acts of defiant opposition to Lords, King, and union. When the poem appeared in later, pro-Royalist printed miscellanies it was probably read as a straightforward anti-Parliament text, without its earlier reservations about the Crown[18]—particularly when titled *"On a FART in the Parliament-House"* and ascribed to the famous Royalist *"Sir JOHN SUCKLIN[G]."*[19] The popularity of this verse was perhaps partly responsible for the several other fart poems in printed miscellanies—including *"Upon a Fart unluckily let,"* and *"On a FART"*[20]—and, through association, might have inclined readers toward an anti-Parliament interpretation of these apparently "nonpolitical" poems.

In fact it is through association rather than explicit, literal articulation that miscellanies generally convey their politics. Those political figures popular in manuscript verse in the first half of the seventeenth century rarely feature in printed miscellanies. Robert Devereux, Earl of Essex; Walter Raleigh; Robert Cecil; the impeached Francis Bacon and Lionel Cranfield; Thomas Wentworth, Earl of Strafford; and the extraordinary Mervyn Touchet, Earl of Castlehaven, were all regular figures in manuscript verse.[21] Most popular—frequent would be a better word—was the vilified George Villiers, Duke of Buckingham, and he *is* represented in printed miscellany poems: *Wit Restor'd* features five, two of which in fact address his assassin, John Felton.[22] But printed miscellanies do not, generally, favor the verse of high politics, nor of political personalities,[23] nor, despite their continued popularity in the 1670s—dubbed by historians the decade of the political party—do they generally offer overt discussion of Tory or Whig.[24] Other types of anthology deal with such explicitly political themes: like *Ratts Rhimed to Death. Or, the Rump-Parliament Hang'd up in the Shambles* (1660); *Rome Rhym'd to Death* (1683); or *A Choice Collection of 120 Loyal Songs. All of them written since the Two late Plots* (1684).

To appreciate miscellanies we need to detect politics through association, connotation, implication—to note actions or modes which, although superficially "nonpolitical," in fact indicate allegiances or tendencies. Drinking, gaming, friendship, and mirth are good examples of politics as cultural phenomenon, of politics not as detached doctrine, not as direct declaration, but as lived, quotidian expression. Similarly, a text's choice of genre, language, tune, or even layout all position a text in terms of other, established modes, and thus convey allegiances, criticism, or some combination of the two.

Lust, Love, and the Ambiguous Royalism of Printed Miscellanies

It is easy to see why the commissioners for the regulation of printing described *Sportive Wit* as "lascivious." Of its ninety-seven poems, fourteen concern sex or lust, including "*Cartwright's* Song of Dalliance Never printed before"; "NARCISSUS. A Song," which describes watching a young man having sex; "On a precise Woman" which tells of a man borrowing money from a husband to buy sex with his wife; "Willy *is gone to the Wood. SONG*," which requires little explanation; and verses beginning "Come, Sweet, and draw the Curtain round," and "I Prethee sweet *Rose* pull up thy cloaths," which substitutes blanks for obviously bawdy words (and thereby compounds their effect).[25] *Choyce Drollery* offers a similar litany, including "*The Maid of* Tottenham," and "*On the Flower-de-luice in* Oxford," which describes a visit to a brothel.[26]

These two books are by no means exceptional with their sustained interest in bawdy verse. Indeed, printed miscellanies established such a connection between printed wit and the lascivious that other, similar publications had to work hard when they sought to distance their playfulness from connotations of the bawdy. As a consequence of texts such as *Choyce Drollery*, Henry Edmundson's *Comes Facundus in Via. The Fellow Traveller through City and Country* (1658) was forced repeatedly to emphasize that its "Wit and Mirth" is "Clean and Innocent," and that while

> Some are of corrupted stomacks, who do most relish broad and obscene Jests, thinking that savoury which is rotten; but here all froth is scummed off, and all things that smell are cast aside and left in their own sinks, not to be brought in before you.[27]

The bawdy was a subject common to university undergraduate manuscript miscellanies from the 1620s and 1630s, and since these texts seem to have been a key source for printed miscellany compilers, it is unsurprising to see the reappearance of the lascivious in collections like *Sportive Wit*. But in the 1650s, licentiousness was more than the occupation of vacant university minds; it was also political critique, since celebrating bawdiness was a defiant challenge to perceptions of Puritan moral reform. There was a consistent stream of overtly anti-Puritan poems flowing through just about all miscellanies, with verses like William Strode's "With face and fashion to be known,"[28] Richard Corbett's "Tell me you anti-Saints why glasse,"[29] and his "Am I mad O noble Festus,"[30] proving particularly popular. The difference in the 1650s was that after initiatives like the Major Generals' 1655–57 attempts to stamp out stage plays, drunkenness, swearing, alehouses, and cock-fighting in the regions, an intrusive, deeply unpopular reforming Puritanism became conflated with Interregnum government. Thus 1650s printed miscellanies, by including verse celebrating, among other things, lust, sex, inconstancy in affection, and general decadence, were issuing a protest to midcentury Puritanism *and* Interregnum government. Printed miscellanies after 1660 continued to present various bawdy scenarios, but here the emphasis of protest altered: Puritans were still mocked, but the anti-government strain desisted. Protest, in other words, became more social than political.

But there is another layer of signification. If we consider bawdy verses as an element of misrule in general—along with drink, riotous behavior, mockery, and a wider rejection of norms or etiquette—it is apparent that "lascivious" verse was not only a means to register anti-Puritan protest and demonstrate hostility to Interregnum government; it was also a way of declaring positive Royalist inclinations.

As has been often discussed, connections between misrule and Royalism were in large part due to popular perceptions of the *Book of Sports*. Issued by James in 1618, and again by Charles in 1633, this document was intended as a means to defend "Lawful Recreations, and Honest Exercises upon *Sundays* and other Holy-Days, after the Afternoon Sermon or Service."[31] James was concerned that Puritan attempts to kill off such activities would both hinder "the Conversion of many"—who would conclude "that no honest Mirth or Recreation is lawful or Tolerable in our Religion"—and

> bareth the common and meaner Sort of People from using such Exercises as may make their Bodies more able for War, when we, or our Successors shall have Occasion to use them; and in Place thereof, sets up filthy Tiplings and Drunkenness, and breeds a number of idle and discontented Speeches in their Ale-Houses.

Consequently,

> after the End of Divine Service our good People be not disturbed, letted or discouraged from any lawful Recreation, such as Dancing, either Men or Women, Archery for Men, Leaping, Vaulting, or any other such harmless Recreation, nor from having of May-Games, Whitson-Ales, and Morris-Dances, and the setting up of May Poles and other Sports.[32]

James's and Charles's *Book of Sports* stemmed from a desire to instil order by allowing a modicum of controlled disorder. It was a moderate document that sanctioned temperate recreation—to be enjoyed only after "having first done their Duty to *God*, and continuing in Obedience to us and our Laws"—as a means to prevent "filthy Tiplings and Drunkenness . . . [and] idle and discontented Speeches." It explicitly prohibited "all unlawful Games . . . [including] Bear and Bull-baitings, [and] Interludes."[33]

The wildly bawdy lifestyle celebrated in printed miscellanies had apparently little to do with these careful sanctions, and would certainly have alarmed James and particularly Charles.[34] But that, really, is not the point. What is significant is that this legitimizing of moderate recreations as a means to control public energies established a link between Royalism and public mirth. Once Royalism was bracketed with activities like "Dancing," "Leaping," "Vaulting," "May-Games" and "Morris-Dances," it was easy for pro-Crown sentiments to be bracketed with more excessive forms of leisure and looser modes of behavior. Bawdy verse, as a celebration of sexual misrule, was thus connected with Royalism—even though such a coupling would have certainly dismayed the Crown. And in the 1650s, by which time the *Book of Sports* had been cast aside along with other initiatives of the Personal Rule, lauding misrule was a potent means of reclaiming a perceived past license that the Puritan government was seeking to overturn.

The literature of opposition to the *Book of Sports* was predicated on this perceived link between Royally sanctioned recreation and debauchery. Thomas Hall, in 1661, offers a sustained invective against festival in general, and, specifically, "the Rise, Root, and Original of May-Games."[35] He presents twenty reasons for opposition, equating festivals with idolatry, with "*That which drives Gods fear out of mens hearts,*" and with "*That which debaseth and debaucheth youth.*"[36] The young, he concedes, do need recreations—but only of a "modest, moderate, manly" variety. May games have nothing to do with such acts of temperance: their "sinful, sensual, sordid Recreations, such as drinking, fighting, dancing, whoring . . . set open the flood-gates to all rudeness, disloyalty, debauchery, & effeminacy."[37] Hall's ardent, sweating protests recall the words of those commissioners for the regulation of printing who described *Sportive Wit* as "scandalous, lascivious, scurrilous," and declared *Choyce Drollery* "profane and obscene . . . [and] tending, to the corruption of manners."[38]

It should be noted that Hall anticipates charges that his critique of May games will prompt allegations of disloyalty to the Crown:

> let me tell thee, the King hath not better friends in the land, than such as oppose those prophane practises; nor more deadly foes, than such as do promote them.[39]

And more significant than the plausibility of his defense is his awareness that an attack on recreations (however excessive they may be) will be construed as anti-Royalist, and thus, implicitly, his acknowledgment that defenders of recreation—even of "sensual . . . whoring . . . debauchery"—are perceived as pro-Crown.

Printed miscellanies' preoccupation with frank discussions of sex and lust, then, was part of a more general celebration of misrule. The bawdy was one of the more extreme means of signaling pro-Crown, anti-Puritan sympathies, and the same allegiances found more moderate expression in poems on May-day games, cock fighting, fox hunting, wilder wedding celebrations, and, more generally, in the incorporation of the language of the *Book of Sports*—"recreation," "sport," "mirth"—in texts like *Wits Recreations, Sportive Wit,* and *Wit and Mirth.*[40] Such celebrations had a particular political charge in the 1650s. After 1660, celebrations of festival and misrule persisted, but with a Crown which had erected a giant royal-crested maypole in the Strand and encouraged Morris dances, they were no longer a means to voice direct opposition to government.[41] Printed miscellany misrule—including those celebrations of the bawdy—was then directed at the social intrusions of Puritans, and religious enthusiasm in general, not the politics of government.[42]

Lust's more decorous sister, love, is also an extremely popular subject in printed miscellanies. In fact, love is by far the most common subject overall—with rather more than one in five verses dealing with happy, unhappy, or would-be couples. Despite its many appearances, though, differences between these manifestations are not great, and love in miscellany verse is limited to a handful of scenarios.

The editor of *The Card of Courtship* (1653), one "Musophilus," is careful to distance the love verse his text has to offer—"these soft numbers"—from the undignified lines peddled by others. "[N]ot a loose line is scatter'd throughout this Volume," he promises, and, by conflating those coarse other works with "the malice of the times," he proposes his anthology as a useful antidote to the troubled contemporary.

> I confess it comes neer to a Syllogisme in these times (when *Mars* and *Bellona* sit as Rectors o're all hearts) to set *Venus* and her Son in opposition against them, as it were to thwart the current of the times: but I hope you (Gentle-men and Ladies, Citizens and Lasses) are not so far in love with the bellowing of the Drum, or the clanger of the Trumpet, that the sweet and harmonious tunes of love shall prove unacceptable to you.[43]

The Card of Courtship's love—decorous, "smooth and pleasing"—is posited as a polite alternative to the bellicose contemporary of drum and trumpet. This contrast is given a clearly political significance when Musophilus describes his offerings as "court-like" and so connects his decorous love with Royalism and, implicitly, "the malice of the times" with Interregnum government.

In fact, love is consistently connected with the court in printed miscellanies. Or, to be more precise, *attempts to procure love* are often placed in a court context. And this is an important distinction. Stable amorous bliss is rarely described. Rather, we read, time and time again, of the male's often frustrated pursuit of that stability of affection, and his lamentations at his insecurities in love—"The Lover angry at his Mistreß unsufferable contempt, may (if he will) thus vent himself, in an invective manner."[44] In their preoccupations these verses recall those late Elizabethan sonnet sequences, like Sidney's *Astrophel and Stella*, which some have argued figured political and social frustrations in romantic terms.[45] What is interesting here is that these printed miscellany verses serve much less to supply the careful allegory of court instability—where failure in love invokes failure at court—and much more to mark involvement in that court life. They become, in other words, emblems of a connection with the elite court world, rather than vignettes of its uncertainty. Thus *The Mysteries of Love and Eloquence* conveys "the Life, . . . [and] Deportments of the most accomplisht Persons"[46] through poems describing the frustrated pleadings of male wooers in the face of female cruelty.[47] Through their inclusion in miscellanies, these poems become not potential allegories of political uncertainty but badges of court life.

Wooing as a specifically courtly activity is further stressed by those poems which mock the faltering attempts to capture love by rural folk: like *Wits Interpreter*'s "A Countrey Suiter to his Love," which depicts the inability of the country male to charm his would-be love in a courtly manner ("Fair Wench, I cannot court thy sprightly eyes").[48] *The Marrow of Complements* includes a whole section devoted to "The Rurall Academy, or Instructions for (and the manner of) the Uulgar . . . Such as Tom Tickle-foot. Lawrence Clod. Peter Puppie. Meg of the Milk paile. Francis of the Apple-loft. Doll of the Darie, and such like,"[49] based around ridicule. Even those verses which deny an interest in court-style wooing—like *Wit Restor'd*'s "*To Phillis*," beginning "Fye on this Courtly life, full of displeasure"—imply a preoccupation through their repeated disavowals.[50]

Thus at the heart of miscellany evocations of court life is the presentation of poems signifying "elite" court manners on the very public stage of the cheap printed book—a presentation that recalls Lois Potter's analysis of the publishing of secrecy, to which this chapter is indebted.[51] While *Wits Interpreter* denounces the idea of including what was already in *print*—"whilst I was in Town to attend the *Press,* I crossed out whatsoever I could hear had been formerly publisht"[52]—to re-present what was *cloistered in manuscript* is presented as a public duty. The text is "a *Collection* of all that for such a time could be ransackt from the private Papers of the *Choicest Wits.*"[53] As has been discussed, there is a tension, if not a contradiction, in making public what was previously private—in presenting the exclusive to everyone. While *The Card of Courtship* conjures the court, it does so for all: it is a text "Fitted to the Humours of all Degrees, Sexes, and Conditions," and its opening prose addresses "the longing Virgins, amorous Batchelors, blithe Widows, kinde Wives, and flexible Husbands, *of what Honour, Title, Calling, or Conversation soever.*"[54]

This paradoxical association with exclusivity is maintained by the use of assumed names and initials. Editors preferred "R.C." to Robert Chamberlain;[55] "I.C" to John Cotgrave;[56] and "H.H." to Henry Herringman.[57] *Merry Drollery the Second Part* is "Collected by *W.N. C.B. R.S. J.G.*"[58] Other collections offer more exotic signatures, including "Musophilus,"[59] or "Nectar."[60] Some prefer, simply, "Your humblest Admirer,"[61] or even no name at all.[62] It was also standard printed miscellany practice to refer to contributors in intriguing initials. Thus *Wit and Drollery* offers the work of "*Sir* J.M.," "Ja.S.," "*Sir* W.D.," and "J.D.,"[63] instead of John Mennes, James Smith, William Davenant, and John Donne.[64] The value of such careful coyness was in the sense of exclusivity it conferred. Shortened names suggest a coterie audience and remove miscellanies from their very public, mass-printed reality. But once again, there is a tension in the reader's relationship to this exclusivity: a tension between the reader as distanced outsider—he or she is, after all, not permitted to know the true identity of compiler or contributor—and the reader as intimate confidant—since abbreviations and assumed names suggest a shared knowledge and a proximity. Initials and conspicuously false names push the reader away, while pulling them in: as we see in *Sportive Wit*'s teasing "*if you can finde out a Christian, and Sirname by the letters in the Title, as they are placed, you will do little leße than devine.*"[65]

Codes function in a similar fashion. Secret writing was the subject of numerous midcentury texts, including John Wilkins's 1641 *Mercury, or the Secret and Swift Messenger*. John Wallis, in his *Discourse*, noted "now there is scarce a Person of Quality, but is more or less acquainted with" ciphers.[66] Miscellanies show a corresponding interest: *Wits Interpreter* includes a detailed (but nebulous) "Cardinal *Richlieus* Key, his manner of writing of Letters";[67] "Another manner of Character difficult to be understood";[68] and methods so "*That a Letter may not be read unleß it be dissolv'd in water,*" and "*That a letter may not be seen by Star-light or Candle-light.*"[69] Even when codes and ciphers are not the explicit subject, miscellanies import a discourse of mystification. *Wits Interpreter* seeks to explain "the whole Mystery of those pleasing *Witchcrafts* of *Eloquence* and *Love*";[70] *The Mysteries of Love and Eloquence* explains "the mode of their Courtly Entertainments ... the Witchcrafts of their perswasive Language, in their Approaches, or other more Secret Dispatches";[71] and we read of countless secret dialogues, intimate letters, whispered exchanges. In "Song 37" of *Windsor Drollery*, the narrator overhears secret promises of love.

Codes and a sense of secrecy were certainly Royalist genres. Secret correspondence had been explicitly connected with the Crown since Parliament's publication of Charles I's covert letters to Henrietta Maria in *The King's Cabinet Opened* (1645),[72] and the idea of secret writing was connected with defiant Royalist sympathies in the 1650s. Thus midcentury miscellanies which advertised secret languages and writings evoked an audience requiring deception and evasion, and implied pro-Crown, anti-Parliament inclinations.

The tension here is, once more, between concealment and revelation: were readers gaining exclusive knowledge, or was exclusive knowledge destroyed by this dissemination? Codes, like compilers' initials, and, more generally, like miscellanies opening up the exclusive to anyone, were treading a fine line between cultivating a sense of the socially eminent and debasing that eminence. This tension must have an effect on our reading of the politics of these texts. It is not sufficient to describe printed miscellanies as simply presenting court connotations and therefore purveying Royalist sympathy. They were also involved in a more complex balancing act that combined lauding court exclusivity with demystification. On one level miscellany evocations of the court are clearly and simply Royalist: they celebrate court manners and exclusivity and adopt a vocabulary of secrecy and codes. On another level, these pro-Crown sentiments are subtly ambiguous: if the court's power came from its restricted access, was not a gesture toward flinging wide its doors a Royalism of a contradictory, even self-defeating sort? Did the act of apparently democratizing court exclusivity, in other words—of redistributing it to a wider, "lower" class—not serve to critique that court world?

In part this question is answered by what I have previously described as printed miscellanies' simultaneous raising of the issue of court access, while denying, implicitly, the possibility of that access. Printed miscellanies gathered status from offering glimpses of court life without really threatening to infiltrate it, and their apparently paradoxical stress on both the practical use of these texts and the importance of maintaining social hierarchy leaves readers, I think, encouraged to appropriate these texts—to include them *within* their existing circumstances—rather than to use them to change those circumstances.

We must note, also, that this simultaneous interest in ideas of application and apparent social mobility, on the one hand, and court life and the regulation or maintenance of society's degrees on the other was most notable in the 1650s and was, to a large part, a reaction to that particular moment: a combination of the sense of possibilities for *social* movement that came about at this time of political revolution, and a means to register protest at those *political* changes through the nostalgic recollection of the banished court and thus the world of maintained hierarchy and degree. It was, in other words, a positive embracing of a sense of social upheaval, alongside a negative reaction to political change. After 1660 miscellanies' boasts of their "use" and thus their apparent sense of the possibility of social mobility declines—in part because these texts had gained a publishing legitimacy they had formerly lacked and, as a consequence, felt less need to position themselves in terms of established types of publications like conduct manuals.

More generally, the idea of education became increasingly problematic after the Civil War. Historians have made the magnificent generalization that education was regarded as a cure for social ills in the sixteenth century, but, post–Civil War, came to be seen as a cause of problems.[73] While I would not want to say that after 1660 printed miscellany compilers were working to anything like so unambiguous a philosophy, the end of talk of readers' social risings and court manners for all, "whosoever thou art,"[74] perhaps had something to do with a more general sense that certain cultural items rightfully belonged to certain social groups, and that distribution across social classes, like education for all, was a dangerous step toward a repetition of the 1640s and 1650s.[75]

However, the fact remains that printed miscellanies of the 1650s, in particular, *did* at least gesture toward a transfer of court culture to a much wider audience. And while they might also emphasize a maintenance of social hierarchy, they thus evinced a paradoxical Royalism, with court connections which were, through their public offering, unsettled. This unsettling was, I think, not a conscious attempt to critique the Crown or the court or elites in general, but rather an inevitable consequence of marketing coterie texts—or texts which purported to be coterie texts—to a mass public.

Love, and other Prisons

Miscellany love poetry most commonly portrays a cruel, powerful woman scorning or torturing a loyal but doomed male wooer—often cast in Petrarchan terms: "You all the arts and pow'rs imqprove / To Tyrant over me, / And make my flames the center of your scorn."[76] This state of male weakness as a result of love is frequently described in an explicitly political vocabulary, as we see in *Wits Interpreter*'s "*The Cavaliers' Husband*":

> And the Star Chamber of her eyes
> Robs Subjects of their liberties.
> Her voyce doth keep mens ears in aw,
> Even like the High-Commission Law.[77]

In those 1650s texts which advertised Royalist sympathies, such verses had an immediate political resonance: the gallant male's harsh fate at the hands of the cruel, female tyrant paralleled a position of political impotence that many Royalists of the time endured.

Interestingly, some texts take the implication of their descriptions of a mistress's cruel rule further. Verses often emphasize that the woman's beauty, and thus her power, are only the *creations of the poet's words*: "I plainly see / ... you'r enthron'd / By me above."[78] In his *Parnassus Biceps*, Abraham Wright suggests his text contains the same potential for generation:

> In this small Glasse you may behold ... a Mistresse of any age, or face, in her created, or uncreated complexion: this mirrour presents you with more shapes then a Conjurers Glasse, or a Limners Pencil. It will also teach you how to court that Mistresse, when her very washings and pargettings cannot flatter her; how to raise beauty out of wrinkles four score years old, and to fall in love even with deformity and uglinesse.[79]

Since poetry can create, it can as easily destroy:

> But yet be wise,
> And don't believe that I
> Doe think your eyes
> More bright than starres can be,
> Or face the Angels face out-vies
> In their celestiall liveries,
> 'Tis all but Poetrie,
> I could have said as much by any she:
> Thou art not beauteous of thy self,
> But art made so by me.[80]

Direct and seductive political readings leap out of such lines: readings that equate poet with public, female with ruler, and so suggest that since a single ruler is only the product of his people's will (recalling Hobbes), a change in the political order is entirely in the hands of the people.

I prefer to think about the relationship between the wooer's sufferings and a text's political stance in less literal terms; more important than direct allegory is the *general condition* of being enthralled to a cruel mistress. Love is repeatedly presented as a prison: "Turn away those sparkling Jems ... Where love from such Imprisonment sets free?";[81] "This silken wreath that circles-in my arms ... This makes my arme your prisoner, that my heart."[82] Love is cast as a restricting opposite to the freedom that friendship, mirth, and wine can induce.

> Ah! What Charmes have those Eyes,
> That a Love so strong can inspire?
> It Mirth, Wit, and Friendship defies;
> And Wine cannot slacken its Fires.
> In spight of my self I must follow him still.[83]

The "him" of the last line is Cupid, and this sense of the *inexorable* prison of love (later comes "I cannot, nay will not retire, / No; though I were sure to be burn'd in the fire") is so often a theme that after reading enough of these verses the *attractiveness* of positions of confinement and exclusion becomes an implicit refrain.

In fact, the inevitability of confinement in love is the most popular instance of the motif of confinement in general—a motif that is rehearsed across various scenarios, and finds its most literal expression in prison verse.[84] In these poems, one of the defining constants is the prisoner's attempt to find strategies to endure his fate: to find some semblance of consolation amid his bondage—like Shakespeare's Richard II, "studying how I may compare / This prison where I live unto the world."[85] Prisoners find comfort not through any vision of release, but rather by converting the condition of imprisonment into a virtuous and potentially rewarding state. This is usually effected in one of two ways.

First, the confinement of prison is translated into an alluring *exclusivity*. Imprisonment is portrayed as a dignified distinctness from the mass, and the prisoner becomes

> Like some high prized *Magerite:*
> Or like some great Mogul or Pope . . .
> *Retiredness is a piece of Majesty;*
> *And thus proud Sultan, I'm as great as thee.*

Interestingly, poets actually employ a vocabulary common to coterie manuscript circulation to describe the solitary prison state:

> That which the world miscalls a Jail,
> A private Closet is to me . . .
> I'm in this Cabinet lock'd up . . .
> . . . cloister'd up from publick, sight.[86]

The poem recalls the language of cabinets, secret transmission, the anti-public—a prestigious discourse often used in miscellany prefaces to infer exclusivity ("thou hast a Cabinet wherein the richest Iewels of our Language are lockt up")[87]—and in so doing transforms the prison cell into a respectable site: part of the world of *"eminent places."*[88]

Second, confinement in prison is presented as a test of character, and, specifically, as a test of the prisoner's loyalty to the King. Consequently, the successful, stoic acceptance of this harsh fate becomes a badge of true Royalism, and the prison becomes a place where the virtuous can display a disdain for the petty sufferings of the day to day and evince a virtue that rises above their condition. The prisoner must act like those "so many noble Sparkes, / Who on their bodies bear the Markes / Of their integrity, / And suffer'd Ruin of estate."[89] The prisoner's stoicism is helped by his innocence—

> a good Conscience is my bail,
> And innocence my liberty:
> *Locks, Bars, and Solitude together met,*
> *Makes me no Pris'ner, but an Anchoret*[90]

and by thoughts of the King—

> A King lives not a braver life
> Then we merry pris'ners doe,
> Though fools in freedome doe conceive
> That we are in want and woe.[91]

But the overwhelming emphasis is on the ability of the prisoner to endure his sufferings without complaint or bitterness:

> How happy's the prisoner that conquers his fate
> With silence, & ne'r on bad fortune complains.[92]

As a consequence, the imprisoned Royalist—despite his evident material misfortunes—is able to prove his greater virtue.

> Let Tyrants wear purple deep dy'd in the blood
> Of those they have slain their Scepters to sway,
> If your cloaths be your own, and our titles good
> to the rags we have on, we'r better than they[.][93]

Prison becomes a place where virtue can be tested and loyalty displayed. In an extreme version of the celebration of the *vita contemplative*, these poems conclude that "bashfull Merit only dwells / In Camps, in Villages and Cells."[94]

There is an initially surprising connection between these rather contorted attempts to transform the superficially bleak prison into a positive space—part of a more general miscellany interest in justifying exclusion—and miscellany preoccupations with anagrams. Anagrams are well represented in printed miscellanies. *Folly in Print* offered three verses which base themselves around somewhat loose scramblings of one "John Bellasyse": "John Bellasyse Anagram. I Bless an Holy"; "John Bellasyse Anagram. His Noble Sayle"; "John Bellasyse Anagram.

Bees is all Hony." For good measure, there is also "On Sir Henry Bellasyse Sonne to my Lord John Bellasyse Anagram. By her Seen Sally." And *J. Cleaveland Revived*'s "*The Definition of a Protector*" bases its attack on Cromwell around the truth an anagram reveals.[95] Lois Potter has noted such lexical juggling was the appropriate literature for those convinced the world was turned upside down.[96] But more than this, anagrams reveal truth through a rearrangement of a superficial reality. They rely on a distance between apparent and actual meaning—a distance which was naturally consoling for a politically oppressed group whose surface offered little comfort. Those codes previously mentioned were doing similar things when they cultivated a sense of mystery and thus implicitly declared that surface signals had little to do with truth. Truth was complex and puzzling; hence, miscellanies seem to suggest, immediate misfortune merely masks a more profound (and perhaps more favorable) condition.[97]

Chronograms, which rearranged dates to reveal meaning, were similarly engaged with hidden consolations and, thus, in finding a reality below the apparent. "*A double* Chronogram *(the one in Latine the other in the English of that Latine) upon the year 1642*," which appeared in *Parnassus Biceps*, reads

> TV DeVs IaM propItIVs sIs regI regnoqVe hVIC UnIVerso. O goD noVV sheVV faVoVr to the kIng anD thIs VVhoLe LanD.[98]

In the 1650s these strategies of reinterpretation and the widespread interest in prison's potential consolations had an immediate resonance as a means to evoke and consider the political displacement of Royalists in Commonwealth England. But what happened after 1660, when this sense of exile was no longer apparent? If one of the defining interests of midcentury printed miscellanies is their sense of confinement—their organization around ideas of exclusion—do Restoration miscellanies give expression to a different preoccupation, given the changing political environment?

The answer to this question is a fairly unequivocal "no." The 1650s spirit of stoic suffering does not disappear, and grievance at exclusion is still generated. What happens, though, is that the source of this discontent changes. Whereas previously Parliament had been the cited cause of all problems, post-1660 miscellanies become preoccupied with the idea of *new courtiers* as catalyst for the true Royalist's dislocation. That is, the apparent loss of immediate *raison d'être* after 1660—when printed miscellanies would surely not need to act as the vehicle for disenfranchised Royalism—was replaced with a more subtle sense of grievance at the *type* of Royalist now favored at court. The sense of complaint was retained, but transferred to a new target. The divide becomes old versus new, rather than Royalist versus Parliamentarian.

Verses contrasting the old and the new courtier became extremely common. In one popular poem which appears in four different texts, the old cavalier is presented as a formidable monument to virtue. He is

> an old worshipful Gentleman who had a great estate,
> Who kept an old house at a beautiful rate,
> And an old porter to relieve the Poor at his gate.

He had "an old study fill'd full of Learned Books," drank "a cup of old Sherry," and offered generous hospitality "With a good old fashion when Christmas is come." But his son, by contrast, "Like a young Gallant inheriting all," "keeps a brace of Whores" and "lieth drunk in a new Tavern till he can neither go nor stand." Instead of his father's fine learned library, he keeps only "a new study stuff'd full of Pamphlets and Plays" (and probably a few miscellanies, too?). And where his father, the old courtier, knew how to keep a fine, welcoming house, this gallant's young wife "never knew what belong'd to good house-keeping or care." (There are plenty of knew/new puns here.) When "*Christmas is come*," the new courtier departs for London,

> And leave noo body at home but our new Porter *John*,
> Who relieves the Poor with a thump on the back with a stone.
> ... good House-keeping is now grown so cold.[99]

The old courtier—aged with moderation, hospitality, generosity, learning; a walking epitome of custom and tradition—is juxtaposed with the new man of court, whose youth and "loose," uneducated profligacy epitomize the breed of post-1660 courtiers. And at court these young figures are those who have come to dominate:

> I went to Court, in hope to find
> Some of my friends in Place;
> And walking there, I had a sight
> Of all the Crew: But, by this light,
> I hardly knew a face!
>
> ...
>
> Not one, upon my life, among
> My old acquaintance ...

> But, truly, There are swarmes of Those,
> Whose chins are beardless, yet their hose
> And Buttocks still wear muffs;
> Whilst the old rusty Cavaleer
> Retires, or dares not once appear
> For want of Coin, and Cuffs.[100]

Pepys repeatedly describes a similar eclipse: in October 1662, he notes a visit

> to Creedes chamber and there sat a good while and drank Chocolate. Here I am told how things go at Court; that the young men get uppermost, and the old serious lords are out of favour.[101]

But in miscellany verse the old "serious" courtier does not complain of being "out of favour": "a calm retreat is best."[102] "He that is a cleare / Cavalier / Will not repine, / Although his fortune grow / So very low." He has only a wry smile for those foolish enough to value Fortune's momentary favor: "Fortune is a Lass, / She will embrace, / And strait destroy; / Free-borne Loyaltie / Will ever be, / Sing vive le Roy." The old courtier displays that same stoicism that formed part of the excluded's reaction to love and to prison in the 1650s: he is the "honest poor Cavalier" who, by bravely enduring his poor condition, proves his true loyalty to the Crown and exudes a spirit of *contemptus mundi*. "Vertue is her own reward, and fortune is a Whore, / There's none but knaves and fools regard / Her, or do her power implore. / A reall honest man, / Might a' bin utterly undone, / To show his Allegiance, / His Love and obedience." The new courtier, like those outside the prison walls in the 1650s, is welcome to the shallow short-term pleasures of temporary preferment (where "Fate will flatter e'm, and will scatter e'm"). While these men offer a Crown loyalty conditional upon worldly rewards, the loyalty of the excluded, "Although he be a ragged Souldier,"[103] is above material hardships:

> This is the constant note I sing,
> I have been faithfull to the King,
> And so shall ever be.[104]

As the prison was made exclusive, so poverty, misfortune, and neglect—"the life of an honest poor Cavalier"[105]—are rendered constituents of virtue, and printed miscellanies, through their sustained meditations on exclusions and potentials for consolation, emerge as a literature of outsiders seeking restoration.[106]

Friendship and Humor

Miscellany constructions of place show the same interest in confined, exclusive spaces, and in the outsider whose virtue stems from this detachment, as prison verse displays. Texts are often careful to associate themselves with exclusive areas—with Windsor, Covent Garden, Holborn (*"send for me to your Chambers, carry me into your Walks or to the Play-House"*[107]). This had clear commercial advantages as readers were offered their little glimpse of lives linked to a topography of "most accomplisht Persons."[108] But along with a general sense of eminence of place are attempts by many texts, particularly those that cluster around midcentury, to connect themselves with an *enclosed* location—with a place that draws attention to its boundaries. This might be the academy (*Academy of Complements, Wits Academy, New Academy of Complements*), or the university (*Parnassus Biceps* represents "some few drops of that Ocean of Wit, which flowed from those two brests of this Nation, the two Universities"[109]), or even the tavern (in poems like "Come away to the Tavern I say"; "Come come away to the Tavern I say"; "I went to the Tavern, and then"[110]). Or it might be a sense of a community apart—in the way that *Musarum Deliciæ* represents "*Sir* John Mennis, *and* Doctor Smiths'" cloistered exchanges,[111] and that *Wit and Drollery* is the product of "*Sir* J.M. *of* Ja.S. *of Sir* W.D. *of* J.D. *and other miraculous Muses of the Times.*"[112]

The sense of a community apart—a community loyal within its walls but closed to outsiders—is often evoked in miscellany discussions of friendship. A celebration of friendship occurs in almost all texts. In particular, printed miscellanies show a sustained interest in group friendship: texts depict a community huddled in opposition to some larger, displacing evil, rarely defined in explicit terms, but sometimes sketched as Interregnum government in the 1650s and new courtiers in the 1660s and 1670s.

Group friendships are invoked as the source of texts. William Hickes decided to *"appear a second time in Print"* since he was *"Urg'd by some friends."*[113] *J. Cleaveland Revived* is "Now at last publisht from his Original Copies, by some of his intrusted Friends," and the editor, E. Williamson, does not apologize that

> Some other Poems are intermixed, such as the Reader shall finde to be of such persons as were for the most part Mr. *Cleavelands* Contemporaries.[114]

Sportive Wit is the product of "*a Club of sparkling Wits, viz. C.J. B.J. L.M. W.T. Cum multis aliis*—," and the reader is assured *"the publishers had no designes beyond thy pleasure, their owne reputation, and the continuation of their sprightly Club."*[115] References to the Order of the Fancy, and to Ben Jonson's groups at the Mermaid, the Devil, and the St. Dunstan taverns—recalled with every cry of "Fetch me *Ben. Johnsons* scull, and fill't with Sack"[116]—invoke an established club context where group friendship was a defining attribute, along with mirth, drink, and (often) a sense of grievance at social exclusion which would, re-created midcentury, acquire a new political charge.

Miscellanies frequently present themselves as the perfect complement to friendship. In the preface to *Wit and Drollery*, the editor declares

> this Wit I present thee with, is such as can onely be in fashion, invented purposely to keep off the violent assaults of Melancholy, assisted by the additionall Engines, and Weapons of Sack and good company.[117]

Texts might even help the reader establish such friendships—*The New Academy of Complements* includes, among other things, model "Eloquent Letters of . . . Friendship,"[118] fit for reapplication.

The reader's relationship to friendship as source, subject, and context for miscellanies is ambiguous. Texts position readers in that by now familiar no-man's-land where they are shown intimacy but not permitted to join, where their sense of near-distance enforces their world apart. Readers were teased with the prospect of joining the "sparkling Wits."[119] There were calls to join the group with verses that begin, for example, "Come all you Gallants that live near the Court"; "My Masters and friends, and good people draw near"; "Come come away to the Tavern I say"; "List you Nobles, and attend"; "Come hither, read (my gentle friend)"; "Oh ho boyes, soh ho boyes"; "Come Lads and Lasses"; "Lets drink, dear Friends, lets drink."[120]

But just as miscellanies appear to offer a path to court while simultaneously littering that very route with obstacles, these invitations to reader participation position the reader as outsider. They are calls to join a group that accentuate the reader as nonmember, that display, close up, a distant world. Scholarly accounts of printed miscellanies tend to conflate the worlds described in verse with the circumstances of readers.[121] In reality, I think, readership was far broader. And a much wider readership inevitably meant a readership that largely could not step up to court—could not "Come come away to the Tavern," nor "List . . . and attend"—and thus a readership whose personal exclusion mirrored miscellany emphasis on boundaries, limits, opposition.

Just as laughter and humor were important constituents of friendship, printed miscellanies in general consistently organize themselves around wit and mirth.[122] Many texts stress their commitment to laughter as a founding principle. *Merry Drollery the First Part* is made up of *"Jovial Poems, Merry Songs, Witty Drolleries. Intermix'd with Pleasant Catches."* A *Jovial Garland* is composed of a "Variety of Songs, full of Mirth and Pleasure." Other collections proclaim "Mirth, Wit, and Eloquence" and are "merry and Jocose." They offer "Pleasant and *Merry Poems*," and consider themselves *"the Meridian of mirth."*[123]

To stress mirth is not to deny an overt seriousness of purpose; a rush toward laughter is also a rush away from *"the violent assaults of Melancholy."*[124] *An Antidote against Melancholy* makes it clear that to "Laugh, and enjoy" a text suggests a world where things are wrong. It is a volume which "Cures the *Spleene* Revives the blood / Puts thee in a *Merry* Mood," and while it may describe its mirth as "Harmeles," it is "a Cordiall On earth" and will help keep away "a *pound* of Sorrow."[125]

Thus miscellany humor is a humor of defiance in the face of melancholy, exemplified in the six printings of Alexander Brome's "Why should we not laugh and be jolly," from *Wits Interpreter* in 1655, to *The Wits Academy* in 1677.[126] While the contexts of these printings changed, and thus their precise resonances altered, there was a consistent commitment to laughter despite the efforts of the everyday. And this commitment was grounded in the idea of a retreat from a bleak contemporary. The very term "drollery," a key constituent in these texts' self-definition, can suggest connotations of the fantastic, the caricaturing, the grotesque.[127] It implied a conscious reaction against—a withdrawal from—a norm. The work of writers associated with the Order of the Fancy which features in printed miscellanies, like James Smith's *"The Love of Hero and Leander"* and *"The Innovation of Penelope and Ulysses,"* are loose "mocks" whose wit, Timothy Raylor has noted, comes from a persistent thwarting of poetic conventions,[128] from the deliberate distance they place between themselves and established modes—while still relying on those established modes as a counterpoint. This commitment to a laughter that is grounded in a sense of opposition receives its most prolonged articulation in *Mock Songs and Joking Poems* (1675), a text "of Mocks to several late Songs about the Town" which bases itself around the verse tradition of parody—providing alternative lyrics to an existing tune—and, in particular, in replacing the original words with a bawdier version.

While formal literary mocks were most popular in this particular collection, the *spirit* of mockery found expression across all texts. Puritans are a consistent target: popular perceptions of their self-importance made them perfect material for the deflations of ridicule and imitation. Hence the popularity of verses like William Strode's *"The Puritan"*—in three midcentury miscellanies[129]—and Richard Corbett's "Am I mad O noble Festus," in four.[130]

Drink and Drunkenness

Drink is the fourth most popular topic for miscellany poems, behind love, death, and women. But if the popularity of drinking verse is a relative constant, a significant shift occurs over time in the ways texts engage with the subject of drink. Early miscellany verses tend to be jokes that use the subject to pursue a few puns. Among its several inclusions, *Wits Recreations* offers

> What's this that's spilt? 'tis clarret wine,
> 'Tis well 'tis spilt, its fall sav'd mine[131]

and

> *Pallas* the off-spring of *Jove's* brain,
> *Bacchus* out of his thigh was ta'en:
> He breaks his brain that learning wins,
> When he that's drunk breaks but his shins.[132]

Given *Wits Recreations*' preoccupation with short, witty epigrams, this preference for instant wit is not surprising. Nonetheless, the change in tone in later collections is remarkable: drinking and drunkenness become refrains; poems consider and reconsider their virtues; and these themes acquire an explicit political charge those earlier verses conspicuously lack.[133]

Drinking is commonly presented as the pastime of the mirthful gallant: a laugh-accompanied pursuit enjoyed by friends ("Come *Harry, George,* and *Jack* take part") and as much a social marker of the young, witty, urban male, as

> Tobacco, Pipe, Artillery,
> A frolick, catch, and Drollery.[134]

It ranks alongside wit, wooing, misogyny, and learning:

> Tis pleasure to drink among these men
> For they have witt and valour good store,
> They all can handle a sword and a pen
> Can court a lady and tickle a whore,
> And in the middle of all their wine,
> Discourse of *Plato,* and *Arretine.*[135]

Pepys, writing in May and October 1660, evoked a similar world:

> After I was in bed, Mr. Sheply and W. Howe came and sat in my cabin, where I gave them three bottles of Marget ale, and sat laughing and very merry till almost one a-clock in the morning; and so good-night.
>
> ...
>
> I met with Sir W. Pen again, and so with him to Redriffe by water and from thence walked over the fields to Deptford (the first pleasant walk I have had a great while); and in our way had a great deal of merry discourse, and find him to be a merry fellow and pretty good-natured and sings very bawdy songs. About noon we dined together and were very merry at table, telling of tales.[136]

The Compleat Angler, too, constructs a world of mirth, drink, learned conversation—where "Mountagne" is quoted—and group friendship: "we shall each be the happier in each others company."[137]

This is the sort of context evoked by miscellany depictions of the coterie exchanges of "Sir J.M. Ja:S. Sir W.D. J.D. And other admirable Wits";[138] of "*the Modern Familie of the Fancies*";[139] of "a Club of sparkling Wits."[140] Within this club context, drinking is not a chaotic Bacchanalian pursuit. A careful sense of order and hierarchy lay at the heart of group drinkers depicted in miscellanies, exemplified in *Wits Interpreter's* "*Bacchus his Schoole, wherein he teaches the Art of drinking by a most learned method.*" This studied explanation of "The eighth liberal Science" is a description of "the art of drinking" as an academic discipline. It offers accounts of syllabi:

If he Studies the English tong	Beer.
If the Dutch,	Ale.
If the Spanish,	He drinks Sack.
...	
If the German,	Renish.

It indicates levels of competence in study: "The degrees attain'd to in this Schoole are these. A fat corpulent fellow, a *Master of Arts*. A leane drunkard, a Batchelour ... " It lists "*Officers in respect and dignity, Civil and Martial,*" and "*Titles proper to the young Schollars of Bacchus, and of certain Orders which he hath bequeathed them for their better Government.*"[141]

Drinking verses pay similar levels of attention to the type of drink being enjoyed. There are hierarchies of alcohol and alcohol connotations—as we read in "*A Catch: By Wine, Ale, and Beer*":

> WINE. I Generous Wine am for the Court.
> BEER. The City calls for Beer:
> ALE. But Ale, bonny Ale, like a Lord of the Soil, In the Countrey shall domineer.[142]

Thus it is a specifically courtly drink that is lauded, rather than the wholesale pursuit of alcohol in general. Printed miscellany verse proclaims wine (or sack or claret or canary) "a Prince . . . In the royal number set,"[143] and judges it an entirely superior libation to "The heresie of Beer."[144] "[G]ive *Calvin* Beer," one poem writes, "And his precise Disciples."[145] Another: "This Beer breeds the Chollick, let us spread / Our Cheeks with Royal Red."[146] A third: "Why should we drop or basely stoop / To popular Ale or Beer?"[147] This disdain for common beer gained particular force in the 1650s when Oliver Cromwell was often described as the beer-drinking son of a tapster, thus enabling a convenient dichotomy between Royal wine and Protectorate beer. "*The Brewer's Praise*" developed out of this tradition, and is particularly interesting since it borrowed tune and structure from "The Blacksmith," and so conjured the sense of injustice, disenfranchisement, and opposition that accompanied that highly popular verse.

> Of all the Professions in the Town,
> This Brewers trade did gain renown,
> His liquor once reacht up to the Crown,
> Which no body, &c.
>
> . . .
>
> Though Honour will be a Princes daughter,
> The Brewer will woe her in bloud and slaughter,
> And win her, or else it shall cost him hot water,
> Which no body, &c.
>
> . . .
>
> And now may all stout souldiers say,
> Farewell the glory of the Dray,
> For the Brewer himself is turn'd to Clay,
> Which no body, &c.[148]

While beer may have been pejoratively linked to Cromwell, the act of drinking was rich with Royalist connotations. Alcoholic oaths of loyalty to the King had a weight of tradition that 1650s Parliament could not dislodge. Even when Royalists were required to subscribe to the Covenant—swearing to resist innovation in religion—and the Negative Oath—vowing to submit to Parliament, and not to help the king, Royalists could usurp Parliamentarian oaths with their own, pro-Crown avowal:

> They force us to take
> Two oaths, but we'll make
> A third, that we ne'er meant to keep 'em. [149]

It is not surprising, then, that drinking poems often connect with the tradition of oaths to the Crown; that drinkers "clear up our Throats for a Health to the King."[150] "Had they been but true Subjects to Drink, and their King," one speculates, the world would have been better.

> A Friend and a Bottle is all my Design,
> Has no room for Treason, that's top-full of Wine.[151]

Another declares,

> What if we drink, let no man think
> There's Treason in the Cup,
> 'Gainst the King is not any thing, 'tis a plot
> To blow our sorrows up.[152]

Only lesser drinks lead to disloyalty.

> Come let's purge our brains from hops & grains
> That do smell of Anarchy[.][153]

Drinking royal wine indicates and inculcates fidelity to the Crown. And naturally enough, drinking was simultaneously a defiant rejection of Puritan intrusions, and thus a further expression of Royalism.

> With wenches and wine
> Our selves we refine,
> From the dross of the Puritan City[.][154]

This pro-Crown loyalty blurs with the noisy loyalty of groups of drinkers. There are pledges that "We'll tipple, my Lads, together";[155] assurances that "Sack and a friend are both divine";[156] declarations that

> By night and by day
> We sport and we play,
> Conferring our notes, conferring our notes,
> Conferring our notes *together*.[157]

The drinking group is a compact group apart, its members fiercely loyal to one another and to the Crown. The group's self-proclaimed "Honesty ... [and] Good-fellowship," and its lack of "selfish preposterous things"[158]—particularly in contrast (and sometimes as antidote) to the solitary union of love (tyrannical, cruel, deceitful, transient)[159]—once more raises the theme of detachment from some dishonest, selfish orthodoxy, and thus rearticulates the sense of protest running through miscellanies.

But alongside the use of controlled drink as an indicator of Royalism, loyalty, and order came a more dramatic characterization of alcohol as an instigator of change—in the effects of drink, and in the truth that drunkenness can create. The most common claim is that drink raises low spirits. Drink "revives sad souls"[160] and renders drinkers "as merry" and "as valiant" as they wish.[161] While *An Antidote against Melancholy* offers itself as a means to good cheer, it has no doubts as to the best antidepressant around.

> There's no Purge 'gainst *Melancholly*,
> But with *Bacchus* to be jolly;
> All else are but Dreggs of Folly.[162]

For gallants, drink "makes a Man witty,"[163] and for poets, this raising of spirits means "Sack both their muse and wit had been."[164] "Sack will the soule of Poetry infuse."[165] Once more the type of drink is significant: "'tis not lousie Beer, Boys, / But Wine that makes a Poet."[166] "*An Epitaph on* John Taylor" notes that the poet's predilections for inferior alcohol meant he was never of the sack-inspired class of Drayton and Jonson.[167]

Like laughter and mirth, alcohol's ability to revive "sad souls" highlights the need for a revival. The cause of the melancholy which drink cures is rarely made explicit, but rather attributed to some vague sense of injustice, displacement, or misfortune. This sense of injustice is rearticulated at different moments, with different effects. Thus readers in the 1650s of

> Rouse thy dull and drowsie spirits,
> Behold the soule reviving streams[168]

were surely likely to connect flagging souls with Royalists' crumbled fortunes. In the 1680s, a similar call to

> Drink, drink, all you that think
> To cure your souls of sadness;

apparently yielded a more general sense of things being out of joint—as the verse goes on to make clear:

> Take up your Sack, 'tis all you lack,
> All worldly care is madness.[169]

But drink does more than raise spirits. It can lead to the appearance of concrete benefits, too, and many miscellany poems celebrate the power of drink to transform. What is transformed, generally, is the unqualified outsider, who after a few drinks considers himself the perfectly equipped social and political highflyer. "Drink," one verse observes, and

> thou shalt be or Lord, or King,
> Rich, stout, kinde, learned, any thing.[170]

Another verse details the various attributes that develop post-drink:

> I am (me thinks)
> In the *Exchequer* now, and hark how it chinks . . .
> Oh admirable Sack! here's dainty sport,
> I am come back from *Westminster* to Court;
> And am grown young again . . .
> I could win a Vestal now, or tempt a Queen to sin . . .
> Sack has tipt
> My tongue with charms.

Money, court position, youth, and wooing eloquence are all restored.

> Inestimable Sack! thou mak'st us rich,
> Wise, amorous, any thing.[171]

And "restored" is, I think, the right term. Drink here, and in general, is lauded as a great reclaimer of what once was, rather than as the creator of an entirely new good fortune. This reflects the conservative nature of miscellany protest: not a call for radical change, not a blueprint for novelty, but a desire for the return to a previous inclusion, for the reapplication of tradition. And this plea for *returns* had a charged political resonance. Robert Herrick's "*A welcome to Sack*" celebrates the return of sack—his "Eternall lamp of love," "my illustrious spouse"—after a long absence. This poem first appeared in print, in *Hesperides*, in 1648, and has been read, recently, as a discussion of inspiration.[172] But its printed miscellany appearance comes later, in *Parnassus Biceps* (1656), and at this date, post-regicide, with the future Charles II hovering in the Low Countries, the lines lamenting the temporary displacement of the object of his reverence acquire a new political gloss.

> Where hast thou been so long from my embraces
> Poor pitied exile, tell me did thy graces
> Fly discontented hence, and for a time
> Did rather chuse to blesse some other clime:
> And was it to this end thou wentst to move me
> More by thy absence to desire and love mee.

In Abraham Wright's Royalist miscellany, the verse defiantly observes

> But to forsake thee ever, could there be
> A thought of such impossibility?[173]

Some pages before, in the same volume, "*An Epitaph on some bottles of Sack and Claret laid in sand*" closed

> Mean while thy friends pray loud that thou maist have
> A speedy resurrection from thy grave.[174]

In the 1650s, poems describing drink as the great restorer must have been read, in part, as expressions of hope for a political return to monarchy. After 1660, calls for restorations acquired a celebratory subtext, while perhaps nostalgically recreating the 1650s sense of exclusion, now presented in terms of social displacement (new courtiers eclipsing the old; religious enthusiasts intruding where they should not).

Alongside celebrations of drink as the key to a restored (but of course fictitious) worldly success is the theme of drink as retreat. Often this retreat is from the prison of love, and drink is consistently cast as a potent antidote to Cupid's fetters: "*We that Bacchus adore, / Envy not . . . the Charms nor Sweets of Love.*"[175]

> The stupid Lovers braines inherits,
> Nought but dull and empty dreames.
> Thinke not then those dismall trances,
> With our raptures can contend.[176]

Another proclaims:

> Prethee friend leave off thy thinking,
> Cast thy cares of Love away,
> Drown thy sorrows all in drinking, [177]

Drink is freedom to love's chains. "'Tis Wine that inspires, / And quencheth Loves fires."[178]

> Then Women make Asses of those that you can
> Ile find out a Comrade, some Jolly brave man;
> When in our full Glasses, we'l laugh and we'l jest,
> And perhps for diversion we'l drink to the best.[179]

Other verses expand this theme to describe not just love but *all the world* as folly—and ascribe to drink the power to reveal this truth. Where drink in other cases gives the illusion of recaptured wealth, youth, and wit—where drink reequipped men for conventional success—alcohol, here, fosters a dignified disdain for those attributes that were lacking.

"When our Glasses flow with Wine," one popular poem observes,

> The Maior of our Towne with his ruffe on,
> What a pox is he better than we? . . .
> Though he Custad may eat,
> And such lubbardly meat,
> Yet our Sacks makes us merrier then he.

And

> Those Cormorants which,
> Are troubled with an itch,
> To be mighty and rich,
> Doe but toile for the wealth which they borrow.[180]

Drink may not be able to offer its imbiber political or social eminence, but like those *contemptus mundi* celebrations of prison and confinement, it can reveal the hollowness of that eminence. Armed with a new awareness of the world's folly—"Since all the world is grown mad,"[181] since "The greatest Kingdoms in Confusion lie"[182]—drinkers prefer an astute *retreat* from the day to day and its futile cares.

This abandonment of the worldly means a withdrawal from serious thought:

> Come let us drink,
> And never think,
> For Care kills a Cat;
> But Wine makes us Fat[,][183]

and, instead, a delight in the superficial:

> Turn off the Glass 'tis a crime to see't full
> Drinking dead liquor, has made us so dull;
> Let slaves and Phanaticks be subject to care
> Deep thoughts, and affairs our fierce enemies are.[184]

Money, meaningless, is shrugged aside—"Come drink, we want no chink"[185]—and the "damn'd money-monger," pointlessly preoccupied with material wealth, is contrasted with

> we that are bonny
> By Sack . . .
> And n ere trouble the scriveners nor Lawyers.[186]

Another observes

> Those are Slaves,
> Fools and Knaves,
> That have Chink,
> And must pay
> For what they say,
> Do, or think;
> Good Fellows account for neither.
> Be we round, be we square,
> We are happier than they are,
> Whose dignity works their Ruine;
> He that well the Bowl rears,
> Can baffle his Cares;
> And a Fig for death or Undoing.[187]

Money, the marker of worldly success, is what the drinker does not have, but the poem transforms this poverty into a wise disengagement—like the translation of prison into an exclusive retreat.

> Our money shall nere indite us,
> Nor drag us to Goldsmiths Hall,
> No Pirates nor wracks can affright us;
> We that have no estates,
> Feare no plunder nor rates

> We can sleep with open gates,
> He that lies on the ground cannot fall.[188]

Goldsmith's Hall Committee was the London body which set fines for those who had supported the King in the 1640s—a machine that was unwieldy, highly unpopular among Royalists, and tainted with charges of corruption.[189] It was a common focus of grievances for Royalists, and was often invoked as the intrusive, punitive body from which drink could offer freedom:

> Since Goldsmiths' Committee
> Affords us no pity,
> Our sorrows in wine we will steep 'em[.][190]

This political freedom, the positive flipside of poverty, is part of a more general political innocence that drinking and intoxication procures.

> A pox of the Fooling and Plotting of late,
> What a pother and stir has it kept in the State;
> Let the Rabble run mad with Suspicions and Fears,
> Let 'em Scuffle and Jar, till they go by the ears;
> Their Grievances never shall trouble my Pate,
> So I can enjoy but my dear Bottle at quiet.[191]

Another poem notes:

> Sobriety and Study breeds
> Suspition in our Acts and Deeds,
> The *Down-right Drunkard* no man heeds.[192]

A third:

> My Masters and Friends, whosoever intends
> To trouble this Room with discourse;
> You that sit by, are as guilty as I,
> Let your talk be better or worse.
> Now lest you should prate of matters of State,
> Or any thing else that might hurt us,
> Rather let us drink off our Cups to the brink,
> And then we shall speak to the purpose.[193]

And here, with serious thoughts and material concerns vanishing, and political innocence secured, drink leads to an end to worries:

> Drink boyes, drink boyes, drink and doe not spare,
> Troule away the bowl, and take no care.
> So that we have meat and drink, and money and clothes
> What care we, what care we how the world goes.[194]

This is not so much a curing of worries, as their renouncement. Drink offers a numbed bliss.

> When thou art arm'd with Sack, thou canst not feel
> Though thunder strike thee; that hath made thee steel.[195]

Here,

> *Bacchus* shall be our Protector,
> And him we'l follow to;
> Being under his Banner, what
> Mischief can ever come to us.[196]

This seems the essence of what drinking verses seek: a retreat from worldly concerns to a numbed happiness—a drunken safe haven—in the immediate. And what is particularly interesting about these verses of withdrawal and restoration is their open celebration of what is known to be illusory. Poems lauding a new alcohol-fostered eloquence acknowledge it as *"Canary-Rhetorick,"* yet the *impression* is still cause for celebration. Verses proclaiming drink which "mak'st us rich ... [and] Wise,"[197] along with those that celebrate the wealth of their poverty, the virtue of their retreat, the freedom of their exclusion—all these poems base their happy conclusions on transient fantasy.

We encounter a similar philosophy in an epigram printed in 1655.[198] It tells of Tom who, despite being on the losing side in battle, decides to tell his prince that he and his comrades secured victory. Celebrations ensue: the kingdom "Rung Bells, made Bonfires as the custome is." But the King soon found the truth. Summoned before the Crown to explain his false account, Tom is unrepentant:

> For where the truth would have brought wailing & weeping;
> My lye hath brought two dayes laughing and sleeping.
> And if you all this year tooke my lye for true,
> To keep you merry, what harme would ensue?

Like the narrators of those drinking poems that draw consolation from the illusory, Tom prefers happy fantasy ahead of painful truth. The imagined acquires a new seriousness.

> Wit and Love are the only things
> Which fill the thoughts of Kings and us;
> Imagination makes us Kings,
> And that is rais'd by drinking thus[.]`199`

We might parallel the hour of drunken happiness—the hour of the excluded living the illusory consolation—with readers spending sixty minutes drifting through a miscellany's pages: through the world of court, eminence, exclusivity; through compliments, lovers' exchanges, songs from the spring balls . . . until the book snaps shut (and the drunkard shudders awake), and, for both, more prosaic realities intrude.

Miscellany verses show ample awareness of the frailty of this mechanism of consolation. At its most candid, this anxiety plainly acknowledges the ephemeral nature of drink's sustenance, even compared with much-maligned love. While

> Love's great Debauch is more lasting and strong,
> For that often lasts a Man all his life long . . .
> . . . the Nights in the Joys of good drinking be past.[200]

But squaring up to the reality of transience, and to drink's ephemeral comfort, is rare. More common are attempts to draw solace from the fact that *everything* is, in fact, transient; that the only consolation is a leveling of meaninglessness that recalls those justifications of drunkenness on the grounds that all the world is mad. Thus

> The changable World to our *Joy* is unjust,
> All *Treasure* uncertain, then down with your dust.
> *In Frolicks dispose your* pounds, shillings, *and* pence,
> *For we shall be nothing a hundred years hence.* [201]

More common still are miscellany verses' bold attempts to actually counter fears of transience. This it sometimes does through an immersion in the moment—through a total engagement with the contemporary and an eschewing of thoughts of the future. Thus:

> Let's banish bus-ness, banish sorrow;
> And leave to whom belongs to morrow.[202]

Alongside these calls for a life lived only in the absolute present are appeals for *endless* drink. "By night and by day," one 1672 verse declares, "We sport and we play."²⁰³ Another: "We'l drink, and we'll kiss, and we'll never have done."²⁰⁴ Others still, from 1677: "And we'll sing till the Morn without rest,"²⁰⁵ "And drink till the Morning appear."²⁰⁶ When the question is put, in 1655, "Now, now, the Sun is fled / Down into *Thetis* bed, / Ceasing his solemn course a while, / What then?" the answer comes "Tis not to sleep but be / Merry all night as wee."²⁰⁷ "Do no longer then delay," another implores, since "*Bacchus* swears it is his will / That we should be drinking still."²⁰⁸ And the view that drinking "is the Profession that never will alter"²⁰⁹ received justification from Abraham Cowley's "The thirsty Earth drinks up the Rain," translated from Anacreon, vindicating alcohol through natural precedent.²¹⁰

A third strategy often summoned in miscellany verse relies on the creation of an alternative time-frame where the order of the outside world—an outside world which has handed the withdrawn drinkers only misfortune—can be evaded.

> Then Come, drink away:
> Be it night, or be it day;
> The time shalt be told as it passes:
> The true hour we shall know
> By the Ebb and the Flow,
> Of the jolly quart pots and the Glasses.²¹¹

The "Ebb and the Flow" of drink can now structure their days. Another verse, from 1669, calls for drinking until time is confused—"Till we baffle the States, and the Sun face about."²¹² A third seeks to displace time through drink: "Come let us drink away the time."²¹³

But perhaps the most intriguing attempt to defeat the clear transience of drink's consolations was the incorporation of a language of religious ceremony into descriptions of drinking. We have already noted a degree of ritual, with drinking as the communal act of a withdrawn, introspective group, bound by its rules and hierarchies, and assembled in its quasi-church (tavern, university, retreat). Although we might expect invocations of Bacchus, reflecting the university educations of drinking group members, the sense of the ceremonial went much further than that. What is more striking is the general description of drinking in sacramental terms. Sack itself is addressed as a god, and drinking becomes the act of letting this god enter the drinker/worshipper. We read in *Parnassus Biceps*:

> Loe I, dread Sack, an humble Priest of thine
> First kisse this cup thy shrine,

> That with more hallowed lips and inlarg'd soule
> I may receive the whole:
> Till *Sibill*-like full with my God I lye[.]

By figuring the act of drinking as the reception of a god, the theme of drink's restorative powers is given a greater charge:

> If thou wouldst prosper, to this Altar bring
> Thy gratefull offring,
> Touch but the shrine, that does the God enclose,
> And streight thy feaver goes.[214]

Even the condition of being "dead drunk" is given a religious respectability.

> To Wine we'll build a Shrine,
> And an Altar divine
> . . . We'll drink off our debts,
> Where he that's dead drunk, shall be
> Laid out in state, as well as he
> Whose dignity the only objects be
> Of new Idolatry.
> . . . Fifty red-faces free, shall his Torch-bearers be;
> Six maudlin mourners his Coffin shall carry,
> There we will tipple free unto the memory
> Of our fraternity drown'd in Canary:
> In the Divel-Tavern we commonly will shew him.[215]

The religious ritualization of drinking brings together certain themes that run through miscellany writings. It is a vivid manifestation of the evocation of orderly communities in retreat: drinkers withdraw in their groups to a place apart, where decorum and rules are maintained. As Lois Potter has made clear, drinking culture reflects a dissatisfaction with the sanctioned ritual of public life, and thus more generally with political, religious, and cultural "orthodoxy."[216] A significant failure of 1650s Parliamentary leaders was their failure to create a popular Commonwealth culture to replace banned activities like those encouraged in the *Book of Sports*.[217] Royalists mocked militantly Protestant schemes like public fasts, and a ceremonial recasting of drink provided an attractive alternative rite by lending respectability and authority to drinking groups and to their protests at Commonwealth culture: they could "drink and pray . . . / For the King in mystical fashions."[218] A language of religious ceremony also presented the transient in transcendent terms—imbuing the momentarily raised glass with a higher, timeless truth.[219] It was perhaps the clearest attempt to make drink's consolation more than fleeting; to defeat time and to render the instant of wine-heartened defiance something more than an exceptional moment amid a larger period of misfortune. It thus, more generally, helped lend meaning to the miscellany voice of protest.

Time

A concern with transience is part of a larger printed miscellany meditation on the competing virtues of past, present, and future. *Wits Recreations*—the earliest of the miscellanies studied here—proudly asserts it is "Selected from the finest Fancies of Moderne MUSES"[220] and makes little attempt to connect with anything but the present (even though its sources were often decades old).[221] Earlier anthologies exhibit an even stronger pride in their moment of production. *A Poetical Rapsodie* (1608), for example, confesses to its readers

> those [poems] *under the name of* Anonymous *were written . . . almost twenty years since, when Poetry was farre from that perfection, to which it hath now attained.*[222]

But by the 1650s, as *The Card of Courtship* makes clear, the contemporary seems to have become a dirty word. That miscellany's editor describes himself as one who has "been forced through whole Forests of bryars, by the malice of the times," and offers his book of decorous and polished compliments in the hope that it will "thwart the current of the times," "when *Mars* and *Bellona* sit as Rectors o're all hearts."[223] Almost every other 1650s miscellany makes a point to distance itself from the present, and instead connects with a sense of the past—recalling Pepys, in 1661: "To hear the discourse of so many high Cavaleers of things past—it was of great content and joy to me."[224]

In part, nostalgia was inevitable. Printed miscellanies were in the business of re-presenting poems culled from various earlier sources, and in the 1650s relied, in particular, on Oxford undergraduates' verse manuscripts, largely composed in the first decades of the seventeenth century. Printed miscellany re-offerings of these earlier texts meant, naturally, that the printed poems vividly recalled those earlier times. Later printed miscellanies drew much more on *contemporary* sources—in particular, on play texts and perhaps performances. Nostalgia was thus less a consequence of their compilation.

But, when evident, nostalgia was often more than a consequence of the mechanics of verse circulation and miscellany compilation. *Wits Interpreter*'s frontispiece includes portraits of "Spencer," "Shakespeare," "S^r. T. More," "L^d. Bacon," and "Sydney." In his address "TO THE READERS," *The Harmony of the Muses*' editor Robert Chamberlain presents his authors as products of a past where "*There were never in one Age so many contemporary Patterns of Invention, or ever Witt that wrought higher or cleerer.*"[225] *Wit and Drollery* is "*a collection from the best Wits, of what above* 15. *yeares since.*"[226] *Parnassus Biceps* came from a better past

> when *Oxford* and *Cambridge* were Universities, and a Colledge more learnd then a Town-Hall; when the Buttery and Kitchen could speak Latine, though not Preach; and the very irrational Turnspits had so much knowing modesty, as not to dare to come into a Chappel, or to mount any Pulpits but their own. Then were these Poems writ, when peace and plenty were the best Patriots and maecenasses to great Wits; when we could sit and make verses under our own Figtrees, and be inspired from the juice of our own Vines.[227]

And *Le Prince d'Amour* finds a transcendence in the past.

> In the whole *Collection* there is not any thing of the gall and venome which has mixed it self with the Ink of these last twenty years, but *wit* born long before our unhappy *intestine divisions,* and has that mark of eternity, that it is not like to grow old.[228]

These common appeals to, and celebrations of, a past—never clearly defined, but generally located in *near* history—had the obvious function of distancing texts from the contemporary and thus implicitly, sometimes explicitly, offering criticism of Interregnum government, and "*these sullen dislaureating times.*"[229] But nostalgia was a *particularly* resonant call since one of the Commonwealth's defining characteristics was its clear lack of precedent, in terms of both political models and an English republican rhetoric. Cromwell, acutely aware of this want in a society which placed great (indeed almost total) emphasis on custom, tradition, and ancient constitutionalism, was forced to justify his actions through awkward appeals to the future.[230] And this culture of anticipation linked novelty with Republicanism, at least in Royalist eyes, and rendered nostalgia a doubly potent means both to laud Crown-ruled England and to discredit the Commonwealth.

After 1660 miscellanies show a quite dramatic reassessment of the merits of past and present. The compiler of *A Jovial Garland* (1670)—one "R.S."—shows little concern with connecting with a better bygone age. He assures readers that "I gathered... [the poems] out of the hands of the youthful and sprightful Youngsters *of these times.*"[231] Texts begin to market themselves as slices of the contemporary: as "a more Exact COLLECTION Of the Newest *Songs, Poems, and Catches,*

Now in Use, Both in CITY and COUNTRY, then any yet Extant"[232]; as "A perfect Collection of all the newest and best Songs, and Catches, that are, and have been lately in request at Court, and both the Theatres."[233] And a claim to novelty even becomes part of the title of later texts. There is *The New Academy of Complements* ("Compiled *By the most refined Wits of the Age*")[234] (1669), *A New Collection of Poems and Songs* (1674), and *A New Collection of the Choicest Songs Now in Esteem in Town or Court* (1676). The virtue of these collections apparently lies in their immediacy.

Folly in Print's deliberately, and jokingly, pessimistic self-presentation (*"Whoever buyes this Book will say, / There's so much Money thrown away: . . . / And to say truth, it is so bad, / A worse is nowhere to be had"*)[235] sees its likely transience as the consequence of the novelty it proclaims:

> When the Gazets are cry'd, we buy in expectation of some thing new, yet though the news be ne're so good, in three days time 'tis laid aside, though we were pleased with our penny worth: I cannot expect a better fortune in this composition[.][236]

One of this collection's poems explores the theme of novelty further by telling "cheerful news to warm . . . [the] blood" of "*Englands rejoycing for* Londons *Rebuilding*"—an optimistic take on the aftermath of the Great Fire. Although the verse fittingly likens London's rise to the ascent of "A Phoenix from her ashes"—and so maintains the restoration motif—the poem makes it clear that the city's novelty, not any nostalgia, is the best of its virtues. New London is a place "Of greater splendour, then the last," where "New Churches with new bels, new tunes shall ring" and "The old are out of fashion now."[237]

The degree of transition in attitudes to the past—that time so lauded in midcentury miscellanies—is apparent when the latest miscellany here considered, *Wit and Mirth* (1682), feels the need to *defend* itself against anticipated charges of printing the products of former times.

> If any object, that many of these *Songs* are old, I answer, if they be so, yet not withstanding they are very good, and herein I imitate the Vintner, who presents you with both old and new Wines, to gain your custom and acceptance.[238]

Last Orders

Printed miscellanies, I have tried to suggest, articulate political concerns in a vocabulary that superficially obscures the political. They offer a politics of association and connotation, not of direct declaration. Thus bawdy verse—for which miscellanies are perhaps best known—is not simply lascivious fun (although it is that as well), but, as part of a larger philosophy of misrule, is an expression of pro-Crown, anti-Puritan, and anti-Interregnum government sentiments. Miscellanies also openly celebrate Royalism: they evoke the court and courtly love, and they laud exclusivity in general. But these celebrations are rendered ambiguous through the apparent demystification of access to this world, through the potentially anarchic transferral of an elite's cultural property to the anonymous mass reader.

Royalism is also evoked in meditations on confinement and exclusion: prison verse in earlier texts and tales of social displacement in later miscellanies construct a world where the true, loyal, Crown-loving man is a victim of misfortune, and so finds consolation in celebrations of withdrawal, exclusivity, and stoicism. Drinking marks out these virtues (loyalty, integrity, separation from the superficial); drunkenness provides further comfort in a world momentarily reordered.

Binding these themes, and so defining these texts, is a sense of grievance. The miscellany voice is a voice of defiant protest, and miscellanies create a literature of outsiders seeking consolation through inclusion, or a denunciation of the excluders. Readers, standing on tip-toes as they peered through court windows, must have felt this sense of exclusion, too.

One last question. To what extent did the English Civil War ensure the popularity of printed miscellanies? To a large degree, miscellanies were the logical consequence of university manuscript verse miscellanies—a product of print technology happening upon these potent sources. They might well have appeared, in some form, Civil War or not—as *Wits Recreations* did, and *The Academy of Complements*, in 1640.

But as we have seen, what defines most miscellanies is their sense of grievance and protest. The Civil War and its consequences thrust a compelling *raison d'être* upon printed miscellanies, and they were able to organize themselves as a voice of disenfranchised Royalism. Consequently, a sense of purpose, mode, and momentum developed, dependent upon the Crown's misfortune. And that ready supply of sources—the university manuscript miscellany—with its Royalism, its club-based wit, and its musings on the more decadent sides of life, offered a fitting vocabulary for protest. Once established, this sense of grievance was sufficiently defining as to be maintained by many later texts, despite changing political contexts. When it did begin to decline, the threads binding printed miscellanies started to loosen, and these books separated away toward new types of texts, like songbooks or political miscellanies. Without Royalist defeat in the Civil War, printed miscellanies would probably have appeared, but as looser, more decorous, duplicates of undergraduate wit—with less anger, less consistency of purpose, and, I am sure, less success.

A consistency of purpose and, more generally, a sense of political advocacy had, I think, relatively little to do with the political agendas of miscellany compilers and publishers. They were a varied bunch: the renowned Humphrey Moseley (of Milton, Vaughan, Cartwright fame), the eccentric William Hickes (dance instructor, tapster, poet), the largely unknown Hobart Kemp, and John Raymond. Any uniformity of printed miscellany politics was, I think, much less an expression of their unified political purpose, and much more the consequence of manuscript being transferred to a broader public; of printing press technology meeting manuscript verse transmission—like a clumsy swimmer clambering into a pool, all noise and splash until, sometime later, a calm begins to emerge.

AFTERWORD

While it is certainly useful to talk of printed miscellanies as a recognizable and to some extent coherent seventeenth-century publishing phenomenon, it has, I hope, become apparent that these books were subject to developments, changes, and movements between 1640 and 1682. While some features of these texts remain constant—their editorial practices; their place within a wider context of verse circulation; their popularity—the printed miscellany was not a static publication, but an evolving form. The early angst-ridden preface, full of contrite justifications for the movement into print, declines. Later prefaces are shorter, more self-assured, more conscious of their text as a legitimate book with its own market and precedents and norms. Self-presentation, in general, becomes far less ornate. Poetry's early accompanying pieces—those jests, riddles, letters, histories—drop from later collections and poetry begins to move away from this practical frame—away from this sense of society yielding new possibilities—and starts to stand on its own. In fact, through the years there is a decline in any declared serious purpose for these collections: formerly presented as guides to social advancement or at least specimens of elite life, they subsequently appear as collections of poems, interesting in themselves and not dependent on constructed connotations, invoked contexts, or grand intentions. Confused shufflings between patron and reader simplify when the latter becomes the former; careful depictions of the prestigious, witty, male, gallant reader drop and there is a more confident embracing of the anonymous owner. Sources alter: new plays offer a wealth of potential verses, and consequently an earlier reliance on undergraduate manuscript collections—or collections related to them—declines.

If printed miscellanies are an identifiable type of publication, at the heart of that identity is a blurring with other texts, an embracing of diversity, an evolution over time.

I stopped my survey at 1682, but this chronological edge is pencil-thin: miscellanies dissipate into subsequent texts, just as they recall literary precedents. Later songbooks, ballad collections, instructional texts, and verse anthologies are full of miscellany poems, titles, tunes, ambitions. *Wit and Mirth* (1682) is a direct ancestor of the hugely popular eighteenth-century *Pills to Purge Melancholy* series, edited by Thomas D'Urfey (6 vols., 1719–20). *Laugh and Be Fat: or, an Antidote against Melancholy* (twelfth edition, 1741) recalls *An Antidote against Melancholy* (1661) which itself invokes earlier collections such as *An Antidote against Melancholy. Or, A Treasury of 53 Rare Secrets & Arts* (1659)—an interesting anthology of health and housekeeping prescriptions: "A most rare Powder to keep teeth from perishing"; "How to make Hair to grow"; "How to make Rats forsake a House"; "How to roast a Capon carried in a Budget at a saddle bow, in the space of riding 5 or 6 miles."[1]

Across the variety of texts included within my 1640–82 parameters, perhaps the most significant function of printed miscellanies is to complicate certain established narratives about the history of seventeenth-century literature.

The rise of the author? But poetry, once in print, "must the peoples not the authors bee."[2] Printed miscellanies largely efface authorship as an organizing principle; they offer unattributed materials that invite readers to look forward to potential moments of use, not back to origins. The triumph of print over manuscript? But Boydell meticulously copied those twisting love poems into his manuscript miscellany ("This is Love, & worth commending"); *Wits Interpreter* announced itself "ransack'd from private papers."[3] Printed miscellanies invoke, draw upon, and supply manuscript collections, and suggest a complicated two-way dynamic between the two media. The capacity of print to fix, set, and stabilize texts? But "*Errour* is an *accident* so *inseparable* from the *Press*."[4] The construction of increasingly passive, acquiescing readers? Miscellany readers are encouraged to adopt, adapt, rewrite, edit, apply, *use* their printed texts; miscellanies suggest active, interventionist readers, removing extracts, reworking print, offering miscellany wit as their own. The separation of printed texts from ideas of social application and utility? "Thou hast choise and select complements set thee downe in a forme which upon an occasion offered thou may imitate or with a little alteration make use of."[5]

Now I certainly do not dispute that these established narratives are important for any account of early modern writing, but miscellanies are significant because they provide moments of resistance to these macro narratives.[6]

In fact, the later texts that developed out of printed miscellanies illustrate the validity of these larger narratives. The most striking difference between mid-seventeenth-century printed miscellanies and these later relatives is the rise of authorship as a category of literary definition and, in general, an increasing interest in origin. *Deliciæ Poeticæ Or, Parnassus Display'd* (1706) matches earlier miscellanies in many respects—in terms of the kind of poetry it includes, and in its intention to make "publick for the Entertainment of others" what had been previously cloistered. What distinguishes the book from earlier miscellanies is the frequency of authorial ascriptions: *"Advice to the City, by Mr. Durfey"*; *"A Song by Mr. Strowd"*; *"An Ode by Mr. Randolph"*; *"A Song on Ingratitude, by Mr. Cowley."*[7] Allan Ramsay's *The Tea-Table Miscellany: Or, A Collection of Scots Songs* (1733) is similarly preoccupied. The collection includes in its index detailed notes on origins: "The Songs mark'd C, D, H, L, M, O, &c. are new Words by different Hands; X, the Authors unknown; Z, old Songs; Q, old Songs with Additions." *The Bee. A Collection of Choice Poems* (1715) is even more assiduous. At the end of "The Cheerful Heart" comes the note *"Brome. ap. Poems. part 2. song 31. p. 104"*; after "Colin's Complaint," *"Rowe. ap. Poems and Translations, by several Hands. Pemberton.1714. p. 88."*[8] And so on, for almost all inclusions. At the end of the volume there is not only a meticulous "Index of Authors" listing names, the years of literary activity of the author, and the textual source (volume, page, edition, date of printing), but also a remarkable authorcentric postscript:

> If any one will be so kind as to send Informations concerning the Authors of Anonymous Pieces, they shall be faithfully inserted; and all Good Poems, directed To The Bee, at the Union Coffee-House, over against the Exchange, shall be carefully printed in Following Collections.

This is a long way from "But let them be writ by whom they will," and printed miscellanies' relaxed indifference to author and origin.[9]

As a consequence of this new prominence afforded to authorship, formalized in the first Copyright Law of 1707, poetry was increasingly separated from ideas of social use. Thus volumes accommodating both poetry and nonverse inclusions—potted histories, jokes, riddles, codes, model letters, notes on mythology—became increasingly rare. *Wits Cabinet: A Companion for Gentlemen and Ladies* appeared some twenty years before the Copyright Law, in 1684, but it illustrates poetry's increasing isolation from ideas of practical use and social advantage. The book offers a range of materials that recalls printed miscellany inclusions: "The Interpretation of Dreams"; "The Art of Physiognomy and Palmistry"; "The Compleat Metalist"; "The Whole Art of Love"; "A Guide to Good Behaviour"; "The Art of Drinking." Poetry, however, is marginalized: a brief selection of songs is included at the very end of the volume, and the title page presents these as a last-minute addition ("To which is added, A Choice Collection of the best Songs")—decorative icing to this practical text, but not a central ingredient.

The place of the printed miscellany is also occupied by collections of explicitly political verse. *A Choice Collection of 120 Loyal Songs* shares with printed miscellanies a Royalist political agenda—the first song begins "Let *Oliver* now be forgotten"—but the collection's political function is far more specific and overt. In an interesting twist on earlier miscellany ideas of social use, the book's ballads are intended "to reduce the deluded Multitude to their just Allegiance" after "the Two late Plots, (viz) The Horrid *Salamanca Plot* in 1678 and the *Fanatical Conspiracy* in 1683." Songs and ballads are deemed the most effective way to catch the ear of "the mis-inform'd Rabble":

> they began to hear Truth in a Song, in time found their Errors, and were charm'd into Obedience. Those that despise the Reverend Prelate in the Pulpit, and the Grave Judge on the Bench; that will neither submit to the Laws of God or Man, will yet lend an itching Ear to a New Song, nay, and often become a Convert by It, when all other means prove ineffectual.[10]

The volume never confronts the awkward paradox of this introduction: are we, as readers, members of "the mis-inform'd Rabble" that the book laments? Are we the mechanism for the subsequent dissemination of materials to this lower group? Or is this political function in fact a fiction to lend charge and significance to a collection of ballads? However this preface is read, the volume's songs and ballads, while overlapping with many printed miscellany inclusions, have a political preoccupation more explicit than the rather amorphous spirit of protest running through printed miscellanies. The same kind of clearly politicized verse is found in *Ratts Rhimed to Death. Or, the Rump-Parliament Hang'd up in the Shambles* (1660) and *Rome Rhym'd to Death* (1683).

As printed miscellanies imply these and other successors, and recall their many precursors, they vividly allude to numerous other, larger projects of scholarship—projects involving broadside ballads; Inns of Court manuscripts; Royalist exiles; songbooks; Derbyshire yeoman; marginalia; theories of textual transmission; popular guides to dance; evolving notions of authorship, reading, media; and countless other topics. And in these vivid allusions, printed miscellanies make apparent the need for organization and communication within the academic community—for the coordinating of information and skills; the marshaling of distant, murmuring voices into something like a conversation.[11] While fault lines of period, specialization, and subject hinder such interdisciplinary projects, the advent of new electronic tools for research and communication—like the online *Index of Poetry in Printed Miscellanies, 1640–1682*, and Steven W. May's magnificent *Bibliography and First-Line Index of English Verse, 1559–1603*—makes acts of coordination far easier. "Such nimble applications, if rightly directed, are most absolutely useful,"[12] and important new projects open up.

APPENDIX

Printed Miscellanies, 1640–1682: Bibliographical Details

Date	Title	Compiler	Printer and Publisher	Place of Publication	Later Editions
1640	Wits Recreations		printed by R[ichard] H[odgkinson][1] for Humphrey Blunden[2]	Castle in Cornhill	1641, 1645, 1650, 1654, 1663, 1667, 1683
1640	The Academy of Complements	Philomuses	printed by TB for H. Mosley	Princes Armes, St. Paul's Church Yard	1641, 1645, 1646, 1650, 1654, 1658, 1663, 1664, 1670, 1684 1685, 1705, 1727, 1750, 1760, 1790, 1795
1653	The Card of Courtship	Musophilus	printed by J.C. for Humphrey Moseley	Princes Armes in St. Paul's Churchyard	
1654	Harmony of the Muses	R[obert] C[hamberlain][3]	TW for William Gilbertson,[4] sold by George Gilbertson	Bible in Giltspur Street	
1655	Wits Interpreter	John Cotgrave[5]	printed for Nath. Brooke	Angel in Cornhill	1662, 1671
1655	Marrow of Complements	Philomuses	printed for Humphrey Moseley	Princes Armes, St. Paul's Churchyard	
1655	Musarum Deliciæ		H[enry] H[erringman][6]	Anchor in the New Exchange	1656
1656	Choyce Drollery		printed by J.G. for Robert Pollard, and John Sweeting	Ben Johnson's head behind the Exchange, and Angel in Popeshead Alley	

Date	Title	Compiler	Printer and Publisher	Place of Publication	Later Editions
1656	Sportive Wit	J[ohn] P[hillips]	printed [John Grismond of Ivy Lane, and Jas. Cotterill of Lambeth Hill] for Nath. Brook.	Angel in Cornhill and the New Exchange, and other places	
1656	Wit and Drollery	John Phillips[7]	printed for Nath. Brook	Angel in Cornhill	1661, 1682
1656	Parnassus Biceps	Abraham Wright[8]	printed for George Eversden	Maidenhead in St. Paul's Churchyard	
1658	Wit Restor'd		printed for R. Pollard, N. Brooks, and T. Dring	Old Exchange and in Fleetstreet	
1658	Mysteries of Love and Eloquence	E[dward] P[hillips][9]	printed for N. Brooks	Angel in Cornhill	1699, as *The Beau's Academy*
1659	J. Cleaveland Revived	E. Williamson	printed for Nathaniel Brooke	Angel in Cornhill	1660
1660	Poems by Pembroke and Ruddier	John Donne, Jr.[10]	printed by Matthew Inman, to be sold by James Magnes	Russel-street, near the Piazza, in Covent Garden	
1660	Le Prince d'Amour	W[illiam] L[eake]	printed for William Leake	Crown in Fleet-street, betwixt the two Temple Gates	
1661	Merry Drollery the First Part	WN, CB, RS, JG	printed by JW for PH	New Exchange, Westminster Hall, Fleetstreet, and Paul's Churchyard	1670, 1691

Date	Title	Compiler	Printer and Publisher	Place of Publication	Later Editions
1661	The Second Part of Merry Drollery	WN, CB, RS, JG	printed by JW for PH	New Exchange, Westminster Hall, Fleetstreet, and Paul's Churchyard	1670, 1691
1661	An Antidote against Melancholy	ND	printed by Mer. Melancholicus	London, Westminster	1669
1667	Folly in Print	[John Raymond?][11]			
1669	The New Academy of Complements		printed for Samuel Speed[12]	near the Inner Temple-gate in Fleetstreet	1671, 1681, 1694, 1715, 1719, 1748
1670	Jovial Garland	R.S.			
1671	Oxford Drollery	William Hickes	printed for J.C., to be sold by Thomas Palmer	Crown in Westminster Hall	1674, 1679
1671	Westminster Drollery		printed for H[enry] Brome[13]	Gun in St. Paul's Churchyard	
1672	New Court Songs	R[obert] V[eel]	printed for R. Paske and W. Cademan	Stationers Arms and Ink-Bottle in Lumbard Street, and the Lower Walk of the New Exchange	
1672	Westminster Drollery the Second Part		printed for William Gilbert, & Thom: Sawbridge[14]	Half-Moon in St. Paul's Churchyard & the three Flower de Luces in Little Britain	

Date	Title	Compiler	Printer and Publisher	Place of Publication	Later Editions
1672	Covent Garden Drollery	A[phra] B[ehn?][15]	printed for James Magnes	near the Piazza in Russel Street	
1672	Windsor Drollery		printed for JM	London and Westminster	
1672	A Collection of Poems		printed for Hobart Kemp	Ship in the Upper Walk of the New Exchange	1673, 1693
1673	London Drollery	W[illiam] H[ickes]	printed for F[rancis] Eglesfield[16]	Marygold in St. Paul's Churchyard	
1673	Methinks the Poor Town				
1673	Holborn Drollery		printed for Robert Robinson	shop near Grays Inne Gate in Holborn	
1674	A New Collection		printed by JC for William Crook	Green Dragon without Temple Bar	1678, as *Melpomene*
1674	Wit at a Venture	CF	printed for Jonathan Edwin[17]	three Roses in Ludgate Street	
1675	A Perfect Collection of the Several Songs now in Mode				
1675	Mock Songs and Joking Poems	by the author of Westminster Drollery	printed for William Birch	the Peacock in the Poultry, near old Jury	

Date	Title	Compiler	Printer and Publisher	Place of Publication	Later Editions
1676	A New Collection				
1677	The Wits Academy			London and Westminster	1696, 1701, 1704
1677	The Last and Best Edition of New Songs				
1682	Grammatical Drollery	W[illiam] H[ickes]	printed for Tho. Fox	Angel and at the Star in Westminster Hall	
1682	Wit and Mirth		printed by A[nn] G[odbid] and J[ohn] P[layford] and sold by Henry Playford	Temple Church	1684

NOTES

Introduction

1. William Andrews Clark Memorial Library, Los Angeles, MS M3835 M3 L651 [1674–76]. The manuscript is unpaginated. Joseph Foster, *Alumni Oxonienses: The Members of the University of Oxford, 1500–1886* (Liechtenstein: Kraus Reprint, 1968), 3:980, records a "Martin, Thomas. s. William, of Ashling, Sussex, minister. QUEENS COLL., matric. 27 May 1669, aged 15; B.A. from NEW INN HALL 1673, MA 1676." Martin signs off a letter "To M^rs AP" "Octob 18 / New in."

2. A letter to his "Loving Sister" from 8 July concludes with Martin bemoaning "the position of your sisters company at Oxon who by her being betwixt chichester & me doth as an unpleasing bulwark stop those letters which would otherwise reach one."

3. Care, *Female Pre-eminence*, 1–2, 7, 22, 28, 35.

4. Ayton's poem first appeared in print in a miscellany: *Wit and Drollery* (1656), 70–71.

5. For another translation of Horace Book 2, ode 14, see John Tutchin, *Poems on Several Occasions* (1685), 43, "Translations OUT OF HORACE." Tutchin begins his version "*Posthumus!* How quick our yeares / Do slide away!"

6. For other expressions of this fashionable theme, see Thomas Flatman's "The Fatigue. A SONG," beginning "Adieu fond World, and all thy wiles," in *Poems and songs* (1686), 106; and, a century later, Edward Perronet's "An Acrostic on the Word 'Acrostic,'" beginning "Adieu, vain world, and all thou art," in *Occasional verse, moral and sacred* (1785), 203.

7. Respectively, verses beginning "Where ever I am or what ever I do"; "Beneath a myrtle shade"; "Oh love if ere thou wilt ease a heart"; "As some brave admirall"; and "After death nothing is & nothing death." For manuscript circulation of the two Rochester poems, see Margaret Crum, ed., *First-Line Index of English Poetry, 1500–1800, in Manuscripts of the Bodleian Library Oxford* (Oxford: Oxford University Press, 1969), 1:34, 84.

8. Poems beginning "The beams of Loves speaking eyes"; "Let Fortune & Phillis frown if they please"; and "Do silly Cupid try again." These poems appear in *New Court Songs* (1672), 3–4, 86–87, and 93. Martin may have turned to another manuscript source which had, in turn, drawn on *New Court Songs*, but the textual correspondence between Martin's verses and this printed miscellany suggests, I think, a direct transference of materials.

Chapter 1

1. Peter Anthony Motteux, John Oldmixon, and Edward Filmer, *The Novelty: Every Act a Play* (1697), act 2, 13.
2. *Academy of Complements*, 55, 133, 179, 46, 124.
3. Note, in particular, *Wits Interpreter, Mysteries of Love and Eloquence*, and *New Academy of Complements* (1669).
4. *Wits Interpreter* (1662), 340–88.
5. *Wit at a Venture*, 29–30, "Impatience. A Song"; *Wits Interpreter*, 15–16, "A Lovers passion" (by—but not here ascribed to—Thomas Carew); *Covent Garden Drollery*, 71, "A SONG."
6. It is worth drawing attention to certain well-known texts I do not include. In order to be considered "core" miscellanies, texts must advertise themselves as multiple-author collections: thus Thomas Carew's *Poems* (1640), while including verses by Robert Herrick, William Strode, Walton Poole, James Shirley, and others, is left out since it offers itself as a single-author edition. By contrast, I do include *J. Cleaveland Revived* since it advertises itself as the work of "*Cleaveland* . . . With some other Exquisite Remains of the most eminent Wits of both the Universities" (title page). I exclude collections in which poetry is a minority constituent: thus, William Winstanley's *The New Help to Discourse* (1672) is omitted. I exclude collections which offer solely dramatic excerpts, such as John Cotgrave's *The English Treasury of Wit and Language* (1655). I exclude translations, such as John Dryden's *Miscellany Poems* (1684) and *Sylvae; or, the Second Part of Poetical Miscellanies* (1685). And I exclude texts with an exclusively educative purpose, like Joshua Poole, *The English Parnassus: Or, A Helpe to English Poesie* (1657). Books commemorating some single event—like *Annalia Dubrensia* (1636), celebrating Robert Dover's Cotswold games—are also omitted, as are the similarly focused "academic miscellanies" such as *Justa Edouardo King* (1638), which included Milton's "Lycidas." For this latter phenomenon, see Alberta T. Turner, "Milton and the Convention of the Academic Miscellanies," *Yearbook of English Studies* 5 (1975): 86–93.
7. V. De Sola Pinto, "*Covent Garden Drollery: A Miscellany of 1672.* Edited G. THORN DRURY," *Review of English Studies* 4 (1928): 468–72.
8. *Facetiæ. Musarum Deliciæ: or the Muses Recreation*, ed. T. Park and E. Dubois, 2 vols. (London: Longman, 1817), which contains editions of three miscellanies—*Musarum Deliciæ, Wit Restor'd*, and *Wits Recreations*. There are three other hybrid editions, ed. Joseph Woodfall Ebsworth: *Merry Drollery compleat* (Boston, 1875); *Westminster Drolleries*, both parts of 1671, 1672 (Boston, 1875); and *Choyce Drollery: Songs and Sonnets. . . . To which are added the extra songs of Merry Drollery, 1661, and an Antidote against Melancholy, 1661* (Boston, 1876).
9. *Facetiæ*, vii.
10. *Facetiæ*, v.
11. H. J. Massingham, *A Treasury of Seventeenth Century English Verse from the Death of Shakespeare to the Restoration (1616–1660)* (London, 1919), xiii.

12. C. C. Smith, "The Seventeenth-Century Drolleries" (PhD diss., Harvard University, 1943). This text found printed expression in Smith's short article "The Seventeenth-Century Drolleries," *Harvard Library Bulletin* 6, no. 1 (1952): 40–51. The most recent call for further study has come from Timothy Raylor, *Cavaliers, Clubs, and Literary Culture: Sir John Mennes, James Smith, and the Order of the Fancy* (London: Associated University Press, 1994), 205. The most helpful recent critical works are Raylor, *Cavaliers, Clubs*, chap. 12, "Drollery in Defeat"; Mary Hobbs, *Early Seventeenth Century Verse Miscellany Manuscripts* (Aldershot: Scolar Press, 1992), 97–104; Arthur Marotti, *Manuscript, Print, and the English Renaissance Lyric* (Ithaca, NY: Cornell University Press, 1995), 265–81; Arthur Marotti, "Malleable and Fixed Texts: Manuscript and Printed Miscellanies and the Transmission of Lyric Poetry in the English Renaissance," and "Manuscript, Print, and the English Renaissance Lyric," in *New Ways of Looking at Old Texts*, ed. W. Speed Hill (New York: Medieval and Renaissance Texts and Studies, 1993), 159–73 and 209–21; A. B. Coiro, "Milton and Class Identity: The Publication of *Areopagitica* and the 1645 *Poems*," *Journal of Medieval and Renaissance Studies* 22, no. 22 (1992): 261–89. Note also five recent facsimile editions of printed miscellanies: Timothy Raylor, ed., *Musarum Deliciæ (1655) and Wit Restor'd (1658)* (New York: Scholars' Facsimiles and Reprints, 1985); Peter Beal, ed., *Parnassus biceps, or Severall choice pieces of poetry, by Abraham Wright 1656* (Aldershot: Scolar Press, 1990); Colin Gibson, ed., *Witts Recreations Selected from the finest Fancies of Moderne Muses 1640* (Aldershot: Scolar Press, 1990); Hilton Kelliher, ed., *J. Cleaveland Revived. Second Edition, 1660* (Aldershot: Scolar Press, 1990); Ernest W. Sullivan, II, ed., *The Harmony of the Muses by Robert Chamberlain* (Aldershot: Scolar Press, 1990).

13. Harold Love, *The Culture and Commerce of Texts: Scribal Publication in Seventeenth-Century England* (Amherst: University of Massachusetts Press, 1998), 8.

14. It is worth noting that nineteenth-century anthologies of early modern ballads, with authorship unavailable as a defining characteristic, are (consequently) much more imaginative in their presentation of poems than author-centered anthologies of the same period: organizing texts thematically; offering textual histories (and making the unusual but wholly logical step of explicitly implicating themselves in the stream of never-neutral reprintings); noting variant readings; and making some efforts toward contextualizations. See Robert Bell, ed., *Early Ballads Illustrative of History, Traditions, and Customs* (London: Bohn's Standard Library, 1877).

15. *Doctor Merry-man: Or, Nothing but Mirth* (1671), Bodleian Wood 382, sig. B3v. My italics. The note is next to the passage "One came to a Wench that was precise, / And by the spirit did the flesh despise, / Moving a secret Match between them two. . . ." This text is not a printed miscellany, but is a similarly cheap, popular text.

16. While I have tried to identify as many poems as I can, many have remained true to their seventeenth-century nature and are still devoid of ascription. Of the 4,639 poems, I have ascribed authors to 1,434 of them.

17. *The Poetical Works of William Strode (1600–1645)*, ed. Bertram Dobell (London: Editor, 1907). Dobell notes, "[I]t gives me much delight to rescue from oblivion another

undeservedly forgotten poet," xiii. Far better than Dobell's text is "A Critical Edition of the Poetical Works of William Strode, Excluding 'The Floating Island,'" ed. M. A. Forey, BLitt thesis (St. Hilda's, Oxford University, 1966).

18. *Wits Interpreter*, sig. A5; *J. Cleaveland Revived*, title page; *Academy of Complements*, sigs. A5–A5v.

19. See my appendix of printed miscellanies, 1640–1682, for a complete list.

20. H. R. Plomer, *A Dictionary of the Booksellers and Printers Who Were at Work in England, Scotland and Ireland, 1641–67* (London: Bibliographical Society, 1907), 34. There is some uncertainty surrounding the involvement of Brooke with *Mysteries of Love and Eloquence* and *Wit Restor'd*: these texts might have been published by Nathan Brooks, bookseller from Bunhill, near Moor Fields, who was tried and convicted in 1664 with Thomas Brewster and Simon Dover for publishing seditious books (Plomer, *Dictionary*, 34–35).

21. Plomer, *Dictionary*, 132–33. See also Marotti, *Manuscript, Print*, 259–65.

22. L. Stephen and S. Lee, eds., *Dictionary of National Biography* (London, 1885, 1908, 1921), 26:360. For an exhaustive account of Hickes, see Smith, "Drolleries," 91–137.

23. There may even have been other lost editions, since the 1641 text calls itself the "Fourth edition," and the 1645 the "Sixth." But such title page claims are often unreliable.

24. Apart from the aforementioned *Academy of Complements* and *Wits Recreations*, these were *Wits Interpreter* (1655, 1662, 1671); *Musarum Deliciæ* (1655, 1656); *Wit and Drollery* (1656, 1661, 1682); *The Mysteries of Love and Eloquence* (1658, 1699); *J. Cleaveland Revived* (1659, 1660); *Merry Drollery the First Part* (1661, 1670, 1691); *Merry Drollery the Second Part* (1661, 1670, 1691); *An Antidote against Melancholy* (1661, 1669); *The New Academy of Complements* (1669, 1671, 1681, 1694, 1715, 1719, 1748); *Oxford Drollery* (1671, 1674, 1679); *A Collection of Poems* (1672, 1673, 1693); *A New Collection* (1674, 1678); *The Wits Academy* (1677, 1696, 1701, 1704); and *Wit and Mirth* (1682, 1684).

25. *Calendar of State Papers Domestic Series, 1655–1656*, ed. M. A. E. Green (London: Longman, 1882), 298.

26. *A Collection of the State Papers of John Thurloe Esq*, ed. Thomas Birch (London, 1742), 4:717. See chap. 4 for more on the political significance of such charges.

27. Twenty-nine of the forty-one printed miscellanies include prefatory material, most of it prose but some in verse. The fullest prefaces come with *Academy of Complements, Wits Interpreter*, and *Mysteries of Love*.

28. *Folly in Print*, sig. A3.

29. *Wit and Drollery*, sig. A3.

30. *Holborn Drollery*, sig. A3v.

31. *Merry Drollery the First Part*, 126–29, "The New Exchange." These lines appear on 127.

32. *Parnassus Biceps*, title page; *Wits Interpreter*, sig. A5. The following dictionary references come via *The Early Modern English Dictionaries Database*, ed. Ian Lancashire (University of Toronto), online at www.chass.utoronto.ca/english/emed/emedd.html.

33. John Florio, *A worlde of wordes, or most copious, dictionarie in Italian and English* (1598).

34. Randle Cotgrave, *A dictionarie of the French and English tongues* (1611).

35. Thomas Thomas, *Dictionarium Linguæ Latinæ et Anglicanæ* (1587).
36. Thomas, *Dictionarium* on "store-house."
37. *Mysteries of Love*, sig. A4.
38. Thomas, *Dictionarium*.
39. *Mysteries of Love*, sig. A6.
40. *Wits Recreations* (1641), "*Ad Lectorem.*"
41. *Mysteries of Love*, sig. A4; *Wits Interpreter*, sig. A5v.

42. Michael Drayton, in his *Poly-Olbion*, showed an awareness of these rhetorical motifs when he declared he was publishing "at this time, when Verses are wholly deduc't to Chambers and nothing is esteemed in this lunatique Age, but what is kept in Cabinets" (noted in Wendy Wall, *The Imprint of Gender* [Ithaca, NY: Cornell University Press, 1993], 180).

43. *Bristol Drollery* (1674), sig. A3. This text is not a printed miscellany but a collection of poems by Matthew Stevenson, which uses printed miscellany presentation techniques to sell itself.

44. *Mysteries of Love*, sig. A3.
45. *Methinks the Poor Town Has Been Troubled Too Long*, sig. A2.
46. *Sportive Wit*, sig. A2.
47. *New Court-Songs*, sig. A3.
48. *Wits Interpreter*, sig. A6.

49. *Wits Interpreter*, "*The PREFACE*" and "THE STATIONER To the READER." The very existence of lengthy prefaces (which decline in later miscellanies) suggests a compiler anxious that his collection might be misread and thus considering his text—to a degree—ambiguous, uncertain, and problematic.

50. *Mock Songs and Joking Poems*, title page.
51. *The Marrow of Complements*, sig. A3.
52. *London Drollery* (1672), sig. A2.

53. *Methinks the Poor Town*, sig. A2v. There is no Epsom Wells drollery. The writer of this preface was probably thinking of *Merry Newes from Epsom-Wells: being a . . . relation of a Lawyers lying with a London Goldsmith's wife, at Epsom* (1663), given that it has been ascribed to John Mennes (Raylor, *Musarum Deliciæ . . . and Wit Restor'd*, 9); another alternative, with a coincidence of publication dates, is Thomas Shadwell's *Epsom-Wells. A comedy* (1673).

54. *Wit and Mirth*, sig. A2.
55. *Mysteries of Love*, sig. A3v.
56. *Wits Academy*, sig. A4.
57. *Wits Academy*, sigs. A4–A5.
58. Folger MS Va 134. The manuscript dates from about 1625.
59. *Wits Recreations*, [3], no. 6, "*To a verse reader.*"
60. Noted in Peter Beal, "Notions in Garrison: The Seventeenth-Century Commonplace Book," in *New Ways*, ed. Speed Hill, 131–47, 139.

61. *Mysteries of Love*, sig. A5. For very useful overviews of the early modern commonplace book, see Sister Joan Marie Lechner, *Renaissance Concepts of the Commonplace* (New York: Pageant Press, 1962), and William Sherman, *John Dee: The Politics of Reading and Writing in the English Renaissance* (Amherst: University of Massachusetts Press, 1995), 60–65. Note also Robert Darnton, "Extraordinary Commonplaces," *New York Review of Books*, 21 December 2000, 82–87. For an interesting discussion of the decline of interest in commonplaces in the later seventeenth century—and thus the emergence of the pejorative connotations surrounding the word in culture today—see Adam Fox, *Oral and Literate Culture in England, 1500–1700* (Oxford: Clarendon, 2000), 167–72.

62. Harry Ransom Center, Pforzheimer MS 2k Box 71. BULSTRODE, Whitelock, Commonplace book, recto fol. 1 (i.e., fol. 1, from the end of the book), "Observanda Sept 1689."

63. 5.1.14. Note also *Hamlet*, 1.5.108: "My tables—meet it is I set it down." Note, too, *A Comedy, called The Marriage Broker: Or, The Pander*, by "M.W. M.A."—published in *Gratiæ theatrales, or A choice ternary of plays* (1662)—3.1.214–15: "To grace you Sir, his outward worth alone / Shall fill large pages in the Common place Book"; and Thomas Tomkis, *Lingva: Or The Combat of the Tongue, And the five Senses for Superiority* (1607), 3.2.85–89: "Yes a company of studious Paper-wormes and leane Schollers, and niggardly scraping Vsurers, & a troupe of heart-eating enuious persons, and those cancker-stomackt spitefull creatures, that furnish up common place-bookes with other mens faults."

64. *The Diary of Samuel Pepys*, ed. Robert Latham and William Matthews (London: Bell and Hyman, 1985), 1:261 (7 October 1660).

65. Robert Burton, *Anatomy of Melancholy* (1621), 4.

66. Mentioned in H. R. Woudhuysen, *Sir Philip Sidney and the Circulation of Manuscripts, 1558–1640* (Clarendon Press: Oxford, 1996), 20–21.

67. BL 3129.c.33. The manuscript notes on tragedy come on the page facing the frontispiece.

68. *Academy of Complements*, 1, 41, 129, 179.

69. *Mysteries of Love*, sig. A5.

70. Bodleian MS Rawl poet 142—probably composed around 1650—for example, contains poems in at least nine hands alongside notes on history, animals, arithmetic, and codes. The whole collection is crammed with marginal notes and additions, often scribbled upside-down. For a valuable discussion of manuscript verse miscellanies, see Woudhuysen, *Sir Philip Sidney*, 153–73.

71. *New Academy of Complements; Academy of Complements*.

72. *Academy of Complements* (1650), sigs. A4v–A5. The reference to "Hocus Pocus tricks" suggests texts such as *Hocus Pocus Junior. The Anatomy of Legerdemain . . . The Art of Juggling set forth in his proper colours, fully, plainly, and exactly* (1654, fourth edition).

73. *The English Treasury of Wit and Language* (1655), "To the Courteous READER."

74. Burton, *Melancholy*, 8–9.

75. William Winstanley, *The New Help to Discourse* (1672), sigs. A2–A2v.

76. Winstanley, *Discourse*, sig. A6v. Christopher Marlowe, *The Famous Tragedy of the Rich Jew of Malta* (1633), sig. B2.

77. See, for instance, F. Whigham, *Ambition and Privilege: The Social Tropes of Elizabethan Courtesy Literature* (Berkeley: University of California Press, 1984). Note also Anna Bryson, *From Courtesy to Civility: Changing Modes of Conduct in Early Modern England* (Oxford: Clarendon Press, 2000).

78. Henry Peacham, *The Complete Gentleman* (1622), sigs. A4–B2.

79. Peacham, *Gentleman*, 78.

80. Peacham, *Gentleman*, 95–96.

81. Harry Ransom Center, Pforzheimer 795.

82. For a survey of the highly popular practical guidebook, see H. S. Bennett, *English Books and Readers, 1603 to 1640* (Cambridge: Cambridge University Press, 1970), 149–59.

83. *Wits Theater of the little World* (1599), "To the Reader," sigs. A3, Av.

84. *Palladis Tamia*, 338v.

85. Note as a contrast to later miscellanies' bawdy verse the poetic offerings of *The Paradyse of Daynty Deuises* (1576), which cover learning, religion, and the virtuous life: offerings like "The Translation of the blessed Saint Barnards verses," "Of the unconstant stay of fortunes giftes," "Finding worldly ioyes but vanities, he wysheth death," and "The complaint of a Synner." For a survey of Elizabethan printed miscellanies, see Elizabeth Pomeroy, *The Elizabethan Miscellanies: Their Development and Conventions* (Berkeley: University of California Press, 1975).

86. The following brief discussion owes much to a very useful article by Frans De Bruyn: "The Classical Silva and the Generic Development of Scientific Writing in Seventeenth-Century England," *New Literary History* 32 (2001): 347–73.

87. De Bruyn, "Silva," 361.

88. *Musarum Deliciæ*, "The Stationer to the Ingenious Reader."

89. *Sportive Wit*, sig. A3v.

90. *A Jovial Garland*, title page.

91. *Wit and Drollery*, sig. A3.

92. The politics of printed miscellanies and, in particular, of drink, pleasure, and disengagement, is discussed in chap. 4.

93. *Sportive Wit*, sig. A4. John Cotgrave attacks collections which "deface the beauty of Po-sie" (*Wits Interpreter*, sig. A3). Donne's poems were, indeed, translated into Dutch, by Constantijn Huygens (1596–1687).

94. *The Last and Best Edition of New Songs*, title page.

95. *Academy of Complements*, sig. A7v.

96. Richard Tottel, *Songes and Sonnettes* (1557), "The Printer to the Reader."

97. *A Collection of Poems: Written upon several Occasions* (1693), sigs. A4–A4v.

98. *Academy of Complements*, sig. A9.

99. *Mysteries of Love*, sig. A5.

100. *Mysteries of Love*, title page.

101. *Academy of Complements*, 245–46.

102. *Academy of Complements* (1650), 59–68.

103. *Wits Interpreter*, 109ff. "Superscriptions for Letters."

104. *New Academy of Complements*, sig. B.

105. *Mysteries of Love*, 142. For an important discussion of the relationship between vocabularies of love and politics, see Arthur Marotti, "'Love Is Not Love': Elizabethan Sonnet Sequences and the Social Order," *English Literary History* 49, no. 2 (1982): 396–428.

106. *Academy of Complements*, 1–40; 91–98; *The Mysteries of Love and Eloquence*, 20–22.

107. *Academy of Complements*, 41–124.

108. *Marrow of Complements*, 22–23.

109. *Academy of Complements*, 245–50, "Fancies, Devices, and flourishing Expressions on Love-Tokens, &c."

110. *Mysteries of Love*, 6.

111. *Mysteries of Love*, 41.

112. *Mysteries of Love*, 2.

113. *New Academy of Complements*, 4, 44–45.

114. *Mysteries of Love*, 338ff.

115. *Wits Interpreter*, "The Labyrinth of Fancies, New Experiements and Inventions," 93–175.

116. *Mysteries of Love*, 165ff, "MISCELLANIA. Fancy awakened: Natural, Amorous, Moral, Experimental, Paradoxical, Enigmatical, Jesting, and Jovial Questions, with their several Answers and Solutions."

117. *Wits Interpreter*, 123–28; 100; *Mysteries of Love*, 193ff; 289ff.

118. *Wits Interpreter*, 1–25. For a similar exposition on logic, see *Mysteries of Love*, 222–88, "The Art of Reason, in the Art of Logick."

119. *Wits Interpreter*, 337–39, 113–22.

120. Peacham, *Gentleman*, sig. A4v.

121. *A Jovial Garland*, title page; *The New Academy of Complements*, title page; *Marrow of Complements*, sig. A2v.

122. *New Academy of Complements*, 62–63.

123. *Marrow of Complements*, 13–14.

124. *Mysteries of Love*, sig. A5.

125. *Wits Interpreter*, sigs. A3v–5.

126. *Academy of Complements* (1650), 40–53. My italics.

127. *Wits Interpreter*, 29.

128. *Marrow of Complements*, sig. A2.

129. *Mysteries of Love*, 150–54.

130. Some of the quotations in this discussion were found with the help of *The English Poetry Full-Text Database* CD-Rom (Chadwyck-Healey, 1995).

131. *Academy of Complements*, 131–36.

132. Thomas Forde, *Love's Labyrinth: A Tragi-Comedy* (1660), act 5, scene 6. The play was first performed in 1660.

133. Richard Brome, *A Jovial Crew, or, the Merry Beggars* (1652), act 2. The play was first performed in 1641 at the Cock-pit in Drury Lane—a year after *The Academy of Complements* first appeared. This miscellany seems to have swiftly established a reputation.

134. Printed miscellanies are also mentioned in Thomas Shadwell's *The Lancashire-Witches* (1682), act 1, where Sir Timothy Shacklehead's "You are the pretty Witch that enchants my heart" is met by Isabella's aside: "Well said, *Academy of Complements*, you are well read I see." For a reference to Tottel's 1557 collection, see Shakespeare's *The Merry Wives of Windsor*: Slender laments, "I had rather than forty shillings I had my Book of Songs and Sonnets here" (I.i.165–66). Smith, "Drolleries," 40, notes some other contemporary references to printed miscellanies.

Chapter 2

1. An anachronism: Brutus would have been reading from a scroll.
2. For example, Smith, "Drolleries," 47–48.
3. *The Character of a Town Gallant* (1675), 1–5.
4. *Mysteries of Love*, sig. A5.
5. Thomas Otway, *Friendship in Fashion* (1678), act 5.
6. *Mysteries of Love*, sig. A3; *Wit and Mirth*, sig. A2; *Holborn-Drollery*, sig. A7v; *An Antidote against Melancholy*, "To the Reader" (unpaginated); *Holborn-Drollery*, title page.
7. See, for example, J. W. Saunders, "The Stigma of Print: A Note on the Social Bases of Tudor Poetry," *Essays in Criticism* 1 (1951): 139–64, and "From Manuscript to Print. A Note on the Circulation of Poetic Manuscripts in the Sixteenth Century," *Proceedings of the Leeds Philosophical and Literary Society* 1, part 8 (1951): 507–28.
8. Puttenham, *Arte*, 61. Qtd. in Rudick, ed., *Poems of Ralegh*, xxiii.
9. B. Castiglione, *The Book of the Courtier*, ed. V. Cox and trans. Sir Thomas Hoby (London: Everyman, 1994), 58–72.
10. *Wit and Drollery*, sigs. A2–A2v.
11. John Taylor's "A comparison betwixt a *Whore* and a *Booke*" reads "For like a *Whore* by day-light, or by Candle, / tis ever free for every knave to handle: / And as a new *whore* is belov'd and sought, / So is a new *Booke* in request and bought / . . . A *Booke* is dedicated, now and than / To some great worthy, or unworthy man: / Yet for all that, tis common unto mee, / Or thee, or hee, or all estates that bee." This text is printed in *The Penguin Book of Renaissance Verse, 1509–1659*, ed. H. R. Woudhuysen (London: Penguin, 1992), 740.
12. For a vigorous critique of the idea of the stigma of print, see Steven W. May, "Tudor Aristocrats and the Mythical 'Stigma of Print,'" in *Renaissance Papers, 1980*, ed.

Leigh Deneed and M. Thomas Hester (Valencia: Southeastern Renaissance Conference, 1981), 11–18.

13. *Antony and Cleopatra*, 5.2.211–12; *Much Ado about Nothing*, 1.1.205–6; *Love's Labour's Lost*, 2.1.15–16.

14. *Academy of Complements* (1650), sigs. A3v–A4.

15. *Academy of Complements* (1650), sigs. A4–A4v.

16. *Wit at a Venture*, title page; *Holborn Drollery*, title page.

17. *Bristol Drollery* (1674), sig. A2.

18. *The Harmony of the Muses*, sigs. A3–A3v.

19. *Sportive Wit*, sig. A3v.

20. *Mysteries of Love*, sig. A4.

21. *Mysteries of Love*, title page. My italics.

22. *Marrow of Complements*, title page. My italics.

23. *Academy of Complements*, sig. A7.

24. *Card of Courtship*, title page and sig. A.

25. *A Jovial Garland*, title page; *New Academy of Complements*, title page; William Wycherley, *The Country Wife* (1675), act 3, scene 2. Noted in Smith, "Drolleries," 48.

26. *Mysteries of Love*, sigs. A6v–A2.

27. *Wits Interpreter*, sig. A3.

28. David Cressy, *Literacy and the Social Order* (Cambridge: Cambridge University Press, 1980), 72–73.

29. Lois Potter, *Secret Rites and Secret Writing: Royalist Literature, 1641–60* (Cambridge: Cambridge University Press, 1989), 25, notes the vitality of (in particular) the London publishing industry. News books, she notes, had a print run of about 10,000, serving a London population of some 500,000. For the rise in titles printed each year in the sixteenth and seventeenth centuries (from 149 in 1560 to 577 in 1640), see F. J. Levy, "How Information Spread among the Gentry, 1550–1640," *Journal of British Studies* 21 (1982): 11–34, esp. 13–14.

30. Handwritten marginal additions in various related texts suggest a price of between 6d and 1s 6d: among them, *A Collection of Poems on Affairs of State* (1689; Bodleian Wood 382) has the note "bought at Oxon 26 Feb 1688—6d." F. R. Johnson, "Notes on English Retail Book-Prices, 1550–1640," *Library*, 5th ser., 5, no. 2 (1950): 83–112, argues that book prices remained fairly constant between the mid-sixteenth and mid-seventeenth centuries.

31. For notes on expanding book ownership in Kent, see Roger Chartier, ed., *A History of Private Life*. Vol. 3, *Passions of the Renaissance* (London: Belknap, 1989), 128–30.

32. Levy, "How Information Spread," 18–20. John Foster's York inventory from 1616 includes Jonson's *Workes* of the same year. For a corresponding survey of a London bookseller's stock, see M. E. Bohannon, "A London Bookseller's Bill: 1635–1639," *Library*, 4th ser., 18, no. 4 (1938): 417–46.

33. For the vital state of the almanac industry—implying a healthy book trade in cheap, popular books more generally—see E. F. Bosanquet, "English Seventeenth-Century Almanacks," *Library*, 4th ser., 10, no. 4 (1930): 361–92. Bosanquet notes high print runs, thousands of editions across the century, and great provincial popularity. Margaret Spufford, *Small Books and Pleasant Histories: Popular Fiction and Its Readership in Seventeenth-Century England* (London: Methuen, 1981), details the vibrant state of the chapbook industry. Note, particularly, *Map 2* (119), showing "Chapmen licensed in England Wales, 1697–8," and indicating a wide reading public—clustering, of course, in major towns like London and Bristol, but strong across wide sweeps of the land. See also Spufford's "First Steps in Literacy: The Reading and Writing Experiences of the Humblest Seventeenth-Century Autobiographers," *Social History* 4, no. 3 (1979): 407–35, which, in an upbeat fashion, argues that while literacy was economically and therefore socially stratified, this limited educational opportunity did not debar at least a few "of the humblest" from developing literacy (and literary) skills. The case rather rests on anecdotal evidence of (presumably exceptional) individuals like John Bunyan and Stephen Duck. For an account of educational opportunities as economically dependent without Spufford's optimistic case studies, see David Cressy, "Educational Opportunity in Tudor and Stuart England," *History of Education Quarterly* 16, no. 3 (1976): 301–20.

34. *Wits Recreations* (1667), Folger M1717b, title page (verso), and sigs. A8, G, O.

35. *Wit at a Venture* (1674), Folger F5, title page.

36. John Playford, *An Introduction to the Skill of Musick* (1674), HN 25416.

37. *Wits Interpreter* (1655), Bodleian Harding C160, final page.

38. For instance, *Wits Interpreter* (1662), Bodleian Jessel, f279, 493.

39. See Cedric C. Brown, "The Two Pilgrimages of the Laureate of Ashover, Leonard Wheatcroft," in *Betraying Our Selves: Forms of Self-Representation in Early Modern English Texts*, ed. Henk Dragstra, Sheila Ottway, and Helen Wilcox (Basingstoke: Macmillan, 2001), 120–35. The Wheatcroft manuscript is in the Derbyshire Record Office at Matlock, DRO, D.253; parts of it are edited in *The Courtship Narrative of Leonard Wheatcroft Derbyshire Yeoman*, ed. George Parfitt and Ralph Houlbrooke (Reading: Whiteknights, 1986). There are of course many instances of (particularly Oxford) students copying verses from print to manuscript. Wheatcroft's significance lies in his distance from such typical cases.

40. *Academy of Complements*, title page.

41. *Academy of Complements*, sigs. A4–A9. My italics.

42. See, for instance, Lawrence Stone, "The Educational Revolution in England, 1560–1640," *Past and Present* 28 (1964): 41–80, and Keith Wrightson, *English Society, 1580–1680* (London: Hutchinson, 1982), 17–38. Stone suggests 2.5 percent of teenage males continued their studies into higher education—a startling figure when it is understood that this level was unsurpassed until after 1945. Wrightson argues that Protestantism's stress on individual study and humanism's educational emphasis, along with widening land markets after the dissolution of the monasteries, and Royal profligacy

with honors, meant that new families could and did join the ranks of the "socially elite."

43. *The Weeding of the Covent-Garden,* published in *Five New Plays* (1659). The lines also appear in two printed miscellanies: *Parnassus Biceps,* 57–58, "*Upon Aglaura Printed in Folio,*" and *Musarum Deliciæ,* 51–52, "*Upon Aglaura in Folio.*" I quote from the *Parnassus Biceps* text. References in Shakespeare's plays show an interest in margins as places for additional information, whether manuscript or print. In *Love's Labour's Lost,* 5.2.6–8, love verses from the King are described: "as much love in rhyme / As would be crammed up in a sheet of paper, / Writ o' both sides the leaf, margin and all." There are several metaphorical notes in the margins in Shakespeare's plays, such as *Romeo and Juliet,* 1.3.87–88: "And what obscured in this fair volume lies / Find written in the margin of his eyes."

44. Sherman, *John Dee,* 53. This distinction between metaphorical and literal margins is noted in H. J. Jackson, "Writing in Books and Other Marginal Activities," *University of Toronto Quarterly* 62, no. 2 (1992–93): 217–31, 217.

45. See, in particular, Woudhuysen, *Sir Philip Sidney,* 22–25.

46. James A. Riddell and Stanley Stewart, *Jonson's Spenser: Evidence and Historical Criticism* (Pittsburgh: Duquesne University Press, 1995). Also of note is Kevin Sharpe, *Reading Revolutions: The Politics of Reading in Early Modern England* (New Haven, CT: Yale University Press, 2000).

47. For Coleridge, note Jackson, "Writing in Books," esp. 221–29, and *Marginalia.* For Jonson, see, for example, R. C. Evans, "Ben Jonson's Library and Marginalia: New Evidence from the Folger Collection," *Philological Quarterly* 66, no. 4 (1987): 521–28, and R. C. Evans, "Jonson's Copy of Seneca," *Comparative Drama* 25, no. 3 (1991): 257–92. For Dee, see Sherman, *John Dee,* 79–100. For other discussions of manuscript marginalia, see A. H. Tricomi, "Philip, Earl of Pembroke, and the Analogical Way of Reading Political Tragedy," *Journal of English and Germanic Philology* 85, no. 3 (1986): 332–45; Anthony T. Grafton, "Gabriel Harvey's Marginalia: New Light on the Cultural History of Elizabethan England," *Princeton University Library Chronicle* LII, no. 1 (1990): 21–24; and Cis Van Heertum, "A Hostile Annotation of Rachel Speght's *A Mouzell for Melastomus* (1617)," *English Studies* 68, no. 6 (1987): 490–96.

48. *Wits Interpreter* (1655), Bodleian Harding C160. While the following account focuses on marginal annotations in printed miscellanies, I also make references to annotations in other related texts, particularly popular, educative books.

49. William Congreve, *The double dealer* (1694), 3.1.506–7: "you may put that into the marginal Notes, / tho' to prevent Criticisms—only mark it with a small asterism."

50. *A Third Collection of the Newest and Most Ingenious Poems, Songs, Catches &c against Popery and Tyranny* (1689), Bodleian Wood 382; *A Collection of Poems on Affairs of State* (1689), Bodleian Wood 382.

51. *Westminster Drollery the Second Part* (1672), BL 11621.a.45, title page; *Wits Recreations* (1645), Folger M1712, sig. I7v; *The Academy of Eloquence* (1656), Huntington 204576, 1;

Academy of Complements (1685), BL 12314.aa.17, title page; *The Diarium, or Journal* (1656), Bodleian Douce DD126, 87; *Covent Garden Drollery* (1672), Bodleian Mal 385, title page; *A New Collection of Poems and Songs* (1674), Folger B5458 copy 1, 1.

52. See, for example, *Wits Interpreter* (1655), Bodleian Harding C160, at various times the property of the aforementioned "Hannah Lea," "Tho: Nicholson," and "Willm Hill, Wye July 30 1760."

53. *Wits Recreations* (1667), Folger M1717b, sig. O, and sig. Y2. The crossings-out are on the title page of the "FANCIES AND Fantasticks" section.

54. BL 238.b.24, sigs. E and B. "Bhild" might also have been the seller of the book.

55. BL 1486.aaa.7.

56. *Wit at a Venture* (1674), Folger F5, title page.

57. *Wit and Mirth* (1684), BL 11623.bb.42. J[ohn] H[orne]'s *The Divine Wooer; or a Poem setting forth The Love and Loveliness of the Lord Jesus* (1673), BL 11626.a.28 has notes of multiple readers: "Charles Peast His Booke Bought Octob 30th Anno Domini 1673"; "Anthony Hingham his Book anno: dominio 1682/3"; and "Edward Bodham his book."

58. *Card of Courtship*, 126–27.

59. *Wits Recreations*, [p. 70] 209, "Another"; *Parnassus Biceps*, 83, "The Catholick."

60. *Wits Interpreter*, 275.

61. *Card of Courtship*, 121–28.

62. *Wit and Drollery*, title page.

63. *Merry Drollery the First Part*, title page. My italics.

64. *Folly in Print*, 59; *Choyce Drollery*, 70–72. Later editions of *Wit and Mirth* include full musical notation.

65. Nathaniel Church, *Cheap Riches, or, A Pocket Companion made of five hundred Proverbial Aphorismes* (1654), sig. A8.

66. *Wits Recreations* (1645), Folger M1712, sig. G8v.

67. *The Diarium, or Journal* (1656), Bodleian Douce DD126. There are also figures on 48, 78, and (upside-down) 102.

68. BL 238.b.24, sig. A5v.

69. Folger 246056, sig. A5.

70. Sherman, *John Dee*, 102–3.

71. *Westminster Drollery* (1671), Bodleian Douce D27.

72. *Academy of Pleasure* (1656), Bodleian VetA3 f315, 1. There are other doodles—sometimes over the printed text—on 38–39, 70, 72; *Wits Recreations* (1663), Folger M1717a, sig. Z5v; *Wits Recreations* (1645), Folger M1712, sig. N7v; *Wits Recreations* (1667), Folger M1717b, sig. F2v; *Musarum Deliciæ* (1656) Folger M1711, 73; *The Diarium, or Journal* (1656), Bodleian Douce DD126, 87.

73. *The Diarium, or Journal* (1656), Bodleian Douce DD126, 42.

74. Gervase Markham, *Markham's Methode, Or Epitome: Wherein is Shewed his approoved Remedies for all Diseases whatsoeuer, incident to Horses, Oxen, Kine, Buls, Calues, Sheepe, Lambs, Goats,*

Swine, Dogs of all kinde, Conies, all sorts of Poultrie, all Water-fowle, as Geese, Ducks, Swans, and the like, Pigeons, all singing Birds, Hawks, of all kinde; and other Creatures seruiceable for the use of man (1616), BL 779.b.10.

75. Markham, *Methode*, title page.

76. Gervase Markham, *The Complete Farriar, Or The Kings High-Way to Horsmanship* (1639), BL 7294.b.47(2), 175 (but unpaginated).

77. HN 14173.

78. *Wit Restor'd* (1658), Bodleian Wood 90, 103.

79. *Musarum Deliciæ* (1655), Folger M1710.

80. *A Collection of the Newest and Most Ingenious Poems* (1689), Bodleian Wood 382. See, for example, 7, "Over the Lord S———rys Door," where "alisbu" has been written in above the blanks.

81. *Wits Recreations* (1654), BL 11601.bb.19. Numbers 183, 272, and 114.

82. *Westminster Drollery the Second Part* (1672), Huntington 105448, 95.

83. *Wits Interpreter* (1662), Bodleian Douce W112, 311.

84. *Wits Recreations* [p. 32] no. 91, "On a Taylour who dy'd of the stitch."

85. *Wits Recreations* (1654), BL 11601.bb.19. Number 126, and epitaph 105, respectively. The Latin couplets come at numbers 311, 325, and 424.

86. *Wit Restor'd* (1658), Folger M1719, 58.

87. BL G.16385.

88. *Wits Recreations* (1641), Folger M1720 copy 1. On sigs. L4, M2v, and M3 this note of preference is crossed out: perhaps a new owner did not want a predecessor's taste, or perhaps the reader changed his mind.

89. *Recreation for Ingenious Head-peeces. Or, a Pleasant Grove for Their Wits to Walk In* (1663), Bodleian Douce W42. This is the title of later editions of *Wits Recreations*. Hands appear next to numbers 270, 271, 272, 317, 323, 346, 361.

90. "Zelmane . . . saw in him [*Dorus*] the glasse of her own miserie, taking the handle of *Philoclea*, and with burning kisses setting it close to her lips (as if it should stande there like a hand in the margine of a Booke, to note some saying worthy to be marked) began to speake these wordes" (*The Countess of Pembroke's Arcadia*, ed. Albert Feuillerat [Cambridge: Cambridge University Press, 1912], book 1, chap. 19, 119).

91. *Wit and Mirth* (1682), Bodleian Douce P452, 7–10.

92. *Wits Interpreter* (1655), William Andrews Clark Memorial Library *PR 3369 C28 W8, 172.

93. *Wits Recreations* (1641), Folger M1720 copy 1, sig. L5.

94. *The New Academy of Complements* (1671), Huntington 399487. There are marks on 153, 155, 191, 192, 294, 295, 297, 300.

95. *Westminster Drollery the Second Part* (1672), Huntington 105448. A "1" is added above "The late Song," 1; "2" above "A late Song," 2; "3" above "The Subtil Girle," 3; "4" above "A Song," 9; "6" above "The Petticoate wagge," 14; "8" above "A woers Expostulation," 28; "9" above " The Matchlesse Maid," 33.

96. *RECREATION FOR Ingenious Head-peeces* (1654), Huntington 147488, sig. A3.

97. *Wits Recreations* (1654), BL 11601.bb.19.

98. *Parnassus Biceps* (1656), Folger W3686. A copy of *Musarum Deliciæ* (1656) in the William Andrews Clark Memorial Library (PR 1209 M98 1656)—owned by one "Jacob Cranpot" (73)—has marks next to sections of stanzas in *"Dr. Smiths Ballet"* (76, 80). On p. 76, the second half of a stanza is marked in the left margin. The lines are "But now my heart is so big it struts / And hold I cannot for my guts; / With as much ease as men crack Nuts / My rimes and numbers meet." On p. 80, five lines of the penultimate stanza are marked with a line and an "x": "Nay, now I have got them within my Clutches, / I'le neither favour Lady nor Dutches, / Although they may think this over-much is, / They are no more to me, then those that goe on crutches. / *I made this staffe too long.*"

99. *Westminster Drollery the Second Part* BL 11621.a.45. There are notes—which, admittedly, may be in a later hand—next to "pink-patticoat" (5); "up and down" (80) and "in and out" (81); "take their kisses back, and give em their own agen" (82); and "My brests never popt up and down so before" (87).

100. *Recreation for Ingenious Head-peeces. Or, a Pleasant Grove for Their Wits to Walk In* (1663), Bodleian Douce W 42, numbers 237 and 239, among others. This is the title of later editions of *Wits Recreations*.

101. *Wits Recreations* (1654), BL 11601.bb.19. Numbers 230, 343, 9, and 386, respectively.

102. *Westminster Drollery the Second Part* (1672), BL 11621.a.45, 2, 19. My thanks to Tim Amos for the Duke Humphrey point. Note that *The New Academy of Complements* (1669), 90, "Mock Song 8"—a poem that mocks the culture of proverbs—concludes "*Duke Humphrey* din'd in *Powls.*" A copy of Izaak Walton's *Reliquiæ Wottonianæ* (1651) in the Huntington—HN 148559—has the notes of an aphorism-hungry reader (perhaps the "Fra. Browne" signed at the start). There are underlinings of phrases including: "that old men live more by memorie than by hope" (1); "there be a satietie in power" (3); "not well plumed in favour for such a flight" (6); "wring out of her Majesty some petty contentments, (as a man would press sowr Grapes)" (9); "naturall choler be but an unruly excuse for roughness with Princes" (51); and "like a stollen taste of something that provoketh appetite" (95).

103. *The Tragedy of Othello, The Moor of Venice*, 2.1.138–41.

104. *A Perfect Collection of the Several Songs Now in Mode* (1675), Bodleian Mal 423, 7. On p. 40 the opposite process seems to occur, as the same hand underlines the final line of "The jealous Mistris"—"*Plunge in true patience, trust me it shews good nature*"—and appears to offer a lengthy, but illegible, commentary underneath. Here, the text is the starting point for further growth—not a garden from which a single flower might be removed.

105. *Westminster Drollery the Second Part* (1672), BL 11621.a.45, 9.

106. *Wits Recreations* [p. 3] no. 6, "To a verse reader."

107. *Apophthegms New and Old* (1625), in *The Works of Francis Bacon*, James Spedding, Robert Leslie Ellis, and Douglas Denon Heath, eds. (London: Longman, 1857–59), 7 vols, vii.123. Qtd. in Fox, *Oral*, 126.

108. Dekker's mock courtesy books, *The Guls Horn-Booke*, describes the would-be courtier as "he that talks all *Adage* and *Apothegme*" (qtd. in Whigham, *Ambition and Privilege*, 27).

109. Henry Edmundson, *Comes Facundus in Via* (1658), sig. a3–a3v.

110. *Parnassus Biceps* (1656), Folger W3686, 43.

111. *Wits Interpreter* (1655), William Andrews Clark Memorial Library, Los Angeles, *PR 3369 C28 W8, 159.

112. *Wits Recreations* (1654), BL 11601.bb.19, no. 342.

113. *Academy of Complements* (1650), Huntington 434443, 134.

114. *Wit Restor'd* (1658), BL C.40.a.1., 66. The line comes in "*The answer, by Dr. Stroad*"—that popular poem beginning "Returne my joyes and hither bring."

115. *Wits Recreations* (1654), BL 11601.bb.19, epitaph 82.

116. *A Collection of Poems* (1672), Bodleian Harding C167, 63. My italics.

117. *Wit and Mirth* (1706), Folger M1738 D4 Cage, 117.

118. *Wit and Drollery* (1682), Bodleian Douce P207, 333.

119. *Wits Recreations* (1641), Folger M1720 copy 1, sig. N.

120. *Sportive Wit* (1656), Bodleian Malone 391, 90–102.

121. *Wit and Mirth* (1682), Bodleian Douce P452, 7–10.

122. Folger MS Va 148, fols. 12v–13.

123. Harry Ransom Center, Pforzheimer 357.

124. *A Collection of Poems* (1673), Folger C5178 is unusual in including these kinds of revisions to lines: see, for instance, 8, 47.

125. For more on this early modern interest in "use" ahead of "meaning," and its place amid long-term changes in attitudes to texts and reading, see Jane P. Tompkins, ed., *Reader-Response Criticism: From Formalism to Post-Structuralism* (Baltimore: Johns Hopkins University Press, 1980), 201–32.

126. Elizabeth Heale, *Wyatt, Surrey and Early Tudor Poetry* (London: Longman, 1998), 42–46. The Devonshire Manuscript is BL Add MS 17492. A copy of Rachel Speght's *Mouzell for Melastomus* (1617) in the Beinecke Library, Yale (Ih Sp 33 617m), contains extensive manuscript annotations that indicate the opposite practice: that is, a misogynous, presumably male reader answering Speght's protofeminist text. For this, see Barbara Kiefer Lewalski, ed., *The Polemics and Poems of Rachel Speght* (New York: Oxford University Press, 1996), 91–107.

127. *Marrow of Complements*, 47ff; *Wit and Drollery*, 19; *London Drollery*, 62; *J. Cleaveland Revived*, 32–33.

128. *Recreation for Ingenious Head-peeces. Or, a Pleasant Grove for their Wits to Walk In* (1663), Bodleian Douce W42, numbers 63, 65, 73, and 81.

129. *Wits Recreations* (1667), Folger M1717b, sigs. Y3–Y5.

130. Harry Ransom Center, Pforzheimer 506.

131. *Doctor Merry-man: Or, Nothing but Mirth* (1671), Bodleian Wood 382, sig. B3v. My italics. The note is next to the passage "One came to wooe a Wench that was precise, / And by the spirit did the flesh despise, / Moving a secret Match between them two . . ."

132. *Wit Restor'd* (1658), Folger M1719, 95. The author is William Strode. The verse begins "When whispering straines doe softly steale," and also appears in *Parnassus Biceps*, 74–75, "*Of Musick.*"

133. See, for example, the initials added to verses in *A Collection of Poems* (1672), Bodleian Firth f92; the penned ascriptions to "D^r. Hen. King" (183) and "B. Jonson" (205) in *Academy of Complements* (1650), Folger G1402; and the few names noted in *Wits Recreations* (1654), BL 11601.bb.19, and *Sportive Wit* (1656), Bodleian Malone 391.

134. *English Treasury of Wit and Language* (1655), BL 1451.c.49. For an analysis of the manuscript additions, see Gerald Eades Bentley, "John Cotgrave's 'English Treasury of Wit and Language' and the Elizabethan Drama," *Studies in Philology* 40, no. 2 (1943): 186–203. Bentley detects at least four hands annotating the text, and finds the ascriptions overwhelmingly accurate. The writers most commonly noted were Shakespeare, Beaumont and Fletcher, Jonson, Chapman, Greville, Webster, Shirley, and Middleton. The spectacular fullness of this single text's annotations should not obscure the general trend which is for a *lack* of interest in authorship and origin.

135. *Choice Drollery* (1656), Huntington 55770, 63.

136. *Wits Recreations* (1665), sigs. P5v–P6v, P7v, Q1, and Folger MS Va 308 fols. 91–92 (for a full discussion of the compelling instance of transmission, see chap. 3); Pepys, *Diary*, 1:302. The former verse, by Henry Hughes, appeared in two printed miscellanies: *New Academy of Complements* (1669), 114, "Song 45," and *Windsor Drollery* (1672), 70–71, "Song 127."

137. See Ann Moss, *Printed Commonplace-Books and the Structuring of Renaissance Thought* (Oxford: Oxford University Press, 1996); and Mary Thomas Crane, *Framing Authority: Sayings, Self, and Society in Sixteenth-Century England* (Princeton, NJ: Princeton University Press, 1993).

138. Only later did "commonplace" acquire its current, pejorative connotations. See, for instance, Thomas Rawlins, *Tom Essence: Or, The Modish Wife* (1677), 3.2.105–6: "hang that dull, common-place / way of making love," and John Dryden, *Secret Love, or The Maiden-Queen* (1668), 3.351: "Away with your old Common-place wit."

139. *Wits Interpreter*, title page.

140. *Marrow of Complements*, 71–72 and 80–81; *Card of Courtship*, 46–47.

141. *Wits Recreations*, [p. 11] 38, "*Ad Scriptorem.*" By John Pyne. For indexes in printed miscellanies, see, for example, *Antidote against Melancholy*, *A New Collection*, and *New Academy of Complements*.

142. Richard Niccols, Epigram IX (lines 12–14), of *Megera*, in *The Furies: With Vertues Encomium. Or, The Image of Honour.*

143. *Oxford Drollery*, 85–87 (beginning, "*Ione* to the May-pole away let us run").

144. *New Court Songs*, 58–59.

145. *Wits Recreations*, no. 165, "*On his Mistris*" (beginning "My love and I for kisses play'd").

146. *Wit Restor'd*, 39–43 (beginning "A Ballet, a ballet! let every Poet"). 112 lines. By William Bagnall.

147. *Musarum Deliciæ*, 72–75. 88 lines.

148. *Academy of Complements*, sig. A6v. My italics.

149. *Wits Recreations*, no. 90.

150. *Hamlet*, 3.2.85–89.

151. *Folly in Print*, sig. A4v.

152. *Mysteries of Love*, sig. A4v.

153. Love, *Scribal Publication*, 149.

154. *Bristol Drollery* (1674), sig. A3.

155. *Marrow of Complements*, 37–40.

156. *Bristol Drollery* (1674), sig. A3.

157. *Holborn Drollery*, sig. A7v.

158. *Wits Recreations*, unpaginated. Other named patrons in printed miscellanies are Ralph Banks in *Sportive Wit*; Edward Pepes [Pepys] (brother of the diarist Samuel) in *Wit and Drollery*; Cristiann, Countess of Devonshire (Christiana Cavendish; widow of William Cavendish, Second Earl of Devonshire; great Royalist supporter; d. 1675) in *Poems of Pembroke and Ruddier*; Richard Mangie in *A Jovial Garland* (1670); and William Wren (1639–89; son of Matthew Wren, Bishop of Ely; knighted in 1685; MP for Cambridge 1685–87) in *Wit at a Venture*.

159. *Wits Recreations*, "The Stationer to the Reader," unpaginated.

160. *Mysteries of Love*, sig. A6v.

161. *Mysteries of Love*, sigs. a2–a4.

162. *Academy of Complements*, sigs. A3v–A4.

163. *Academy of Complements*, sigs. A3v–A4.

164. *Academy of Complements*, sig. A3v.

165. *Marrow of Complements*, sig. A2.

166. *Marrow of Complements*, sig. A2v.

167. *Folly in Print*, sig. A4.

168. *Wits Interpreter*, sig. A4v.

169. *Mysteries of Love*, sig. A4v.

170. *Mysteries of Love*, sig. A4.

171. *Mysteries of Love*, sig. A5.

172. Joshua Poole, *The English Parnassus: Or, A Helpe to English Poesie* (1657), sig. a4.

173. Whitney, *A Choice of Emblemes* (1586), 171.

174. *Academy of Complements*, sig. A7v.

175. *Wits Interpreter* (1662), Bodleian Jessel f279, 493.

176. For an account which places more emphasis on the genuinely transformative potential of conduct manual literature, see Whigham, *Ambition and Privilege*.

177. *Mysteries of Love*, sig. a4. *Wits Academy* has an understanding (and maintenance) of hierarchy at its core: it is a book "helpful for the inexpert to imitate, and pleasant to those of better Judgement, at their own leisure to peruse" (title page).

178. *Mysteries of Love*, title page.

179. In fact, *Mysteries of Love* contains three separate prefaces which show an awareness of rank: "The Preface. To the Youthful Gentry"; "To those Cruel Fair ones, that triumph over the distresses of their loyal Lovers, the Author wisheth more Clemency; and to their afflicted Servants, more magnanimity and Roman Fortitude"; and, lastly, "A short Advertisement to the Reader, by way of Introduction, for his better understanding of the Mysteries of Eloquence and Complementing."

180. *Wits Interpreter*, title page.

181. *Wits Interpreter*, sig. A4v.

182. For more thoughts on this tension, and, in particular, its political and social significance, see chap. 4.

183. *Mysteries of Love*, sigs. a2–3.

184. *Mysteries of Love*, sig. A5.

185. *Card of Courtship*, "To the longing Virgins, amorous Batchelors, blithe Widows, kinde Wives, and flexible Husbands, of what Honour, Title, Calling, or Conversation soever, within the REALM OF GREAT BRITAIN" (unpaginated).

186. There are exceptions: *The Wits Academy*, for example, has the explicitly functional aim of helping readers "to discourse . . . with the critical sort of people, which live in this censorious Age."

187. *Mysteries of Love*, title page.

188. *Wits Interpreter*, title page.

189. *Mock Songs and Joking Poems*, title page.

190. *Windsor Drollery*, title page.

191. *A New Collection of Poems and Songs*, title page.

192. *Wits Academy* (1704), 53–54, 71–72, 56–57, 59–60, 146–49.

193. *Holborn Drollery* finds "*Drollery* to have its moveable Scenes, as *Windsor, Westminster* and *Covent-Garden*" (sig. A3v). Earlier, 1650s miscellanies do talk of baser rival publications but with much less specificity: the sense of a known and established tradition is stronger among later texts.

194. For discussions of printed marginal notes, see Evelyn B. Tribble, *Margins and Marginality: The Printed Page in Early Modern England* (Charlottesville: University Press of Virginia, 1993); D. C. Greetham, ed., *The Margins of the Text* (Ann Arbor: University of Michigan Press, 1997); Anthony Grafton, *The Footnote: A Curious History* (London: Faber and Faber, 1997); Lawrence Lipking, "The Marginal Gloss," *Critical Inquiry* 3, no. 4 (1977): 609–55; William W. E. Slights, "The Edifying Margins of Renaissance English Books," *Renaissance Quarterly* 42, no. 4 (1989): 682–716; and G. K. Hunter, "The Marking of *Sententiæ* in Elizabethan Printed Plays, Poems, and Romances," *Library*, 5th ser., 6, nos. 3–4 (1951): 171–88.

195. "Epigrammes" I, "TO THE READER."

196. Discussed in Tribble, *Margins*, 130–56.

197. Tribble, *Margins*, 146–54.

198. Tribble, *Margins*, 11–55.

199. Miguel de Cervantes Saavedra, *The Adventures of Don Quixote*, trans. J. M. Cohen (London: Penguin, 1950), 29. *Don Quixote* contains a wealth of mocking points about the practice of adding printed notes to texts. See 27–30.

200. For other cases of printed miscellanies using printed marginal notes, see *Antidote against Melancholy*, 59–61, "The Medley of Nations," where stanzas are labeled; *Wits Interpreter* (1662), 326–28, "A tale of a Tub, and a Gyant," where details are added to help the reader; *Wit and Mirth*, 84, part of "The FOUR-LEGG'D QUAKER," which includes explanatory notes; *Wit and Mirth* (1707), 93–95, "A New SONG, upon the Robin-redbrest's attending Queen Mary's Hearse in Westminster Abby," 240 "A SONG" where, beside the line "Fye! nay! *Pish be not unlucky!" is the instruction "*Pish *must not be utter'd not sung*," 292, "Bacchus's *Health*" which includes notes that "*At this Star they all bow to each other, and sit down. †At this Dagger all the Company beckons to the Drawer." The printed marginal notes in this later text mark the movement from printed miscellany to songbook that occurred in the last decades of the seventeenth century. Other related texts with printed notes include *Ratts Rhimed to Death* (1660), 4, 5, 6, part of "ARSY VERSY," and 60–65, "A Display of the Headpiece and Codpiece Valour, of the most Renowned, Colonel *Robert Jermy*, late of *Bafield*"; *Academy of Pleasure* (1656), 43, part of "SONG X. *The Conceited Lover*"; [Samuel Holland], *Wit and Fancy In a Maze. Or The Incomparable Champion of Love and Beautie. A Mock Romance* (1656), which features many marginal notes offering comic or mock information; and *Naps upon Parnassus* (1658).

201. *Sportive Wit*, 90–102; *Mysteries of Love*, 82–89; *Wit and Drollery*, 46–56; *Wit and Mirth* (1706), 8–15. The verse also appears in editions of *Wit and Mirth* in 1707, 1709, and 1719.

202. This quotation is from *Mysteries of Love* text.

203. Quotations from the *Wit and Mirth* (1706) edition.

204. Other printings of this poem more willingly dropped or altered notes than verse. In fact, there is an eighteenth-century ballad version—*The Tombs in Westminster Abbey. As Sung by Brother Popplewell in the manner of Chanting in a Cathedral* (London [1775]; Roxburghe Collection, 3.476)—with no marginal asides at all.

205. *Wit and Drollery*, 3–5; *Wit Restor'd*, 149–56. For details of Smith's life, see Raylor, *Cavaliers, Clubs*, 50–67, and 157–73. For an excellent account of this verse, see 142–53.

206. I quote from the *Wit Restor'd* text.

207. *Wit Restor'd*, 139–40, "To his Worthy Friend Mr. J.S. upon his happy Innovation of *Penelope* and *Ulysses*."

208. *Wit Restor'd*, 142.

209. *A History of Reading in the West*, ed. Guglielmo Cavallo and Roger Chartier and trans. Lydia G. Cochrane (Amherst: University of Massachusetts, 1999), 27–28.

210. A central tenet of Adrian Johns's *The Nature of the Book* (Chicago: University of Chicago Press, 1998), is that it is anachronistic to consider print an *inevitable* force for fixing and stabilizing texts.

211. The words are James Howell's, in an address to the Earl of Dorset from 1651. Qtd. in David Cressy, *Education in Tudor and Stuart England* (London: Edward Arnold, 1975), 27.

212. *Mysteries of Love*, sig. a4.

213. Roger Chartier, "Texts, Printing, Readings," in *The New Cultural History*, ed. L. Hunt (Berkeley: University of California Press, 1989), 154–75, 171.

214. See also Roger Chartier, "Reading Matter and 'Popular' Reading: From the Renaissance to the Seventeenth Century," in Cavallo and Chartier, *History of Reading*, 269–83.

Chapter 3

1. *Methinks the Poor Town*, sigs. A2–A2v.

2. Isaac Walton, *The Compleat Angler* (1653), 243; 1661, 251. For a very useful discussion of textual instability in manuscript and print, see Marotti, *Manuscript, Print*, 135–208. My chapter owes much to this important account.

3. See J. Lowenstein, "The Script in the Marketplace," *Representations* 12 (fall 1985): 101–14.

4. *CSPD 1655–1656*, 298.

5. Birch, *State Papers*, 717–18. Brooke refers to 1–5, "*The Maids Portion*," and 27–31, "*The hunting of the Gods. To the Tune of* Room for Cuckolds."

6. *Wits Interpreter*, sig. A6.

7. *A Perfect Collection of the Several Songs now in Mode*, sig. A2v.

8. *A Jovial Garland*, sig. A2.

9. *A Jovial Garland*, sig. A2.

10. *Wits Interpreter*, sig. A4v.

11. *London Drollery* and *Grammatical Drollery*, title pages.

12. *Mysteries of Love*, sig. A3.

13. *Academy of Complements*, sigs. A6–A9.

14. *Academy of Complements*, sig. A9. My italics.

15. On 1–3, 54, 121–22, 122–24, 128, and 126–27.

16. *Oxford Drollery*, title page.

17. *Oxford Drollery*, 85–87; *New Court Songs*, 58–59; *Academy of Complements*, sig. A6v.

18. *The English and Latin Poems of Sir Robert Ayton*, ed. C. B. Gullans (Edinburgh: William Blackwood and Sons, 1963), 297–300.

19. J. B. Leishman, "'You Meaner Beauties of the Night.' A Study in Transmission and Transmogrification," *Library*, 4th ser., 26, no. 2 (1945): 99–121.

20. Ted-Larry Pebworth, "Sir Henry Wotton's 'O Faithles World': The Transmission of a Coterie Poem and a Critical Old-Spelling Edition," *Analytical and Enumerative Bibliography* 5, no. 4 (1981): 205–31.

21. Mary Hobbs, "Early Seventeenth-Century Verse Miscellanies and Their Value for Textual Editors," in *English Manuscript Studies, 1100–1700*, ed. Peter Beal and Jeremy Griffiths, 1:182–210, 183 (Oxford: Basil Blackwell, 1989).

22. I am conscious that my use of the term "variant" to describe printed miscellany texts might also be said to invoke such a textual hierarchy, but I would wish the

term to suggest, more neutrally, a departure from, rather than a corruption of, an earlier text.

23. For this, see, in particular, D. F. McKenzie's *Bibliography and the Sociology of Texts* (London: British Library, 1986). Note also Arthur Marotti, "Manuscript, Print, and the English Renaissance Lyric," in *New Ways*, ed. Speed Hill, 209–21, esp. 209–11, which surveys recent trends in bibliography; Love, *Scribal Publication*, 313–56 ("Editing Scribally Published Texts"); and Anna R. Beer, *Sir Walter Ralegh and his Readers in the Seventeenth Century* (Basingstoke: Macmillan, 1997).

24. For some notes on other possible uses of the index, see my "An Online *Index of Poetry in Printed Miscellanies, 1640–1682*," *Early Modern Literary Studies* 8, no. 1 (2002).

25. *The Poems and Masques of Aurelian Townshend with Music by Henry Lawes and William Webb*, ed. Cedric C. Brown (Reading: Whiteknights, 1983), 115–17.

26. For an excellent discussion of the interactions between print, manuscript, and orality, see Arthur F. Marotti and Michael D. Bristol, eds., *Print, Manuscript, and Performance: The Changing Relations of the Media in Early Modern England* (Columbus: Ohio State University Press, 2000).

27. Thanks to Cedric C. Brown for alerting me to this interesting history.

28. I quote from *Townshend*, ed. Brown, 19. Brown bases his text on BL Add MS 25303, fol. 129; Add MS 21433, fol. 119; Harl. 3910, fol. 112v.

29. For an instance of a printed text retaining the poem's triangular relationship, see John Playford, *The Musical Companion, in Two Books* (1673), 120. G. C. Moore, "Aurelian Townshend," *Modern Language Review* 12 (1917): 426–27, transcribes an answer to "Victorious Beauty" from BL Egerton 2725, fol. 65v. John Benson's reworked version of Shakespeare's Sonnets appeared as *Poems: Written by Wil. Shake-speare. Gent* (1640). Of course, Cotgrave may have turned to a source which had already introduced the changes to Townshend's text, but it is still significant that *Wits Interpreter* conveys this radically altered text to a wide readership.

30. *Wits Interpreter*, 272–73, 304.

31. *Wits Interpreter*, 101 [281]. Sir John Harrington, *The Most Elegant and Witty Epigrams* (1618), epigram 39.

32. *Wits Interpreter*, 307.

33. *Marrow of Complements*, 80–81; *Card of Courtship*, 46–47.

34. *Oxford Drollery*, 15–20.

35. James Howell, *Poems on several Choice and Various Subjects* (1663), 80–81.

36. *Wit at a Venture*, 52.

37. *Parnassus Biceps*, 30. Henry King, *Poems, Elegies, Paradoxes, and Sonnets* (1657), 95–96.

38. *Parnassus Biceps*, sig. A2. However, Hobbs, *Verse Miscellany Manuscripts*, 100, notes that the *Parnassus Biceps* text is close to the version in the notebook of Thomas Manne—Henry King's amanuensis—and speculates that the omission of the lines may reflect a direct borrowing from this source.

39. *Parnassus Biceps*, 68–70. Carew, *Poems* (1640), 190–91.

40. *Mysteries of Love*, 138–39. Benson, *Poems*, sonnets 23, 6, 4, 5, 11. Noted in *The New Variorum Edition of Shakespeare: The Sonnets*, ed. H. E. Rollins (Philadelphia, 1944), 2:330, and *Shakespeare's Sonnets*, ed. Katherine Duncan-Jones (Oxford: Arden, 1997), 74. The final couplet of Benson's sonnet 92 is included in this same letter, lines 17–18.

41. *Academy of Complements*, 146. Michael Drayton, *Englands Heroicall Epistles* (1598), fol. 30r–v. Drayton's text was reprinted at various dates, but textual variants indicate *The Academy of Complements* was drawing on—directly or indirectly—the 1598 text.

42. *Academy of Complements*, 141, "Of Musicke and Love." Sir Philip Sidney, *The Countess of Pembroke's Arcadia (The Old Arcadia)*, ed. Katherine Duncan-Jones (Oxford: Oxford University Press, 1985), 51–52.

43. *Academy*, 147; Marlowe, *Hero and Leander* (1598), lines 235–36. Marlowe's text reads "Like untun'd golden strings *all* women are" (my italics).

44. *Marrow of Complements*, sig. A3.

45. Other writers whose works are borrowed are William Cartwright (*The royal slave* [1639], *The ordinary* [1651], *Poems* [1651], *The siedge* [1651]); James Howell (*A New Volume of Familiar Letters* [1655]); Thomas Heywood (*The rape of Lucrece* [1638]); John Fletcher (*The mad lover* [1647], *The elder brother* [1679]); Francis Beaumont, *The knight of the burning pestle* [1679]); John Fletcher and Philip Massinger (*The Little French Lawyer, The false one* [1647]); John Fletcher (*The captaine* [1647]); John Fletcher and William Rowley (*The maid in the mill* [1647]); Thomas Middleton and William Rowley (*Wit at severall weapons* [1647]); and Samuel Rowlands (*The knave of Clubbs* [1611]).

46. There was a later edition in 1818.

47. *Marrow of Complements*, "THE STATIONER TO THE READER."

48. *Marrow of Complements*, 37–41.

49. *Marrow of Complements*, 38 "7. Her Lips." From Wither, lines 1009–10.

50. *Marrow of Complements*, 38. Wither, lines 969–80.

51. *Marrow of Complements*, 38–39. Wither, lines 1015–24.

52. *Wits Interpreter*, sig. B1.

53. *Wits Interpreter*, 14–15, "SONG" (beginning "He that loves a rosie-cheek"), in *Poems* (1640), 29.

54. *Wits Interpreter*, 50–51, "*Age not to be rejected*" (beginning "Am I despis'd because you say"), in *Hesperides* (1648), 68.

55. *Wits Interpreter*, 108 [untitled], beginning "Why shouldst thou swear I am forsworn," in *Lucasta* (1649), 15–16.

56. *Wits Interpreter*, 24 [untitled] (beginning "A maiden fair I dare not wed"), in Thomas Deloney, *The Pleasant History of John Winchomb. In his Yonger Years Called, Jack of Newbery* (1672), sigs. Bv–B2.

57. The following references to and quotations from *The Workes* come from the 1616 edition. The ordering of the 1640 edition is, for the poems I discuss, the same.

58. Again, it is possible *Wits Interpreter* employed a manuscript which had already made this conflating error, although I have found no such reading elsewhere.

59. Walter J. Ong, *Orality and Literacy* (New York: Routledge, 1982), esp. 29.

60. See, for instance, R. C. Newton, "Jonson and the (Re-)Invention of the Book," in *Classic and Cavalier: Essays on Jonson and the Sons of Ben*, ed. C. J. Summers and T-L. Pebworth (Pittsburgh: University of Pittsburgh Press, 1982), 31–55; Joseph Loewenstein, "The Script in the Marketplace," *Representations* 12 (fall 1985): 101–14.

61. *Wits Interpreter*, 305, 317, 136–37, 272–73, 316–17, 305.

62. For Jonson as controller, see the aforementioned Newton, "Jonson and the ... Book." Note also J. Brady and W. H. Herendeen, eds., *Ben Jonson's 1616 Folio* (London: Associated University Presses, 1991); and Richard Helgerson, *Self-Crowned Laureates* (Berkeley: University of California Press, 1983), chap. 3, "Self-Creating Ben Jonson," 101–84.

63. "Epigrammes" I, "TO THE READER."

64. It is a neat irony that the popularity of Jonson's verse in printed miscellanies was in part a consequence of the publication of his supposedly fixing *Workes*.

65. *Wits Interpreter*, sigs. A5–6; *Mysteries of Love*, sig. A4.

66. Birch, *State Papers*, 717–18.

67. I quote from *New Academy of Complements*, 229–30.

68. Folger MS Va 124, fols. 36–37.

69. Folger MS Va 162, fol. 39.

70. Respectively, Bodleian MS Ashmole 36, 37, fol. 145v; Bodleian MS Rawl poet 26, fol. 5; and BL Add MS 25303, fol. 70v.

71. The poem appears in *Marrow of Complements*, 171–73; *Wit and Drollery*, 21–23; *Folly in Print*, 86–88 [96–98]; *New Academy of Complements*, 229–30; *A Jovial Garland*, sigs. D3–D3v; *Westminster Drollery the Second Part*, 74–75.

72. *Wits Interpreter*, 68, 40–41. For a discussion of this poem's various manifestations, see Charles B. Gullans, "Ralegh and Ayton: The Disputed Authorship of 'Wrong Not Sweete Empress of My Heart,'" *Studies in Bibliography: Papers of the Bibliographical Society of the University of Virginia* 13 (1960): 191–98; and Michael Rudick, ed., *The Poems of Walter Ralegh: A Historical Edition* (Tempe, AZ: Renaissance English Texts Society, 2000), lx–lxi.

73. *Wits Interpreter*, 122–23, 289.

74. BL Add MS 54332, fols. 199, 194. For more on answer poetry, see Marotti, *Manuscript, Print*, 159–71.

75. Unless otherwise noted, I quote from the *Wit and Drollery* text.

76. *Wit and Drollery*, 70–71; *Merry Drollery the Second Part*, 1–2; *New Academy of Complements*, 213; *Windsor Drollery*, 65–66.

77. In manuscript we find another answer verse, but here the two poems—original and answer—have been conflated. "Dieing Louer pro et contra" (BL MS Harley 3991, fols. 3v–4) presents a dialogue, offering assertion and denial of the anti-Petrarchan line with stanzas labelled "Song" and "Answere" (or "S" and "A").

78. *Wit and Mirth*, 121.

79. *Mock Songs and Joking Poems*, 1–2; *Antidote against Melancholy*, 49–50.

80. *Merry Drollery the First Part*, 81–84; *Choyce Drollery*, 61.

81. *New Court Songs*, 115–16. William Wycherley's *Love in a Wood*, act 1, scene 2.

82. *Wits Interpreter*, 20–21. This local sequence of verse and answer on the theme of assertion continues until p. 22.

83. *Wits Interpreter*, 73–74.

84. *Wits Interpreter*, 10–11. The answer can be found in Bodleian MS CCC 327, fol. 32.

85. *Parnassus Biceps*, 134–35.

86. *Wit and Drollery* 54–57; *Wit and Drollery* 56–58.

87. Bodleian MSS Eng poet c50, Rawl poet 142, Malone 21, Rawl D1092; BL MS Sloane 1792.

88. See E. F. Hart, "The Answer-Poem of the Early Seventeenth Century," *Review of English Studies* 7, no. 25 (1956): 19–29.

89. Bodleian MS Ashmole G.16 [4]. Discussed in Simpson, *Ballad*, 319–20.

90. Fox, *Oral*, 319. *Antidote against Melancholy*, 35–37. "Tom a Bedlam" lines quoted from *Wit and Mirth*, 56–57.

91. *Mock Songs and Joking Poems*, 2–132 [3], "SONG. 2. A Mock to a Lover I am, and a Lover I'le be. And to that Tune."

92. 2, "The second Song in the Masque at Court."

93. 6–7, "Song 9."

94. *Windsor Drollery*, 132, "Song 252," and *Westminster Drollery*, 1–2, "The first Song in the Ball at Court."

95. *Mocks Songs*, 132 [3]-4, "SONG 3. A Mock, to I pass all my hours in a shady old Grove. And to that Tune."

96. *Mock Songs*, 85, "SONG 29. A Mock to a Lover I am, and a Lover I'le be, in the praise of Tobacco: And to that Tune."

97. *Westminster Drollery*, 2, "The second Song in the Masque at Court"; *Windsor Drollery*, 6–7, "Song 9."

98. *Westminster Drollery*, 16–17, "The Wooing Rogue. The Tune is, My Freedom is all my Joy."

99. *Merry Drollery the Second Part*, 45; *Mock Songs and Joking Poems*, 6–7; *Oxford Drollery*, 65–66.

100. *Wit and Drollery*, 6–10, *Wit Restor'd*, 156–162; *Antidote against Melancholy*, 11–14; *Merry Drollery the Second Part*, 40–44; and *Wit and Mirth*, 21–24. The verse also appeared as (at least) three broadside ballads (and probably many more), and is found in one midcentury manuscript verse miscellany. As a broadside ballad it appears three times: twice titled *The bonny Black-smiths delight: OR, A Noble Song in praise of the Black-smiths* (reprinted in Pepys's Ballads, 4:264; also in Bodleian Rawlinson 191), and *A merry new Ballad, both pleasant and sweet, In praise of the Black-smith, which is very meete* (British Library's Roxburghe Ballads, 1:250–51). The latter has been dated at about 1650 (Wing 1870A). It is also included in one manuscript: Bodleian MS Ashmole 36–37 (fols. 195–96)—the carefully constructed midcentury verse miscellany of Elias Ashmole (1617–92). It is significant that

in these four versions the poem is unaccompanied by any note of its original club contexts.

101. Raylor, *Cavaliers, Clubs*, 69–110.

102. Raylor, *Cavaliers, Clubs*, 103.

103. Raylor, *Cavaliers, Clubs*, 98.

104. For a very useful extended discussion, see Raylor, *Cavaliers, Clubs*, 142–53.

105. *Wit and Drollery*, 1–5, offers a similar, although less detailed, frame, including "*The Preface to that most elaborate piece of Poetry entituled* Penelope Ulysses" and ending "*Here endeth the Preface, and now beginneth the Book*" with "Whoop, is there a Song? let's ha't: it followeth," but titling "The Blacksmith" simply "*SONG*," with no communal ascription.

106. Bodleian MS Ashmole 36–37, fol. 196.

107. *The Rump, or Collection of Songs and Ballads, made upon those who would be a PARLIAMENT, and were but the RUMP of an House of Commons, five times dissolv'd* (1660), 1–5.

108. Simpson, *British Broadside Ballad*, 269. Later the tune came to be titled "And is not Old England grown New," and "Lulla by baby" (from a 1688 ballad *A New Song of Lulla By, or Father Peter's Policy Discovered*). Noted in Simpson, *British Broadside Ballad*, 276. Hobbs, *Verse Miscellany Manuscripts*, 35, expands on this point: "The tune of the love song 'Greensleeves' was taken over by the Puritans as a carol (a seasonal one only, since they had abolished the keeping of Christmas), 'The old year now hath past away': it is still sung today." This Puritan use of the tune is particularly interesting given the anti-Puritan connotations the same tune, titled "The Blacksmith," acquired: see below.

109. *Antidote against Melancholy*, 62–64. The verse also appeared in *Merry Drollery the Second Part*, 35–38.

110. Pepys, *Diary*, 1:114.

111. *Merry Drollery the Second Part*, 77–80; *Merry Drollery the Second Part* 70–72; *Covent Garden Drollery*, 29–30; *Folly in Print*, 63–64; *Parnassus Biceps*, 159–60; *Merry Drollery the First Part*, 85–86. Other printed miscellany poems that use the "Which no body can deny" refrain include (by first line) "Nick Culpepper, and William Lilly," *Merry Drollery the First Part*, 56–60, "Admiral Deans Funeral"; "Oh fire, fire, fire, where?" *Choyce Drollery*, 33–37, "Upon a House of Office over a River, set on fire by a Coale of TOBACCO"; "The Papist cannot take one oath," *Folly in Print* (1667), 63–64 [untitled]; "There's many a blinking verse was made," *Merry Drollery the Second Part*, 35–38, "*The Brewers praise*."

112. *Ratts Rhimed to Death* (1660), 60–65. See also *A Pill to purge State-Melancholy: or, a Collection of Excellent New Ballads* (1725), 122–25, "A New Ballad, to the Old Tune of, Which no body can deny, &c." The opening of "The Blacksmith"—"Of all the . . ."—also seems to have become established as a known model to follow. Numerous printed miscellany inclusions adopt a similar beginning, including "Of all the brave Birds that ere I did see," *Windsor Drollery*, 50, "Song 74," and "Of all the rare juices," *Sportive Wit*, 45–46, "On CANARY" (by Alexander Brome).

113. *Merry Drollery the Second Part*, 35–38, "*The Brewers praise*"; *Antidote against Melancholy*, 62–64, "THE BREWER. *A Ballad made in the year*, 1657. *To the Tune of the Blacksmith*"; *Wit and Mirth*, 25–27, "*The BREWER.*"

114. *Folly in Print*, 52–53.

115. *Choyce Drollery*, 68–69. This tune is discussed in Simpson, *British Broadside Ballad*, 643–46.

116. Fox, *Oral*, 319, notes some significances conveyed by the referents "Tom of Bedlam" (which "mocked the idiocy of a libel victim") and "Fortune my Foe" ("known to everyone as "the hanging tune" because of its performance at public executions").

117. Noted briefly in Raylor, *Cavaliers, Clubs*, 219. Houlbrook's story is recounted by Raymond Lister, *The Loyal Blacksmith* (Cambridge, UK: Golden Head Press, 1957).

118. Houlbrook draws those eight stanzas from "Of all the Sciences beneath the Sun," printed in *Merry Drollery the Second Part*. Houlbrook's stanza two corresponds (loosely) to *Merry Drollery*'s stanza eight; three to twelve; four (loosely) to seven; six to ten; seven to eight; eight to thirteen; nine to fourteen. The last two stanzas do not correspond.

119. Houlbrook, *A Black-smith* (1677), 71–72.

120. Walton, *Angler*, 165–66.

121. Walton, *Angler*, 117–20.

122. Francis Davison, *A Poetical Rhapsody* (1611), 161–62, "A song in praise of a Beggars life"; *Windsor Drollery* 97–98, "Song 168"; *Card of Courtship* 109–10, "Song 19. Sung by three Beggers."

123. John Playford, *The Musical Companion, in two books* (1673), 49.

124. Birch, *State Papers*, 717–18.

125. *Wit and Mirth*, 68–69, "*The* EPICURE." A theorbo is a kind of large lute.

126. As noted in Hobbs, "Verse miscellanies," 192–93, and *Early Seventeenth Century Verse Miscellany Manuscripts* (Aldershot: Scolar Press, 1992), 105–8, musical settings to poems often led to textual changes. For discussion of music meetings in the 1640s (semipublic performances which might have been important moments in the dissemination of verses like "Come with our Voyces"), and their part in catalyzing Playford's publications, see Mary Chan, "Mid-Seventeenth-Century Music Meeting and Playford's Publishing," in *The Well Enchanting Skill: Music, Poetry and Drama in the Culture of the Renaissance: Essays in Honour of F. W. Sternfeld*, ed. J. Caldwell, E. Olleson, and S. Wollenberg, 231–44 (Oxford: Clarendon, 1990).

127. *Ben Jonson: The Complete Poems*, ed. G. Parfitt (Middlesex: Penguin, 1975), 463.

128. 173. It is not included in the 1616 edition of Jonson's *Workes*. I have used a British Library copy of the 1640 *Workes*, cataloged 79.l.4.

129. Unless otherwise indicated, verse quotations come from the 1640 *Workes* text.

130. 62–63, 94–95, and 27, respectively.

131. My italics.

132. *Ben Jonson*, C. H. Herford, Percy Simpson, and Evelyn Simpson, eds. (Oxford: Clarendon, 1925–1952), 8:11. Extant manuscripts offer examples of such a text: Bodleian MS Eng poet c53, British Library Add MS 30982, and St. John's College, Cambridge MS S.23, for example, present "Two Ladies invitinge each other to singe," "Two Ladies ioyning each other to sing," and "A dialog betweene two Ladies. B.J." All omit what was the second stanza in *The Workes*.

133. For example, Bodleian MS Eng poet c53, fol. 2v; British Library Add MS 30982, fol. 37v; St. John's College, Cambridge, MS S.23, fol. 53r–v.

134. *The Harmony of the Muses,* 62–63.

135. For example, British Library MSS Add 25707, fols. 4v–5; Add 15227, fol. 88v; Sloane 1446, fol. 55. Folger MS Vb43, fols. 28v–29. Stoughton MS, 101–2.

136. Love, *Scribal Publication,* 35–39.

137. John Playford, *The Musical Companion, in Two Books* (1673), sig. A4v.

138. BL Add MS 29396, f.76. Noted in Hobbs, "Verse Miscellanies," 192–93.

139. *Love's Labour's Lost,* V.2.869–902. *New Academy of Complements,* 178, "Song 160," and 180, "Song 163"; *Windsor Drollery,* 7, "Song 10," and 135–36, "Song 222."

140. Bodleian MS Mus Sch C142, fols. 1–4.

141. Bodleian MS Mus b1, fols. 81–83. For notes on this folio manuscript, see Hobbs, *Verse Miscellany Manuscripts,* 50–51. Peter Beal, *Index of Literary Manuscripts.* Vol. 1, *1450–1625* (London: Mansell, 1980), part 2, 233, notes the existence of a copy of Jonson's *Workes* (1616), now in the Pierpont Morgan Library, inscribed "To his most worthy, & learned Friend M^r: John Wilson."

142. Of course each musical performance of the poem would have been different, as every reading of even the same text is different. Alongside the lost manuscripts, then, must be placed each lost moment of performance and reading, every one a new text in its own right.

143. See, for example, Ian Spink, "English Seventeenth-Century Dialogues," *Music and Letters* 38, no. 2 (1957): 155–63.

144. For a brief discussion, see Marotti, *Manuscript, Print,* 143–44.

145. Walton, *Angler,* 255–57.

146. Pepys, *Diary,* 8:521–22.

147. Pepys, *Diary,* 9:195.

148. *The Works of John Dryden,* gen. ed. H. T. Swedenberg, Jr. (Berkeley: University of California Press, 1978), 11:411–12.

149. *The Conquest of Granada* (1672), 127–28.

150. *Westminster Drollery,* 14–15, and *New Academy of Complements* (1671), 316–17.

151. Love, *Scribal Publication,* 69. Love's excellent discussion of the scribal publication of play texts (on which my brief notes draw) appears on 65–70. See also Woudhuysen, *Sir Philip Sidney,* 134–45.

152. There are, however, other ways in which the song might have been transmitted: the play might have recirculated an already known song, with a previous oral, printed, or manuscript history. In this instance, my sketch of printed miscellanies drawing on a performance (or drawing on texts which themselves drew on a performance) is challenged.

153. I quote from the 1673 quarto.

154. For a discussion of date and the once vexed issue of authorship, see David J. Lake, *The Canon of Thomas Middleton's Plays* (Cambridge: Cambridge University Press,

1975), 38–43. Lake fixes the date of the play's composition "by parallels and a topical reference to the execution of Mrs. Turner in November 1615" (39). For a (relatively) recent edition, see *The Works of Thomas Middleton*, ed. A. H. Bullen, 8 vols. (London: John C. Nimmo, 1885), 5:117–235.

155. As evidence of this song's popularity, note that it also appeared in *Merry Drollery the Second Part*, 44–45, as "The Gypsies, a Catch."

156. *Wits Interpreter*, 69–70, "The theifes Song"; *Choyce Drollery*, 60, "The High-way mans Song"; *New Academy of Complements*, 135, "Song 84"; *Windsor Drollery*, 134–35, "Song 257."

157. William Andrews Clark Memorial Library *PR 1213 P74, no. 66.

158. *Parnassus Biceps* seems to have a close relationship with Folger MS Va 97 (a miscellany from the late 1630s); *The Harmony of the Muses* perhaps borrowed extensively and sequentially from Oxford MS CCC 328. For a discussion of manuscript verse miscellanies, see Hobbs, *Verse Miscellany Manuscripts*; Marotti, *Manuscript, Print*; Woudhuysen, *Sir Philip Sidney*, 153–73. For a helpful analysis of (among other things) the relationships between one manuscript miscellany and its printed counterparts, see Randall Louis Anderson, "'The Merit of a Manuscript Poem': The Case for Bodleian MS Rawlinson poet. 85," in Marotti and Bristol, *Print*, 127–71.

159. Respectively, HM 116, 13, "How to choose a Wife"; 16–18, "Sr Gwalter Raleigh to ye sole Gouernours of his Affection"; 19–20, "Upon a faire Gentlewoman walking in ye Snow," ascribed to "Dr Corbet."

160. Harry Ransom Center, University of Texas at Austin, MS Killigrew, T Misc B. For a brief discussion of this manuscript, see Nancy Cutbirth, "Thomas Killigrew's Commonplace Book?" *Library Chronicle of the University of Texas*, n.s., no. 13, 1980, 31–38.

161. BL Add MS 27419.

162. The most significant overlaps come at HM 198 part 1, 138–47, and *Poems of Pembroke and Ruddier*, 3–22.

163. *Poems of Pembroke and Ruddier*, sig. A.

164. For brief notes on this manuscript, see Beal, *Index . . . 1450–1625*, 253; and C. M. Armitage, "Donne's Poems in Huntington Manuscript 198: New Light on 'The Funeral,'" *Studies in Philology* 63 (1966): 697–707.

165. HM 198, Part 1, 163, 158–59, 196–97.

166. Brown, "The Two Pilgrimages." For Brown's notes on overlaps between the manuscript and printed miscellanies, see pp. 129–30.

167. Folger MS Va 308, fol. 124v.

168. These images appear in all post-1640 editions of *Wits Recreations*.

169. The images appear in *Wits Recreations* (1665), sigs. P5v–P6v, P7v, Q1; Folger MS Va 308 fols. 91–92.

170. Folger MS Va 308, fols. 93–95v.

171. Folger MS Va 308, fol. 125r–v; *Wits Recreations* (1665), sigs. X8v–Y2v.

172. Folger MS Va 308, fols. 126–129v; *Wits Recreations* (1665), sigs. L4–P4.

173. Folger MS Va 308, fol. 3.
174. Folger MS Va 308, fol. 139; *Wits Interpreter* (1671), 99.
175. Folger MS Va 308, fol. 139v; *Wits Interpreter* (1671), 62.
176. Folger MS Va 308, fol. 139; *Wits Interpreter* (1671), 74–75.
177. Folger MS Va 308, fols. 57, 131.
178. For another example of manuscript appropriating print, see the account book of Charles C. Jones, written between 1662 and 1665 (Clark MS J765 M3 M294 1662–1665 Bound). This text includes a miscellaneous bundling of "Certaine Rules to be Obserued for the more Elagant Compossing ... of Latine" (fol. 2); legal templates for future use ("A Bill oobligatory . . . Be it knowne unto all men by these p^{r}sente, that I A.B. of &c doe owe & am indebted unto C.D. of &c. in the summe of &c" [fol. 8v]); accounts ("for 2 hoggs" [£], "2 paire of stockings" [4s 6d], "A mouse trapp" [3s] [fol. 11v]); "Select obseruations taken out of diuerse Authors for my private use" (fol. 14r–v); and, five pages from the end, a meticulous duplication of the title page of the highly popular *The young Clerkes guide: or, An exact collection of choice English presidents, according to the best forms now used, for all sorts of Indentures, Letters of Atturney, Releases, Conditions &c. Compiled by Sr R.H. Counsellor* (1651). The next eight pages of the manuscript are transcripts from the opening of this printed book.
179. For example, *Wits Recreations* (1641), sig. L3v.
180. BL Add MS 37719, fol. 163. Among the other printed images pasted into Gibson's manuscript are a small printed page on astrology, probably from an almanac, supplemented with Gibson's own notes ("The world runs round" and "Like an old Alminacke quite out of date / I am forgot! such is my ridged state. / JG.") (fol. 190v); two oval vignettes, depicting Christ going to Emmaus and St. George slaying the dragon, around which Gibson has added his own verse (fol. 283); the frontispiece to Lancelot Andrewes's *Private Devotions* (1647), with related manuscript verses (fol. 204b); the title page of the *Whole Duty of Man* (1659), to which Gibson has added red coloring to the images and the lines, "Albion I leaue Thee, wallowinge in thy bloud! / Once famous for a Church; when King, and Bishops stood" (fol. 203); and an image of Charles II to which has been added the manuscript note "Charles the second; 1 Englands splendor, / 2 Britains Glorye, / 3 ffaiths Defendor" (fols. 183, 185).
181. Other letters in these books exhibit similar parallels. Compare *Mysteries of Love*, 37–38, "To make an Acquaintance"; 38–39, "A Visit"; 40, "To invite a Friend to Dinner"; and 40–41, "Another form of Invitation"; with, respectively, *New Academy of Complements*, 9–10, "Instructions how to become acquainted upon accidentally meeting any Person"; 10–11, "When one makes a Visit"; 11, "To invite a Friend to Dinner"; and 12, "Another from whom the Invitation is accepted."
182. *Wits Interpreter*, 307–8.
183. *Coffee-House Jests* (1677), BL 12314.df.40, 102.
184. *A Jovial Garland*, sigs. G4v–G5v.

185. Playford, *Dancing Master*, 47. *Antidote against Melancholy*, 73–74; *Windsor Drollery*, 30–31.

186. Borges, *Labyrinths*, 92–94.

Chapter 4

1. *CSPD*, 298. The defendant's replies are printed in Birch, *State Papers*, 4:717–18.
2. *CPSD*, 314.
3. Joseph Frank, *Hobbled Pegasus. A descriptive bibliography of Minor English Poetry, 1641–1660* (Albuquerque: University of New Mexico Press, 1968), 4. Frank's text is a consideration of all "minor" (broadly, "noncanonical") poetry, and not merely printed miscellanies. He defines *Wits Interpreter, Musarum Deliciæ, Wit and Drollery, Parnassus Biceps,* and *Le Prince d'Amour* as "Non-political" (343, 348, 355, 359, 448.)
4. John Wardroper, ed., *Love and Drollery* (London: Routledge and Kegan Paul, 1969), x.
5. Raylor, *Cavaliers, Clubs*, 205. There have of course been several excellent studies of the political significance of (more broadly) seventeenth-century mirth and misrule, including Leah S. Marcus, *The Politics of Mirth: Jonson, Herrick, Milton, Marvell, and the Defense of Old Holiday Pastimes* (Chicago: University of Chicago Press, 1986).
6. *Wit and Drollery*, "To the Reader" (unpaginated).
7. Note, for example, *Harmony of the Muses*, 63–64, "A Sonnet in praise of Musick," which begins, "Hail, sacred *Musick*! Queen of Souls!," and *Academy of Complements*, 134, "On her Armes," which reads, "Her Twinne-like armes, that stainlesse paire, / Fit for a Kings embraces are."
8. Marika Keblusek is editing Honywood's catalog, to be published as *Honywood in Holland* (Cambridge, UK: Libri Pertinentes). My thanks to Marika for sharing her research with me.
9. *J. Cleaveland Revived*, 35–36, by Josias Howe (beginning "Make big the bon-fires, for in this one Son"); 96–97, by Jasper Mayne (beginning "The Prince hath now an equal, and may see"); 41–42, by Jasper Mayne (beginning "That Children are like Olive-branches, we"); 64–65, by Martin Lluelyn (beginning "Great Queen, / Whom tumults lessen not, whose womb, we see"); 97–99, by Jasper Mayne (beginning "After the Princes birth, admired Queen").
10. *J. Cleaveland Revived*, 9–10.
11. *Parnassus Biceps*, 50–53.
12. *A Jovial Garland*, sigs. F3–F5, "SONG LXI."
13. *Oxford Drollery*, 170–72.
14. James Loxley, *Royalism and Poetry in the English Civil Wars: The Drawn Sword* (Basingstoke: Macmillan, 1997), 21–57. The poems of William Cartwright and Jasper Mayne are particularly associated with this kind of publication.

15. *Parnassus Biceps*, 36–38.

16. *Wit Restor'd*, 16–17. "Supposed to be made by Mr. William Murrey of His Majesties Bedchamber."

17. A preoccupation with original authorship has not only led to a low level of interest in printed miscellanies; it has stunted wider considerations of the politics of re-presentation in general—despite it being crucial to early modern texts in their material, transmitted reality. Any discussion of manuscripts, songbooks, and plays—which frequently re-present existing verse—should acknowledge the importance of changing contexts. Reissued single-author texts also demand careful, distinct contextualizings—texts like Ben Jonson's *Workes*, in 1616 and 1640.

18. A point made by Marotti, *Manuscript, Print*, 113–15.

19. *Wit and Mirth*, 65–66. The poem also appears in *Musarum Deliciæ*, 65–67, "The Fart censured in the Parliament House," and *Le Prince d'Amour*, 93–99, "The Censure of the Parliament Fart."

20. *Musarum Deliciæ*, 37–79; *Westminster Drollery the Second Part*, 127–29. Note also *Wits Interpreter*, 273, "On a Fart."

21. Marotti, *Manuscript, Print*, 94–112. Note also Pauline Croft, "The Reputation of Robert Cecil: Libels, Political Opinion and Popular Awareness in the Early Seventeenth Century," *Transactions of the Royal Historical Society* (1991), 43–69.

22. *Wit Restor'd*, 56, "Upon Iohn Felton's hanging in Chaines at Portsmouth, for killing the Duke of Buckingham"; 56–58, "To Felton in the Tower"; 58, "To the Duke of Buckingham"; 58, "To the Same"; 92–93, "To the Duke of Buckingham."

23. There are a few exceptions, of course, like *Wit Restor'd*, 65, "On the death of the Lord Treasurer," and *Wits Interpreter*, 270, "On old Cecil."

24. For rare references note *Wit and Mirth*, 107–9, "IGNORAMUS. An Excellent new Song" ("Since Reformation"); 117–18, "10 *Catch* to the same Tune" ("Oh the Presbyterian Whiggs"); and 123, "26 *Catch*" ("We'l laugh and we'l Sing . . . And a fart for the Whigs").

25. *Sportive Wit*, sigs. C6v–C7, C7v–C8v, 11–12, 125–26, C–C5v, 30–31.

26. *Choice Drollery*, 45–47; 16.

27. Henry Edmundson, *Comes Facundus in Via* (1658), title page and sig. A7.

28. *Parnassus Biceps*, 143–45, "A Song of the Precise Cut"; *Sportive Wit*, 37–38, "The Tub-Preacher"; *J. Cleaveland Revived*, 91–93, "The Puritan."

29. *Parnassus Biceps*, 81, "On Faireford Windows," and *Westminster Drollery*, 87–88, "On Fairford *curious Church-Windows, which scap'd the War and the Puritan.*" Note also *Parnassus Biceps*, 3–12, "A Poem, In defence of the decent Ornaments of Christ-Church Oxon, occasioned by a Banbury brother, who called them Idolatries," beginning "You that prophane our windows with a tongue."

30. *Le Prince d'Amour*, 171–77, "The distracted Puritane"; *Merry Drollery the Second Part*, 50–52, "The mad Zealot"; *Antidote against Melancholy*, 35–37, "A Song Of the hot-headed ZEALOT. To the Tune of Tom a Bedlam"; *Wit and Mirth*, 87–89, "The DISTRACTED PURITAN."

31. *The Book of Sports as Set Forth by Charles the I. with Remarks upon the Same* (London, 1709), 2.

32. *Book of Sports*, 3.

33. *Book of Sports*, 4.

34. Marcus, *Politics of Mirth*, 14, notes the contrast between Crown-sanctioned recreation and Charles's personal disdain for misrule.

35. Thomas Hall, *The Downfall of the May Games* (1661), 6.

36. Hall, *Downfall*, 8–10.

37. Hall, *Downfall*, 31–34.

38. *CSPD*, 298 and 314.

39. Hall, *Downfall*, 34.

40. For miscellany examples, see *Mysteries of Love*, 7–9, "Upon the fatall disaster that befell the Gallants upon May-day last in Hide Park"; *Wit and Drollery*, 70–75 [110–15], "A match at Cock-fighting . . . T.R."; *Merry Drollery the First Part*, 29–30, "The Hunting"; *Merry Drollery the Second Part*, 127 [125]–26 [128], "Arthur of Bradly." Ronald Hutton, *The Rise and Fall of Merry England. The Ritual Year 1400–1700* (Oxford: Oxford University Press, 1994), 196, notes that the *Book of Sports* was sometimes referred to as "the Book of Recreation."

41. Hutton, *Merry England*, 225.

42. The tale of the Quaker "*that to the shame of his Profession, attempted to buggar a Mare near* Colchester" (originally by John Denham) appeared in three texts: *J. Cleaveland Revived*, 72–73; *Merry Drollery the First Part*, 48–51; and *Wit and Mirth*, 14–16. The same topic appears later in *Wit and Mirth*, 81–85, "The FOUR-LEGG'D QUAKER." *Wit and Mirth*, 74–78, "The MADMAN" is a satire on all religious sects who wrongly turn from truth to novel religions. *The Wits Academy* includes 85–88, "The Quakers Song, CI."

43. *Card of Courtship*, "To the longing Virgins, amorous Batchelors, blithe Widows, kinde Wives, and flexible Husbands, of what Honour, Title, Calling, or Conversation soever, within the REALM OF GREAT BRITAIN" (unpaginated).

44. *Card of Courtship*, 46–47.

45. Marotti, "Love Is Not Love."

46. *Mysteries of Love*, title page.

47. See, e.g., "Song" (55–56); "A Fond Design" (65–66); "Not to be Alter'd" (67–68); and "Loves Martyr" (68).

48. *Wits Interpreter*, 14.

49. *Marrow of Complements*, 47ff.

50. *Wit Restor'd*, 105–6.

51. Potter, *Secret Rites*.

52. *Wits Interpreter*, sig. A5.

53. *Wits Interpreter*, sig. A5. *J. Cleaveland Revived* similarly offers printings of former manuscripts but is careful that those that "were before in print . . . in this second Edition I have crossed them out, only reserving them that were excellently good, and never

before extant" (sig. A5). T. Walkington, in *The optick glasse of humors* (1639), sees a clear sense of duty in this printing of manuscripts: "[K]nowledge concealed and not broched for a publique use, is like to a peerelesse gem interred in the center of the earth; whereof no man knowes but he that hid it" (qtd. in Bennett, *English Books*, 219).

54. My italics.

55. *The Harmony of the Muses*, sig. A3v.

56. *Wits Interpreter*, sig. A5v.

57. *Musarum Deliciæ*, "THE STATIONER TO THE Ingenious READER" (unpaginated).

58. *Merry Drollery the Second Part*, title page.

59. *Card of Courtship*, "To the longing Virgins, amorous Batchelors, blithe Widows, kinde Wives, and flexible Husbands, of what Honour, Title, Calling, or Conversation soever, within the REALM OF GREAT BRITAIN" (unpaginated).

60. *Sportive Wit*, sig. A4.

61. *Holborn Drollery*, sig. A6v.

62. As was the case with, for example, the first and second parts of *Merry Drollery* which sign their "TO THE READER"s simply "Farewell." The use of initials or anonymity by compilers might also indicate an anxiety about government reaction to their texts, particularly after the 1656 burnings—although the majority of initials are clearly intended to recall illustrious (and unaware) *authors*; and the use of initials continues after 1660, when such fears would not have been so great.

63. *Wit and Drollery*, title page.

64. One copy of *Musarum Deliciæ*—Folger M1710—includes a reader's title page manuscript note that "Sr J.M. and Ja: S" correspond to "Mr John Mennes and Dr James Smith."

65. *Sportive Wit*, "To the Reader," sigs. A3–A4.

66. Qtd. in Potter, *Secret Rites*, 39.

67. *Wits Interpreter*, 123–25.

68. *Wits Interpreter*, 125–26. Interestingly, a 1662 edition of *Wits Interpreter*—Bodleian Jessel f279—contains manuscript additions around this section (in this text, on p. 493), suggesting a reader actively practicing the codes and so, perhaps, considering them not just mere badges of an elite, but useful, applicable tools.

69. *Wits Interpreter*, 126.

70. *Wits Interpreter*, title page.

71. *Mysteries of Love*, title page.

72. Potter, *Secret Rites*, 58–59.

73. See, e.g., Cressy, "Educational Opportunity," and John Morrill, ed., *Revolution and Restoration: England in the 1650s* (London: Collins and Brown, 1992), 109–10. Morrill notes that Hobbes and the Earl of Clarendon both saw an overeducated public as a key cause of the Civil War. The same post-1660 fear of democracy was a founding suspicion in Roger L'Estrange, *Considerations and Proposals In Order to the Regulation of the Press. Together with Diverse Instances of Treasonous, and Seditious Pamphlets, Proving the Neceßity thereof*

(London, 1663). Christopher Hill, *Some Intellectual Consequences of the English Revolution* (Madison: University of Wisconsin Press, 1980), notes post-revolution hostility toward ideas of "enthusiasm" and, in literature, "inspiration," which parallels this sense of a fear of intellectual freedom.

74. *Wits Interpreter*, sig. A3.

75. James Howell, a Royalist whose career was rudely upset by the Civil War, wrote in 1651 to Edward Sackville, Earl of Dorset, that "It were to be wished that there reigned not among the people of this land such a general itching after book-learning, and I believe so many Free-Schools do rather hurt than good; nor did the art of printing much avail the Christian commonwealth, but may be said to be well near as fatal as gunpowder, which came up in the same age" (qtd. in Cressy, *Education*, 27).

76. *Wits Interpreter*, 1–2. The verse is by Alexander Brome.

77. *Wits Interpreter*, 63–64.

78. *Wits Interpreter*, 1–2.

79. *Parnassus Biceps*, sigs. A3–A3v. A similar theme finds expression in *Windsor Drollery*, 53–54, "Song 81," by Thomas Carew (beginning "Know CÆLIA since thou art so proud"); and Sir Charles Sedley's poem opening "As in those Nations, where they yet adore," printed in *New Academy of Complements*, 85, "Song 1," and *A Collection of Poems*, 43–44, "To Celia."

80. *Wits Interpreter*, 1–2.

81. *Wit at a Venture*, 6, "To Silvia, on the Tyranny of her Looks. A Song."

82. *Wit Restor'd*, 222–23, "On a Ribband," by Thomas Carew.

83. *Methinks the Poor Town*, 28.

84. For a very useful discussion, see Potter, *Secret Rites*, 135–40.

85. *Richard II*, 5.5.1–2.

86. *Wit and Drollery*, 11–14; *Westminster Drollery*, 96–98; *Parnassus Biceps*, 107–10.

87. *Academy of Complements*, sig. A7. Note also *Holborn Drollery*, sig. A7: "Understanding These were Condemn'd to the Preß, which I presum'd had been design'd no farther then my Cabinet"; and *Wit and Drollery*'s "To The Truly Noble Edward Pepes, Esq.," which observes how the patron "shuns the vulgar wayes of being made publick to the world."

88. *Mysteries of Love*, sig. A4.

89. *Merry Drollery the First Part*, 45–46, "The Cavaleer's Complaint."

90. *Wit and Drollery*, 11–14, "Loyalty confin'd"; *Westminster Drollery*, 96–98, "The Loyal Prisoner"; *Parnassus Biceps*, 107–10 "The Liberty and Requiem of an imprisoned Royalist." This verse is perhaps by Roger L'Estrange.

91. *Wits Interpreter*, 22–23, "The Prisoners song," and *New Academy of Complements*, 195–96, "Song 181."

92. *Choyce Drollery*, 93–96, "The contented Prisoner his praise of Sack"; *Merry Drollery the First Part*, 101–3, "A Song"; *A Jovial Garland*, sigs. B4v–B5v, "SONG XVI"; *Windsor Drollery*, 74–75, "Song 134"; *The Wits Academy*, 34–35, "SONG XLII." This poem comes from act 3, scene 2, of *Cromwell's Conspiracy. A tragi-comedy, relating to our latter times.*

93. *Choyce Drollery*, 93–96, "*The contented Prisoner his praise of Sack*"; *Merry Drollery the First Part*, 101–3, "*A Song*"; *A Jovial Garland*, sigs. B4v–B5v, "SONG XVI"; *Windsor Drollery*, 74–75, "*Song 134*"; *The Wits Academy*, 34–35, "SONG XLII."

94. *Merry Drollery the First Part*, 46–48, "*An Eccho to the Cavaleers complaint.*"

95. *Folly in Print*, 67–70; *J. Cleaveland Revived*, 78–79. *Wits Recreations* includes a sequence of anagram couplets, from numbers 195 [p. 65] to 201 [p. 67]. Among them are "*Thomas Egerton. 1 anagr. Honors met age*"; "*Phineas Fletcher. 5 anagr. Hath Spencer life? Or Spencer hath life*"; and "*Mrs. Elizabeth Noell 6 anagr. holinesse be still my star.*"

96. Potter, *Secret Rites*, 50–51. Potter notes a Frenchman constructed 400 anagrams of the names of English kings. All were pejorative. For a wider discussion of manipulations of the printed word to reveal new meanings, see Martin Elsky, *Authorizing Words* (Ithaca, NY: Cornell University Press, 1989), esp. 147–83, "5. The Space of the Hieroglyph: George Herbert and Francis Bacon."

97. Anagrams are common in seventeenth-century manuscript miscellanies and commonplace books. Folger MS Va 147—the manuscript miscellany of Theophilus Alye composed between 1679 and 1716 has various anagrams (f.5v) of names including "Sir Edmund Bury Godfrey" transformed into "I fynd murder'd by rogues," and "Sir Edmund Boey Godfrey" rendered "By Rome's rude finger dy'd." At the foot of the page is the note "These Anagrams I haue compared, & find them, by the letters, to be exactly true"—suggesting both that the rearrangements of letters is accurate, and that the sentiments conveyed are apt. The sense that anagrams might be genuinely revelatory is implicit in many manuscript miscellanies.

98. *Parnassus Biceps*, 161.

99. *Wits Academy*, 145–48, "SONG CLIX"; *New Academy of Complements*, 225–28, "*Song 213*"; *Antidote against Melancholy*, 14–16, "*An Old Song of an Old Courtier and a New*"; *Wit and Mirth*, 43–45, "*The OLD and NEW COURTIER.*"

100. *Merry Drollery the First Part*, 45–56, "*The Cavaleer's Complaint*"; *Antidote against Melancholy*, 49–50, "The CAVALIERS Complaint. To the Tune of *I'le tell thee Dick, &c.*"; *New Academy of Complements*, 238–39, "*Song 226.*"

101. Pepys, *Diary*, 17 October 1662, 3:226–27.

102. *Merry Drollery the First Part*, 46–48, "*An Eccho to the Cavaleers complaint.*"

103. *Westminster Drollery the Second Part*, 48–51, "*On Loyalty in the Cavaliers*," and *Wit and Mirth*, 95–97, "*The CAVALIERS SONG.*"

104. *Merry Drollery the First Part*, 46–48, "*An Eccho to the Cavaleers complaint.*"

105. *Westminster Drollery the Second Part*, 48–51, "*On Loyalty in the Cavaliers*," and *Wit and Mirth*, 95–97, "*The CAVALIERS SONG.*"

106. I should stress that I am not claiming that the phenomena described here are exclusive to this moment: comparisons between new- and old-style courtiers were around before, and love was, perhaps, always a prison. For a thesis that suggests that a sense of exclusion was common among many university graduates in the (early) seventeenth century, given the lack of church vacancies relative to numbers leaving Oxford

and Cambridge, see Mark H. Curtis, "The Alienated Intellectuals of Early Stuart England," *Past and Present*, no. 23 (November 1962): 25–43.

107. *Holborn Drollery*, sig. A7v.

108. *Mysteries of Love*, title page.

109. *Parnassus Biceps*, sig. A2.

110. *Antidote against Melancholy*, 67, "6. A Catch," by John Suckling; *Oxford Drollery* 21–22, "*Two Parliament Troopers who lay sick in* Scotland: *In Imitation of the Song of* Bow Bells," by William Hickes; *Westminster Drollery the Second Part*, 54–56, "Song."

111. *Musarum Deliciæ* "THE STATIONER TO THE Ingenious READER" (unpaginated).

112. *Wit and Drollery*, sig. A3v.

113. *Oxford Drollery*, "To the *READER*" (unpaginated).

114. "To the Discerning *READER*," sigs. A3–A5.

115. *Sportive Wit*, title page, sig. A3v.

116. *Antidote against Melancholy*, 57–59, "On the vertue of *SACK*, By D.R. H.E."; *Wit and Mirth*, 59–61, "*The Virtue of SACK. By Dr. Hen. Edwards.*" The verse is by Dr. Henry Edwards.

117. *Wit and Drollery*, sig. A3.

118. *New Academy of Complements*, title page.

119. *Sportive Wit*, "To the Reader," sigs. A3–A4.

120. *The Wits Academy*, 96–98, "SONG CIX"; *Wit and Drollery*, 97–99, "*A Song. To the Tune of Packingtons Pound*"; *Antidote against Melancholy*, 67, "6. A Catch," by John Suckling; *Choyce Drollery*, 20–30, "Jack of Lent's Ballat"; *Wit Restor'd*, 64, "Upon a Cobler"; *Wits Recreations*, [p. 24], "67. On a Cobler"; *Sportive Wit*, 131–32, "*A SONG*"; *London Drollery*, 26–28, "*A Song to the first Figure Dance at Mr. Young's Ball in Feb. 72.*"; *Westminster Drollery the Second Part*, 80–82, "*The Rurall Dance about the May-pole. The Tune, the first Figure dance at Mr. Young's Ball in May 1671*"; *Methinks the Poor Town*, 16, "*A Drinking Catch.*"

121. Smith, "The Seventeenth-Century Drolleries," 47.

122. "Wit and mirth" is one of those neat couplings that crops up again and again in preface, title page, and verse; a rhetorical regular, like "profit and delight," and "variety." (See, e.g., prefaces to *Wits Interpreter, Card of Courtship, Mysteries of Love*, and many others.) Consequently, caution is needed not to overinterpret what was in some ways standard marketing cant. But still, a potential for mirth was something like a miscellany constant and thus demands enquiry.

123. *Merry Drollery the First Part*, title page (my italics); *A Jovial Garland*, title page; *Wits Academy*, title page; *Wit and Mirth*, sig. A2; *Wit and Drollery*, sig. A3.

124. *Wit and Drollery*, sig. A3.

125. *Antidote against Melancholy*, "To the Reader" (unpaginated).

126. *Wits Interpreter*, 61–63, [untitled]; *Wit and Drollery*, "112"–"14" [152–54], "Another"; *Merry Drollery the Second Part*, 136–37, "The merry Goodfellow"; *New Academy of Complements*, 100–101, "Song 22"; *Windsor Drollery*, 128–30, "Song 214"; *The Wits Academy*, 80–82, "SONG XCVII."

127. See Raylor, *Cavaliers, Clubs,* 118.

128. For a thorough discussion of these poems, see Raylor, *Cavaliers, Clubs,* 136–53.

129. *J. Cleaveland Revived,* 91–93, "*The Puritan*"; *Parnassus Biceps,* 143–45, "*A Song of the Precise Cut*"; and *Sportive Wit,* 37–38, "*The Tub-Preacher.*" The verse begins "With face and fashion to be known."

130. *Le Prince d'Amour,* 171–77, "*The distracted Puritane*"; *Merry Drollery the Second Part,* 50–52, "*The mad Zealot*"; *Antidote against Melancholy,* 35–37, "*A Song Of the hot-headed ZEALOT. To the Tune of* Tom *a* Bedlam"; *Wit and Mirth,* 87–89, "*The DISTRACTED PURITAN.*"

131. *Wits Recreations,* 71, "*212. On Clarret wine spilt.*"

132. *Wits Recreations,* 73, "*220. On Pallas and Bacchus Birth.*"

133. See Potter, *Secret Rites,* 134–40, for a discussion of the political significance of drink. For a detailed consideration of ideas about drinking in seventeenth-century lyric poetry, see Joshua Scodel, *Excess and the Mean in Early Modern English Literature* (Princeton, NJ: Princeton University Press, 2002), 199–252. Note also my *Drink and Conviviality in Seventeenth-Century England* (Suffolk: Boydell and Brewer, forthcoming in 2004).

134. *Folly in Print,* 52–53, "*A CATCH, To the Tune of, Old Poets Hipocrene Admire.*"

135. *Wit Restor'd* (1658), 16–17, "*The Gallants of the Times. Supposed to be made by* Mr. William Murrey *of His Majestie's Bed-Chamber.*"

136. Pepys, *Diary,* 7 May 1660, 1:131; 9 October 1660, 1:262.

137. *Compleat Angler* (1655), sig. Bv.

138. *Wit and Drollery,* title page.

139. *Wit Restor'd,* 156.

140. *Sportive Wit,* title page.

141. *Wits Interpreter,* 324–32. This text also contains a drinking game on p. 100, where dice determine drinks to be downed. It concludes, "O Where is the Wine, come fill up the Glass, / For here is the Man that hath thrown [double one]." It also bases its drinking around clear rules and thus at its heart has a sense of order.

142. *London Drollery,* 46.

143. *Merry Drollery the First Part,* 114–16, "*Canary Crowned.*" *Windsor Drollery,* 44, "*Song 65,*" begins "Sack is the Prince of Wales."

144. *Wit and Drollery,* "68"–"70" [108–10], "*Upon the fall of the Miter in Cambridge*"; *Wit and Mirth,* 58–59, "*Of The DOWNFAL of one part of the MITRE-TAVERN in CAMBRIDGE, or the SINKING thereof into the CELLAR. By Mr. Tho. Randolph.*" The verse is by Thomas Randolph.

145. *Antidote against Melancholy,* 57–59, "*On the vertue of SACK, By D.R. H.E.*"; *Wit and Mirth,* 59–61, "*The Virtue of SACK. By Dr. Hen. Edwards.*" The verse is by Dr. Henry Edwards.

146. *Merry Drollery the Second Part,* 65–67, "*In praise of Sack.*"

147. *Merry Drollery the First Part,* 114–16, "*Canary Crowned.*"

148. *Merry Drollery the Second Part*, 35–38, "*The Brewers praise*"; *Antidote against Melancholy*, 62–64, "The BREWER. A *Ballad* made in the year, 1657. To the Tune of the *Blacksmith*"; *Wit and Mirth*, 25–27, "*The* BREWER." Note also *Merry Drollery the First Part*, 119–23, "A Medly of Nations," especially p. 121. (A verse by Thomas Jordan, also printed in *Antidote against Melancholy*, 59–61, "The Medley Of the NATIONS," and *A Jovial Garland*, sigs. C–C2v, "SONG XXII.")

149. Qtd. in Paul H. Hardacre, *The Royalists during the Puritan Revolution* (The Hague: Martinus Nijhoff, 1956), 22.

150. *Wit and Mirth*, 120, "18 *Catch.*" Note also *Folly in Print*, 47–48, "*A Catch made before the* KINGS *coming to* Worcester *with the* Scottish *Army*": "The Round-heads drink a health / To their new Common-wealth, / And swear the Kings must be forgot; / But the pot shall be bang'd / When the Rogues are all hang'd / Here's a Health to the King and the Scot."

151. *Wit and Mirth*, 93–94, "*The Claret Drinkers SONG*," by John Oldham.

152. *Wit and Mirth*, 115, "4 *Catch.*"

153. *Merry Drollery the First Part*, 114–16, "Canary Crowned."

154. *Wits Academy*, 13–14, "*A Drinking Catch.*"

155. *Windsor Drollery*, 47, "Song 70."

156. *Folly in Print*, 52–53, "A CATCH, To the Tune of, *Old Poets Hipocrene Admire.*"

157. *Windsor Drollery*, 126, "Song 244." My italics.

158. *Wit and Mirth*, 68–69, "*The* EPICURE."

159. See, e.g., *Methinks The Poor Town*, 28, "A Song" (beginning "*From Friends, all inspir'd with brisk* Burgundy *Wine*").

160. *Wits Interpreter*, 116–17, "*A Bacchanal*"; *Antidote against Melancholy*, 39, "*A Glee, In praise of WINE.*"; *Merry Drollery the Second Part*, 31–32, "The Virtue of Wine"; *A Jovial Garland*, sigs. E7v–E8, "SONG LVI"; *Windsor Drollery*, 48–49, "Song 73"; *Wit and Mirth*, 100–101, "*A GLEE to BACCHUS. By Ben. Johnson.*" This is the chorus to Aurelian Townshend's highly popular verse beginning "Bacchus, Iacchus, fill our braines" or "Let Souldiers fight for pay and praise." For a modern edition of this verse, see *Aurelian Townshend*, ed. Brown, 115–17.

161. *Wit and Mirth*, 113, "CATCHES."

162. *Antidote against Melancholy*, "To the Reader" (unpaginated).

163. *Wits Academy*, 13–14, "*A Drinking Catch.*"

164. *Parnassus Biceps*, 158–59, "*A Song upon a Winepot.*"

165. *Parnassus Biceps*, 60–63, "*An Ode in the praise of Sack.*"

166. *Windsor Drollery*, 7, 9 "Song 141."

167. *Sportive Wit*, 130, "*An Epitaph on* John Taylor, *who was born in the City of* Glocester, *died in* Phænix *Alley, in the 75. yeare of his age; you may finde him, if the worms have not devoured him, in* Covent Garden *Churchyard.*" The verse begins with typically unmerciful wit: "Here lies *John Taylor*, without rime or reason."

168. *Wits Interpreter*, 104–5 [untitled]; *Wit and Drollery*, 67–68, "*A SONG.*"

169. *Wit and Mirth*, 113, "*CATCHES.*"

170. *Holborn Drollery*, 75–76, "*The Humours of the Tavern.*"

171. *Antidote against Melancholy*, 57–59, "On the vertue of *SACK*, By D.R. H.E."; *Wit and Mirth*, 59–61, "*The Virtue of SACK. By Dr. Hen. Edwards.*" The verse is by Dr. Henry Edwards.

172. A. B. Coiro, *Robert Herrick's "Hesperides" and the Epigram Book Tradition* (Baltimore: Johns Hopkins University Press, 1988), 128–29.

173. *Parnassus Biceps*, "96"[95]–97. The verse appears in *The Poetical Works of Robert Herrick*, ed. F. W. Moorman (London: Humphrey Milford, 1921), 77–79.

174. *Parnassus Biceps*, 63, by Robert Wild.

175. *Windsor Drollery*, 42, "*Song 62.*"

176. *Wits Interpreter*, 104–5 [untitled]; *Wit and Drollery*, 67–68, "*A SONG.*"

177. *Oxford Drollery*, 137–38, "*A Song call'd the Cup of Claret.*"

178. *Antidote against Melancholy*, 54, "*In the praise of WINE*"; *Wit and Mirth*, 102, "*In the praise of WINE.*" By Roger Boyle, Earl of Orrery.

179. *Wit and Mirth*, 122, "*25 Catch.*"

180. *Wits Interpreter*, 61–63 [untitled]; *Wit and Drollery*, "112"–"14" [152–54], "*Another*"; *Merry Drollery the Second Part*, 136–37, "*The merry Goodfellow*"; *New Academy of Complements*, 100–101, "*Song 22*"; *Windsor Drollery*, 128–30, "*Song 214*"; *The Wits Academy*, 80–82, "SONG XCVII."

181. *Wits Interpreter*, 61–63 [untitled]; *Wit and Drollery*, "112"–"14" [152–54], "*Another*"; *Merry Drollery the Second Part*, 136–37, "*The merry Goodfellow*"; *New Academy of Complements*, 100–101, "*Song 22*"; *Windsor Drollery*, 128–30, "*Song 214*"; *The Wits Academy*, 80–82, "SONG XCVII."

182. *Windsor Drollery*, 75–77, "*Song 135.*"

183. *Wit and Mirth*, 120, "*18 Catch.*"

184. *Wits Academy*, 73, "*The double Health*," and *New Court Songs*, 63, "*The Double Health.*"

185. *Westminster Drollery the Second Part*, 85–86.

186. *Wits Interpreter*, 61–63 [untitled]; *Wit and Drollery*, "112"–"14" [152–54], "*Another*"; *Merry Drollery the Second Part*, 136–37, "*The merry Goodfellow*"; *New Academy of Complements*, 100–101, "*Song 22*"; *Windsor Drollery*, 128–30, "*Song 214*"; *The Wits Academy*, 80–82, "SONG XCVII."

187. *Windsor Drollery*, 47, "*Song 70.*"

188. *Wits Interpreter*, 61–63 [untitled]; *Wit and Drollery*, "112"–"14" [152–54], "*Another*"; *Merry Drollery the Second Part*, 136–37, "*The merry Goodfellow*"; *New Academy of Complements*, 100–101, "*Song 22*"; *Windsor Drollery*, 128–30, "*Song 214*"; *The Wits Academy*, 80–82, "SONG XCVII."

189. See, for example, C. H. Firth, "The Royalists under the Protectorate," *English Historical Review* 52 (1937): 634–48, especially 637–39.

190. Qtd. in Hardacre, *Royalists*, 22. Included in Thomas Weaver's "*On the Goldsmiths-Committee*" (beginning "Come Drawer, some wine") in *Merry Drollery the Second Part*, 29–30.

191. *Wit and Mirth*, 93–94, "*The Claret Drinkers SONG*," by John Oldham. Contrast love as a path to trouble: "Blind Love will blab what he in secret did" (*Wit and Drollery*, 71–72, "*De Vino & Venere*").

192. *J. Cleaveland Revived*, 99–101, "*A Song of SACK*," by Charles Cotton.

193. *Windsor Drollery*, 32–33, "*Song 48. The Politick Drinker.*" Note also *London Drollery*, 111, "*A Catch*," especially "But there's no deciet in a *Brimmer*, / Truth in the bottom does lie."

194. *Choice Drollery*, 42, "*A CATCH.*"

195. *Parnassus Biceps*, 60–63, "*An Ode in the praise of Sack.*"

196. *London Drollery*, 17–19, "*A Song in Praise of Drinking.* Tune, Mr. Smith's Jig, call'd Mris. Madge's Jig."

197. *Antidote against Melancholy*, 57–59, "On the vertue of *SACK*, By D.R. H.E."; *Wit and Mirth*, 59–61, "*The Virtue of SACK. By Dr. Hen. Edwards.*" The verse is by Dr. Henry Edwards.

198. *Wits Interpreter*, "197" [297].

199. *Windsor Drollery*, 55–56, "*Song 83.*"

200. *Wit and Mirth*, 95, "*The Delights of the Bottle*"; *The Wits Academy*, 3, "*SONG III.*"

201. *Wit and Mirth*, 68–69, "*The EPICURE.*" Note also *The Wits Academy*, 43–46, "*SONG LIII*," and *Wit and Mirth*, 90–92, "*SONG*," which tell of the nothingness of everything. There are many verses lamenting the madness of the world—like *The Wits Academy*, 74–75, "*SONG XC*"; *Windsor Drollery*, 99–100, "*Song 170*"; and *Windsor Drollery*, 75–77, "*Song 135.*"

202. *Windsor Drollery*, 14, "*Song 23.*" A related sense of living for the moment is seen in 17, "*Song 27. A Catch*," originally by Alexander Brome, out of Anacreon. (Also printed in *The Wits Academy*, 13, "*A Catch. XIV.*")

203. *Windsor Drollery*, 126, "*Song 244.*"

204. *Windsor Drollery*, 145, "*Song 267.*"

205. *Wits Academy*, 103, "*SONG CXIV.*"

206. *Wits Academy*, 15, "*A drinking Catch.*"

207. *Marrow of Complements*, 67–68, "*SONG. Sung by a Company of Cup-shaken Corybants.*"

208. *Oxford Drollery*, 137–38, "*A Song call'd the Cup of Claret.*"

209. *Wit and Mirth*, 93–94, "*The Claret Drinkers SONG*," by John Oldham. These two strategies to defeat transience—on the one hand, living only in the present moment; on the other, living in the eternal—in some ways parallel love poetry's division between those *carpe diem* poems that seek an immersion in immediate (and momentary) physical pleasure and those that pledge a timeless, Platonic love.

210. *New Academy of Complements*, 95–96, "*Song 17*"; *Windsor Drollery*, 135, "*Song 258*"; *Wit and Mirth*, 115, "*5 Catch . . . Mr. A. Cowley*"; *A Jovial Garland*, sig. D, "*SONG XXXIII.*"

211. *Windsor Drollery*, 55, "*Song 82*"; *Wits Academy*, 25, "*A Tavern Song.*"

212. *New Academy of Complements*, 251–52, "*Song 241.*"

213. *J. Cleaveland Revived*, 99–101, "*A Song of SACK*," by Charles Cotton.

214. *Parnassus Biceps*, 60–63, "An Ode in the praise of Sack."

215. *Merry Drollery the Second Part*, 65–67, "In Praise of Sack."

216. Potter, *Secret Rites*, 138–39.

217. See Marcus, *Politics of Mirth*.

218. Qtd. in Potter, *Secret Rites*, 148. The poem, "The Cock Crowing at the Approach of a Free Parliament," is in *Rump* (1662), 2:176.

219. Potter, *Secret Rites*, 138.

220. *Wits Recreations*, title page.

221. *Wits Recreations* borrows extensively from Thomas Bastard, *Chrestoleros* (1598); John Davies, *The Scourge of Folly* (1611?); Henry Parrot, *Laquei Ridiculosi* (1613); Henry Fitzgeffrey, *Certain Elegies* (London, 1618); and Robert Hayman, *Certain Epigrams* (London, 1628). See *Witts Recreations*, ed. Gibson, "Introduction."

222. *A Poetical Rapsodie* (1608), "To the Reader," sig. A4.

223. *Card of Courtship*, "To the longing Virgins" (unpaginated).

224. Pepys, *Diary*, 8 March 1661, 2:51.

225. *The Harmony of the Muses*, sigs. A3–A3v.

226. *Wit and Drollery*, sig. A3v.

227. *Parnassus Biceps*, sigs. A2–A2v.

228. *Le Prince d'Amour*, sigs. A3v–A4.

229. *Academy of Complements*, sig. A3v.

230. Morrill, *Revolution and Restoration*, 13. See also chap. 2, "The English Republican Imagination," by Jonathan Scott, 35–54.

231. *A Jovial Garland*, sig. A2. My italics.

232. *Windsor Drollery*, title page.

233. *Wits Academy*, title page.

234. *New Academy of Complements*, title page.

235. *Folly in Print*, title page.

236. *Folly in Print*, sigs. A3v–A4.

237. *Folly in Print*, 76–79.

238. *Wit and Mirth*, sig. A2.

Afterword

1. *An Antidote against Melancholy: Or, A Treasury of 53 Rare Secrets and Arts* (1659), 1–3.

2. *Wits Recreations*, no. 90.

3. *Wits Interpreter*, sig. A5.

4. *Methinks the Poor Town*, sig. A2.

5. *Academy of Complements*, sig. A6v.

6. Some of these narratives are articulated in Elizabeth Eisenstein's crucial but controversial *The Printing Press as an Agent of Change: Communication and Cultural Transforma-

tion in Early Modern Europe, 2 vols. (Cambridge: Cambridge University Press, 1979). For useful reflections on some of these larger issues, see Marotti and Bristol, *Print*, 1–29.

7. *Deliciæ Poeticæ; Or, Parnassus Display'd* (1706), title page, and 58, 84, 86, 113.

8. *The Bee: A Collection of Choice Poems* (1715), 3, 7.

9. Walton, *Angler* (1653), 243.

10. *A Choice Collection of 120 Loyal Songs* (1684), title page, sigs. a2–a2v.

11. Love, *Culture and Commerce*, 9, discusses "undiscovered public knowledge," and the need for its coordination.

12. *Mysteries of Love*, sig. A5.

Appendix

1. Hodgkinson was three times in trouble with the Star Chamber: in 1635, when his press and letters were seized, and twice in 1637, over a payment dispute with Arthur Nicholls, and for printing Dr. John Cowell's *Interpreter*. His reputation was subsequently restored. See Plomer, *Dictionary*, 99.

2. Blunden's other publications include several theological books (including work by Henry Vaughan), Thomas Jordan's *Poetical Varieties*, Robert Davenport's comedy *A New Trick to Catch the Devil*, and John Johnson's *The Academy of Love*. During the Civil War Blunden published political pamphlets and was editor of the news sheet that became known as "Blunden's Passages." See *Witts Recreations*, ed. Gibson, ix.

3. Chamberlain (*fl.* 1640–60) was a poet and popular wit at Oxford University in the late 1630s. He published apothegms, a comedy, some short poems, and collections of ancient jokes. See the introduction to *The Harmony of the Muses*, E. W. Sullivan II, ed.

4. Gilbertson also published ballads in partnership with T. Vere, John Wright, and Francis Coles.

5. Cotgrave—unrelated, it seems, to his better-known namesake Randolph—also published *The English Treasury of Wit and Language* (1655), a collection of quotations from dramatic sources, and *The Muses Mistresse* (1660), a small book of two staunchly Royalist poems.

6. Herringman (1628–1704) is better known as the publisher of John Dryden and an associate and sometimes partner of Humphrey Moseley.

7. Phillips (1631–1706) was the younger brother of Edward Phillips. He made a name for himself with his scathing satire on Puritanism, *Satyr against Hypocrites* (1655).

8. Wright (1611–90) was a Royalist who gained a reputation at Oxford University as an eloquent writer and preacher, and as a strident defender of university learning. (Wright seems to have regarded his poems in *Parnassus Biceps* as models for rhetoric.) Wright delivered a speech welcoming Charles I to the new library of St. Johns, Oxford, in August 1636. His other publications include an anthology of Latin verse (*Delitiæ Delitiarum*), sermons (in 1656, *Five Sermons*), and theological commentaries. See *Parnassus Biceps*, Beal, ed., ix–xvii.

9. Phillips (1630–[96]) was the brother of John Phillips and the nephew of John Milton, and is well known for his *A New World of Words, or a General Dictionary* (1658).

10. Donne (1604–62), son of the poet John Donne, was a miscellaneous writer notorious for his dissipated habits. During the Civil War, he was an object of suspicion for parliament. A handwritten note at the start of the British Library copy 11446 of *Poems by Pembroke and Ruddier* records that Donne edited the volume at the request of Christiana, Countess of Devonshire.

11. The Bodleian Library catalog suggests (the otherwise unknown?) Raymond as the compiler of *Folly in Print* (1667), relying, it seems, on references in poems in the volume.

12. In 1666 Speed courted trouble by selling law books printed under the Commonwealth and was subsequently imprisoned. See Plomer, *Dictionary*, 169–70. Plomer notes that Speed was active between 1658 and 1667, but Speed's *New Academy* was published in 1669.

13. Brome's other publications include broadsides, poetry, and plays. He was not related to Alexander or Richard Brome, although their work did appear among Henry Brome's books (and in several printed miscellanies).

14. Sawbridge was a prolific publisher and was well known, in particular, for the books he produced between 1678 and 1681 with Benjamin Tooke, John Dunmore, T. Dring, and Charles Mearne. See Plomer, *Dictionary*, 263.

15. The case for Behn's involvement is uncertain. *Covent Garden Drollery* was "Compiled by A.B." Some have suggested "A.B." indicates Alexander Brome, but this is impossible since Brome died in 1666, six years before this miscellany appeared. There is, perhaps, a hint at Behn's authorship in the preface to *Bristol Drollery* (1674) with the lines "*But if she* [i.e., *Bristol Drollery*] *finds*——— / *No favour mongst you slighting, jeering men,* / *(twixt her and I) I have advis'd her then,* / *Humbly to cast her self no Madam* Behn" (sig. A3v). However, "A.B." was often used in Renaissance publications as contemporaries employ "John Doe"—as an established means to convey anonymity. I suspect *Covent Garden Drollery*'s ascription may be an example of this.

16. Eglesfield's other publications include theological texts and Robert Herrick's *Hesperides*.

17. Edwin was a Royalist and Churchman, and published several books critical of Presbyterians and Dissenters.

BIBLIOGRAPHY

Primary Texts

Manuscripts

Bodleian Library, Oxford
Bodleian Malone 21
Bodleian MS Ashmole 36–37
Bodleian MS Ashmole G.16 [4]
Bodleian MS Eng poet c50
Bodleian MS Eng poet c53
Bodleian MS Mus b1
Bodleian MS Mus Sch C142
Bodleian MS Rawlinson poet 26
Bodleian MS Rawlinson poet 142
Bodleian Rawlinson 191
Bodleian Rawlinson D1092

British Library, London
BL Add MS 15227
BL Add MS 25303
BL Add MS 25707
BL Add MS 27419
BL Add MS 30982
BL Add MS 37719
BL Add MS 54332
BL MS Harley 3991
BL MS Sloane 1446
BL MS Sloane 1792

Christ Church College, Oxford
Oxford MS CCC 327
Oxford MS CCC 328

William Andrews Clark Memorial Library, Los Angeles
MS J765 M3 M294 1662–65 Bound
MS M3835 M3 L651 [1674–76]

Folger Shakespeare Library, Washington, DC
Folger MS Va 124
Folger MS Va 134
Folger MS Va 147
Folger MS Va 148
Folger MS Va 162
Folger MS Va 308
Folger MS Vb43
Folger MS Va 97

Harry Ransom Center, University of Texas, Austin
MS Killigrew, T Misc B
Pforzheimer MS 2k Box 71

Huntington Library, San Marino, California
HM 93
HM 116
HM 198 part 1

St. John's College, Cambridge University
St. John's MS S.23

Printed Books (including modern editions of early modern texts)

The Academy of Complements. 1640, 1641, 1645, 1646, 1650, 1654, 1658, 1663, 1664, 1670, 1684, 1685, 1705, 1727, 1750, 1760, 1790, 1795.
The Academy of Pleasure. 1656.
Against Popery and Tyranny. 1689.
Allott, Robert. *Wits theater of the little World.* 1599.
———. *Englands Parnassus: Or the Choysest flowers of our moderne poets.* 1600.
An Antidote against Melancholy. Or, A Treasury of 53 Rare Secrets & Arts. 1659.
An Antidote against Melancholy. 1661, 1669.
Ayton, Robert. *The English and Latin Poems of Sir Robert Ayton.* Edited by C. B. Gullans. Edinburgh: William Blackwood and Sons, 1963.
Bacon, Francis. *The Works of Francis Bacon.* Edited by James Spedding, Robert Leslie Ellis, and Douglas Denon Heath. 7 vols. London: Longman, 1857–59.
The Bee: A Collection of Choice Poems. 1715.

Bell, Robert, ed. *Early Ballads Illustrative of History, Traditions, and Customs*. London: Bohn's Standard Library, 1877.

The Book of Sports as Set Forth by Charles the I. with Remarks upon the Same. London, 1709.

Borges, Jorge Luis. *Labyrinths: Selected Stories and other Writings*. Edited by Donald A. Yates and James E. Irby. London: Penguin, 1970.

Brome, Richard. *A Jovial Crew, or, the Merry Beggars*. 1652.

Bullen, A. H., ed. *Speculum Amantis: Love-Poems From Rare Song-Books and Miscellanies of the Seventeenth Century*. London: Privately printed, 1902.

Burton, Robert. *The Anatomy of Melancholy*. 1621.

The Card of Courtship. 1653.

Care, Henry. *Female Pre-eminence; or, the Dignity and excellency of that sex*. 1670.

Carew, Thomas. *Poems*. 1640.

Castiglione, B. *The Book of the Courtier*. Edited by V. Cox. Translated by Sir Thomas Hoby. London: Everyman, 1994.

de Cervantes Saavedra, Miguel. *The Adventures of Don Quixote*. Translated by J. M. Cohen. London: Penguin, 1950.

Chamberlain, Robert. *The Harmony of the Muses*. 1654.

———. *The Harmony of the Muses by Robert Chamberlain*. Edited by Ernest W. Sullivan II. Aldershot: Scolar Press, 1990.

The Character of a Town Gallant. 1675.

A Choice Collection of 120 Loyal Songs. 1684.

Choyce Drollery. 1656.

Choyce Drollery: Songs and Sonnets. . . . To which are added the extra songs of Merry Drollery, 1661, and an Antidote against Melancholy, 1661. Edited by Joseph Woodfall Ebsworth. Boston, 1876.

Church, Nathaniel. *Cheap Riches, or, A Pocket Companion made of five hundred Proverbial Aphorismes*. 1654.

A Collection of Poems. 1672, 1673, 1693.

A Collection of Poems on Affairs of State. 1689.

A Collection of the Newest and Most Ingenious Poems. 1689.

Congreve, William. *The Double Dealer*. 1694.

Cotgrave, John. *The English Treasury of Wit and Language*. 1655.

———. *Wits Interpreter*. 1655, 1662, 1671.

The Court of Venus. 1538.

Covent Garden Drollery. 1672.

Davison, Francis. *A Poetical Rhapsody*. 1602.

Deliciæ Poeticæ; Or, Parnassus Display'd. 1706.

The Diarium, or Journal. 1656.

Doctor Merry-man; Or, Nothing but Mirth. 1671.

Donne, John, Jr., *Poems of Pembroke and Ruddier*. 1660.

Dover, Robert. *Annalia Dubrensia*. 1636.
Drayton, Michael. *Englands Heroicall Epistles*. 1598.
Dryden, John. *Miscellany Poems*. 1684.
———. *Sylvae; or, the Second Part of Poetical Miscellanies*. 1685.
———. *The Works of John Dryden*. Edited by H. T. Swedenberg, Jr. Berkeley: University of California Press, 1956–.
Edmundson, Henry. *Comes Facundus in Via*. 1658.
L'Estrange, Roger. *Considerations and Proposals in Order to the Regulation of the Press. Together with Diverse Instances of Treasonous, and Seditious Pamphlets, Proving the Neceßity thereof*. 1663.
Facetiæ. Musarum Deliciæ: or the Muses Recreation. Edited by T. Park and E. Dubois. 2 vols. London: Longman, 1817.
Flatman, Thomas. *Poems and Songs*. 1686.
Forde, Thomas. *Love's Labyrinth: A Tragi-Comedy*. 1660.
Green, M. A. E., ed. *Calendar of State Papers Domestic Series, 1655–1656*. London: Longman, 1882.
Hall, Thomas. *The Downfall of the May Games*. 1661.
Harrington, John. *The Most Elegant and Witty Epigrams*. 1618.
Herrick, Robert. *The Poetical Works of Robert Herrick*, ed. F. W. Moorman. London: Humphrey Milford, 1921.
Hickes, William. *Oxford Drollery*. 1671, 1674, 1679.
———. *London Drollery*. 1673.
———. *Coffee-House Jests*. 1677.
———. *Grammatical Drollery*. 1682.
Holborn Drollery. 1673.
Holland, Samuel. *Wit and Fancy In a Maze. Or the Incomparable Champion of Love and Beautie. A Mock Romance*. 1656.
Horne, John. *The Divine Wooer; or a Poem Setting forth the Love and Loveliness of the Lord Jesus*. 1673.
Howell, James. *Poems On several Choice and Various Subjects*. 1663.
Hocus Pocus Junior. The Anatomy of Legerdemain . . . The Art of Juggling set forth in his proper colours, fully, plainly, and exactly. 4th ed. 1654.
Jonson, Ben. *Workes*. 1616, 1640.
———. *Ben Jonson*. Edited by C. H. Herford, Percy Simpson, and Evelyn Simpson. 11 vols. Oxford: Clarendon, 1925–52.
———. *The Complete Poems*. Edited by G. Parfitt. Middlesex: Penguin, 1975.
Jovial Garland. 1670.
King, Henry. *Poems, Elegies, Paradoxes, and Sonnets*. 1657.
Lancashire, Ian, ed. *The Early Modern English Dictionaries Database*. Available from University of Toronto, www.chass.utoronto.ca/english/emed/emedd.html.
The Last and Best Edition of New Songs. 1677.

Leake, William. *Le Prince d'Amour.* 1660.
Ling, Nicholas. *Politeuphuia, Wits Common-Wealth.* 1598.
Markham, Gervase. *Markham's Methode, Or Epitome.* 1616.
———. *The Complete Farriar, Or The Kings High-Way to Horsmanship.* 1639.
Marlowe, Christopher. *The Famous Tragedy of The Rich Jew of Malta.* 1633.
The Marrow of Complements. 1655.
Meres, Frances. *Palladis Tamia. Wits Treasury.* 1598.
Merry Drollery the First Part. 1661, 1670, 1691.
Merry Drollery the Second Part. 1661, 1670, 1691.
Merry Drollery Compleat. Edited by Joseph Woodfall Ebsworth. Boston, 1875.
Merry Newes from Epsom-Wells: being a . . . relation of a Lawyers lying with a London Goldsmith's wife, at Epsom. 1663.
Methinks the Poor Town Has Been Troubled for Too Long. 1673.
Middleton, Thomas. *The Works of Thomas Middleton.* Edited by A. H. Bullen. 8 vols. London: John C. Nimmo.
Mock Songs and Joking Poems. 1675.
Motteux, Peter Anthony, John Oldmixon, and Edward Filmer. *The Novelty: Every Act a Play.* 1697.
Musarum Deliciæ. 1656.
Naps upon Parnassus. 1658.
The New Academy of Complements. 1669, 1671, 1681, 1694, 1715, 1719, 1748.
A New Collection. 1674, 1676, 1678.
Otway, Thomas. *Friendship in Fashion.* 1678.
Palladis Palatium: Wisedoms Pallace. Or the Fourth Part of Wits Commonwealth. 1604.
The Paradyse of Daynty Deuises. 1576.
Peacham, Henry. *The Complete Gentleman.* 1622.
Pepys, Samuel. *The Diary of Samuel Pepys.* Edited by Robert Latham and William Matthews. 11 vols. London: Bell and Hyman, 1985.
A Perfect Collection of the Several Songs now in Mode. 1675.
Perronet, Edward. *Occasional verse, moral and sacred.* 1785.
Phillips, Edward. *The Mysteries of Love and Eloquence.* 1658, 1699.
Phillips, John. *Sportive Wit.* 1656.
———. *Wit and Drollery.* 1656, 1661, 1682.
A Pill to purge State-Melancholy: or, a Collection of Excellent New Ballads. 1725.
Playford, John. *The Dancing Master.* 1651.
———. *The Musical Companion, in Two Books.* 1673.
———. *An Introduction to the Skill of Musick.* 1674.
Poole, Joshua. *The English Parnassus: Or, A Helpe to English Poesie.* 1657.
Ralegh, Walter. *The Poems of Walter Ralegh: A Historical Edition.* Edited by Michael Rudick. Tempe, AZ: Renaissance English Texts Society, 2000.

Ratts Rhimed to Death. 1660.
Raylor, Timothy, ed. *Musarum Deliciæ (1655) and Wit Restor'd (1658)*. New York: Scholars' Facsimiles and Reprints, 1985.
Raymond, John(?). *Folly in Print*. 1667.
Rawlins, Thomas. *Tom Essence: Or, The Modish Wife*. 1677.
The Rump, or Collection of Songs and Ballads, made upon those who would be a PARLIAMENT, and were but the RUMP of an House of Commons, five times dissolv'd. 1660.
Shadwell, Thomas. *Epsom-Wells. A comedy*. 1673.
———. *The Lancashire-Witches*. 1682.
Shakespeare, William. *Poems: Written by Wil. Shake-speare. Gent*. Edited by John Benson. 1640.
———. *Shakespeare's Sonnets*. Edited by Katherine Duncan-Jones. Oxford: Arden, 1997.
———. *The New Variorum Edition of Shakespeare: The Sonnets*. Edited by H. E. Rollins. Philadelphia: Lippincott, 1944.
Stevenson, Matthew. *Bristol Drollery*. 1674.
Strode, William. *The Poetical Works of William Strode (1600–1645)*. Edited by Bertram Dobell. London: Editor, 1907.
———. *A Critical Edition of the Poetical Works of William Strode, Excluding "The Floating Island."* Edited by M. A. Forey. BLitt thesis, St. Hilda's, Oxford, 1966.
A Third Collection of the Newest and Most Ingenious Poems, Songs, Catches &c. 1689.
The Tombs in Westminster Abbey: As Sung by Brother Popplewell in the manner of Chanting in a Cathedral. 1775.
Tomkins, Thomas. *Lingva: Or The Combat of the Tongue, And the Five Senses for Superiority*. 1607.
Tottel, Richard. *Songes and Sonnettes*. 1557.
Townshend, Aurelian. *The Poems and Masques of Aurelian Townshend with Music by Henry Lawes and William Webb*. Edited by Cedric C. Brown. Reading: Whiteknights, 1983.
Tutchin, John. *Poems on Several Occasions*. 1685.
Veel, Robert. *New Court Songs*. 1672.
Walton, Isaac. *The Compleat Angler*. 1653.
———. *Reliquiæ Wottonianæ*. 1651.
Wardroper, John, ed. *Love and Drollery*. London: Routledge and Kegan Paul, 1969.
Westminster Drollery. 1671.
Westminster Drollery the Second Part. 1672.
Westminster Drolleries, both parts of 1671, 1672. Edited by Joseph Woodfall Ebsworth. Boston: 1875.
The Courtship Narrative of Leonard Wheatcroft Derbyshire Yeoman. Edited by George Parfitt and Ralph Houlbrooke. Reading: Whiteknights, 1986.
Whitney, Geoffrey. *A Choice of Emblemes*. 1586.
Williamson, E. J. *Cleaveland Revived*. 1659, 1660.
———. *J. Cleaveland Revived. Second Edition, 1660*. Edited by Hilton Kelliher. Aldershot: Scolar Press, 1990.
Windsor Drollery. 1672.

Wycherley, William. *Love in a Wood, or, St. James's Park.* 1672.
Winstanley, William. *The New Help to Discourse.* 1672.
Wit and Mirth. 1682, 1684.
Wit at a Venture. 1674.
Wit Restor'd. 1658.
Wither, George. *Faire-Virtue, the Mistress of Philarete.* 1622, 1633.
The Wits Academy. 1677, 1696, 1701, 1704.
Wits Recreations. 1640, 1641, 1645, 1650, 1654, 1663, 1667, 1683.
Witts Recreations Selected from the Finest Fancies of Moderne Muses 1640. Edited by Colin Gibson. Aldershot: Scolar Press, 1990.
Wits Theater of the Little World. 1599.
Woudhuysen, H. R., ed. *The Penguin Book of Renaissance Verse, 1509–1659.* London: Penguin, 1992.
Wright, Abraham. *Parnassus Biceps.* 1656.
———. *Parnassus biceps, or Severall choice pieces of poetry, by Abraham Wright, 1656.* Edited by Peter Beal. Aldershot: Scolar Press, 1990.

Secondary Texts

Anderson, Randall Louis. "'The Merit of a Manuscript Poem': The Case for Bodleian MS Rawlinson poet. 85." In *Print, Manuscript, and Performance: The Changing Relations of the Media in Early Modern England,* ed. Arthur F. Marotti and Michael D. Bristol, 127–71. Columbus: Ohio State University Press, 2000.
Armitage, C. M. "Donne's Poems in Huntington Manuscript 198: New Light on 'The Funeral.'" *Studies in Philology* 63 (1966): 697–707.
Beal, Peter. *Index of Literary Manuscripts.* Vol. 1, 1450–1625. London: Mansell, 1980.
———. "Notions in Garrison: The Seventeenth-Century Commonplace Book." In *New Ways of Looking at Old Texts,* edited by Speed Hill, 131–47. New York: Medieval and Renaissance Texts and Studies, 1993.
Beer, Anna R. *Sir Walter Ralegh and His Readers in the Seventeenth Century.* Basingstoke: Macmillan, 1997.
Bennett, H. S. *English Books and Readers, 1603 to 1640.* Cambridge: Cambridge University Press, 1970.
Bentley, Gerald Eades. "John Cotgrave's 'English Treasury of Wit and Language' and the Elizabethan Drama." *Studies in Philology* 40, no. 2 (1943): 186–203.
Birch, Thomas, ed. *A Collection of the State Papers of John Thurloe Esq,* by John Thurloe. 7 vols. 1742.
Bohannon, M. E. "A London Bookseller's Bill: 1635–1639." *Library,* 4th ser., 18, no. 4 (1938): 417–46.
Bosanquet, E. F. "English Seventeenth-Century Almanacks." *Library,* 4th ser., 10, no. 4 (1930): 361–92.

Brady, J., and W. H. Herendeen, eds. *Ben Jonson's 1616 Folio*. London: Associated University Presses, 1991.

Brown, Cedric C. "The Two Pilgrimages of the Laureate of Ashover, Leonard Wheatcroft." In *Betraying Our Selves: Forms of Self-Representation in Early Modern English Texts*, edited by Henk Dragstra, Sheila Ottway, and Helen Wilcox, 120–35. Basingstoke: Macmillan, 2001.

Bryson, Anna. *From Courtesy to Civility: Changing Modes of Conduct in Early Modern England*. Oxford: Clarendon Press, 2000.

Cavallo, Guglielmo, and Roger Chartier, eds. *A History of Reading in the West*. Translated by Lydia G. Cochrane. Amherst: University of Massachusetts, 1999.

Chan, Mary. "Mid-Seventeenth-Century Music Meeting and Playford's Publishing." In *The Well Enchanting Skill: Music, Poetry and Drama in the Culture of the Renaissance: Essays in Honour of F. W. Sternfeld*, edited by J. Caldwell, E. Olleson, and S. Wollenberg, 231–44. Oxford: Clarendon Press, 1990.

Chartier, Roger, ed. *A History of Private life*. Vol. 3, *Passions of the Renaissance*. London: Belknap, 1989.

———. "Texts, Printing, Readings." In *The New Cultural History*, edited by L. Hunt, 154–75. Berkeley: University of California Press, 1989.

Coiro, A. B. *Robert Herrick's "Hesperides" and the Epigram Book Tradition*. Baltimore: Johns Hopkins University Press, 1988.

———. "Milton and Class Identity. The Publication of *Areopagitica* and the 1645 *Poems*." *Journal of Medieval and Renaissance Studies* 22, no. 22 (1992): 261–89.

Crane, Mary Thomas. *Framing Authority: Sayings, Self, and Society in Sixteenth-Century England*. Princeton, NJ: Princeton University Press, 1993.

Cressy, David. *Education in Tudor and Stuart England*. London: Edward Arnold, 1975.

———. "Educational Opportunity in Tudor and Stuart England." *History of Education Quarterly* 16, no. 3 (1976): 301–20.

———. *Literacy and the Social Order*. Cambridge: Cambridge University Press, 1980.

Croft, Pauline. "The Reputation of Robert Cecil: Libels, Political Opinion and Popular Awareness in the Early Seventeenth Century." *Transactions of the Royal Historical Society* (1991): 43–69.

Crum, Margaret, ed. *First-Line Index of English Poetry, 1500–1800, in Manuscripts of the Bodleian Library Oxford*. 2 vols. Oxford: Oxford University Press, 1969.

Curtis, Mark H. "The Alienated Intellectuals of Early Stuart England." *Past and Present* 23 (November 1962): 25–43.

Cutbirth, Nancy. "Thomas Killigrew's Commonplace Book?" *Library Chronicle of the University of Texas*, n.s., no. 13 (1980): 31–38.

Darnton, Robert. "Extraordinary Commonplaces." *The New York Review of Books*, 21 December 2000, 82–87.

De Bruyn, Frans. "The Classical Silva and the Generic Development of Scientific Writing in Seventeenth-Century England." *New Literary History* 32 (2001): 347–73.

De Sola Pinto, D. "*Covent Garden Drollery: A Miscellany of 1672.* Edited G. THORN DRURY." *Review of English Studies* 4 (1928): 468–72.

Eisenstein, Elizabeth. *The Printing Press as an Agent of Change: Communication and Cultural Transformation in Early Modern Europe.* 2 vols. Cambridge: Cambridge University Press, 1979.

Elsky, Martin. *Authorizing Words.* Ithaca, NY: Cornell University Press, 1989.

Evans, R. C. "Ben Jonson's Library and Marginalia: New Evidence from the Folger Collection." *Philological Quarterly* 66, no. 4 (1987): 521–28.

———. "Jonson's Copy of Seneca." *Comparative Drama* 25, no. 3 (1991): 257–92.

Firth, C. H. "The Royalists under the Protectorate." *English Historical Review* 52 (1937): 634–48.

Foster, Joseph. *Alumni Oxonionses: The Members of the University of Oxford, 1500–1886.* 4 vols. Liechtenstein: Kraus Reprint, 1968.

Fox, Adam. *Oral and Literate Culture in England, 1500–1700.* Oxford: Clarendon Press, 2000.

Frank, Joseph. *Hobbled Pegasus: A Descriptive Bibliography of Minor English Poetry, 1641–1660.* Albuquerque: University of New Mexico Press, 1968.

Grafton, Anthony. *The Footnote: A Curious History.* London: Faber and Faber, 1997.

———. "Gabriel Harvey's Marginalia. New Light on the Cultural History of Elizabethan England." *Princeton University Library Chronicle* 52, no. 1 (1990): 21–24.

Greetham, D. C., ed. *The Margins of the Text.* Ann Arbor: University of Michigan Press, 1997.

Gullans, Charles B. "Ralegh and Ayton: The Disputed Authorship of 'Wrong Not Sweete Empress of My Heart.'" *Studies in Bibliography. Papers of the Bibliographical Society of the University of Virginia* 13 (1960): 191–98.

Hardacre, Paul H. *The Royalists during the Puritan Revolution.* The Hague: Martinus Nijhoff, 1956.

Hart, E. F. "The Answer-Poem of the Early Seventeenth Century." *Review of English Studies*, n.s., 7, 25 (1956): 19–29.

Heale, Elizabeth. *Wyatt, Surrey and Early Tudor Poetry.* London: Longman, 1998.

Helgerson, Richard. *Self-Crowned Laureates.* Berkeley: University of California Press, 1983.

Hill, Christopher. *Some Intellectual Consequences of the English Revolution.* Madison: University of Wisconsin Press, 1980.

Hobbs, Mary. "Early Seventeenth-Century Verse Miscellanies and Their Value for Textual Editors." In *English Manuscript Studies, 1100–1700*, vol. 1, edited by Peter Beal and Jeremy Griffiths, 182–210. Oxford: Basil Blackwell, 1989.

———. *Early Seventeenth Century Verse Miscellany Manuscripts.* Aldershot: Scolar Press, 1992.

Hunter, G. K. "The Marking of *Sententiæ* in Elizabethan Printed Plays, Poems, and Romances." *Library*, 5th ser., 6, nos. 3–4 (1951): 171–88.

Hutton, Ronald. *The Rise and Fall of Merry England: The Ritual Year, 1400–1700.* Oxford: Oxford University Press, 1994.

Jackson, H. J. "Writing in Books and Other Marginal Activities." *University of Toronto Quarterly* 62, no. 2 (1992–93): 217–31.

———. *Marginalia: Readers Writing in Books.* New Haven, CT: Yale University Press, 2001.
Johns, Adrian. *The Nature of the Book.* Chicago: University of Chicago Press, 1998.
Johnson, F. R. "Notes on English Retail Book-Prices, 1550–1640." *Library,* 5th ser., 5, no. 2 (1950): 83–112.
Lake, David J. *The Canon of Thomas Middleton's Plays.* Cambridge: Cambridge University Press, 1975.
Lechner, Sister Joan Marie. *Renaissance Concepts of the Commonplace.* New York: Pageant Press, 1962.
Leishman, J. B. "'You Meaner Beauties of the Night.' A Study in Transmission and Transmogrification." *Library,* 4th ser., 26, no. 2 (1945): 99–121.
Levy, F. J. "How Information Spread among the Gentry, 1550–1640." *Journal of British Studies* 21 (1982): 11–34.
Lewalski, Barbara Kiefer, ed. *The Polemics and Poems of Rachel Speght.* New York: Oxford University Press, 1996.
Lipking, Lawrence. "The Marginal Gloss." *Critical Inquiry* 3, no. 4 (1977): 609–55.
Lister, Raymond. *The Loyal Blacksmith.* Cambridge, UK: Golden Head Press, 1957.
Love, Harold. *The Culture and Commerce of Texts. Scribal Publication in Seventeenth-Century England.* Amherst: University of Massachusetts Press, 1998.
Lowenstein, J. "The Script in the Marketplace." *Representations* 12 (fall 1985): 101–14.
Loxley, James. *Royalism and Poetry in the English Civil Wars: The Drawn Sword.* Basingstoke: Macmillan, 1997.
Marcus, Leah S. *The Politics of Mirth: Jonson, Herrick, Milton, Marvell, and the Defense of Old Holiday Pastimes.* Chicago: University of Chicago Press, 1986.
Marotti, Arthur. "'Love Is Not Love': Elizabethan Sonnet Sequences and the Social Order." *English Literary History* 49, no. 2 (1982): 396–428.
———. "Malleable and Fixed Texts: Manuscript and Printed Miscellanies and the Transmission of Lyric Poetry in the English Renaissance." In *New Ways of Looking at Old Texts,* edited by Speed Hill, 159–73. New York: Medieval and Renaissance Texts and Studies, 1993.
———. "Manuscript, Print, and the English Renaissance Lyric." In *New Ways of Looking at Old Texts,* edited by Speed Hill, 209–21. New York: Medieval and Renaissance Texts and Studies, 1993.
———. *Manuscript, Print, and the English Renaissance Lyric.* Ithaca, NY: Cornell University Press, 1995.
———, and Michael D. Bristol, eds. *Print, Manuscript, and Performance: The Changing Relations of the Media in Early Modern England.* Columbus: Ohio State University Press, 2000.
Massingham, H. J. *A Treasury of Seventeenth Century English Verse from the Death of Shakespeare to the Restoration (1616–1660).* London: Macmillan, 1919.
May, Steven W. "Tudor Aristocrats and the Mythical 'Stigma of Print.'" In *Renaissance Papers 1980,* edited by A. Leigh Deneed and M. Thomas Hester, 11–18. Valencia: Southeastern Renaissance Conference, 1981.

McKenzie, D. F. *Bibliography and the Sociology of Texts.* London: British Library, 1986.
Moore, G. C. "Aurelian Townshend." *Modern Language Review* 12 (1917): 426–27.
Morrill, John, ed. *Revolution and Restoration: England in the 1650s.* London: Collins and Brown, 1992.
Moss, Ann. *Printed Commonplace-Books and the Structuring of Renaissance Thought.* Oxford: Oxford University Press, 1996.
Newton, R. C. "Jonson and the (Re-)Invention of the Book." In *Classic and Cavalier: Essays on Jonson and the Sons of Ben,* edited by C. J. Summers and T-L. Pebworth, 31–55. Pittsburgh: University of Pittsburgh Press, 1982.
Ong, Walter J. *Orality and Literacy.* New York: Routledge, 1982.
Pebworth, Ted-Larry. "Sir Henry Wotton's 'O Faithles World': The Transmission of a Coterie Poem and a Critical Old-Spelling Edition." *Analytical and Enumerative Bibliography* 5, no. 4 (1981): 205–31.
Plomer, H. R. *A Dictionary of the Booksellers and Printers Who Were at Work in England, Scotland and Ireland, 1641–67.* London: Bibliographical Society, 1907.
Pomeroy, Elizabeth. *The Elizabethan Miscellanies: Their Development and Conventions.* Berkeley: University of California Press, 1975.
Potter, Lois. *Secret Rites and Secret Writing: Royalist Literature, 1641–60.* Cambridge: Cambridge University Press, 1989.
Raylor, Timothy. *Cavaliers, Clubs, and Literary Culture: Sir John Mennes, James Smith, and the Order of the Fancy.* London: Associated University Press, 1994.
Riddell, James A., and Stanley Stewart. *Jonson's Spenser: Evidence and Historical Criticism.* Pittsburgh: Duquesne University Press, 1995.
Saunders, J. W. "The Stigma of Print: A Note on the Social Bases of Tudor Poetry." *Essays in Criticism* 1 (1951): 139–64.
———. "From Manuscript to Print: A Note on the Circulation of Poetic Manuscripts in the Sixteenth Century." *Proceedings of the Leeds Philosophical and Literary Society* 1, part 8 (1951): 507–28.
Scodel, Joshua. *Excess and the Mean in Early Modern English Literature.* Princeton, NJ: Princeton University Press, 2002.
Scott, Jonathan. "The English Republican Imagination." In *Revolution and Restoration: England in the 1650s,* edited by John Morrill, 35–54. London: Collins and Brown, 1992.
Sharpe, Kevin. *Reading Revolutions: The Politics of Reading in Early Modern England.* New Haven, CT: Yale University Press, 2000.
Sherman, William. *John Dee: The Politics of Reading and Writing in the English Renaissance.* Amherst: University of Massachusetts Press, 1995.
Simpson, C. M. *The British Broadside Ballad and Its Music.* New Brunswick, NJ: Rutgers University Press, 1966.
Slights, William W. E. "The Edifying Margins of Renaissance English Books." *Renaissance Quarterly* 42, no. 4 (1989): 682–716.
Smith, C. C. "The Seventeenth-Century Drolleries." PhD dissertation, Harvard University, 1943.

———. "The Seventeenth-Century Drolleries." *Harvard Library Bulletin* 6, no. 1 (1952): 40–51.

Smyth, Adam. "An Online Index of Poetry in Printed Miscellanies, 1640–1682." *Early Modern Literary Studies* 8, no. 1 (2002).

Spink, Ian. "English Seventeenth-Century Dialogues." *Music and Letters* 38, no. 2 (1957): 155–63.

Spufford, Margaret. "First Steps in Literacy: The Reading and Writing Experiences of the Humblest Seventeenth-Century Autobiographers." *Social History* 4, no. 3 (1979): 407–35.

———. *Small Books and Pleasant Histories: Popular Fiction and Its Readership in Seventeenth-Century England.* London: Methuen, 1981.

Stephen, L., and S. Lee, eds. *Dictionary of National Biography.* London: Smith, Elder, 1885, 1908, 1921.

Stone, Lawrence. "The Educational Revolution in England, 1560–1640." *Past and Present* 28 (1964): 41–80.

Tompkins, Jane P., ed. *Reader-Response Criticism: From Formalism to Post-Structuralism.* Baltimore: Johns Hopkins University Press, 1980.

Tribble, Evelyn B. *Margins and Marginality: The Printed Page in Early Modern England.* Charlottesville: University Press of Virginia, 1993.

Tricomi, A. H. "Philip, Earl of Pembroke, and the Analogical Way of Reading Political Tragedy." *Journal of English and Germanic Philology* 85, no. 3 (1986): 332–45.

Turner, Alberta T. "Milton and the Convention of the Academic Miscellanies." *Yearbook of English Studies* 5 (1975): 86–93.

Van Heertum, Cis. "A Hostile Annotation of Rachel Speght's *A Mouzell for Melastomus* (1617)." *English Studies* 68, no. 6 (1987): 490–96.

Wall, Wendy. *The Imprint of Gender.* Ithaca, NY: Cornell University Press, 1993.

Whigham, F. *Ambition and Privilege: The Social Tropes of Elizabethan Courtesy Literature.* Berkeley: University of California Press, 1984.

Woudhuysen, H. R. *Sir Philip Sidney and the Circulation of Manuscripts, 1558–1640.* Oxford: Clarendon Press, 1996.

Wrightson, Keith. *English Society, 1580–1680.* London: Hutchinson, 1982.

INDEX

Academy of Complements, The, 1, 9, 10, 14, 17, 20, 23, 24, 28, 29, 30, 31, 34, 36, 39, 50, 55, 58, 75, 85–86, 171
Academy of Pleasure, The, 43
Acrostics, xix, 121
Allott, Robert, *Englands Parnassus*, 20, 41, 42
Almanacs, 43
Anacreon, 166
Anagrams, 147–48. *See also* Chronograms
Answer poems, transmission of, 93–97. *See also* Mocks
Antidote against Melancholy, An, 100, 153, 158, 174
Antidote against Melancholy. Or, A Treasury of 53 Rare Secrets & Arts, An, 174
Atkins, James, 99
Authors: Ben Jonson as author, 87–90; challenges to, xxi, 174; legal elision of, 74; miscellany resistance to, 5, 73–77; noted in readers' marginal additions, 46; readers' attitudes toward, 52, 55–56; reasons for popularity of some, 8; relationship with compilers, 75–76; represented in miscellanies, 6–8
Ayton, Sir Robert, xx, 7–8; "Wrong not dear Empress of my heart," 92–93, 119; "No man Love's fiery Passions can approve," 93–94

Bacon, Francis, 35, 75, 135; *Sylva Sylvarum*, 21
Bagnall, William, 99

Ballads, 52–53; "Towzer Discover'd," 96; "The Blacksmith," 52–53, 79, 97–103, 156
Bastard, Thomas, 7
Bawdiness, 136–44. *See also* Misrule
Bee. A Collection of Choice Poems, The, 175
Benson, John, 82
Bickerstaffe, Isaac, *Love in a Village*, 31
Bond, William, "An Answer to the Letter of the Cloake," 95
Book of Sports, The, 137–40, 167
Borges, Jorge Luis, 73, 131
Boydell, John, 121–26, 174
Brome, Alexander, 8, 79; "Stay shutt ye gate," 110; "Why should we not laugh and be jolly," 79, 153
Brome, Richard, 39; *Joviall Crew, or, The Merry Beggars*, 31
Brooke, Nathaniel, 9, 10, 74, 75, 90, 132
Bulstrode, Whitelock, 15–16
Burton, Robert, *Anatomy of Melancholy*, 16

Calverley, Henry, manuscript of, 119
Cambridge University, and manuscript miscellanies, 17
Card of Courtship, The, 10, 36, 42, 140, 141, 168
Care, Henry, *Female Pre-eminence*, xvii–xviii
Carew, Thomas, 8, 17, 79, 87; "In her faire cheekes two pits doe lye," 85
Castiglione, Baldassare, *The Courtyer*, 19, 33
Cavendish, William, 30; *The Triumphant Widow*, 29
Cecil, Robert, 135

Cervantes, Miguel de, *The Adventures of Don Quixote*, 65
Chapbooks, 34
Chartier, Roger, and Guglielmo Cavallo, *A History of Reading in the West*, 69–72
Choice, as printed miscellany virtue, 11–12
Choice Collection of 120 Loyal Songs, A, 136, 175–76
Choyce Drollery, 9, 52, 117–18, 132, 136, 139
Chronograms, 148. See also Anagrams
Civil War, 144, 171–72
Clubs, 99–103, 151. See also Drinking; Friendship; Order of the Fancy, The
Codes, 142. See also Secrecy
Coleridge, Samuel Taylor, 40
Collection of the Newest and Most Ingenious Poems, A, 45
Collection of Poems, A, 22, 50, 63
Commonplace books: construction of, 15–17; printed commonplace books, 16; problems with definition of, 130–31; reading habits induced, 53–54; similarities with printed miscellanies, 15–16, 17, 18
Conduct manuals, 18
Copyright Law, 175
Corbett, Richard, 8, 96; "Am I mad O noble Festus," 137, 154; "Tell me you anti-Saints," 137
Cotgrave, John, 37, 82; *The English Treasury of Wit and Language*, 18, 27, 46, 55, 89
Court of Venus, The, 20
Court: depicted in printed miscellanies, 141–44; courtiers, new versus old, 148–50. See also Royalism
Covent Garden Drollery, 36
Cowley, Abraham, "The thirsty Earth drinks up the Rain," 166
Cranfield, Lionel, 135
Cressy, David, 37

Cromwell, Oliver, 101, 156, 169
Cromwell's Conspiracy, 115

Davenant, William: *Love and Honour*, 86; *The Tempest* (with John Dryden), 114, 142
Davison, Francis, *A Poetical Rhadsody*, 20, 104, 168
De Bruyn, Frans, 21
Dee, John, 40
Deliciæ Poeticæ; Or, Parnassus Display'd, 174–75
Deloney, Thomas, *Jack of Newbury*, 87
Devereux, Robert, Earl of Essex, 135
Devonshire, Cristiana, Countess of, 120
Devonshire Manuscript, 51
Dialogues, in printed miscellanies, 25, 28, 115–17, 126–27; "In a Pastorall Dialogue," 105–14
Diaries, used as printed miscellanies, 43
Doctor Merry-man: Or, Nothing but Mirth, 52
Donne, John, 142
Drama: depicting printed miscellany readers, 29–31; texts containing excerpts from, 46–47; transmission of dramatic texts, 114–18
Drayton, Michael, 85
Drinking, 154–68; beer, 101, 156; and ceremony, 166–68; and disengagement, 160–64; endless, 165–66; and exclusivity, 162–63; groups, 157–58; as instigator of change and revival, 158–59; oaths, 156–57; politicized, 156–57; rules of, 155–56; sack, 156; significance of particular drinks, 155–56; taverns, 151–52
Drollery, 153
Dryden, John, *The Conquest of Granada*, 96, 115–17; *The Tempest* (with William Davenant), 114

INDEX

D'Urfey, Thomas, *Pills to Purge Melancholy*, 174

Editing, theories of, 76–78
Edmundson, Henry, *Comes Facundus in Via*, 49, 137
Electronic texts, 69–72
Englands Heroicall Epistles, 85
English language, celebrated, 22
Errata, notes of and attitude toward, 56

Fart, parliamentary, 135
Felton, John, 46, 136
Fire, Great, 170
Fitzgeffrey, Henry, 7
Folly in Print, 10–11, 55–56, 59, 92, 147, 170
Forde, Thomas, *Love's Labyrinth*, 30, 63
Foxe, John, *Pandectae locorum communion*, 16
Friendship, as printed miscellany theme, 25–26, 42, 151–54, 155. *See also* Clubs; Laughter

Games, explained in printed miscellanies, 26; and tricks, 123–24, 142
Gansforde, Thomas, "A description of Women," 95
Gascoigne, George, *A Hundreth Sundrie Flowres*, 21
Genre, movement of texts between genres, 126–31
Gibson, Sir John, and his manuscript commonplace book, 126
Goldsmith's Hall Committee, 163
Grammatical Drollery, 10, 75
Guazzo, Stephano, *The Civile Conversation*, 19

Hall, Thomas, 139
Harmony of the Muses, The, 35, 105–9, 169
Harrington, Sir John, 83
Heale, Elizabeth, 51

"Hence all ye vain delights," 95; William Strode's answer, 95–96
Herrick, Robert, 99; and drink, 159–60; *Hesperides*, 86, 87
Hickes, William, 7, 10, 33, 75, 76, 83, 128, 151, 172
Hobbs, Mary, 77
Hocus Pocus Junior. The Anatomy of Legerdemain, 124
Hodgeson, Marmaduke, *A Treatise of Practical Gauging*, 41
Holborn Drollery, 11, 35, 57
Honywood, Michael, 132–33
Horti Carolini Rosa Altera, 134
Houlbrook, William, 102–3
Howell, James, 83–84

Index of Poetry in Printed Miscellanies, 1640 to 1682 (online), 78, 174
Inns of Court, and manuscript miscellanies, 17

J. Cleaveland Revived, 9, 134, 148, 151
Jackson, H. J., *Marginalia: Readers Writing in Books*, 40
Jonson, Ben, 8, 40, 45, 65, 75, 83, 86; and clubs, 152; *Conversations with William Drummond*, 105; *Cynthias Revells*, 83; and fragmentation of *Workes*, 87–90, 105–14; "On an English Monsieur," 89; "On Banck the Usurer," 88; "On something that walkes somewhere," 89; "The Musicall strife; In a Pastorall Dialogue," 104–14; *Part of King James His Royall and Magnificent Entertainment*, 65; *Sejanus*, 65; *Time vindicated to himselfe*, 86; "To Person Guiltie," 88
Jovial Garland, A, 27, 129, 134, 153, 169

Kemp, Hobart, 172

Killigrew, Thomas, *The Parson's Wedding*, 115; his manuscript miscellany, 119, 124
King, Henry, "On Prince Henry's Death," 84
King's Cabinet Opened, The, 142

L'Estrange, Roger, 50, 96
Laugh and Be Fat, 174
Laughter, as printed miscellany theme, 21, 152–53; jokes, 26, 128; and drink, 154. *See also* Friendship
Leishman, J. B., 77
Letter writing, xv–xvi; concerns over privacy, xvi
Ling, Nicholas: *Englands Helicon*, 51; *Politeuphuia, Wits Common-Wealth*, 20
Literacy rates, 37
Logic, explained in printed miscellanies, 26
London Drollery, 10, 13, 75
Love, Harold, 5, 56, 109, 116
Love: dramatic depictions of wooing, 29–31; as miscellany theme, 3, 91–92, 93–94, 136–46; Petrarchan love verses, 80, 93–94, 144; politicized, 24, 140–46; wooing instructions in printed miscellanies, 24–25
Lovelace, Richard, *Lucasta*, 87
Lowe, Edward, 110

Major Generals, 137
Manuscripts: circulation of, 90–93; manuscript culture compared to print culture, 87–90; miscellany reliance on, 9, 90–93; BL Add MS, 27419, 119; Bod MS Ashmole, 36–37 52–53; Bod MS Mus b1, 111, 112; Bod MS Mus Sch C142, 111; Folger MS Va 96, 53; Folger MS Va 124, 91; Folger MS Va 162, 91; Folger Va 308, 54, 120; HM 93, 119; HM 116, 119; HM 198, part I, 119–20; Trinity College, Cambridge, MS B.14.22, 109. *See also* Commonplace books; Devonshire Manuscript; Miscellanies (manuscript)
Marbeck, John, *Booke of Notes and Common places*, 16
Marginalia: calligraphy practiced in printed miscellanies, 43; depictions of, 39–40; past studies of, 40; printed marginal notes, 65–69; readers', in printed miscellanies, 37–38, 40–59
Markham, Gervase: *The Complete Farrier*, 44; *The English House-Wife*, 19; *Markham's Methode*, 44; *The whole art and trade of husbandry*, 19
Marlowe, Christopher: "Come live with me and be my love," 96, 113; *Hero and Leander*, 86
Marrow, as printed miscellany description, 12
Marrow of Complements, The, 10, 12, 27, 28, 36, 56–57, 59, 86, 87, 105–9, 141
Martin, Thomas, xv–xxii; letter-writing, xv–xvi; book buying, xvii; verse composition, xviii–xx; transcription of poems, xx–xxi
Massinger, Philip, 99
May, Steven W., and *Bibliography and First-Line Index of English Verse, 1559–1603*, 176
Mayne, Jasper, *The amorous warre*, 86
Memory, and role in textual transmission, 103–14
Mennes, Sir John, 35, 45, 68, 99, 133, 142
Meres, Francis, 20
Merry Drollery . . . The First Part, 53, 153
Methinks the Poor Town Has Been Troubled Too Long, 73

Middleton, Thomas, *The Widdow*, 117–18
Miscellanies (manuscript), 17, 90–93; relationship with printed miscellanies, 118–126
Miscellanies (printed), sixteenth-century, 20
Misrule, 137–40. See also Bawdiness
Mocks, 153; and transmission of 96–97. See also Answer poems
Mock Songs and Joking Poems, 13, 96–97, 153
More, Thomas, 75
Moseley, Humphrey, 10, 172
Munsey, William, 7
Musarum Deliciæ, 35, 43, 45, 55, 151
Music: celebrated in printed miscellanies, 104; political significance of ballad tunes, 100–103; role in textual transmission, 103–14
Mysteries of Love and Eloquence, The, 9, 14, 15, 25, 27, 35, 36, 56, 58, 60, 61, 66, 75, 85, 90, 126, 129, 141, 142

New Academy of Complements, The, 24, 27, 36, 47, 49, 81–82, 110–11, 115–18, 152, 170
New Academy of Complements: Or, The Lover's Secretary, The, 126–27
New Collection, A (1674), 63, 170
New Collection, A (1676), 170
New Court-Songs, xxi, 94
Niccols, Richard, 55

"O Love whose power and might," 91–92, 95, 96
Ong, Walter J., 88
Oral culture, 42; printed miscellanies rely upon, 97
Order of the Fancy, The, 79, 99–103, 152, 153
Otway, Thomas, *Friendship in Fashion*, 33

Oxford Drollery, 10, 76, 83, 93–94, 95, 97, 134
Oxford University: and manuscript miscellanies, 17; as site of verse transmission, xv, 91–92

Palladis palatium: wisedoms palace, 20
Paradyse of Daynty Deuises, The, 20
Parnassus Biceps, 48, 49, 76, 84, 89, 134, 145, 148, 159–60, 166, 169
Parrot, Henry, 7
Patrons, and changing relationship to readers, 57–59
Peacham, Henry, *The Compleat Gentleman*, 19, 26
Pebworth, Ted-Larry, 77
Pepys, Samuel, 54; and ballads, 100; and dance, 129; and drama, 114–15; and laughter, 155; and new courtiers, 150; and nostalgia, 168
Perfect Collection of the Several Songs now in Mode, A, 48
Phillips, Edward, 75, 85
Playford, John: *Choice Ayres, Songs, and Dialogues*, 44; *The Dancing Master*, 128–29; *An Introduction to the Skill of Musick*, 37; *The Musical Companion*, in two books, 104, 110, 129
Poems by Pembroke and Ruddier, 104, 119–20
Poems On several Choice and Various Subjects, 83
Politics: of ballad tunes, 100–103; of drinking, 156–57; of printed miscellanies, 132–72. See also Friendship; Laughter; Misrule
Pollard, Robert, 9
Poole, Joshua, *The English Parnassus*, 60
Popular verses in printed miscellanies, 78–81; reasons for popularity of particular poems, 80–81
Potter, Lois, 141, 148, 167
Practical handbooks, 19–20, 38–39

Prince d'Amour, Le, 169
Print culture: and the dissemination of texts, 73–131, 71, 92–93; compared to manuscript culture, 87–93; as force for fixity asserted and challenged, 69–72, 87–90, 174; as force for textual malleability, 73–74, 76–78
Printed miscellanies: contents of, 2–3; definition of, 2; destruction of, 10, 132; editorial approaches to, 76–78; literary precedents, 12–13, 15–21, 63; and politics, 132–72; popularity of, 10–11; previous studies, 5; publishers of, 9–10; purpose of (declared), 21–29; readers of (constructed and actual), 29–31, 32–72; rivalry between miscellanies, 14; self-presentation of, 11–15; and social mobility, 60–64; textual descendants of, 173–76; and textual transmission, 73–131
Prisons, 146–47, 162
Publishers of printed miscellanies, 9–10
Publishing industry, vitality of, 9, 37; regional booksellers, 37
Puritans, criticized in printed miscellanies, 21, 96, 101, 137–40, 153–54
Puttenham, George, *The Arte of English Poesie*, 33
Pye, John, 7

Quarles, Francis, *The Virgin Widow*, 86

Raleigh, Walter, 93, 135
Ramsay, Allan, *The Tea-Table Miscellany: Or, A Collection of Scots Songs*, 175
Randolph, Thomas, 75
Ratts Rhimed to Death, 100, 136, 176

Raylor, Timothy, 99, 153
Raymond, John, 172
Reading: commonplace culture reading methods, 16, 53–54; depictions of printed miscellany readers, 29–31; reading and sex, 57; reading habits of printed miscellany readers, 32–72, 174; readers encouraged to alter printed texts, 55–56; vast number of new books, 18; women readers 27–28, 37, 51. *See also* Sententiæ and aphorisms
Richelieu, Cardinal, 75, 142
Riddell, James A., and Stanley Stewart, *Jonson's Spenser: Evidence and Historical Criticism*, 40
Rome Rhym'd to Death, 136, 176
Royal Society, 21
Royalism: laments for, 101; as miscellany theme, 133–44; potentially debased, 142–44; royal births celebrated, 134–35; Royalist readers, 133–34. *See also* Court
Rump, The, 100

Second Part of Merry Drollery, The, 53, 100, 141
Secrecy, 141–42. *See also* Codes
Sententiæ and aphorisms, 15, 17, 18, 42–43, 48, 49
Shakespeare, William, 8, 75, 82; *Antony and Cleopatra*, 34; *As You Like It*, 86; *Love's Labour's Lost*, 16, 86, 110; *Merry Wives of Windsor*, 86; *Much Ado About Nothing*, 34, 86; *Sonnets*, 85; *Twelfth Night*, 86; *The Winter's Tale*, 129
Shape poems, 42, 121–22
"She lay all naked in her bed," 95
Sherman, William, *John Dee. The Politics of Reading and Writing in the English Renaissance*, 40

INDEX

Shirley, James, 134; excerpts from *The Cardinal*, 96
Sidney, Philip, 8, 35, 75; *Astrophel and Stella*, 140; *The Countesse of Pembroke's Arcadia*, 85
Silva tradition, 20–21
Smith, James, 35, 45, 99, 142, 153; *The Innovation of Penelope and Ulysses*, 67–69
Social mobility: possibility denied, 61–64, 71–72, 141–43; printed miscellanies promise to enable, 23–29, 38–39, 54–55, 60–64, 141–43, 174; ridiculed, 28–29, 31; of women, condemned, 27
Solis Britannici Perigaeum, 134
Sowter, John, xvi–xix
Spenser, Edmund, 8, 40, 75
Sportive Wit, 9, 10, 35, 50, 52, 66, 74, 90, 104, 132, 136, 137, 139
Stadius, Joannes, *Ephemerides novae*, 43
Stevenson, Matthew, *Bristol Drollery*, 35, 56–57
Stigma of print, 33–35, 70, 90
Stoats, 31
Strode, William, 8, 42, 48, 50, 154; "I saw fair Chloris walk alone," 104, 119, 129; "Keep on your Mask, and hide your eye," 78, 85, 93; "Return my joys and hither bring," 95–96; "With face and fashion to be known," 137
Suckling, Sir John, 99, 135; *Aglaura*, 39

Time, competing merits of past and present in printed miscellanies, 168–70
Tottel, Richard, *Songes and Sonnettes*, 20, 22, 51
Touchet, Mervyn, Earl of Castlehaven, 135

Townshend, Aurelian: "Let Souldiers fight for pay or praise," 78, 135; "Victorious beauty, though your eyes," 81–82, 129
Trigge, Thomas, *Calendarium Astrologicum: or an Almanack for the Year of our Lord, 1666*, 43

Variety, as printed miscellany virtue, 12
Villiers, George, Duke of Buckingham, 46, 135–36

Waller, Edmund, 44
Wallis, John, *Discourse*, 142
Walton, Isaac, *The Compleat Angler*, 74, 103–4, 112–13, 155
Wentworth, Thomas, Earl of Strafford, 75, 135
Westminster Drollery, 13, 43, 45, 48–49, 96, 115–17
Westminster Drollery the Second Part, 48
Wheatcroft, Leonard, 38, 54, 120–21, 124
Whitney, Geoffrey, *Choice of Emblems and other Devises*, 60
"Why should we boast of Arthur and his Knights," 79
Wilkins, John, *Mercury, or the Secret and Swift Messenger*, 142
Wilson, John, 111
Windsor Drollery, 96, 122, 125, 142
Winstanley, William, *The New Help to Discourse*, 18
Wit and Drollery, 9, 21, 34, 50, 53, 66, 68, 92, 95, 132, 142, 151, 152, 169
Wit and Mirth, 14, 41, 47, 50, 53, 66, 139, 170, 174
Wit at a Venture, 41, 83–84
Wit Restor'd, 9, 44, 46, 52, 68, 99, 136, 141
Wither, George, 7; *Faire-Virtue*, excerpts in printed miscellany, 86–87

Wits Academy, 63
Wits Academy, The, 14, 72, 153
Wits Cabinet: A Companion for Gentlemen and Ladies, 174
Wits Interpreter, 9, 13, 24, 27, 30, 35, 37, 40, 42, 45, 46, 54, 61, 62, 75, 82, 83, 87–89, 92–93, 92–93, 94, 105–9, 117–18, 123–24, 125, 128, 141, 142, 144, 153, 155, 168–69, 174
Wits Recreations, 37, 41, 42, 43, 45, 46, 47, 48, 49–50, 51, 52, 54, 55, 57, 120–22, 124, 125, 126, 133–34, 154, 168, 171
Women: and marginalia, 39–40; printed miscellanies described as, 56–57; printed miscellany praise of, 24; as readers of printed miscellanies, 27–28, 36–37, 51; and social mobility (condemned), 27
Wotton, Henry, "You Meaner Beauties of the Night," 77
Woudhuysen, H. R., *Sir Philip Sidney and the Circulation of Manuscripts, 1558–1640*, 40, 85–86
Wright, Abraham, 76, 84, 145, 160
Wycherley, William: "A Wife I do hate," from *Love in a Wood*, 94, 115; *The Country Wife*, 36